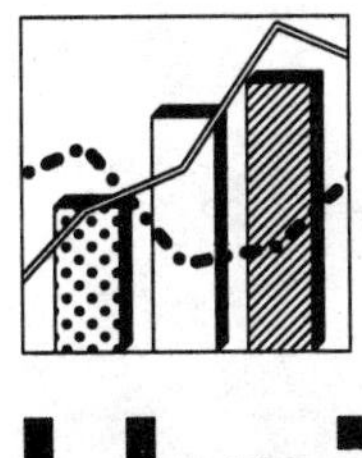

Mastering United States History Skills

Gerard J. Pelisson
Former Social Studies Teacher
Adlai E. Stevenson High School
New York City

AMSCO SCHOOL PUBLICATIONS, INC.
315 Hudson Street / New York, N.Y. 10013

For my wife Margaret

About the Author

GERARD J. PELISSON taught social studies in New York City high schools for more than 20 years. In addition, he coordinated teacher training and student skills development programs for the High School Division of the New York City Board of Education. Mr. Pelisson is also the author of *Mastering Social Studies Skills* and *Mastering American History Skills,* a text for senior high school students.

Reviewers

JOAN KOPCZA ANDREJKO
6th Grade Social Studies Teacher
Cohoes Middle School
Cohoes, New York
New York Geographic Consultant

RIC CANER
Columbus, Ohio, Public Schools
Monroe Traditional School

WILLIAM MCKEE
Chairperson, Social Studies
Brockport High School
Brockport, N.Y.

When ordering this book, please specify:
either **R 659 W** *or* MASTERING UNITED STATES HISTORY SKILLS

ISBN 1-56765-605-6
New York City Item 56765-605-5

Printed in the United States of America

2 3 4 5 6 7 8 9 10 03 02 01 00 99

PREFACE

New approaches to learning and new technology require today's students of United States history to possess skills unimagined by previous generations of students. *Mastering United States History Skills* offers in one volume a comprehensive approach to the latest and most important skills needed to study United States history.

In 25 chapters, *Mastering United States History Skills* teaches a wide range of skills:

READING SKILLS: Separating Fact From Opinion, Comparing and Contrasting, Recognizing Cause and Effect, Taking a Test, Making Generalizations, and Drawing Conclusions and Making Inferences

WRITING SKILLS: Summarizing, Taking Notes, Outlining, Writing an Essay, and Writing a Research Paper

RESEARCH SKILLS: Using Primary and Secondary Sources, Using the Library (including the Library Computer Catalog), Using Reference Books, Preparing a Portfolio, and Using the Internet

ANALYSIS SKILLS: Understanding Time Lines and Dates, Interpreting Charts and Graphs, Interpreting Drawings and Photographs, Interpreting Political Cartoons, Using the Movie and Television Media, and Solving Problems

MAP SKILLS: Recognizing Landforms and Water Forms, Using Directions, and Interpreting Relief, Product, and Population Maps

Each chapter of this book:

- assumes that students are starting with little knowledge of the skill to be taught.
- begins with a simple example of a skill and leads to a more complex example.
- asks questions throughout the chapter so that students can see if they are understanding a skill as it develops. (Answers and their explanations are given in each chapter. By checking their answers against the ones given, students can see immediately if they are learning the skill.)
- contains at least five exercises at the end of the chapter, giving students ample opportunity to demonstrate their understanding of each skill. (Answers to the exercises are included in a separate answer key.)

In addition to the skills chapters, the book contains a glossary and an index. The glossary contains important skill terms as well as difficult words. In general, words italicized in the text are listed in the glossary.

Teachers can use *Mastering United States History Skills* at the beginning of a term to teach all the skills at once, or to supplement any standard textbook throughout the term. They can teach each chapter in the book as a full class lesson or allow students to work independently at their own pace.

The book can also help prepare for standardized tests and competency examinations in United States history. Students who master the skills in this book will have a much better chance of doing well in all their schoolwork.

The author wishes to thank the following for their advice and assistance in the preparation of this book: Sr. Kathleen Carlin, O.P., Principal, St. Agnes Cathedral School, Rockville Centre, New York, and Robert W. DiLorenzo, Social Studies teacher, DeWitt Clinton High School, New York City.

Gerard J. Pelisson

CONTENTS

CHAPTER 1

Recognizing Landforms and Water Forms

Studying the history of the United States can be enjoyable and rewarding. It is an opportunity to learn about many interesting people and about events that have shaped our nation and the world. How much you learn will depend greatly on the skills you possess. A skill is something a person does well. This book will help you develop the skills needed to study the history of the United States.

Let us begin with map skills. In this chapter, you will learn to use maps to locate landforms and water forms in and around the United States. On the landforms, people live, grow food, and manufacture products. The water forms provide water for drinking and for growing crops, routes for travel, and sea animals for food. Many of these landforms and water forms have affected the history of the United States. So it is a valuable skill to be able to recognize them on a map.

Landforms

CONTINENTS. The largest landforms on the earth are called *continents.* The map below shows all seven continents: Asia, Africa, North America, South America, Antarctica, Europe, and Australia. Your country, the United States, is located in North America. The map on page 2 shows that North America also includes the countries of Canada and Mexico. In addition, the seven countries of Central America are part of North America. These countries are Panama, Costa Rica, Honduras, Guatemala, Nicaragua, Belize, and El Salvador.

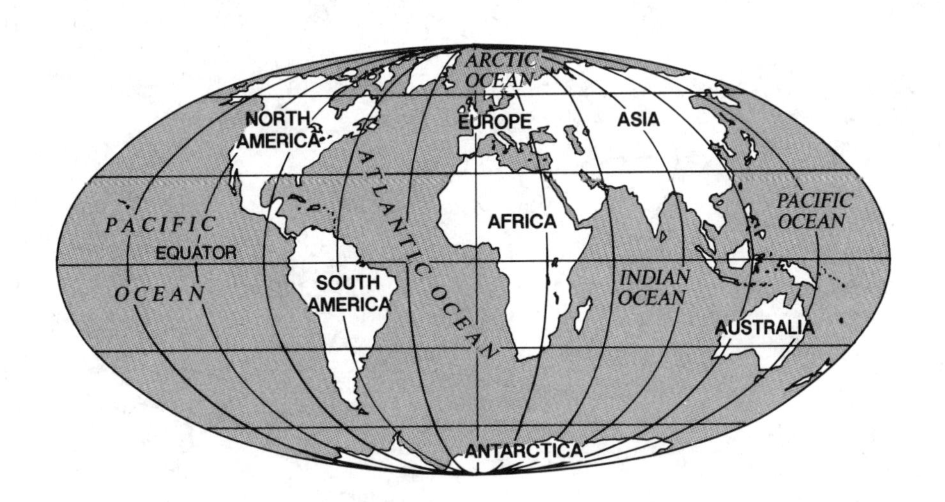

ISLANDS. An *island* is a body of land completely surrounded by water. Most islands belong to a particular continent. For example, Greenland is part of North America. Find Greenland on the map below.

A group of islands that are near each other is called an *archipelago.* Look for the archipelago labeled West Indies on the map below. What are the names of some of the islands that make up this archipelago?

PENINSULAS. A body of land extending into the sea and almost completely surrounded by water is called a *peninsula.* Florida, for example, is a peninsula. Locate it on the map below.

CAPES. A *cape* is a point of land that extends into the sea. One example is Cape Cod. It is shown on the map below.

ISTHMUSES. An *isthmus* is a narrow strip of land connecting two large landforms. The Isthmus of Panama connects North America and South America. Find the Isthmus of Panama on the map below.

Let us see how much you have learned about landforms. Write the letter of the correct choice on the line next to the number of the question.

North America

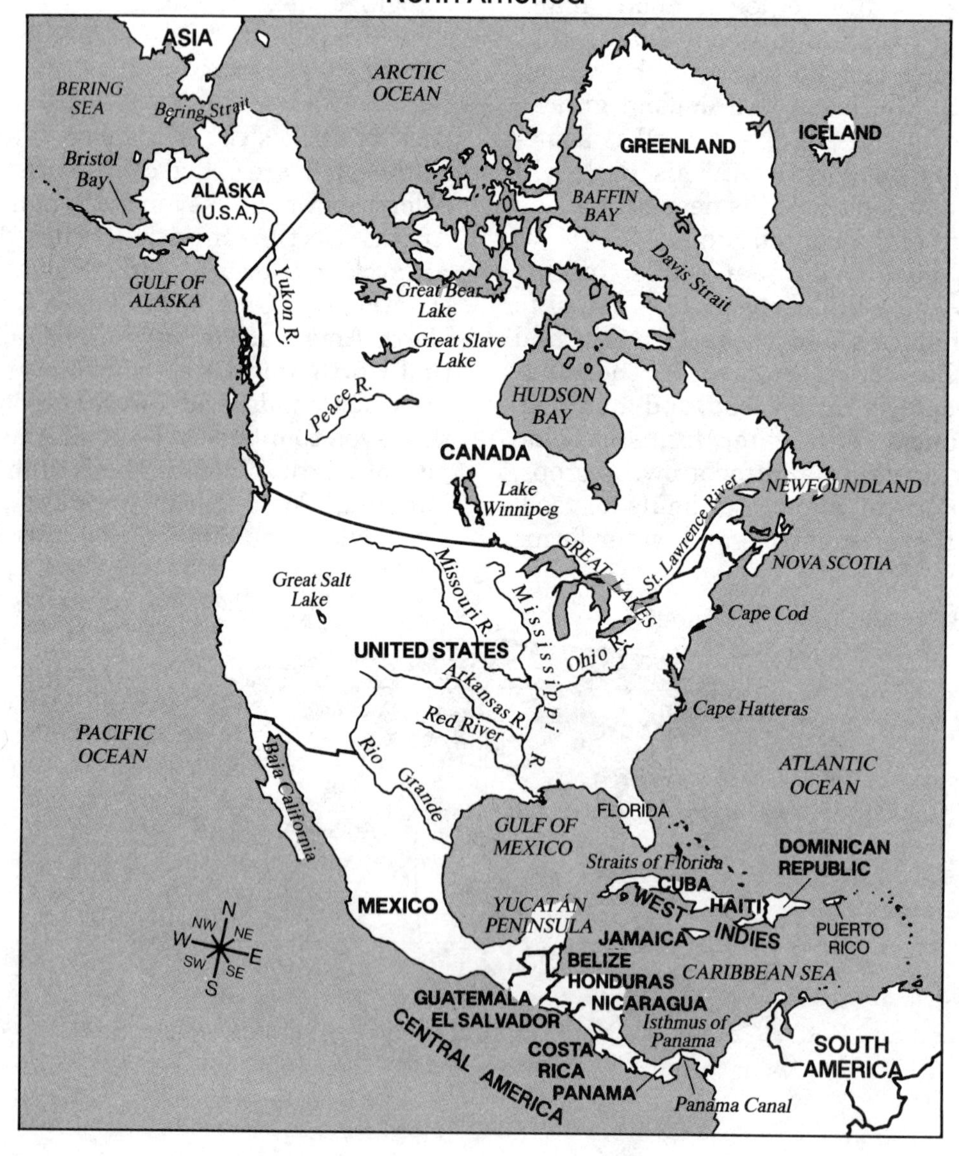

____ 1. North America is
(a) an island.
(b) an archipelago.
(c) a continent.
(d) a country.

Which answer did you choose? You read in this chapter that an island is a body of land completely surrounded by water. North America is not completely surrounded by water. It is connected to South America by the Isthmus of Panama, as shown on the map on page 2. Because North America is not an island, it cannot be an archipelago, which is a group of islands. The great size of North America fits the definition of a continent, the largest landform on the earth. So *(c)* could be the answer. But what about *(d)* a country? Some countries are very large, but they are not natural landforms. Countries are created by governments. They are usually found within continents and separated from other countries by boundary lines determined by governments. Choice *(d)* cannot be the answer. Therefore, the answer to question 1 must be *(c)*.

2. Baja California is part of Mexico, as shown on the map on page 2. Is it a cape or a peninsula?

____

What is your answer? A cape is a point of land that extends into the sea. A peninsula is a body of land extending into the sea and almost completely surrounded by water. Baja California is more than a point of land. It is a long body of land that extends far into the sea. Therefore, Baja California is a peninsula.

Water Forms

OCEANS. The largest bodies of water (or water forms) on the earth are called *oceans.* As you can see on the map on page 1, there are four oceans: the Pacific, the Atlantic, the Indian, and the Arctic. Three of these oceans touch the United States. Can you name them?

SEAS, GULFS, BAYS. Three other large water forms are usually parts of oceans. They are *seas, gulfs,* and *bays.* (Some seas are completely surrounded by land, and some bays are parts of lakes.) Most of them are partly surrounded by landforms or extend deep into landforms. On the map on page 2, find the Bering Sea, the Gulf of Alaska, and Bristol Bay. These large bodies of water are part of the Pacific Ocean.

STRAITS AND CANALS. *Straits* and *canals* are narrow stretches of water connecting two larger bodies of water. A strait is a natural water form, while a canal is a water route made by humans. The map on page 2 shows the Bering Strait connecting the Arctic Ocean and the Bering Sea. It also shows the Panama Canal, which ships can use to sail between the Atlantic Ocean and the Pacific Ocean.

LAKES. Many bodies of water lie within landforms. A body of water completely surrounded by land is called a *lake.* (A few seas are also surrounded by land.) The map on page 2 shows the Great Lakes, located between Canada and the United States.

RIVERS. Another important water form found inside land is a *river.* On a map, a river is usually shown by a blue or black line.

The close-up map of the Mississippi River on page 4 reveals a number of interesting details about rivers.

The place where a river begins is called its *source.* This source may be water running down from mountains or a lake. In the case of the Mississippi River, the source is Lake Itasca in Minnesota.

The place where a river ends is called its *mouth.* The Mississippi River flows in a generally southerly direction. Its mouth is where the river empties into the Gulf of Mexico.

A large area of fertile soil at the mouth of a river is called a *delta.* It is usually a good area for growing crops. Find the Mississippi Delta on the close-up map on page 4.

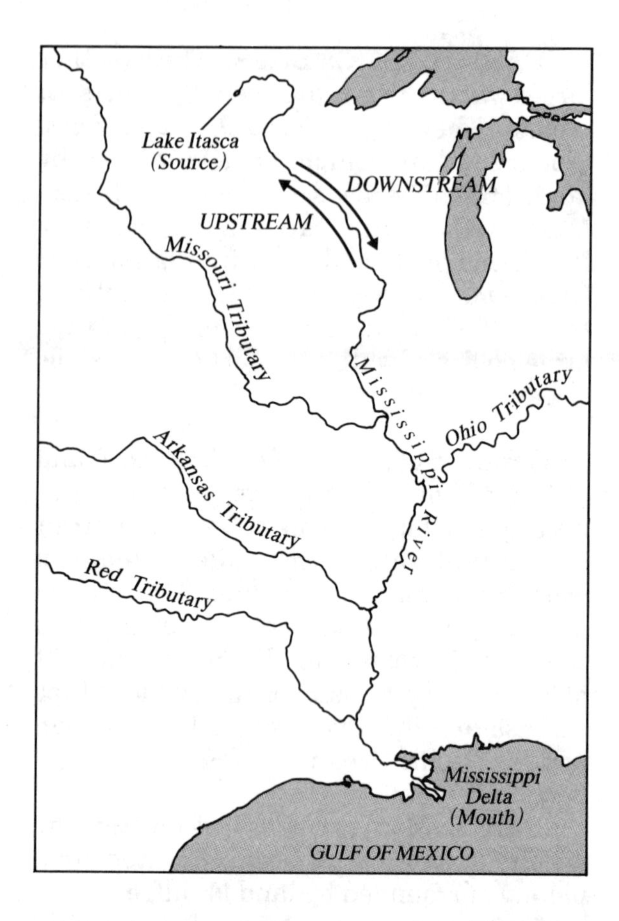

Smaller rivers that flow into a large river are called *tributaries.* Name some of the major tributaries of the Mississippi River.

Two other important terms relating to rivers are shown on the close-up map. They are *downstream* and *upstream.* Downstream is the direction in which a river flows. When you travel downstream on the Mississippi River or on any river, you are traveling away from the source and toward the mouth. Upstream means traveling against the flow of a river. When you travel upstream, you are moving away from the mouth and toward the source.

Let us find out how much you have learned about water forms.

____ 3. A body of water that extends into the land is called a
(a) strait.
(b) lake.
(c) river.
(d) bay.

Which answer did you choose? Do you know the meaning of each water form listed in the choices? Straits are narrow, natural stretches of water connecting two larger bodies of water. Lakes are bodies of water completely surrounded by land. Rivers are water forms that start inside land and flow to the sea. Bays, like seas and gulfs, are parts of oceans that extend into the land. By definition, choice *(d)* must be the answer to question 3.

4. Match the terms related to rivers in Column B with their meanings in Column A.

Column A

____ 1. the place where a river begins

____ 2. a smaller river flowing into a larger river

____ 3. the direction in which a river flows

____ 4. the place where a river ends

____ 5. an area of fertile land near where a river ends

____ 6. the direction opposite to, or against, the flow of a river

Column B

a. downstream
b. delta
c. tributary
d. upstream
e. source
f. mouth

An explanation of each of these terms is given in this chapter. Read over the chapter if you have forgotten their meanings. The correct answers are 1. *e,* 2. *c,* 3. *a,* 4. *f,* 5. *b,* 6. *d.*

Directions

In locating landforms and water forms on a map, it is valuable to know how to use directions. The direction compass on the map on page 2 shows the four *cardinal* (main) directions—north (N), south (S), east (E), west (W)—and the four *intermediate* (in-between) directions—northeast (NE), southeast (SE), southwest (SW), northwest (NW). With the help of the direction compass, you can see that Baffin Bay is north of Hudson Bay and that Hudson Bay is west of Newfoundland. If you travel from Florida to the West Indies, you travel in a southeast direction. In which direction do you travel from the West Indies to Florida? The answer is in a northwest direction. If you travel from the Yucatán Peninsula in Mexico to Florida, you travel in a northeast direction. So, in which direction do you travel from Florida to the Yucatán Peninsula?

In this chapter, you have learned how to locate and name landforms and water forms on a map. The following exercises will give you more practice is using this valuable skill.

USING YOUR SKILLS

A. Write the letter of the correct choice on the line next to the number of each question.

____ 1. As shown on the map on page 2, the three largest countries on the North American continent are
(a) the United States, Canada, and Costa Rica.
(b) Canada, the United States, and Mexico.
(c) Mexico, the United States, and Nicaragua.
(d) the United States, Alaska, and Mexico.

____ 2. The term for the largest landform is
(a) island. *(c)* peninsula.
(b) country. *(d)* continent.

____ 3. Which of the following is a landform?
(a) strait *(c)* canal
(b) bay *(d)* isthmus

____ 4. Which of the following water forms is most like a gulf?
(a) sea *(c)* lake
(b) strait *(d)* river

____ 5. Which of the following is made by humans?
(a) gulf *(b)* strait *(c)* canal *(d)* tributary

____ 6. Which ocean does NOT touch any part of the United States?
(a) Arctic Ocean *(c)* Indian Ocean
(b) Atlantic Ocean *(d)* Pacific Ocean

____ 7. When you are traveling downstream on a river, you are going
(a) with the flow of the river away from the source.
(b) with the flow of the river heading toward the source.
(c) against the flow of the river.
(d) away from the mouth of the river.

____ 8. In which direction are you going if you travel directly from Mexico to Canada?
(a) north *(b)* south *(c)* east *(d)* west

____ 9. The letters that stand for the direction northeast are
(*a*) NW. (*c*) WN.
(*b*) NE. (*d*) EN.

____ 10. A peninsula is a
(*a*) group of islands.
(*b*) narrow strip of land connecting two larger land areas.
(*c*) body of land completely surrounded by water.
(*d*) body of land extending into the sea and almost completely surrounded by water.

B. Locating Landforms and Water Forms.

B-1. Landforms. Using the map on page 2 as a reference, match the examples in Column B with their landforms in Column A. One example does not match any landform.

Column A	*Column B*
____ 1. continent	*a.* Yucatán
____ 2. island	*b.* Panama
____ 3. archipelago	*c.* Newfoundland
____ 4. peninsula	*d.* North America
____ 5. cape	*e.* Hudson
____ 6. isthmus	*f.* West Indies
	g. Hatteras

B-2. Water Forms. Using the map on page 2 as a reference, match the examples in Column B with their water forms in Column A. One example does not match any water form.

Column A	*Column B*
____ 1. ocean	*a.* Rio Grande
____ 2. sea	*b.* Caribbean
____ 3. gulf	*c.* Winnipeg
____ 4. bay	*d.* Cuba
____ 5. strait	*e.* Baffin
____ 6. river	*f.* Mexico
____ 7. lake	*g.* Arctic
	h. Florida

C. Next to the name of each country on the North American mainland, write the number that matches its location on the map below. If you need help, look at the map of North America on page 2.

Countries of North America

_____Belize

_____Canada

_____Costa Rica

_____El Salvador

_____Guatemala

_____Honduras

_____Mexico

_____Nicaragua

_____Panama

_____United States

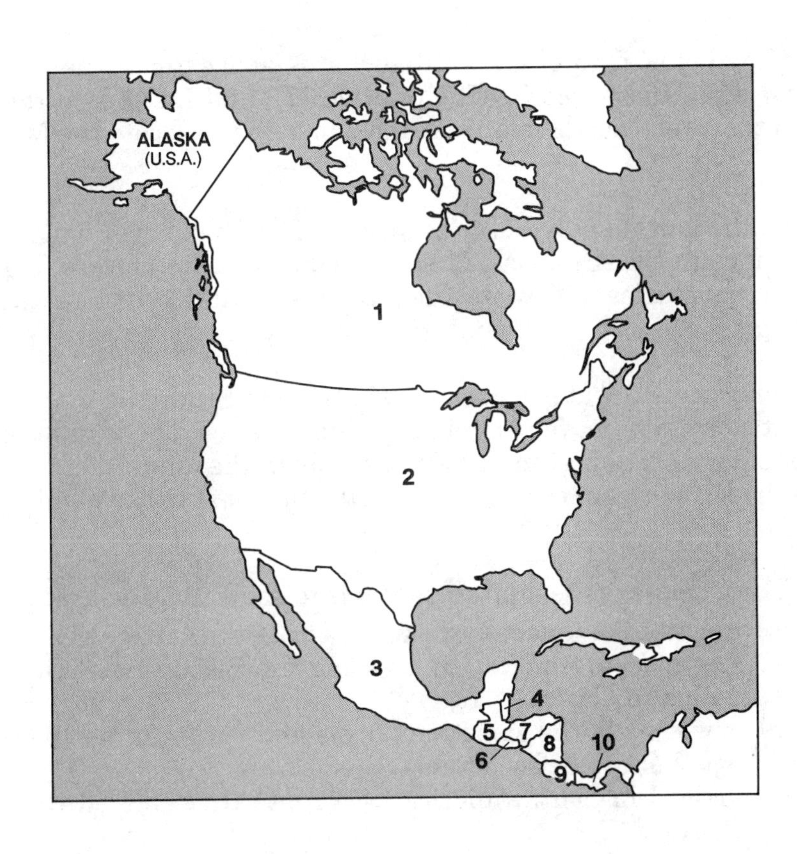

D. Terms Related to Rivers.

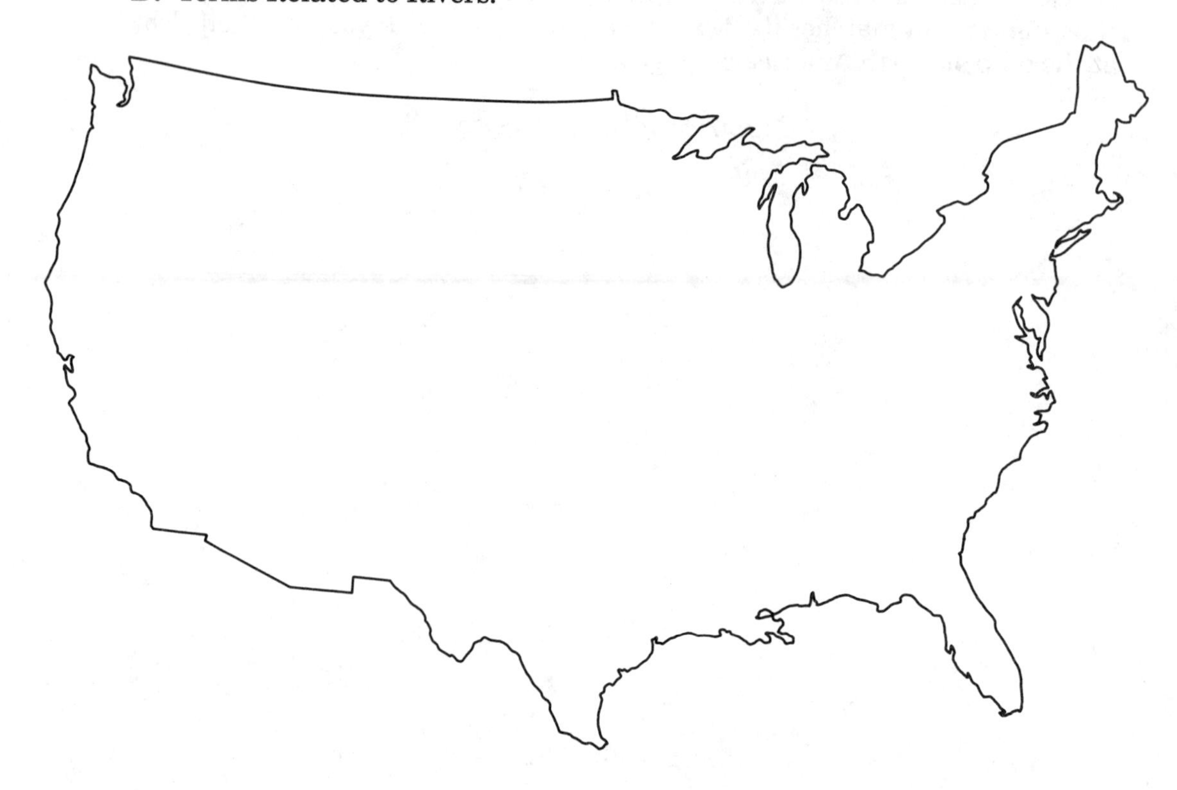

D-1. On the blank map of the United States above, draw the Mississippi River and write the terms SOURCE, MOUTH, and DELTA in the correct places on the river. Use the map on page 2 to help you locate the Mississippi River.

D-2. Find the four main tributaries of the Mississippi River on the map on page 2. They are the Arkansas, Missouri, Ohio, and Red rivers. Then draw these four tributaries and write their names in the correct places on the blank map.

E-1. Landforms and Water Forms in U.S. History. Study the map on page 9 of the first *migration* (movement of people) to America. The *key* at the bottom of the map provides important information about the map.

Write the letter of the correct choice on the line next to the number of each question.

_____ 1. The purpose of the map on page 9 is to show that the first people
- *(a)* migrated to America by sailing across the Arctic Ocean.
- *(b)* migrated to America by crossing the Bering Land Bridge from Asia into Alaska.
- *(c)* saw exactly the same landforms and water forms 15,000 years ago that can be seen today.
- *(d)* arrived in South America by a route that crossed the Atlantic Ocean.

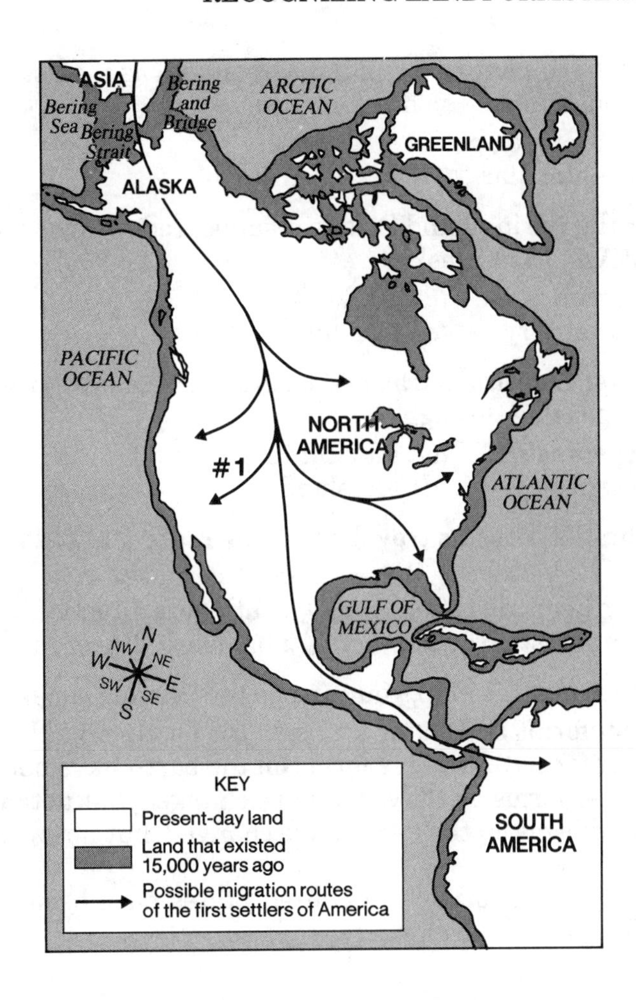

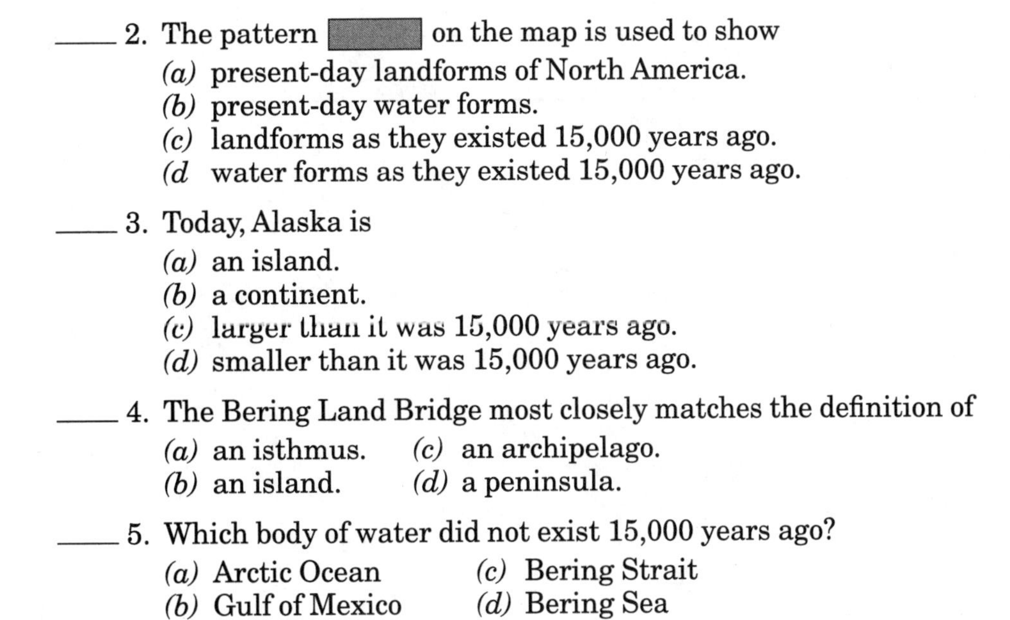

_____ 2. The pattern [gray box] on the map is used to show

(a) present-day landforms of North America.
(b) present-day water forms.
(c) landforms as they existed 15,000 years ago.
(d water forms as they existed 15,000 years ago.

_____ 3. Today, Alaska is

(a) an island.
(b) a continent.
(c) larger than it was 15,000 years ago.
(d) smaller than it was 15,000 years ago.

_____ 4. The Bering Land Bridge most closely matches the definition of

(a) an isthmus. (c) an archipelago.
(b) an island. (d) a peninsula.

_____ 5. Which body of water did not exist 15,000 years ago?

(a) Arctic Ocean (c) Bering Strait
(b) Gulf of Mexico (d) Bering Sea

_____ 6. Today, Greenland is an island. Greenland as it existed 15,000 years ago would have been described as
(*a*) an archipelago. (*c*) a cape.
(*b*) a peninsula. (*d*) a continent.

_____ 7. After the Bering Land Bridge disappeared, which water form separated Asia from Alaska?
(*a*) a river (*c*) a lake
(*b*) a tributary (*d*) a strait

_____ 8. The first Americans traveled from North America into South America by passing through
(*a*) a peninsula. (*c*) an isthmus.
(*b*) a cape. (*d*) an island.

_____ 9. The first Americans traveling on the route marked #1 were headed in a
(*a*) northeast direction. (*c*) southwest direction.
(*b*) southeast direction. (*d*) northwest direction.

_____ 10. By studying this map, you can see that during thousands of years,
(*a*) landforms and water forms on the earth have changed.
(*b*) landforms and water forms on the earth have not changed.
(*c*) water forms on the earth have changed, but not landforms.
(*d*) landforms on the earth have changed, but not water forms.

E-2. How might the history of the United States have been different if the Bering Land Bridge had never existed?

____

____

____

____

CHAPTER 2
Using Relief Maps

The maps you see throughout this book are called flat maps because they are drawn on flat paper. But the surface of the earth is not completely flat. Some land features are higher or lower than others.

High land features include:

- *mountains:* landmasses much higher than nearby areas
- *mountain ranges:* mountains close together in a row
- *volcanoes:* mountains with an opening in the top or side, through which melted rock, steam, and ashes are forced out from inside the earth
- *plateaus:* high, flat landmasses
- *hills:* high, rounded landmasses, usually less tall than mountains

There are also two important lower land features:

- *valleys:* long, narrow areas, usually formed by rivers
- *basins:* wide, deep areas, sometimes enclosed by mountain ranges

Where there are no high land features, there may be *plains*—areas of level or rolling land. Plains that are good for growing crops or raising animals are sometimes called *prairies.*

Another important land feature is a *coastline* (shoreline). A coastline is the land found all along the edge of a body of water such as an ocean or a lake.

How can you draw these land features on a flat map? One way is to make a relief profile (side view). It shows the shape and *altitude* (height above sea level) of land features.

Figure A below is a relief profile of the United States. It shows the shapes of many of the land features listed at the beginning of this chapter. The measurements (2,000, 5,000, 10,000, and 12,000 feet) on each end of the profile are used to show the altitudes of the land features. For example, find the altitude of the Sierra Nevada, a mountain range in the western United States. Place your finger on the Sierra Nevada on the profile. Then run your finger straight across to the measurement on the left side of the profile. The top of the Sierra Nevada nearly matches the 10,000-feet mark on the measurement. So, the Sierra Nevada range reaches an altitude of nearly 10,000 feet.

The measurement 10,000 feet means 10,000 feet above *sea level.* When measuring land features, it is important to start from the same level on the ground. But the ground levels of land are very different in

Figure A

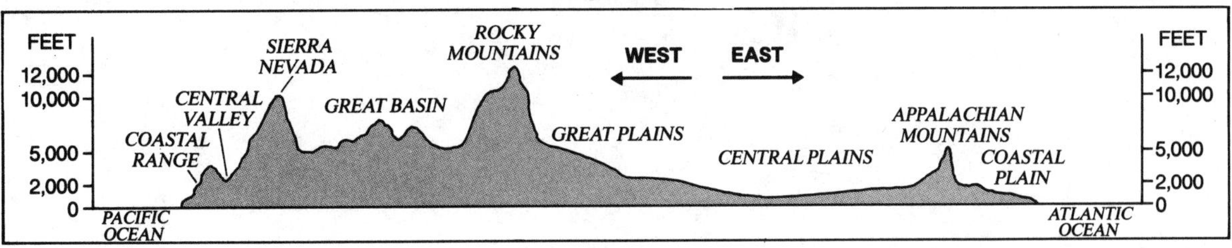

different parts of the world. Only the surface of the ocean waters is more or less the same throughout the world. Therefore, the measurement of altitude starts on the surface of the oceans, or sea level.

Find out how much you have learned about side-view relief maps. Use Figure A on page 11 to help you answer the following questions.

_____ 1. Which area of the United States has higher land features?

(a) East *(b)* West

Which answer did you choose? Find the words WEST/EAST on the figure. The arrows below these direction words will show you where the eastern and western areas of the United States are located. By studying the profile, you should see that there are higher land features in the western areas of the United States than in the eastern areas. Therefore, the answer to question 1 is *(b)*.

_____ 2. The Rocky Mountains reach an altitude

(a) of less than 2,000 feet

(b) between 2,000 and 5,000 feet.

(c) between 5,000 and 10,000 feet.

(d) of more than 10,000 feet.

Which answer did you choose? Locate the Rocky Mountains on Figure A and then run your finger across to the measurements on the side of the profile. You can see that the Rocky Mountains reach an altitude of more than 10,000 feet. Therefore, the answer to question 2 is *(d)*.

Most relief maps use a top view of an area rather than a side view. Map A below and Map B on page 13 are two types of top-view relief maps.

Map A is a simple map. The symbol [mountain symbol] shows the location of high land features, mostly mountains. The map also shows the altitude of specific land features. For example, find Mount Whitney on Map A. The name and altitude of the mountain are shown like this: *Mount Whitney* + 14,494 The sign (+) means *above*. So, Mount Whitney has an altitude of 14,494 feet above sea level. In some areas of the United States, dry land is actually below sea level. Death Valley is one example. Higher land around the valley keeps it from being flooded by ocean water. Find Death Valley on Map A. The name and altitude are shown like this: *Death Valley* – 282 The sign (–) means *below*. So, Death Valley is 282 feet below sea level.

Map A

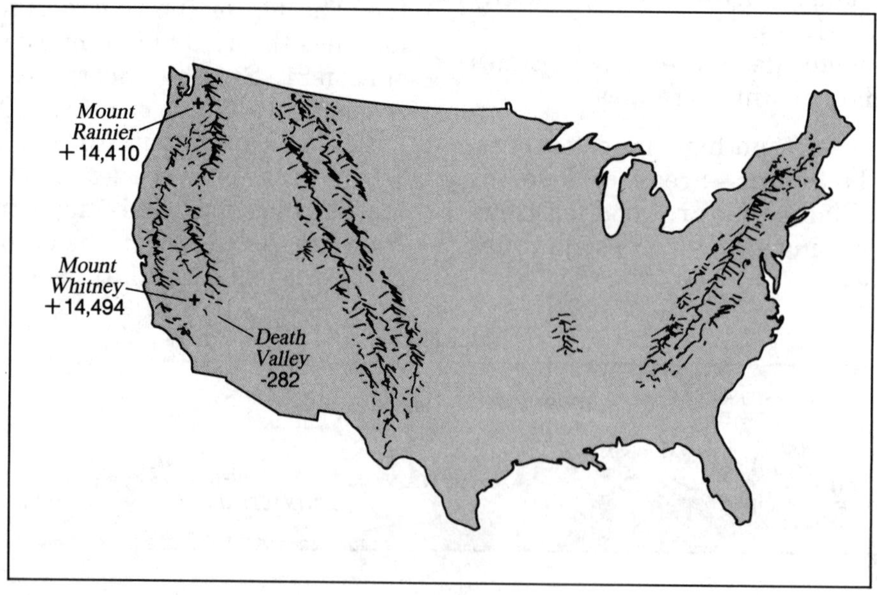

Map A does not show the altitude of large areas of land. Map B, on the other hand, uses different patterns to show the altitudes of large areas of land. The key on the map gives the altitudes that each pattern represents. By using the key, you can see how high the land areas are.

Using Figure A, Map A, and Map B as references, answer the following questions.

_____ 3. Which mountain has a higher altitude?

(a) Mount Whitney
(b) Mount Rainier

What was your answer? Very high mountains are often shown on a map with their exact altitudes written near them. Find Mount Whitney and Mount Rainier on Map A. You can see that Mount Whitney is 14,494 feet above sea level and that Mount Rainier is 14,410 feet above sea level. Therefore, Mount Whitney has a higher altitude, and the answer to question 3 is *(a)*.

_____ 4. The pattern [dotted pattern] on Map B stands for an altitude

(a) of sea level to 1,000 feet.
(b) between 1,001 and 5,000 feet.
(c) between 5,001 and 10,000 feet.
(d) of more than 10,000 feet.

Which answer did you choose? The key shows that the pattern [dotted pattern] stands for an altitude between 5,001 and 10,000 feet. This means that every area on the map with this pattern has an altitude between 5,001 and 10,000 feet above sea level. Therefore, the answer to question 4 is *(c)*.

_____ 5. Most of the United States is

(a) very mountainous.
(b) covered by plains and rolling hills.
(c) covered by high plateaus.
(d) made up of high volcanoes.

Which answer did you choose this time? Figure A and Map B can help you find the

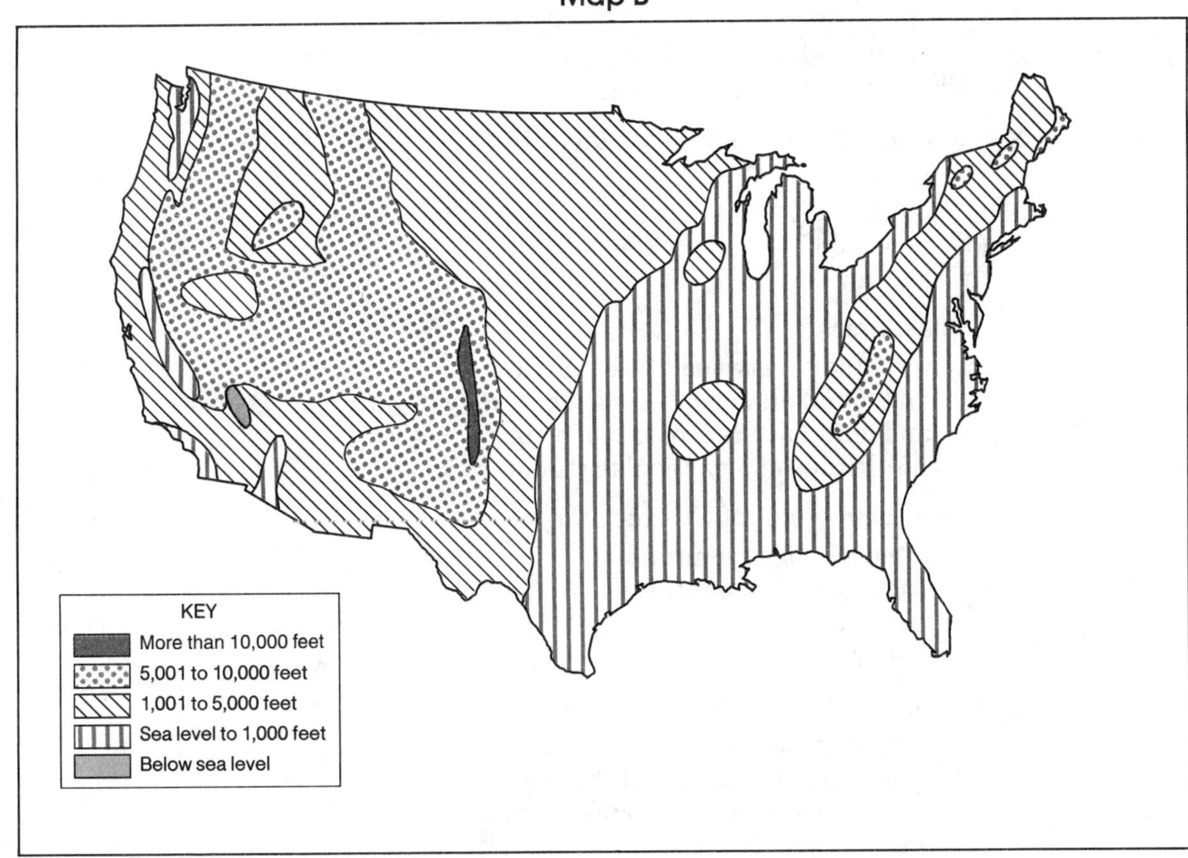

answer. Most of the land that Figure A identifies as plains is less than 5,000 feet above sea level. And most of the land on Map B is covered by the patterns [diagonal-line pattern] and [vertical-line pattern]. These patterns also represent land that is less than 5,000 feet above sea level. Mountains, high plateaus, and high volcanoes usually have altitudes of more than 5,000 feet. Plains, as shown in Figure A, and rolling hills usually have altitudes of less than 5,000 feet. Since most of the land in the United States has altitudes of less than 5,000 feet, most of that land must be covered by plains and rolling hills. Therefore, the answer to question 5 is *(b).*

The lives of Americans have been and continue to be affected by this country's land features. For example, the Rocky Mountains slowed the movement of early explorers and settlers. Think of how difficult it has always been to grow crops in mountainous areas. Even athletes have to train in special ways to compete in the thinner air of high altitudes.

Being able to identify land features on a relief map and to measure their altitude are worthwhile skills. The following exercises will give you practice in developing these two skills.

USING YOUR SKILLS

A. Write the letter of the correct choice on the line next to the number of each question.

_____ 1. A relief profile shows
(a) how many people live in an area of land.
(b) why people live on high land features.
(c) the altitudes of land features.
(d) the crops grown in a country.

_____ 2. Which one is NOT a high land feature?
(a) prairie
(b) plateau
(c) mountain
(d) volcano

_____ 3. A coastline is
(a) a boundary between two countries.
(b) land found all along the edge of a body of water.
(c) land found in the center of a country.
(d) the altitude of a particular mountain range.

_____ 4. The measurement of altitude starts
(a) at the foot of a mountain.
(b) at the top of a mountain.
(c) below sea level.
(d) at sea level.

_____ 5. The phrase "below sea level" means
(a) at the edge of the sea.
(b) lower than the surface of the oceans.
(c) below the level of any body of water.
(d) at the bottom of the sea.

B. Match the shapes of the land features in the drawing with their names in the following list.

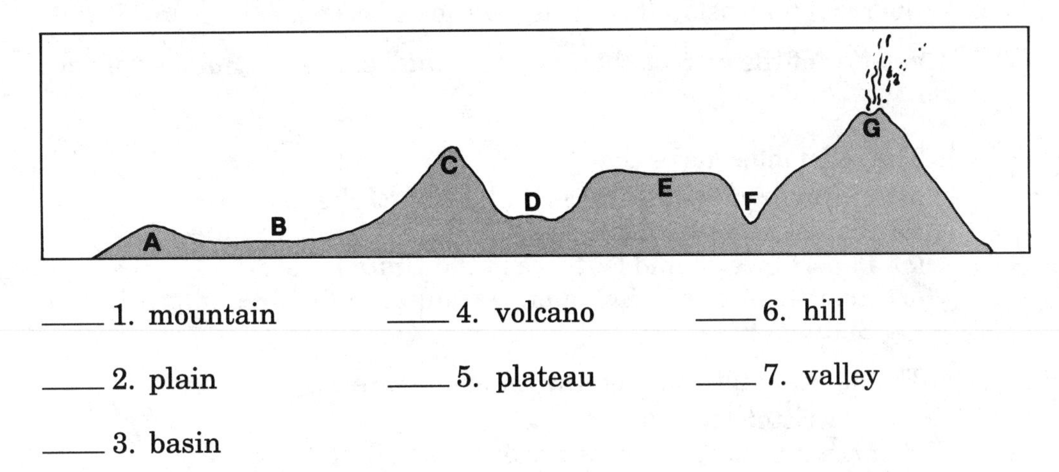

_____ 1. mountain _____ 4. volcano _____ 6. hill

_____ 2. plain _____ 5. plateau _____ 7. valley

_____ 3. basin

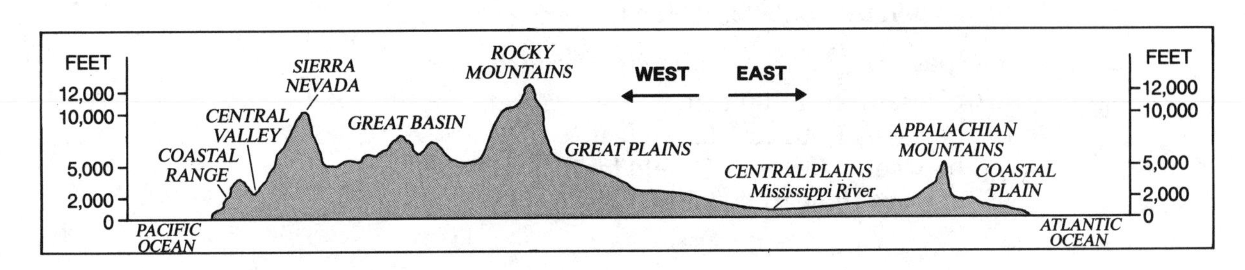

C. Studying a Relief Profile.

Write the letter of the correct choice on the line next to the number of each question.

_____ 1. Which mountain range is located in the eastern United States?
(a) Rocky Mountains *(c)* Sierra Nevada
(b) Appalachian Mountains *(d)* Coastal Range

_____ 2. The Mississippi River flows through the
(a) Rocky Mountains. *(c)* Appalachian Mountains.
(b) Coastal Plain. *(d)* Central Plains.

_____ 3. The land between the Sierra Nevada and the Rocky Mountains is called
(a) a valley. *(c)* a basin.
(b) a lowland area. *(d)* a plain.

_____ 4. According to the profile, the Appalachian Mountains reach an altitude of
(a) 2,000 feet. *(c)* 10,000 feet.
(b) 5,000 feet. *(d)* 12,000 feet.

_____ 5. Which mountain range on the profile has the highest altitude?
(a) Appalachian Mountains *(c)* Sierra Nevada
(b) Rocky Mountains *(d)* Coastal Range

D. Studying a Top-View Relief Map.

Look at the relief map below. Then answer the questions.

Write the letter of the correct choice on the line next to the number of each question.

____ 1. The relief map shows the
(a) altitudes of land features in the United States.
(b) distances between land features in the United States.
(c) importance of land features in the United States.
(d) number of people living on certain land features in the United States.

____ 2. The different altitudes on the relief map are
(a) all written out in words.
(b) shown by patterns that are explained in the key.
(c) shown by patterns that are not explained in the key.
(d) shown by symbols, such as [mountain symbol].

____ 3. The pattern [diagonal-line pattern] stands for altitudes
(a) of less than 1,000 feet.
(b) between 1,001 and 5,000 feet.
(c) between 5,001 and 10,000 feet.
(d) of more than 10,000 feet.

A Relief Map of the United States

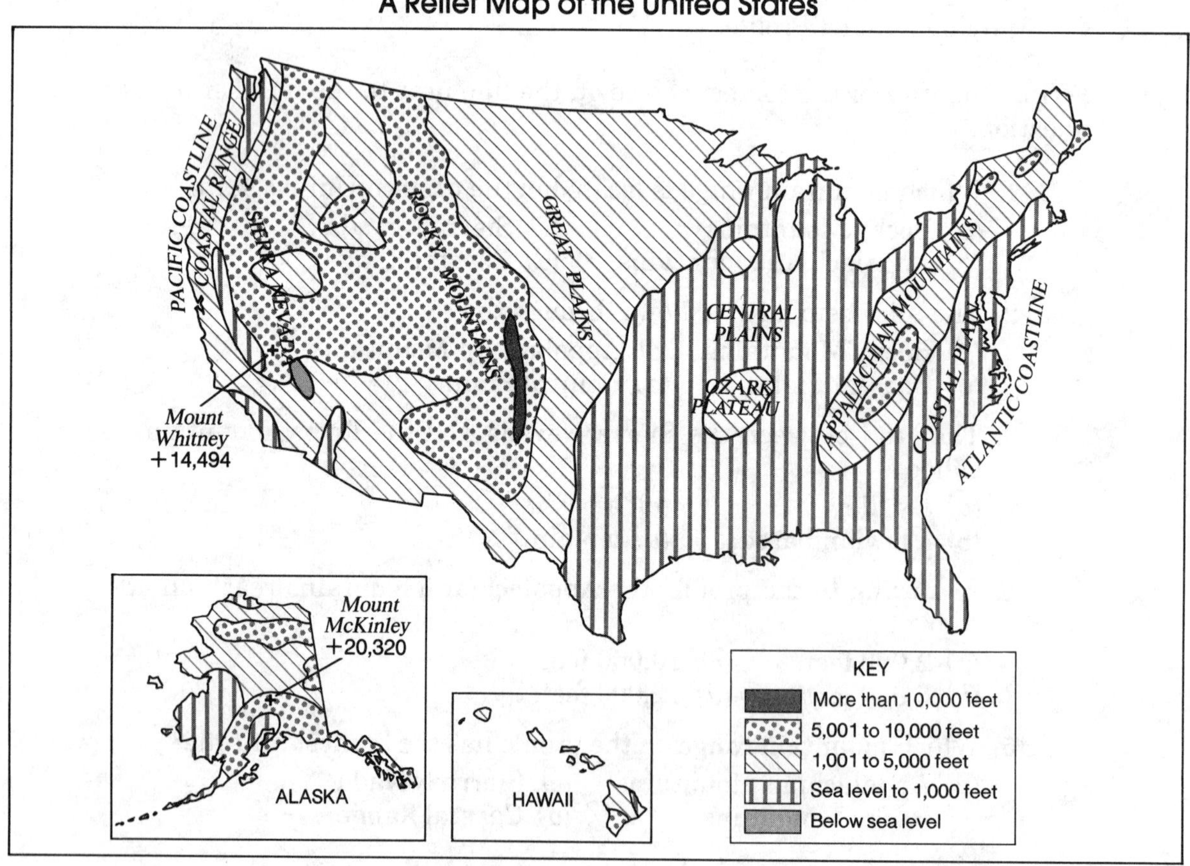

____ 4. A land feature 6,500 feet above sea level would be shown by the pattern
(a) [vertical-striped pattern] *(c)* [dark pattern]
(b) [gray pattern] *(d)* [dotted pattern]

____ 5. Most of Alaska is covered by
(a) land below sea level. *(c)* high mountains.
(b) land at sea level. *(d)* high flat lands, hills, and mountains.

____ 6. The Ozark Plateau has altitudes
(a) below sea level.
(b) between sea level and 1,000 feet.
(c) between 1,001 and 5,000 feet.
(d) between 5,001 and 10,000 feet.

____ 7. Most of the Atlantic Coastline area is covered by
(a) plains. *(c)* valleys.
(b) mountains. *(d)* plateaus.

____ 8. Which land feature reaches altitudes of more than 10,000 feet?
(a) Appalachian Mountains *(c)* Rocky Mountains
(b) Central Plains *(d)* Coastal Range

____ 9. Which mountain has the higher altitude?
(a) Mount Whitney *(b)* Mount McKinley

____ 10. Which area has the highest altitude?
(a) Atlantic Coastal Plain *(c)* Great Plains
(b) Central Plains

E-1. Land Features in U.S. History. Study the map on page 18 of European exploration in the New World. The term "New World" was the name once used by historians to describe North and South America.

Write the letter of the correct choice on the line next to the number of each question. Some of the questions deal with landforms and water forms as well as land features.

____ 1. The purpose of the map is to show
(a) that all European explorers arrived in the New World at the same time.
(b) that many of the European explorers must have met one another.
(c) where European explorers lived in the New World.
(d) the travel routes taken by European explorers in the New World.

____ 2. Which two explorers ended voyages in the same year?
(a) Columbus and Verrazano *(c)* De Soto and Coronado
(b) Pizarro and Cartier *(d)* Cabrillo and La Salle

____ 3. The line ⟶ represents the exploration route used by
(a) Verrazano. *(c)* Pizarro.
(b) Columbus. *(d)* Cabrillo.

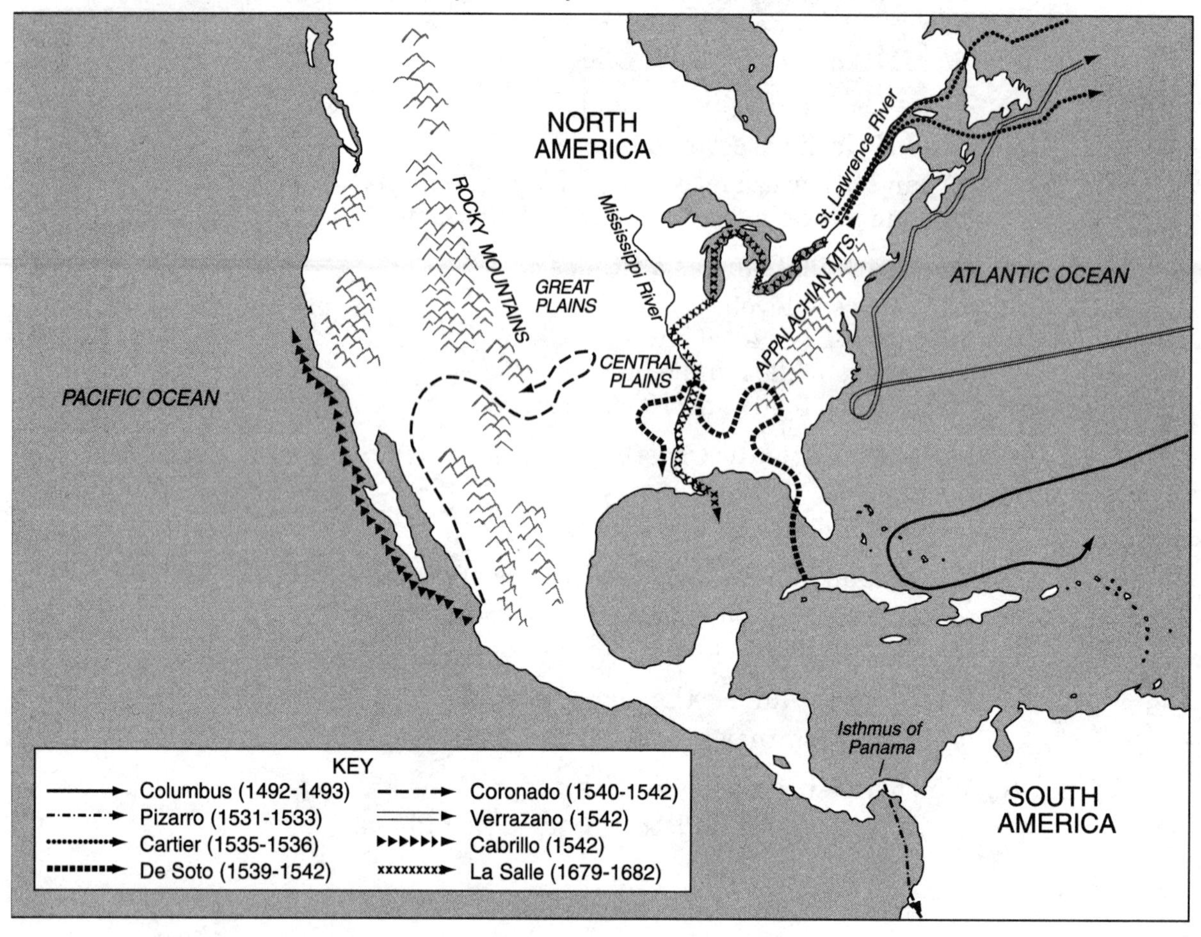

____ 4. Which of the explorers listed sailed along the Atlantic Coastline?
(*a*) La Salle (*c*) Verrazano
(*b*) Cabrillo (*d*) Coronado

____ 5. Which explorer sailed part of the way up the St. Lawrence River?
(*a*) Cartier (*c*) De Soto
(*b*) Verrazano (*d*) Pizarro

____ 6. De Soto and, later, La Salle explored
(*a*) the Great Plains.
(*b*) the Appalachian Mountains.
(*c*) the Mississippi River.
(*d*) most of South America.

____ 7. The Pacific Coastline was explored by
(*a*) Columbus. (*c*) Cartier.
(*b*) La Salle. (*d*) Cabrillo.

____ 8. The map shows that Pizarro crossed the
(*a*) Great Plains. (*c*) Appalachian Mountains.
(*b*) Isthmus of Panama. (*d*) Mississippi River.

_____ 9. Which explorer crossed the Rocky Mountains and part of the Great Plains?

(a) De Soto *(c)* La Salle
(b) Columbus *(d)* Coronado

_____ 10. Which explorer traveled through part of the Central Plains?

(a) De Soto *(c)* Cabrillo
(b) Cartier *(d)* Pizarro

E-2. More About Land Features in U.S. History. Land features sometimes helped European explorers in their travels; sometimes they held the explorers back. Name an explorer on the map who may have been helped or held back by land features. Explain your answer.

____

____

____

____

CHAPTER 3

Using Historical Maps

Illinois, Iowa, and Delaware are the names of three states in the United States. But where did these states get their names? The answer can be found on the map below.

This map is called a *historical map* because it shows what the United States looked like at a particular time in history, namely, the year 1600. (Of course, the United States did not yet exist as a country in 1600, but the land shown on the map eventually became the United States.)

The title of the map tells you that it shows Native American tribes and *culture areas* in 1600. Each tribe name on the map is in the place where the tribe settled. Find the Illinois, Iowa, and Delaware tribes on the map. Now you know that the states of Illinois, Iowa, and Delaware were named for three Native American tribes. Can you find any other Native American tribes on the map that gave their names to U.S. cities and states?

Native American Tribes and Culture Areas, 1600

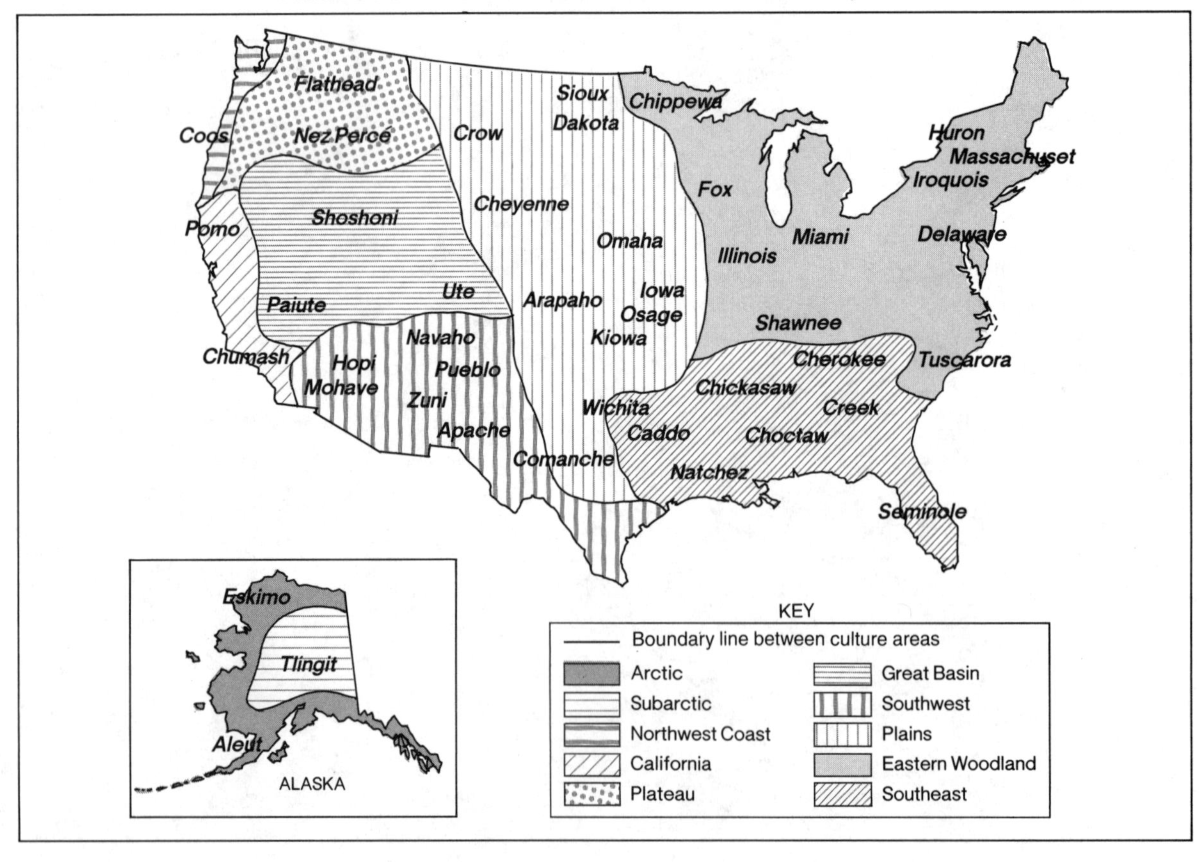

To locate the culture areas on the map, you must study the key. It is important to study the key on any map if you want to understand the map fully.

On this map, the key uses patterns to show different Native American culture areas. For example, the Eastern Woodland culture area is represented by the pattern . The Native American tribes that lived in the Eastern Woodland area shared a similar *culture.* This means that they shared a common way of living, as in their dress, their forms of art, and their religious beliefs and practices. In many cases, they spoke related languages.

Use the historical map on page 20 to answer the following questions.

1. TRUE or FALSE: If the underlined word makes the statement true, write TRUE on the line to the left of the statement. If the underlined word makes the statement false, write on the line to the left the word or words that will make the statement true.

______________ This historical map shows the location of Native American tribes <u>today</u>.

What was your answer? Perhaps the most important fact on a historical map is the date. The date tells you what year or time period the information on the map reflects. The year 1600 appears in the map title. This means that the map shows the location of Native American tribes in 1600. Therefore, the underlined word <u>today</u> is false and should have been changed to *in 1600.*

____ 2. Which two tribes belong to the Southwest culture area?
(a) Crow and Omaha
(b) Huron and Iroquois
(c) Hopi and Navaho
(d) Flathead and Nez Percé

Which answer did you choose? Find the pattern on the key that matches the Southwest culture area. You can see that the Southwest culture area is represented by the pattern . Now find that pattern on the map. You should see that the Hopi and Navaho belong to the Southwest culture area. Therefore, the answer to question 2 is *(c).*

Notice that lines are used to show the boundaries where a culture area begins and ends. The boundary lines on this map are drawn as follows: ————. Other maps may use different lines, such as: ------ or —·—·—·—. The key on a map should identify the line used to show the boundary.

Historical maps can be drawn to show the United States at different times in history. The map below shows British colonies in America in 1750. Once again, the key explains what the map shows. See if you understand the key, and then answer the following questions.

____ 3. Which pattern represents the land settled by the British?
(a)
(b)

British Colonies in America in 1750

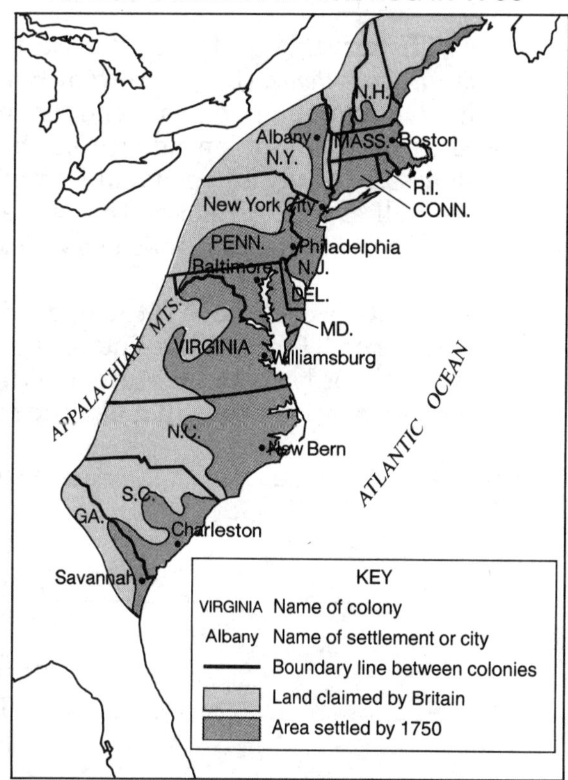

Which answer did you choose? The key shows that the pattern [gray pattern] represents the land settled by the British. Therefore, the answer to question 3 is *(b)*.

____ 4. According to the map, Williamsburg was

(a) the name of a colony.
(b) the name of a settlement or city.
(c) located in Pennsylvania.
(d) located in the Appalachian Mountains.

Which answer did you choose this time? Find Williamsburg on the map. Notice that it is spelled with only the first letter capitalized. The key shows that colony names are spelled in all capital letters, so *(a)* cannot be the answer. According to the key, places spelled with only the first letter capitalized are the names of settlements or cities. This seems to make *(b)* the answer, but you should always check the remaining choices. The map shows that Williamsburg is in Virginia, not Pennsylvania, so choice *(c)* is incorrect. Choice *(d)* is also wrong because the map shows that Williamsburg is far from the Appalachian Mountains. Now we are sure that the answer to question 4 is *(b)*.

Notice also that each settlement and city on the map is shown with a dot •. Dots are often used on maps to show cities. Stars * are sometimes used to show capital cities. When necessary, the key will explain dots and stars.

Historical maps are used more than any other kind of map in the study of U.S. history. In this chapter, you have learned the importance of the key on a historical map. You also have learned how important it is to know the year or time period of the map. The following exercises will give you practice in using historical maps.

USING YOUR SKILLS

A. Historical Map. The United States fought the Revolutionary War to gain its *independence* (freedom) from Britain. In 1783, the two nations signed a *treaty* (formal agreement) ending the war. In this treaty, Britain officially recognized the independence of the United States. The map on page 23 shows the newly independent United States. It also shows lands in the eastern half of North America that were claimed by the United States, Britain, and Spain, as well as lands not yet explored by Europeans.

A-1. TRUE or FALSE: If the underlined word or words make the statement true, write TRUE on the line to the left of the statement. If the underlined word or words make the statement false, write or draw on the line to the left the information that will make the statement true.

____________________ 1. In 1783, the newly independent United States extended from the Atlantic Ocean to the <u>Pacific Ocean</u>.

____________________ 2. The area of the United States covered by the pattern [gray pattern] was kept as a <u>Native American reserve</u>.

____________________ 3. The pattern [hatched pattern] is used to represent land claimed by <u>Britain</u>.

The United States in 1783

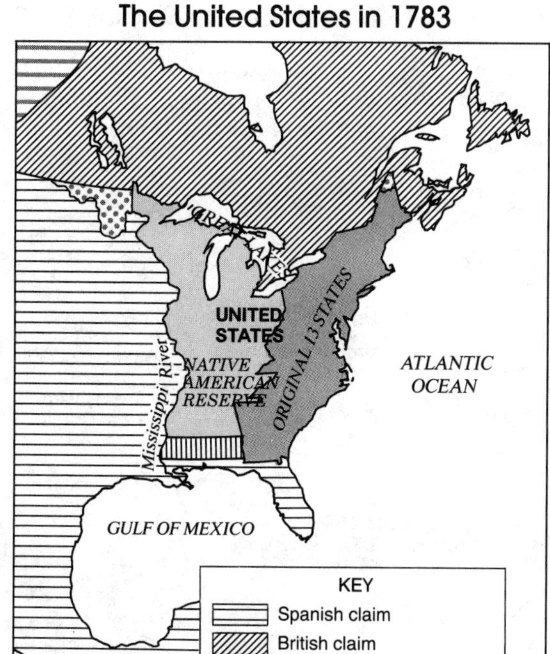

________________ 4. Land claimed by both the United States and Spain is shown by the pattern ______.

________________ 5. The land west of the Mississippi River eventually became part of the United States, but in 1783 nearly all that land was claimed by Spain.

A-2. How does the map show that water forms were used to determine boundaries of the United States?

____

____

____

B. Historical Map. *Manifest destiny* was the 19th-century belief that Providence (God) chose the United States to govern all the land between the Atlantic Ocean and the Pacific Ocean. The map on page 24 shows how the United States "fulfilled" its manifest destiny. Study the map and then answer the questions.

United States, Manifest Destiny

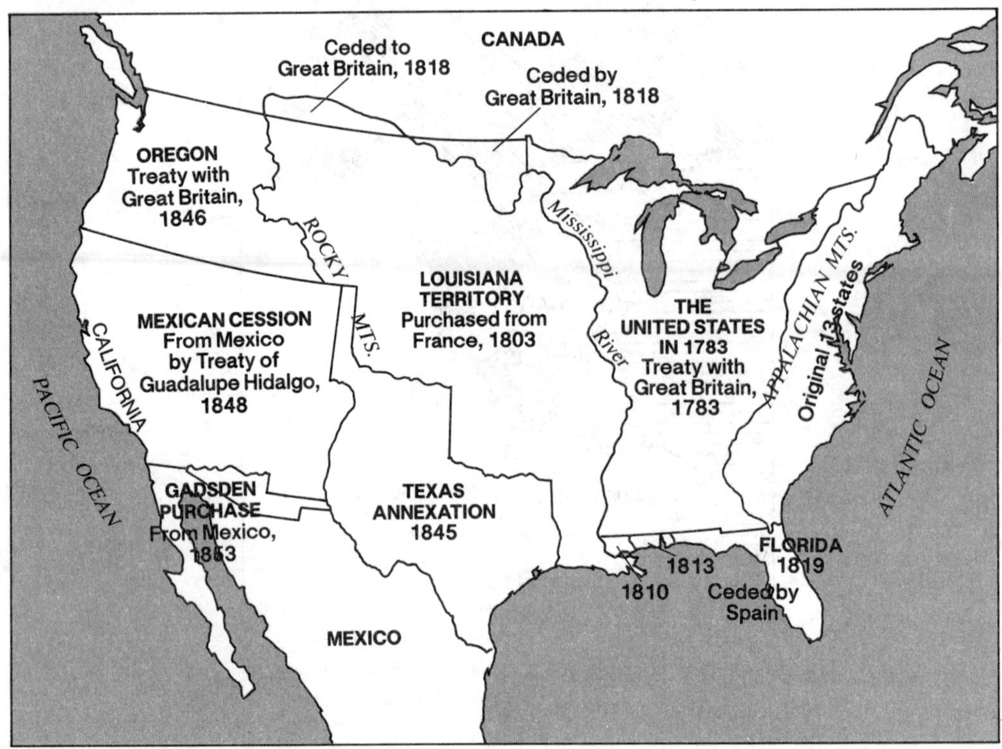

Write the letter of the correct choice on the line next to the number of each question.

_____ 1. According to the idea of manifest destiny, the United States
(*a*) had to acquire all new land through treaties.
(*b*) had no right to purchase Louisiana from France.
(*c*) respected all Mexican land claims in North America.
(*d*) claimed a right to control all of the land shown on the map.

_____ 2. In 1783, the United States extended from the Atlantic Ocean to the
(*a*) Appalachian Mountains. (*c*) Rocky Mountains.
(*b*) Mississippi River. (*d*) Pacific Ocean.

_____ 3. As a result of the Louisiana Purchase, the United States
(*a*) approximately doubled in land size.
(*b*) lost land west of the Mississippi River.
(*c*) extended to the Pacific Ocean.
(*d*) gained Texas.

_____ 4. In 1818, the United States ceded (gave up) to Great Britain an area of land next to Canada. At the same time,
(*a*) the United States ceded land to France.
(*b*) Great Britain ceded land to the United States.
(*c*) the United States ceded land to Mexico.
(*d*) Great Britain ceded land to Mexico.

_____ 5. In 1819, Florida was ceded to the United States by
(*a*) France. (*b*) Mexico. (*c*) Spain. (*d*) Great Britain.

_____ 6. Which area did the United States annex (take over) in 1845?
(*a*) Oregon (*c*) Gadsden Purchase
(*b*) Mexican Cession (*d*) Texas

_____ 7. The United States gained Oregon after signing a treaty with
(*a*) Great Britain. (*c*) Mexico.
(*b*) Spain. (*d*) France.

_____ 8. As a result of the Treaty of Guadelupe Hidalgo, the United States acquired
(*a*) Louisiana.
(*b*) the Mexican Cession.
(*c*) the Gadsden Purchase.
(*d*) the original 13 states.

_____ 9. The last area on the map gained by the United States was
(*a*) Texas. (*c*) the Mexican Cession.
(*b*) Oregon. (*d*) the Gadsden Purchase.

_____ 10. In which year did the United States finally reach from the Atlantic Ocean to the Pacific Ocean?
(*a*) 1803 (*b*) 1819 (*c*) 1846 (*d*) 1853

C. Historical Map. Study the map on this page and then answer the questions.

The United States at the Outbreak of the Civil War, 1861

Write the letter of the correct choice on the line next to the number of each question.

____ 1. The map is for the year
(*a*) 1850. (*b*) 1860. (*c*) 1861. (*d*) 1871.

____ 2. Areas with the pattern were the
(*a*) Border States.
(*b*) Union States.
(*c*) Union Territories.
(*d*) Confederate States.

____ 3. How many states belonged to the Confederate States of America?
(*a*) 10 (*b*) 11 (*c*) 12 (*d*) 13

____ 4. Richmond, Virginia, was the capital of the
(*a*) Confederate States.
(*b*) Union.
(*c*) Border States.
(*d*) Union Territories.

____ 5. Which territory supported the Confederacy?
(*a*) Washington (*c*) Colorado
(*b*) Dakota (*d*) New Mexico

____ 6. On the map, Kentucky is shown as a
(*a*) slave territory.
(*b*) slave state loyal to the Union.
(*c*) member of the Confederate States of America.
(*d*) territory supporting the Confederacy.

____ 7. In which group are there only Union states?
(*a*) Massachusetts, Ohio, Louisiana, Georgia
(*b*) Alabama, Mississippi, Arkansas, Texas
(*c*) Illinois, Connecticut, Florida, Virginia
(*d*) Maine, New York, Indiana, Iowa

____ 8. Which statement is TRUE?
(*a*) In 1861, there were more Union Territories than Confederate States.
(*b*) In 1861, there were more Confederate States than Union States.
(*c*) In 1861, five states that permitted slavery supported the Union.
(*d*) In 1861, the New Mexico Territory supported the Union.

____ 9. Which area was a state in 1861?
(*a*) Utah (*c*) Nevada
(*b*) Kansas (*d*) New Mexico

____ 10. The admission of West Virginia to the Union in 1863 brought the number of Union States and Border Slave States loyal to the Union to a total of
(*a*) 20. (*b*) 22. (*c*) 24. (*d*) 26.

D. Historical Map. Study the map below and then answer the questions.

The United States and Its Possessions in 1917

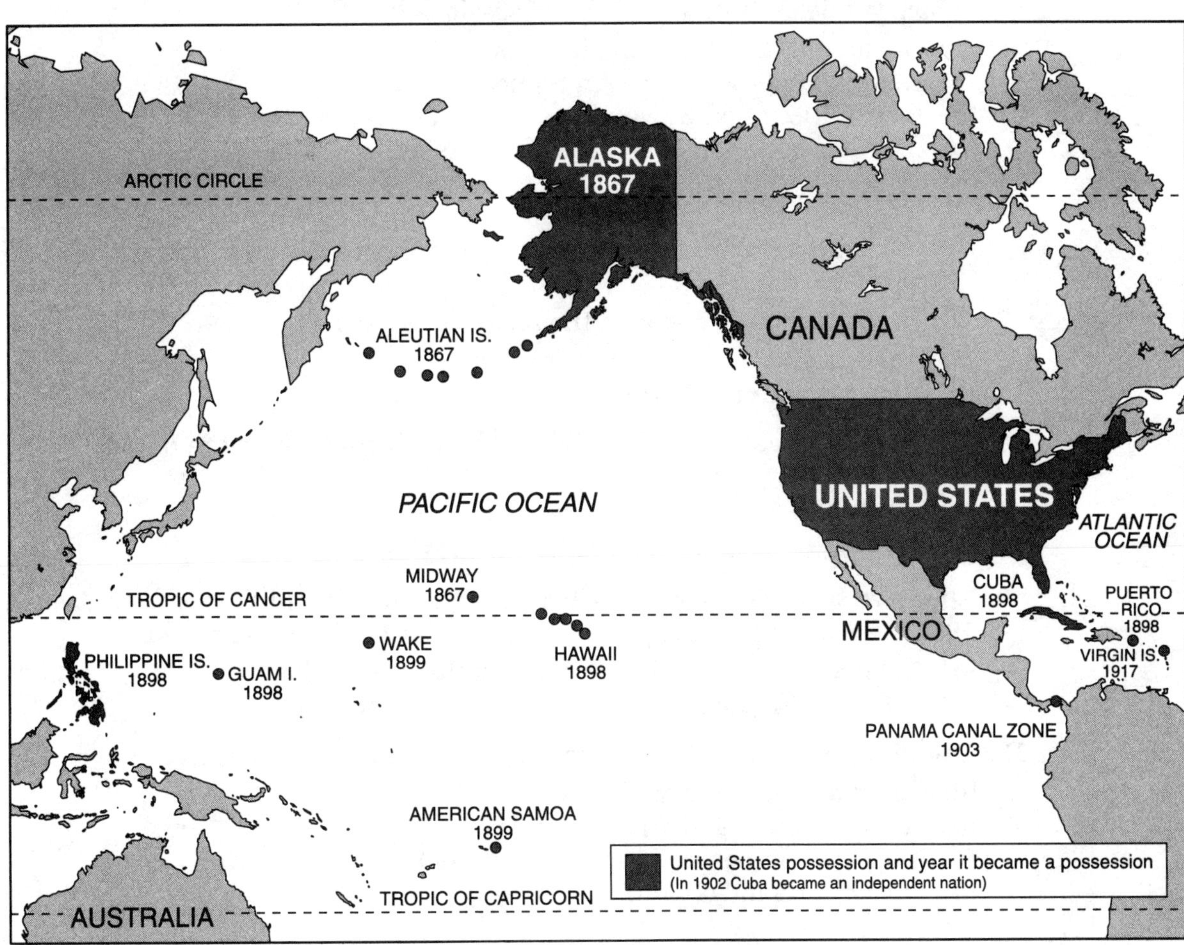

Write the letter of the correct choice on the line next to the number of each question.

_____ 1. Possessions of the United States are shown by the pattern
(a) [vertical-stripe pattern]. *(b)* [light gray pattern]. *(c)* [crosshatch pattern]. *(d)* [black pattern].

_____ 2. The map shows overseas possessions of the United States
(a) in thc Atlantic Ocean only.
(b) in the Pacific Ocean only.
(c) in the Atlantic Ocean and the Pacific Ocean.
(d) in neither the Atlantic Ocean nor the Pacific Ocean.

_____ 3. The number 1898 under the Hawaiian Islands represents
(a) the date when the Hawaiian Islands became a U.S. possession.
(b) the date when the Hawaiian Islands became independent of the United States.
(c) the total square miles of the Hawaiian Islands.
(d) the total population of the Hawaiian Islands today.

____ 4. The map contains information as of
(*a*) 1867. (*c*) 1903.
(*b*) 1898. (*d*) 1917.

____ 5. Which two islands became U.S. possessions in 1899?
(*a*) Guam and the Philippine Islands
(*b*) Wake Island and American Samoa
(*c*) Puerto Rico and Midway Island
(*d*) the Aleutian Islands and the Virgin Islands

____ 6. Alaska became a U.S. possession in
(*a*) 1867. (*c*) 1899.
(*b*) 1898. (*d*) 1903.

____ 7. Which U.S. possession was in the Atlantic Ocean?
(*a*) Wake Island (*c*) Puerto Rico
(*b*) Midway Island (*d*) Guam

____ 8. Which U.S. possession would not be shown if this map were dated 1910?
(*a*) the Philippine Islands (*c*) the Hawaiian Islands
(*b*) the Virgin Islands (*d*) Midway Island

____ 9. Theodore Roosevelt served as President of the United States from 1901 to 1909. During his presidency, the United States acquired
(*a*) Alaska. (*c*) the Panama Canal Zone.
(*b*) American Samoa. (*d*) the Virgin Islands.

____ 10. The Philippines became a U.S. possession in the same year as did
(*a*) Guam and Wake Island.
(*b*) Midway Island and Wake Island.
(*c*) American Samoa and the Hawaiian Islands.
(*d*) Puerto Rico and Guam.

E-1. Historical Map. The Rio Pact, or the Inter-American Treaty of Reciprocal Assistance, was signed in Rio de Janeiro, Brazil, on September 2, 1947. It was the first defense system that the United States joined after World War II. Its purpose was to protect member countries from foreign *aggression* (warlike acts). Study the map on page 29 and then answer the questions.

Write the letter of the correct choice on the line next to the number of each question.

____ 1. This map is dated
(*a*) 1942. (*b*) 1945. (*c*) 1947. (*d*) 1949.

____ 2. The pattern [shaded box] represents
(*a*) members of the United Nations.
(*b*) all the countries of South America.
(*c*) members of the Rio Pact.
(*d*) countries that are not members of the Rio Pact.

The Rio Pact, 1947

____ 3. Boundary lines between countries on this map are shown by

(a) ———— *(c)* —··—··—··—
(b) – – – – – – *(d)* ····················

____ 4. Chile shares a border with

(a) Uruguay. *(c)* Colombia.
(b) Brazil. *(d)* Argentina.

____ 5. Which of the following is NOT a member of the Rio Pact?
(a) Chile *(c)* Mexico
(b) Jamaica *(d)* Haiti

____ 6. In which group are all of the countries members of the Rio Pact?
(a) Colombia, Nicaragua, Argentina, Dutch Guiana
(b) British Honduras, Honduras, Venezuela, Paraguay
(c) Bolivia, French Guiana, Costa Rica, Mexico
(d) Panama, Dominican Republic, Peru, Chile

____ 7. Which country would be least likely to have a navy?
(a) Mexico *(c)* Argentina
(b) Bolivia *(d)* Brazil

____ 8. According to the map, how many Rio Pact members are there on the continent of South America?
(a) 9 *(b)* 11 *(c)* 13 *(d)* 15

____ 9. How many members of the Rio Pact are shown on this map?
(a) 11 *(b)* 16 *(c)* 19 *(d)* 21

____ 10. Today, Nicaragua, Ecuador, the nation of Trinidad and Tobago, and the Bahama Islands are members of the Rio Pact, and Cuba is no longer a member. How many nations are now members of the Rio Pact?
(a) 20 *(b)* 21 *(c)* 22 *(d)* 23

E-2. Historical Map. The Rio Pact is more formally called the Inter-American Treaty of Reciprocal Assistance. Now that you have studied the map on page 29 and answered the questions in E-1, what do you think "Inter-American" and "Reciprocal" mean?

Inter-American ____

____

____

Reciprocal ____

____

____

CHAPTER 4

Understanding Historical Population and Product Maps

Historical Population Maps

When George Washington became the first president of the United States in 1789, our country was much smaller in size and population than it is today. As you have learned, historical maps can show the size and shape of the United States as George Washington knew it. Maps can also show how many people lived in the United States during the years Washington was president. This kind of map is called a *historical population map.*

Below is a map of the United States in 1790, one year after Washington became president. In a way, it looks like other maps you have studied because it shows states, *territories,* boundary lines, and important cities. But the key tells us that this map gives population data. The key includes symbols commonly used to show population figures for cities. Notice that each symbol stands for a different number of people.

The United States in 1790

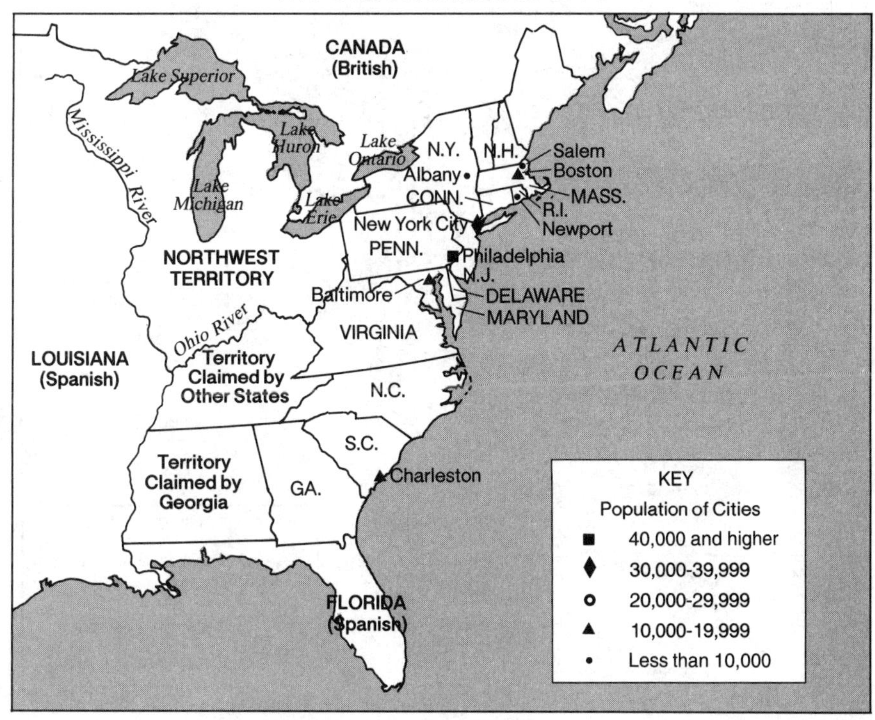

Now, use this map and key to answer the following questions.

_____ 1. In 1790, Boston, Massachusetts, had a population

(*a*) under 10,000.
(*b*) between 10,000 and 19,999.
(*c*) between 20,000 and 29,999.
(*d*) between 30,000 and 39,999.
(*e*) of 40,000 and higher.

Which answer did you choose? On the map, look for Boston, Massachusetts. The symbol next to Boston is ▲. The key shows that this symbol represents a population between 10,000 and 19,999. Therefore, the answer to question 1 is *(b)*.

_____ 2. How many cities had a population of more than 30,000 in 1790?

(*a*) two
(*b*) three
(*c*) four
(*d*) five

Which answer did you choose? Look at the key to see which symbol or symbols are used to show cities with a population of more than 30,000. There are two symbols, ♦ and ■, that represent such a population. Now look on the map to see if there are any cities marked with either symbol. The symbol ♦ is next to New York City, and the symbol ■ is next to Philadelphia. Therefore, two cities have populations of more than 30,000, and the answer to question 2 is *(a)*.

Another kind of historical population map could be used to show the population of each state and territory in 1790.

On the *population distribution map* below, patterns are used to represent population figures for each state and territory. The key explains the population figures represented by each pattern.

Answer the following questions by using the information on this population map.

_____ 3. In 1790, the Northwest Territory had a population of

(*a*) less than 100,000.
(*b*) between 100,000 and 249,999.
(*c*) between 250,000 and 499,999.
(*d*) 500,000 and higher.

Population Distribution in the United States, 1790

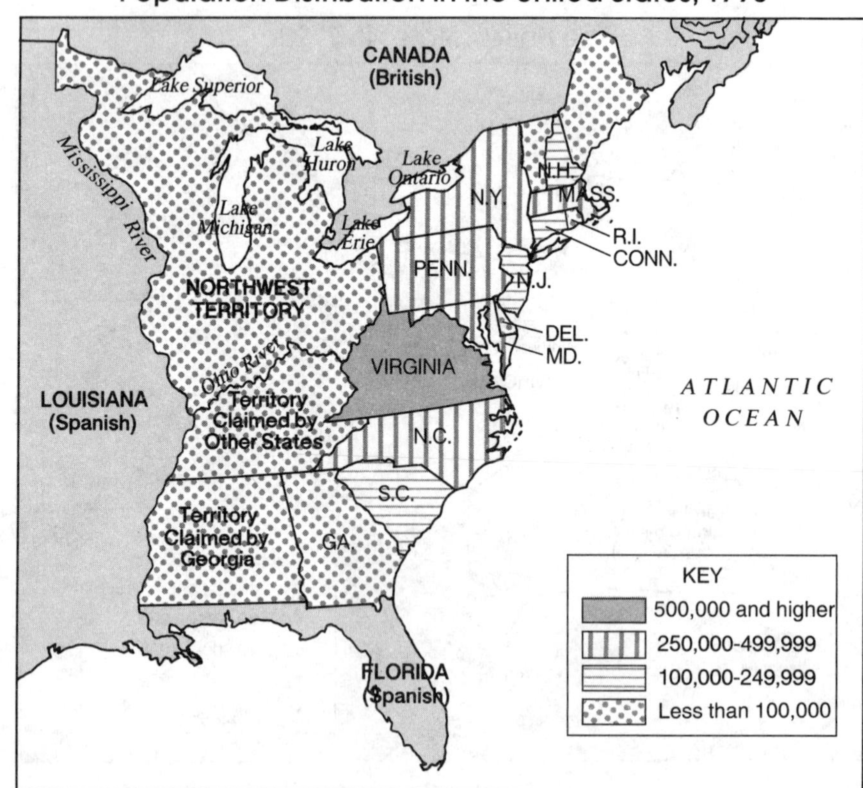

Which answer did you choose? Find the Northwest Territory on the map. You can see that the Northwest Territory is covered by the pattern . Now find this pattern on the key. It represents a population of less than 100,000. Therefore, the answer to question 3 is *(a)*.

____ 4. Which state had the largest population in 1790?
(a) Rhode Island
(b) South Carolina
(c) New York
(d) Virginia

Which answer did you choose? On the map, you can see that Rhode Island is covered by the pattern , South Carolina by , New York by , and Virginia by . The key shows that the pattern represents the largest population (500,000 and higher). Therefore, Virginia had the largest population, and the answer to question 4 is *(d)*.

The map on page 32 gives population figures for each state and territory in 1790, but it does not tell you how many people lived in certain areas of each state and territory. Some such areas have larger populations than other areas. Historical population maps can be drawn to show the population of different areas of a state or territory. This kind of map is called a *population density map.* (Population density means the average number of people living on a certain area of land, usually a square mile. An area with a dense population is heavily populated.)

The map below shows the population density of the United States in 1790. Patterns are used to show how many people per square mile lived in certain areas of each state and territory. The key tells you the population figures represented by each pattern.

After studying this population density map, answer the following questions.

Population Density in the United States, 1790

____ 5. A population of 25 people per square mile is shown on the map by the pattern

(a) ▭.
(b) ▭.
(c) ▭.

Which answer did you choose? The key shows the population figures represented by each pattern. A population of fewer than 6 people per square mile is represented by the pattern ▭, a population between 6 and 45 by the pattern ▭, and a population of more than 45 by the pattern ▭. A population of 25 people per square mile is represented by the pattern ▭ because 25 is in the number range between 6 and 45. Therefore, the answer to question 5 is *(b)*.

____ 6. Which of the following states is covered by all three patterns?

(a) Delaware
(b) South Carolina
(c) Virginia
(d) Rhode Island

Which answer did you choose? The map shows that two states, New York and Virginia, are covered by the three patterns. Since only Virginia is named in the question, the answer to question 6 is *(c)*.

You saw on the population distribution map on page 32 that Virginia had a population of 500,000 and higher, but you could not tell where the people lived in that state. The population density map shows that the heaviest population was in the eastern areas of the state.

Historical Product Maps

The historical population maps in this chapter show you where people lived in the United States in 1790. Why were some areas of the United States more populated than other areas? Before you can know why people lived in certain cities, states, or territories, you need to know more about these places. In general, people lived where they could grow crops and earn a living. A map that shows what goods are produced in certain areas is called a *historical product map.*

On the product map on page 35, picture symbols represent the different goods produced in the United States in 1790. The key explains what each symbol represents. Some picture symbols stand for crops. For example, the symbol 🍃 stands for tobacco. That symbol appears in the states where tobacco was grown. The map also shows goods other than crops. For example, the symbol ▼ appears in the states and territories where animals were trapped for their fur.

After looking at the product map, answer the following question.

____ 7. How does the map show that farming was a more important way of earning a living in the Southern states than in the Northern and Middle states?

____

____

____

____

What did you write? First of all, you have to know which were the Northern, Middle, and Southern states. In 1790, the Northern states were Massachusetts, Connecticut, New Hampshire, and Rhode Island. The Middle states were New York, New Jersey, Pennsylvania, and Delaware. The Southern states were Maryland, Virginia, North Carolina, South Carolina, and Georgia. A careful study of the map shows that the Southern states have more crop symbols (🍃 ✎ ♦ ✕) than the Northern and Middle states. The map uses crop symbols to show where people earned a living by farming. Because the Southern states have more crop symbols, you can say that farming was a more important way of earning a living in the Southern states than in

Product Map of the United States, 1790

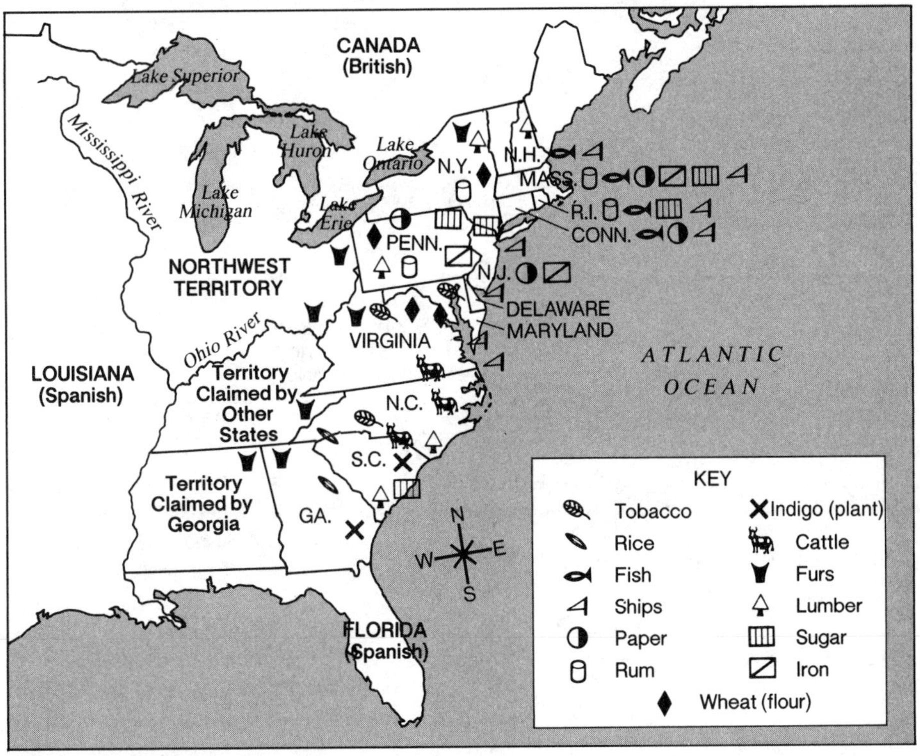

the Northern and Middle states. If your answer contains these ideas, you wrote a good answer to question 7.

Why did farming become so important in the Southern states? The answer is that much of the land is flat and easy to farm. Southern states also have a warmer climate and a longer growing season than Northern and Middle states. These conditions help explain why farming was an important way of earning a living for people in the Southern states.

In this chapter you have seen how maps can show the population and products of the United States in 1790. As you will see in the following exercises, historical population and product maps can be drawn for other years or time periods in U.S. history. Be sure you know what year or time period the map is showing.

USING YOUR SKILLS

A. Historical Population Map.

Write the letter of the correct choice on the line next to the number of each question.

_____ 1. The map on page 36 shows population figures for the United States
(a) in 1790. *(b)* in 1830. *(c)* in 1890. *(d)* today.

_____ 2. According to the map on page 36, Charleston, South Carolina, had a population
(a) of less than 40,000.
(b) between 40,000 and 89,999.
(c) between 90,000 and 139,999.
(d) between 140,000 and 189,999.

The United States in 1830

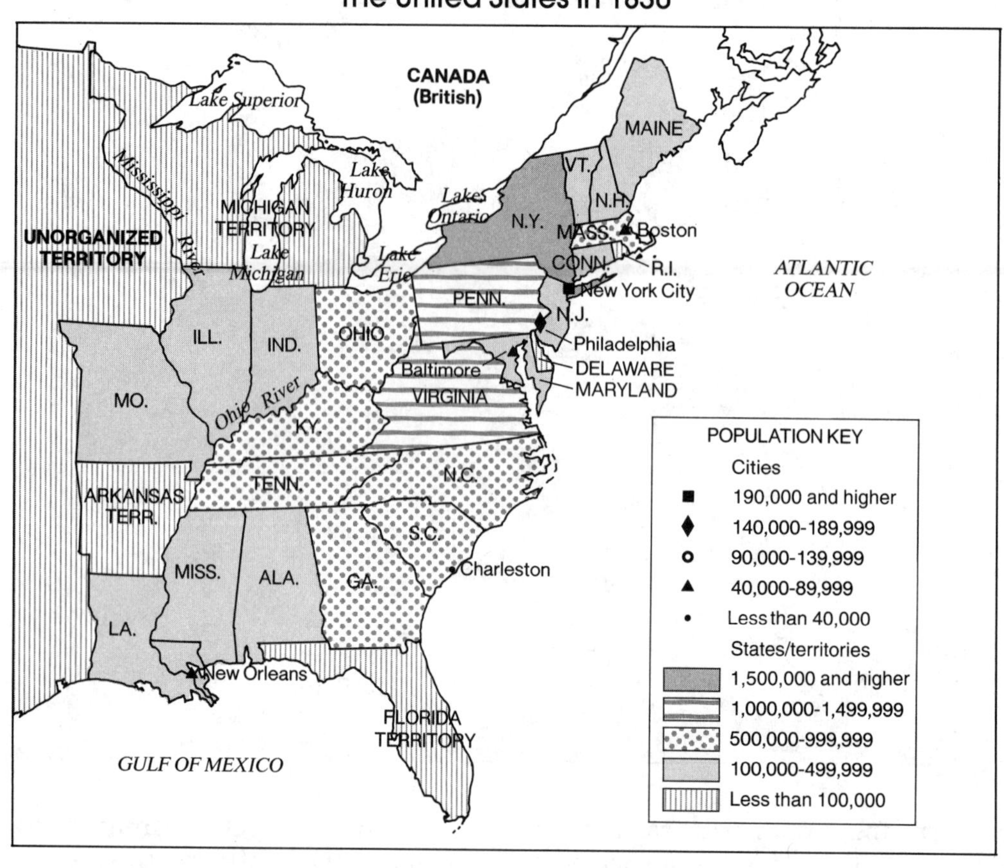

_____ 3. How many cities on the map had a population between 40,000 and 89,999?

(*a*) one (*b*) two (*c*) three (*d*) four

_____ 4. Which population figures are represented by the pattern ?

(*a*) less than 100,000
(*b*) 100,000 to 499,999
(*c*) 500,000 to 999,999
(*d*) 1,000,000 to 1,499,999

_____ 5. The pattern is used to show the population figures for

(*a*) New York.
(*b*) Pennsylvania.
(*c*) Mississippi.
(*d*) Tennessee.

_____ 6. Which state had the largest population?

(*a*) Missouri (*b*) Virginia (*c*) New York (*d*) Georgia

_____ 7. Which three states had a population between 500,000 and 999,999?

(*a*) North Carolina, Virginia, and Maine
(*b*) Georgia, Ohio, and Massachusetts
(*c*) Illinois, Indiana, and South Carolina
(*d*) Pennsylvania, Massachusetts, and Virginia

_____ 8. All the areas on the map marked as territories had populations

(*a*) of less than 100,000.
(*b*) between 100,000 and 499,999.
(*c*) between 500,000 and 999,999.
(*d*) of 1,500,000 and higher.

____ 9. Which of the following Northeastern states had the largest population?
(*a*) Maine (*c*) Rhode Island
(*b*) Massachusetts (*d*) Vermont

____ 10. The city of Philadelphia had a larger population than
(*a*) the state of New York.
(*b*) North Carolina and South Carolina combined.
(*c*) the Florida Territory.
(*d*) all the other cities on the map combined.

B. Historical Population Density Map.

B-1. Write the letter of the correct choice on the line next to the number of each question.

____ 1. The purpose of the map below is to show the
(*a*) population density of the United States in 1830.
(*b*) total population of each state in 1830.
(*c*) cities in territories in 1830.
(*d*) geographical features affecting population distribution in 1830.

Population Density in the United States, 1830

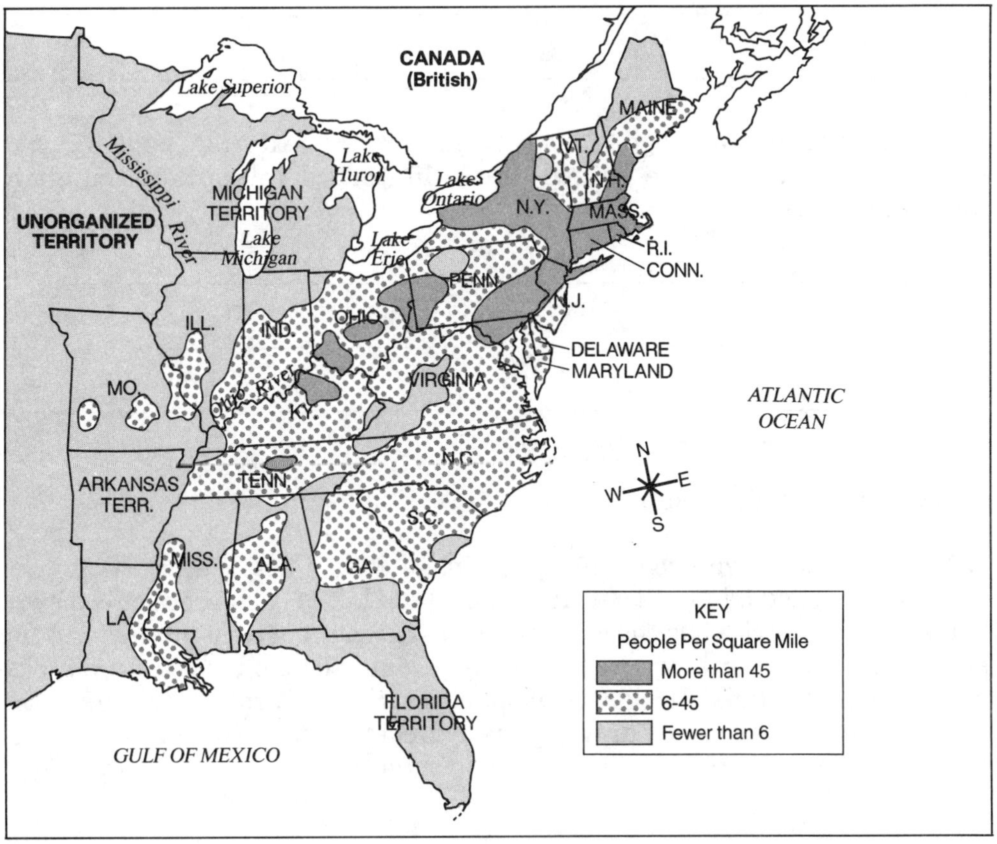

KEY
People Per Square Mile
More than 45
6-45
Fewer than 6

_____ 2. The pattern [ ] stands for
(*a*) fewer than 6 people per square mile.
(*b*) 6 to 45 people per square mile.
(*c*) more than 45 people per square mile.

_____ 3. Which of the following states is covered by all three patterns?
(*a*) Maine (*c*) Mississippi
(*b*) Maryland (*d*) Missouri

_____ 4. Which of the following states or territories had an area or areas with a population between 6 and 45 people per square mile?
(*a*) Florida
(*b*) Arkansas Territory
(*c*) Missouri
(*d*) Michigan Territory

_____ 5. The population density in the United States in 1830 was highest in the
(*a*) Northwest. (*c*) Southeast.
(*b*) Northeast. (*d*) Southwest.

B-2. Use the 1790 population density map on page 33 and the 1830 population density map in this exercise (page 37) to answer the following question. How do the two population density maps show that between 1790 and 1830 many Americans moved westward?

____

____

____

B-3. Both the map on page 36 and the map in this exercise (page 37) give population figures for the United States in 1830. Explain how these two maps are different.

____

____

____

C. Historical Product Map.

C-1. Draw Your Own Product Map. On page 40 is a list of products grown, made, or supplied by Americans in 1830. To the left of each product is a symbol. For example, rice has the symbol ✎. To the right of each product are the states and/or territories where this product could be found. For example, rice was grown in Georgia, Florida, Louisiana, and South Carolina. Complete the product map on page 39 by drawing the symbol for each listed product in the states and/or territories where that product was found.

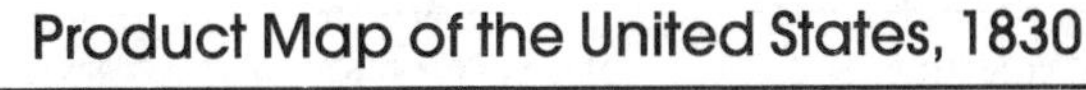

C-2. Write the letter of the correct choice on the line next to the number of each question.

_____ 1. According to the 1830 product map above, which you completed, corn was grown in

(a) Tennessee and Arkansas. (c) Florida and Rhode Island.
(b) New Hampshire and Virginia. (d) Indiana and Massachusetts.

_____ 2. In which state did people grow cotton and rice and raise cattle?

(a) Louisiana (c) New York
(b) South Carolina (d) Ohio

SYMBOL	PRODUCTS	PRODUCING STATES/TERRITORIES
	Rice	Florida, Georgia, Louisiana, South Carolina
	Wheat	Illinois, Maine, Maryland, Michigan, New Hampshire, New York, Pennsylvania, Vermont, Virginia
	Corn	Arkansas, Delaware, Georgia, Illinois, Indiana, Kentucky, Louisiana, Maryland, Missouri, Ohio, Tennessee
	Cotton	Alabama, Arkansas, Georgia, Louisiana, Mississippi, North Carolina, South Carolina, Tennessee
	Tobacco	Kentucky, Maryland, Missouri, North Carolina, Tennessee, Virginia
	Sugar	Florida, Georgia, Louisiana, South Carolina
	Cattle	Kentucky, Mississippi, New Jersey, New York, North Carolina, Ohio, Pennsylvania, Rhode Island, South Carolina
	Fish	Massachusetts, New Hampshire, New York
	Ships	Connecticut, Delaware, Massachusetts, New Hampshire, New York, Rhode Island, Virginia
	Iron	Delaware, Georgia, New York, North Carolina, Ohio, Rhode Island, Virginia
	Coal	Pennsylvania
×	Textiles	Maryland, Massachusetts, Pennsylvania

____ 3. According to the 1830 product map, cotton was grown in
(*a*) every state. (*c*) the Northern states.
(*b*) every territory. (*d*) the Southern states.

____ 4. According to the 1830 product map, which of the following states was an important farming state?
(*a*) Massachusetts (*c*) Georgia
(*b*) Connecticut (*d*) New Hampshire

____ 5. Which of the following products appears on the 1830 product map on page 39 but not on the 1790 product map on page 35?
(*a*) fish (*b*) rice (*c*) cotton (*d*) iron

D. Historical Mineral Resource and Product Map. Study the map on page 41. Then answer the questions.

TRUE or FALSE: If the underlined information makes the statement true, write TRUE on the line to the left of the statement. If the underlined infor-

Mineral Resources and Products of the United States, 1870–1900

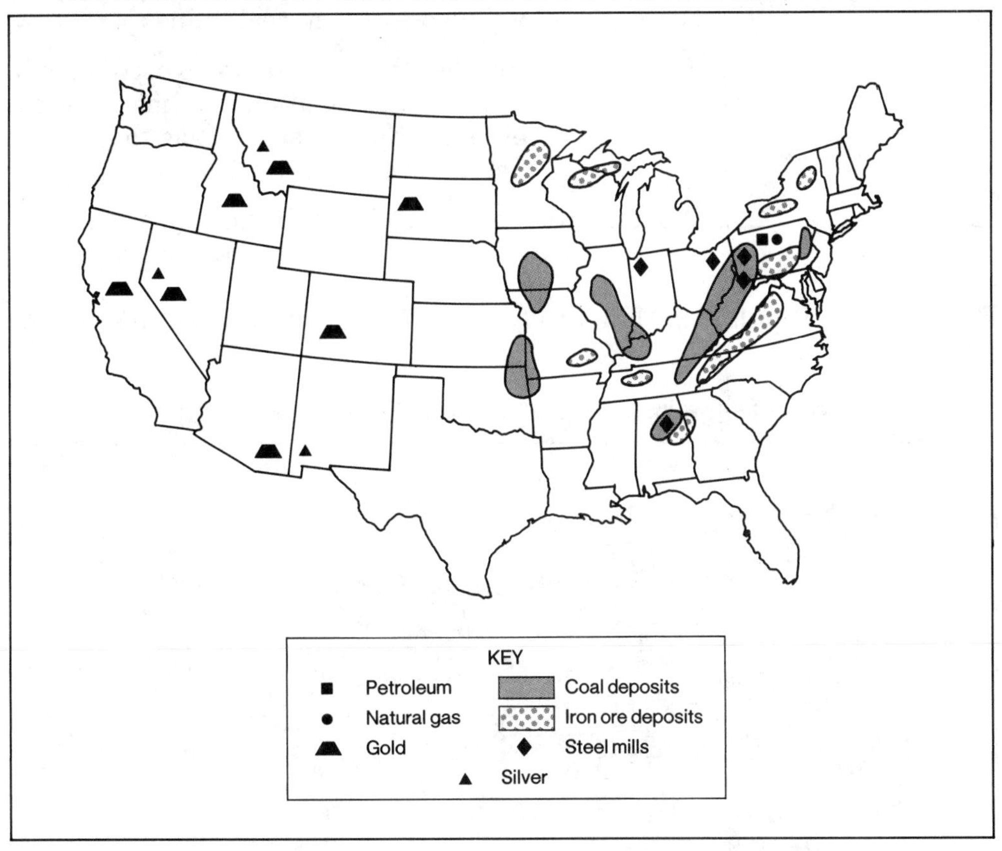

mation makes the statement false, write or draw on the line to the left the information that will make the statement true.

__________ 1. Petroleum is represented by the symbol __▲__.

__________ 2. The symbol ◆ represents silver.

__________ 3. According to the map, gold was found only in the western half of the United States.

__________ 4. The pattern ▬ represents iron-ore deposits.

__________ 5. The Northeast had more steel mills than any other area of the United States.

To answer questions 6 through 10, use the map in Exercise E (page 42) to help you find the location of certain states and territories.

__________ 6. Nevada was a leading producer of silver and gold.

__________ 7. According to the map, Minnesota had coal deposits.

_______________ 8. A major occupation in West Virginia was working in coal mines

_______________ 9. Because the map shows no petroleum in Texas, it can be assumed that the great oil fields that exist in Texas today were not discovered until after 1870.

_______________ 10. Coal, petroleum, natural gas, and iron ore were all found in Pennsylvania.

E. Historical Population Map. Study the following map. Then answer the questions.

Population Distribution in the United States, 1900

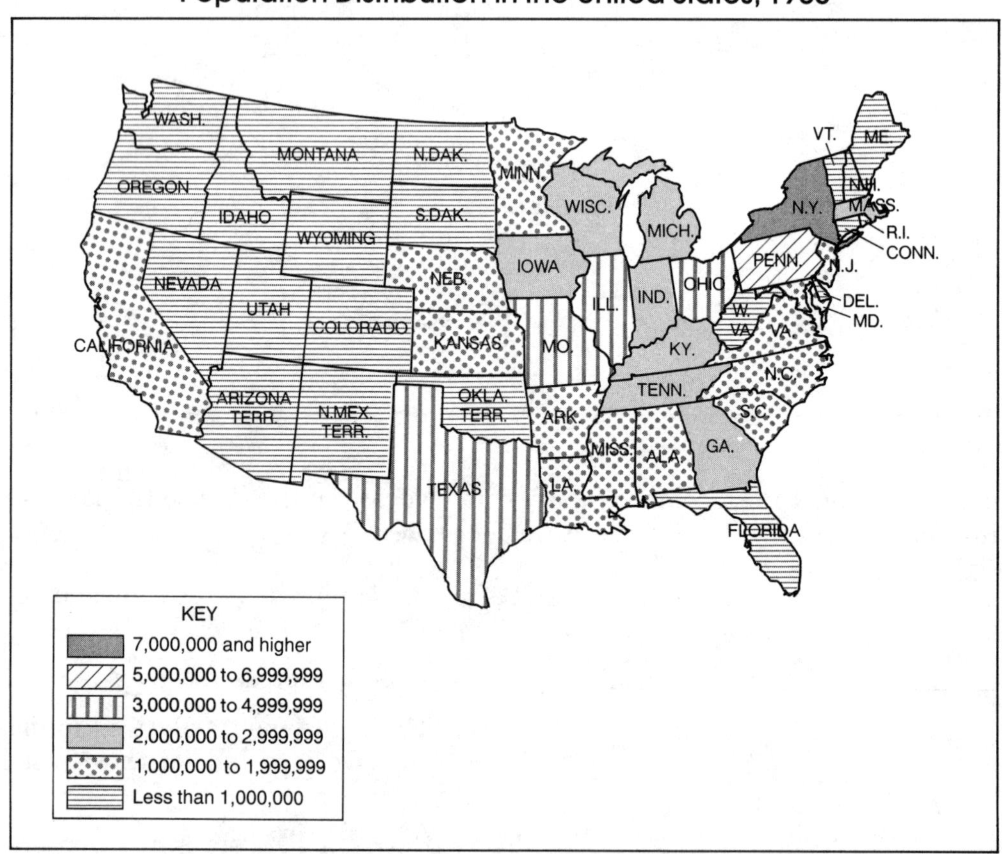

E-1. For questions 1 through 5, write the letter of the correct choice on the line next to the number of each question.

____ 1. On the map above, which population figures are represented by the pattern [ ]?

(a) 7,000,000 and higher
(b) 5,000,000 to 6,999,999
(c) 3,000,000 to 4,999,999
(d) 2,000,000 to 2,999,999

____ 2. Which state had a population between 3,000,000 and 4,999,999?

(a) Illinois
(b) Virginia
(c) New Jersey
(d) California

____ 3. Which three states each had a population of less than 1,000,000?
- *(a)* Wyoming, Kentucky, and Maryland
- *(b)* Tennessee, Washington, and Ohio
- *(c)* South Dakota, South Carolina, and Alabama
- *(d)* Utah, Colorado, and Maine

____ 4. All the territories on the map are covered by the same pattern. Which is it?
- *(a)* [vertical lines pattern].
- *(b)* [dotted pattern].
- *(c)* [horizontal lines pattern].
- *(d)* [gray shaded pattern].

____ 5. Which of the following pairs of states had the largest population?
- *(a)* Texas and California
- *(b)* Colorado and Utah
- *(c)* Missouri and California
- *(d)* Texas and Missouri

E-2. Arrange the following states by placing the state with the highest population first, the next highest second, and so on.

Georgia, Texas, Pennsylvania, Wyoming, California

1. ____________________
2. ____________________
3. ____________________
4. ____________________
5. ____________________

E-3. In 1830, no state had a population of more than 2,000,000. In 1870, only four states (New York, Pennsylvania, Ohio, and Illinois) had a population of more than 2,000,000. List the 14 states on the 1900 map on page 42 that had populations of more than 2,000,000.

____________________ ____________________

____________________ ____________________

____________________ ____________________

____________________ ____________________

____________________ ____________________

____________________ ____________________

____________________ ____________________

CHAPTER 5
Separating Fact From Opinion

Statement 1

More people in the United States are killed each year by guns than by all other weapons put together.

Statement 2

Banning the sale of guns in the United States would result in more crime, not less.

One of these statements is a fact. The other is an opinion. How can you tell the difference? A *fact* is something that is true or that really happened. A fact can be proved to be true. An *opinion* is something that a person believes to be true or a particular point of view held by a person. An opinion cannot be proved to be true. If an opinion could be proved true, it would become a fact.

So which of the above statements is a fact and which is an opinion?

Government and private studies show that more people in the United States are killed each year by guns than by all other weapons put together. This information proves that Statement 1 is a fact.

Some people believe that banning the sale of guns in the United States would result in more crime, not less. But other people believe the opposite. Even if the crime rate increases after guns are banned, the increase might be due to reasons other than the gun ban. It would be difficult to prove Statement 2. Therefore, you should view it as an opinion.

Writers and speakers sometimes state opinions as if they were facts, but now you know that some things you read or hear are not facts. Statements in books, newspapers, and magazines are not necessarily facts. Neither is everything broadcast on the radio or television. In this chapter, you will learn how to separate facts from opinions and avoid mistaking one for the other.

Recognizing Opinions

One way to know that an opinion is being expressed is to look for key words such as "think" and "believe."

"I think that the punishment for having an illegal gun isn't tough enough."

"We believe that crime has more to do with poverty than with how many people own guns."

A writer or speaker may not use such key words. Then you have to decide by other means if the statement is a fact or an opinion. You might, for instance, look for words that express values, such as "fortunate," "noble," and "good."

"We are fortunate to live in a country where a person still can own a gun."

"Fighting against gun control is a noble cause."

"Good people will support gun control."

People are likely to disagree about what is "fortunate," "noble," or "good." Therefore, statements that claim that someone or something is "fortunate," "noble," or "good" are generally opinions.

Interpreting Facts

Very often people use the same facts to form different opinions. This is known as "interpreting facts." Read the following selections to see how the same facts can be interpreted differently. As you read, you will see that in Selection 1 certain facts are used to support a ban on gun sales. In Selection 2 the same facts are used to argue against a ban on gun sales.

Selection 1

The Second Amendment to the U.S. Constitution states, "A well-regulated militia being necessary to the security of a free State, the right of the people to keep and bear arms shall not be infringed [interfered with]." Therefore, as an American citizen, I have a right to bear firearms. I have a right to own the smallest hand gun and the most powerful automatic rifle. If we forbid the sale of guns or rifles, only criminals will have them. A ban on firearms won't end crime any more than the present ban on cocaine and heroin has ended their use. Some people argue that gun control would have kept Lee Harvey Oswald from assassinating President John Kennedy. Believe me, assassins can always find ways to get their weapons of choice.

The important question is, What happens to me if I can't own a gun? I know the police are supposed to protect us, but a police officer cannot be in my home 24 hours a day. If a killer enters in the middle of the night, do I have to hope the police will arrive before I'm killed?

Some people say that only certain firearms, such as semiautomatic rifles, should be banned. But once the government starts banning things, it doesn't know when to stop. It has already gone too far in regulating who can own what kind of firearm. The government would be wise to go after the criminals and leave the guns alone. I'll tell you what I would support, a ban against criminals.

Selection 2

Please! Don't tell me that the Second Amendment gives us the right to carry semiautomatic rifles. The Second Amendment states, "A well-regulated militia being necessary to the security of a free State, the right of the people to keep and bear arms shall not be infringed." Some people love to emphasize the second part and ignore the first part. The way I read it, the people have a right to bear arms in order to provide for a well-regulated militia. But we no longer need a well-regulated militia of private citizens who own firearms. We now have police departments to protect us, as well as the Army, the Navy, and the Marines. All of which makes the Second Amendment completely outdated.

> At the very least, the government is right in regulating who can own what kinds of firearms. But banning extremely dangerous and unnecessary weapons is also needed. It is true that banning cocaine and heroin has not ended their use in this country. But it has surely reduced their use. Banning certain firearms and regulating ownership of firearms will not end crime, but please don't tell me that it won't help lower the crime rate. Don't tell me that it won't keep firearms out of the hands of crazy people. Think about this: President John F. Kennedy might not have been assassinated had Lee Harvey Oswald had a harder time buying a rifle.

Did you notice that both selections share the same facts? Two of these shared facts are in the following list. Add three more facts that can be found in both selections.

1. The Second Amendment to the U.S. Constitution states, "A well-regulated militia being necessary to the security of a free State, the right of the people to keep and bear arms shall not be infringed."

2. Police departments exist to protect citizens from criminals.

3. ______________________________

   ____

4. ______________________________

   ____

5. ______________________________

   ____

What facts did you find? Both selections state that President John F. Kennedy was assassinated. This is easy to prove. Both agree that banning cocaine and heroin has not ended their use. This, too, can be proved to be true. Both also state that the government regulates who can own what kinds of guns. This is also provable.

Did you also notice that each selection interprets these five facts differently? Let us see how well you can pick out the different interpretations. Answer the following questions based on the two selections you just read. Write the number of the correct selection on the line to the left of the question.

_____ 1. Which selection argues that the Second Amendment to the U.S. Constitution has no reason to exist anymore?

_____ 2. Which selection argues that banning firearms would reduce the crime rate?

_____ 3. Which selection argues that controlling the sale of guns would not have kept Lee Harvey Oswald from assassinating President Kennedy?

Question 1

Both selections accept that the Second Amendment to the Constitution provides for a well-regulated militia made up of private citizens who own firearms. But Selection 2 argues that "The Second Amendment is completely outdated" because "We now have police departments to protect us . . ." Therefore, the answer to question 1 is Selection 2.

Question 2

Both selections admit that banning certain firearms won't put an end to crime, but Selection 2 states, "please don't tell me that it won't help lower the crime rate." So the answer to question 2 is Selection 2.

Question 3

Both selections state that Lee Harvey Oswald assassinated President Kennedy, but Selection 1 argues that gun control would not have kept Oswald from getting a weapon. Therefore, the answer to question 3 is Selection 1.

We live in a world in which books, magazines, radio, television, movies, and computers bombard us with facts and opinions, as well as opinions offered as facts. In learning how to separate fact from opinion, you are learning a valuable skill that will be useful throughout your schooling and your life. The following exercises will give you more practice in this valuable skill.

USING YOUR SKILLS

A. The following selection is about Benjamin Franklin's attempt to unite the 13 colonies. After you have read the selection, try to separate the facts from the opinions.

Trying to Unite the 13 Colonies

The opening shots of the French and Indian War in 1754 set Britain against France in a struggle for control of the eastern half of North America. They also forced the people of the 13 British colonies to think about forming a union. No colony was strong enough by itself to fight the French and their Indian *allies* (supporters). Only by cooperating with one another could the colonies hope to defend themselves.

Shortly after the war began, Benjamin Franklin sought to unite the 13 colonies. Under his leadership, representatives from 7 of the 13 colonies met in Albany, New York, to plan for a common defense against the French. Franklin proposed that the colonists form a permanent union. The representatives accepted Franklin's plan—called the Albany Plan of Union—as a way of uniting the colonies to fight against the French. The plan was a good one, but when it was presented to the colonial assemblies for approval, they rejected it. The colonial assemblies were afraid that such a union would cost them their right to act independently. They also feared that such a union would mean more taxes.

These excuses for rejecting the Albany Plan made no sense. Though Franklin's plan failed, it caused many colonists to think about the advantages of uniting. Less than 15 years after the end of the French and Indian War in 1763, the colonists would be ready to form a union. This time they united in their struggle for independence from Great Britain.

Each of the following statements is based on the selection you just read. If the statement is a fact, put an **F** in front of it. If the statement is an opinion, put an **O** in front of it. It is important to remember the meaning of fact and opinion. Not everything you read is a fact.

_____ 1. No colony was strong enough by itself to fight the French and their Indian allies.

_____ 2. Representatives from 7 of the 13 colonies met in Albany, New York, to plan for a common defense against the French.

_____ 3. Benjamin Franklin's Albany Plan of Union was a good plan.

_____ 4. The colonial assemblies rejected the Albany Plan of Union.

_____ 5. The excuses for rejecting the Albany Plan of Union made no sense.

B. On July 4, 1776, the Second Continental Congress formally adopted the Declaration of Independence. By this act, the 13 colonies declared themselves a free and independent country. Some colonists supported the Declaration of Independence, while other colonists opposed it. The following two selections deal with this subject. The writers used the same facts but interpreted them differently. Read each selection carefully.

Selection 1

Admit it, my friends, we are at war. We have no other choice but to fight. Parliament has overtaxed us. We have been denied our rights as British subjects. British soldiers have fired on and killed colonists. There is no turning back. We are no longer fighting to protest a few unjust laws. We are now fighting for our freedom—for our independence. I urge all of you to support the Declaration of Independence that was adopted by the Congress on July 4. This declaration will help us gain the support of other countries. Perhaps France and Spain will send us arms and money for the fight against the British.

We have a mighty cause. Surely, God is on our side, and history will judge us a brave people. The time has come to fight for our independence.

Selection 2

I fear we have made a tragic error in declaring our independence. The Declaration of Independence, adopted by the Congress on July 4, will mean death and the destruction of property. This cry for independence comes from a mob of people who do not care about law and order. Who will protect us and our property if British soldiers withdraw from our cities and villages?

At first, I supported the fighting. Parliament should not have taxed us. I regretted that innocent people were killed by British soldiers. But independence is out of the question. After all, are we not British ourselves? Is not the British king our king?

War is serious business. Do not forget that if we lose this struggle, many could be hanged. We would be better off to avoid this war and to try to make peace with our king.

B-1. As you read the selections, you should have seen that both writers agreed on certain facts. In the following spaces, list three facts on which both writers agreed.

1. ______________________________

____

2. ______________________________

____

3. ______________________________

____

B-2. Can you remember the different opinions reached by the two writers? Place the number of the correct selection on the line to the left of each statement.

_____ 1. The colonists' rights as British subjects are being denied.

_____ 2. A declaration of independence might bring the support of other countries.

_____ 3. Mobs of people might destroy property.

_____ 4. If the struggle for independence is lost, many colonists could be hanged.

_____ 5. History will judge the supporters of independence to be a brave people.

B-3. Write the letter of the correct choice on the line next to the number of each question.

____ 1. Which statement best summarizes the opinion of the person who wrote Selection 1?

(*a*) War is serious business.
(*b*) The Declaration of Independence will mean death and the destruction of property.
(*c*) We are not fighting to protest a few unfair taxes but to win our freedom.
(*d*) All British subjects should obey their king.

____ 2. Which statement best summarizes the opinion of the person who wrote Selection 2?

(*a*) It is a tragic error to declare our independence.
(*b*) Parliament has placed too many taxes on the colonists.
(*c*) God is on the side of the king.
(*d*) The right to run the government should be given to the people.

C. The following selection is about the treatment of Native Americans during the development of the American West. After you have read the selection, try to separate the facts from the opinions.

The Shameful Story of the Native Americans

Before the 1850s, the Native Americans of the Great Plains had little to fear from settlers from the East. The Great Plains, from the western Missouri River to the Rocky Mountains and from Canada to Texas, were ignored by settlers. They considered these regions unsuitable for farming. But on the plains lived great herds of buffalo. The Native Americans depended on the buffalo for food, clothing, and shelter.

In the early 1850s, increasing numbers of wagon trains crossed the Great Plains on their way to California and Oregon. It soon became clear to the travelers that much of this land was indeed suitable for farming. This discovery was most unfortunate for the Native Americans living there. Farmers and ranchers began to settle the land on which the Native Americans hunted buffalo.

While some settlers just took over Native American lands, others tried to gain land through legal means. They encouraged the U.S. government to *negotiate* (work out) treaties with the Native Americans. According to the treaties, the Native Americans would give up certain lands and agree to live only in other areas. In exchange, they would be paid yearly allowances of money and supplies. Though many tribes signed such treaties, they quickly discovered that the treaties were not worth the paper they were written on. The supplies given to the Native Americans were of poor quality. To make matters worse, the buffalo that the Native Americans depended on were slaughtered by the people who came to build railroad lines.

Native Americans had no other choice but to react to this shameful treatment by raiding and killing settlers and soldiers. Perhaps the most famous example was the Battle of the Little Big Horn in Montana. On June 25, 1876, Lieutenant Colonel George Custer led 264 men in an attack on what appeared to be a small Sioux camp near the Little Big Horn River. To the soldiers' surprise, they were met by Chief Sitting Bull, Chief Crazy Horse, and 2,500 warriors. Custer and all of his men were killed.

Despite the Little Big Horn, the Native Americans could not hold out against the modern weapons of the U.S. Army. During the Indian Wars, which lasted from the early 1860s to 1890, the Army defeated one Native American tribe after another. The Native Americans were then forced to live on *reservations,* areas of public land set aside by the federal government.

While some Americans had no pity for the Native Americans, all decent Americans began to realize that the United States had acted shamefully. Many thought that the only way to help the Native Americans was to "Americanize" them. In 1887, Congress passed the Dawes Act. It officially abolished tribes and stated that each Native American family could claim 160 acres of reservation land as a farm. It was hoped that the Native Americans would give up their tribe loyalties, become U.S. citizens, and adopt the American way of life.

From the beginning, "Americanization" of the Native Americans was a total failure. The Native Americans were given land but never taught how to farm it. And many male Native Americans felt that farming was not a proper way of life. They were hunters. Traditionally, women grew crops. Because the federal government did not provide the Native Americans with proper health care, many died from disease and poor nutrition. In the Native American schools, Native American cultures were usually belittled, and Native Americans were made to think as "Americans." Native American children were torn between their home culture and the American ways taught at school. This conflict created many problems for Native Americans that still exist today. The story of the treatment of Native Americans was and remains a shameful chapter in the history of the United States.

Each of the following statements is based on the selection you just read. If the statement is a fact, put an **F** in front of it. If the statement is an opinion, put an **O** in front of it.

____ 1. Before the 1850s, settlers from the East ignored the Great Plains because they considered the plains unsuitable for farming.

____ 2. The discovery by settlers that the land of the Great Plains was suitable for farming was most unfortunate for Native Americans.

_____ 3. While some settlers just took over Native American lands, others tried to gain land through treaties.

_____ 4. The treaties signed by the Native Americans and the U.S. government were not worth the paper they were written on.

_____ 5. Native Americans had no choice but to react to their poor treatment by raiding and killing settlers.

_____ 6. On June 25, 1876, Lt. Col. George Custer led 264 men in an attack on a Sioux camp near the Little Big Horn River.

_____ 7. While some Americans had no pity for the Native Americans, all decent Americans began to realize that the United States had acted shamefully.

_____ 8. In 1887, Congress passed the Dawes Act, which officially abolished tribes and stated that each Native American family could claim 160 acres of reservation land as a farm.

_____ 9. From the time it began, "Americanization" of Native Americans was a total failure.

_____ 10. The story of the treatment of Native Americans was and remains a shameful chapter in the history of the United States.

D. The following two selections deal with American involvement in Vietnam from the 1950s to the 1970s. The selections use many of the same facts, but they express opposite points of view. Read each selection carefully. Then answer the questions.

Selection 1

For hundreds of years, the people of the country we know today as Vietnam struggled to be independent. They had to resist Chinese invasions, French rule, and, during World War II, Japanese occupation. Even after the defeat of Japan, Vietnam did not gain its independence. The country was again ruled by France, forcing the Vietnamese to continue their struggle for independence. Finally, in 1954, a peace agreement was reached between Vietnam and France. The agreement gave Vietnam independence but divided it into North Vietnam and South Vietnam. The North was led by Ho Chi Minh, a *Communist* and *nationalist,* who had fought more than 30 years to rid Vietnam of foreign influence. The South was led by Emperor Bao Dai, chosen by the French.

According to the 1954 agreement, an election was to be held within two years to form a government for all of Vietnam. Shortly after the agreement went into effect, Ngo Dinh Diem overthrew Bao Dai. Diem said he would not allow the election to take place because he had not signed the agreement. Understandably, various groups then attacked Diem's government.

Most of the opposition came from South Vietnamese Communists, called the Viet Cong, who were aided by Ho Chi Minh. Fearing that South Vietnam would fall to *communism,* President Dwight D. Eisenhower sent U.S. military advisers to aid Diem in 1955. This was a great mistake because the conflict between the North and the South was a civil war. Our fear of communism blinded us to the fact that the Vietnamese had to solve their own problems. (Communism is a political system that abolishes private property and in which one party controls state-owned means of production.)

When fighting between North and South Vietnam worsened in the early 1960s, President John F. Kennedy raised the number of military advisers to 17,000. By 1966, the military advisers were replaced by 200,000 American combat troops with orders to fight. The number of U.S. combat troops in Vietnam eventually reached about 550,000.

As the death toll of American troops rose, opposition to the war grew at home and around the world. Demonstrations across America urged the U.S. government to pull out of Vietnam. According to some observers, those demonstrations encouraged the Communists. Perhaps they did. But perhaps they also forced the U.S. government to seek peace talks, for on January 27, 1973, President Richard Nixon announced that the United States and North Vietnam had agreed to a *cease-fire.* The United States would withdraw its troops from South Vietnam, and North Vietnam would release American prisoners of war. The 1973 cease-fire was merely a way for the United States to pull out of Vietnam and save face. In 1975, the expected happened. North Vietnam invaded and conquered South Vietnam. The side with the greater will to win finally won.

U.S. involvement in Vietnam and the final Communist victory left many Americans frustrated and bitter. Some 58,000 Americans died in Vietnam, and 300,000 were wounded. The war cost more than $150 billion. What a terrible waste of lives and resources! All Americans should honor the brave men and women who served in Vietnam. But, sadly, the truth is that they should never have been sent there in the first place. All that was needed in Vietnam was to allow it to exist as a united, independent country.

Selection 2

War is a terrible thing, but there are things worse than war. One is to live without freedom. For nearly 20 years, the United States tried to protect the freedom of South Vietnam. A 1954 peace agreement divided Vietnam into North Vietnam and

South Vietnam. The North was led by Ho Chi Minh, a Communist, and the South by Emperor Bao Dai. According to the agreement, an election was to be held within two years to form a government for all of Vietnam. When it became obvious that Communist North Vietnam would win the election, the new leader of South Vietnam, Ngo Dinh Diem, refused to allow the election to take place. The South Vietnamese Communists (the Viet Cong), aided by Ho Chi Minh, then attacked Diem's government. Their goal was to overthrow Diem and unite all of Vietnam in a Communist dictatorship.

In 1955, President Dwight D. Eisenhower sent U.S. military advisers to aid Diem in holding back the Communist attack. Little by little, the United States increased its support of Diem's government. In the early 1960s, President John F. Kennedy raised the number of military advisers to 17,000. By 1965, President Lyndon Johnson feared that the South Vietnamese government had become too weak to fight the Communists. The United States could not stand by as two Communist giants (the Soviet Union and China) aided North Vietnam. So, in 1966, 200,000 American troops were sent to South Vietnam ready for combat. In time, the total number of U.S. troops in Vietnam reached about 550,000.

Let's be honest. Anyone who thinks this was merely a civil war between two parts of the same country is a fool. When you find Russian- and Chinese-made rifles on the bodies of dead Viet Cong, you are talking about more than civil war. The United States had to respond.

For the brave men and women who went to Vietnam, fighting the war was hard enough. What made it worse were the so-called peace demonstrations back in the United States. They played right into the hands of the enemy. The Viet Cong could shoot at American soldiers from the front while anti-war demonstrators stabbed them in the back. Whatever Americans thought of the war, they should have supported their soldiers by supporting their war.

Then, in 1973, there was that disgraceful cease-fire agreed to by President Richard Nixon. The United States would withdraw its troops from South Vietnam, and North Vietnam would release American prisoners of war. Was there ever a doubt that the cease-fire merely allowed the United States to withdraw from Vietnam and save face? No one was surprised when North Vietnam invaded and conquered South Vietnam in 1975.

The final Communist victory in Vietnam left many Americans bitter and frustrated. I'm one of those angry souls. Some 58,000 Americans died and 300,000 were wounded for nothing. The war could have been won, but we didn't have the will to win it. When will we learn that any person's struggle for freedom is our struggle for freedom? I only hope that when it's our turn to need help, other countries will respond to our call.

D-1. While reading, you should have seen that both writers agreed on certain facts. In the following spaces, list five facts on which they agreed. (More than five shared facts can be found in the selections.)

1. ______________________________

2. ______________________________

3. ______________________________

4. ______________________________

5. ______________________________

D-2. Can you remember the different opinions expressed by the two writers? Write the number of the correct selection on the answer line to the left of each question.

_____ 1. In which selection did the writer state that the United States could not ignore South Vietnam as long as two Communist giants were aiding North Vietnam?

_____ 2. In which selection did the writer claim that anti-war demonstrations made it more difficult for U.S. soldiers in combat?

_____ 3. In which selection did the writer explain why various groups, such as the Viet Cong, attacked Ngo Dinh Diem's government?

_____ 4. In which selection did the writer claim that the United States did not have the will to win the war in Vietnam?

_____ 5. In which selection did the writer believe that the war in Vietnam was a civil war that should have been left to the Vietnamese to solve on their own?

D-3. Write the letter of the correct choice on the line next to the number of each question.

_____ 1. Which statement best describes the opinion of the person who wrote Selection 1?

(a) The war in Vietnam was a continuation of Vietnam's long struggle for independence.
(b) The United States should have committed only military advisers and not combat troops to Vietnam.
(c) North Vietnam would not have forced the people of South Vietnam to live under communism.
(d) The U.S. soldiers who fought in Vietnam deserve pity but not praise.

____ 2. Which statement best describes the opinion of the person who wrote Selection 2?
(*a*) I would not have wanted my child to fight in Vietnam.
(*b*) Freedom does not come cheaply.
(*c*) The United States did not betray the people of South Vietnam.
(*d*) U.S. support for South Vietnam led to Soviet and Chinese support for North Vietnam.

____ 3. Which statement best describes an opinion shared by both writers.
(*a*) The United States should never have become involved in the war in Vietnam.
(*b*) The Communist North would not have won the election required by the 1954 peace agreement.
(*c*) The 1973 cease-fire was merely a way for the United States to pull out of Vietnam and let the North conquer the South.
(*d*) By not winning the war in Vietnam, the United States let 58,000 soldiers die in vain.

E. On the following lines, write two new statements that are facts and two new statements that are opinions. These statements can deal with anything in U.S. history or with anything to do with the United States today. (Do not use any fact or opinion stated in this chapter.)

FACTS

1. ____

____

2. ____

____

OPINIONS

1. ____

____

2. ____

____

CHAPTER 6

Comparing and Contrasting

Life in America today is very different from what it was 200, 100, or even 50 years ago. But it is not completely different. You can learn how certain aspects of American life have changed or not changed by using the skills of comparing and contrasting. *Comparing* means examining how things are alike and how they are different. For example, by comparing the United States in 1776 and today, you could see both how it has changed and remained the same. *Contrasting,* on the other hand, means examining only how things are different rather than how they are alike or different.

Comparing

First, let us take a look at the skill of comparing. Read the following selection comparing colonial Americans and Americans today. As you read, pay attention to the similarities (how things are alike) and the differences stated in the selection.

Colonial America or Convenience America?

Americans today share with colonial Americans a love of freedom and adventure. They also share a respect for hard work and a desire to do a job well. What they do *not* share is a life of convenience. Americans today have conveniences that the colonists could not have imagined. Colonists were used to making the things they needed. Almost all clothes were made by the family. A colonist who wanted a new shirt or dress had to wait until someone in the family cut the cloth and sewed the pieces together. Few Americans today make their own clothes. We usually go to stores and choose our clothes from a wide selection of styles, fabrics, sizes, and colors.

Americans today also go to stores to buy food, most of which is already packaged in bags, boxes, or cans. The colonists had to kill the chickens, cattle, and sheep they needed for meat. They had to grow their own vegetables and fruits.

Today, Americans expect to travel in air-conditioned automobiles, buses, airplanes, and trains. Colonial travelers had to rely on horses for land travel. Now we take electricity for granted; we can flick a switch and have our homes glow with light. Colonial homeowners needed candles to light their dwellings, and most of the time they had to make their own candles. If we want to listen to music, we turn on a radio or a stereo. Colonial Americans had to go where musicians were playing or invite musicians into their homes.

It might be fun to imagine what life was like 250 years ago. But few Americans would want to give up today's conveniences for life in colonial America.

What similarities and differences did you find as you read? Two ways in which colonial Americans and Americans today are similar are given in the following list. Add two more similarities found in the reading selection.

SIMILARITIES

1. Colonial Americans and Americans today share a love of freedom.
2. They share a love of adventure.
3. ______________________________

____
4. ______________________________

____

What did you write? In the first paragraph, you read that both groups share a respect for hard work and a desire to do a job well. These are the two similarities you should have listed.

But we know from the reading selection that colonial Americans and Americans today do not share a life of convenience. In this area, their lives are very different. Two examples of such differences are given in the following lists. Add two more differences found in the reading selection.

DIFFERENCES

Colonial Americans	*Americans Today*
1. If colonial Americans wanted to hear music, they had to go where musicians were playing or invite musicians to their homes.	1. Americans today can hear music by turning on a radio or stereo.
2. Colonial Americans lighted their homes with candles.	2. Americans today use electric lights.
3. ______________________________	3. ______________________________
______________________________	______________________________
______________________________	______________________________
4. ______________________________	4. ______________________________
______________________________	______________________________
______________________________	______________________________

What other differences did you find? Almost all clothes were made by the colonial family, while nearly all Americans today buy their clothes in stores. Colonial Americans killed animals for meat and grew fruit and vegetables. Americans today buy most of their food in stores. Colonial Americans relied on horses for land travel, while Americans today travel in air-conditioned automobiles, buses, airplanes, and trains. You should have chosen two of these differences.

So far you have learned that comparing can be used to identify similarities and differences. With this skill, you can study different periods in U.S. history, as well as various happenings in the same period.

Contrasting

Contrasting examines differences only. This skill is also helpful in studying about different periods in U.S. history, as well as various happenings. Let us use it here to learn about two labor movements that began during the 20-year period following the Civil War. (The Civil War ended in 1865.)

The Rise of the Labor Movement in the United States

In the years following the Civil War, the United States became a wealthy industrial power. Very little of that wealth went to the millions of workers whose labor made American industries grow. Instead, they endured poor, sometimes dangerous, working conditions, long hours, and low wages.

In 1869, Uriah Stephens organized the Knights of Labor for the improvement of workers' lives. All workers, skilled and unskilled, were admitted to the Knights of Labor. Local branches were made up of workers who lived near one another, no matter what their job or skill. This way of organizing was not successful. Members of a local branch did not always have the same economic interests. When unskilled workers went on strike, they were easy to replace, so the strikes often failed. At its peak, in 1886, the Knights of Labor had 700,000 members. But less than ten years later, the organization had disappeared.

Samuel Gompers had a different approach to organizing workers. In 1881, he began the American Federation of Labor (AFL). It admitted mostly skilled workers and organized them into separate craft unions, such as carpenters or plumbers. When the skilled workers went on strike, they were more successful because they could not be replaced easily. In 1890, the American Federation of Labor had only 100,000 members, but by 1920, it had four million. It still exists today.

The following lists give two differences between the Knights of Labor and the American Federation of Labor. Add two more differences found in the reading selection above.

DIFFERENCES

Knights of Labor	*American Federation of Labor*
1. Skilled and unskilled workers were admitted.	1. Mostly skilled workers were admitted.
2. The strikes of unskilled workers often failed.	2. The strikes of skilled workers were usually more successful.
3. ______________________________	3. ______________________________
4. ______________________________	4. ______________________________

What other differences did you find? Members in local branches of the Knights of Labor, whether skilled or unskilled, were grouped by area. Members in local branches of the American Federation of Labor were all skilled and were organized according to their craft. The Knights of Labor disappeared by 1895, and the American Federation of Labor still exists. These are the two differences that you should have listed.

You have seen in this chapter that one way to learn about something is to compare or contrast it with something else. Let us see how well you can compare and contrast in the following exercises.

USING YOUR SKILLS

A. Read the following selection, which compares colonial life in Massachusetts and Virginia.

A Visit to Massachusetts and Virginia

Today, June 15, 1750, I sail back to Great Britain after spending a year in America. I divided my time between visiting my aunt and uncle in Massachusetts and my brother and his wife in Virginia. When I arrived in America, I expected life to be the same in all the colonies. Oh, it was true that certain practices existed throughout all the colonies. For example, nearly all colonists had farms. Most owned their own farms. Also, each colonial family tended to be self-sufficient, in that it produced most of its own food, clothing, and other necessities.

Even though the colonies had much in common, I was surprised to see how different life was in Massachusetts and Virginia.

Climate and geography were partly responsible for the differences. In Massachusetts, the climate was quite cool. The land was very rocky, making it difficult to grow crops. Farms were not large, and farmers grew mainly small amounts of wheat, barley, oats, and corn. In Virginia, the climate was warmer, and the land was better for farming. I saw many large farms, called plantations. The major crops were tobacco, rice, and indigo (a plant used to make a blue dye).

One part of the trip that bothered me was seeing slaves, in both Massachusetts and Virginia. Many blacks worked as skilled laborers in Massachusetts, but they were still slaves. In Virginia, most slaves worked very hard in the fields of the large plantations.

I learned a great deal about the colonies during my visit. The most important thing I learned was that the colonies were developing their own separate ways.

Compare colonial life in Massachusetts and Virginia. First show how life in both places was similar. Then show how it was different.

SIMILARITIES

1. ______________________________

____

2. ______________________________

____

3. ______________________________

____

4. ______________________________

____

DIFFERENCES

Massachusetts	*Virginia*
1. ______________	1. ______________
______________	______________
______________	______________

Massachusetts	*Virginia*
2. ______________________	2. ______________________
______________________	______________________
______________________	______________________
3. ______________________	3. ______________________
______________________	______________________
______________________	______________________
4. ______________________	4. ______________________
______________________	______________________
______________________	______________________

B. Read the following selection, which compares immigration between 1830 and 1860 and immigration between 1880 and 1920.

Comparing Old Immigration and New Immigration

Between 1880 and 1920, 23 million immigrants came to the United States during the so-called period of *New Immigration.* The 10 million people who immigrated to the United States between 1830 and 1860 belong to the period called the *Old Immigration.*

For the most part, the "old" and "new" immigrants came for the same reasons. They wanted to escape hardships at home. Some left because they could not find work or save enough money to buy a farm that could support a family. Others wanted to get away from the political persecution they suffered for having views different from their government's. So they came to America, hoping to improve their lives—to find work, land, and freedom.

While many immigrants did find a better way of life in America, it was not always easy. Some native-born Americans were unwilling to accept foreigners who did not fit quickly into the existing American culture. As a result, many immigrants faced some form of *discrimination* (unfair treatment of a minority by the majority). There was much more opposition to the "new" immigrants than to the "old." The "old" immigrants had come chiefly from northern Europe: Great Britain, Germany, Holland, Scandinavia, and Ireland. They were mostly Protestant, as were most native-born Americans. The Irish immigrants were an exception; most of them were Roman Catholics.

The "new" immigrants came chiefly from southern and eastern Europe: Italy, Poland, Russia, and Hungary. They were mostly Roman Catholic, Jewish, or Eastern Orthodox. They held on to their European traditions and usually took a longer time to learn English than the "old" immigrants.

Many of the "old" immigrants were skilled workers who came to the United States with money in their pockets. The Germans and Dutch were generally well educated, and the Scandinavians were usually skilled farmers. Many of the "new" immigrants were poor. Some did not even know what money was. In their homelands, they had traded the goods they possessed for the goods they needed. Most had little education and possessed few skills.

Some Americans demanded an end to the flow of "new" immigrants into the United States. Some of these critics came from families that had been "old" immigrants. Although laws were passed in the 1920s to limit future immigration, the many millions already here could not be sent back to their homelands. Today, more than half of the American people are descendants of the "old" and "new" immigrants.

SIMILARITIES

1. ____________________
____

2. ____________________
____

3. ____________________
____

DIFFERENCES

Old Immigration	*New Immigration*
1. ____________	1. ____________
2. ____________	2. ____________
3. ____________	3. ____________
4. ____________	4. ____________

C. Read the following selection, which contrasts a young immigrant girl's life with that of a young American-born woman. The story takes place in New York City about 1910.

The American Dream

I remember the first day I saw her. It was a beautiful spring day and she was wearing a pretty, pale pink dress. Since then I have seen her once a week—and each time she has worn something different. I am always in the same dress. The last time I had a new dress was two years ago when I came with my family from Italy.

It is not possible for my family to buy me many new clothes. My father cannot always find work. Things are so bad right now that my mother makes artificial flowers in our kitchen and sells them on street corners just to make a little money. I help her make and sell the flowers.

This is how I came to see the young woman who dresses so well. She passes in front of the place where we sell our flowers. One day she stopped to tell us how lovely they were and to buy some. She spoke so well. I wouldn't speak to her because my English is still so poor.

As the young woman walked away with her flowers, my mother said to me, "Maybe someday, if you work hard, you will be like her. This is America. You are only 12. You are young."

"That's right!" said an elderly woman who had stopped to look at our flowers. "Listen to your mother. Work hard and you'll do well."

"Pardon me," my mother said to the elderly woman, "but do you know the young woman who just bought flowers?"

"Oh, yes," said the elderly woman. "She's the daughter of a wealthy banker. The family lives in a mansion just off Fifth Avenue. I hear she's a very generous woman . . . gives much of her time to helping orphans."

I was pleased that the young woman helped orphans. I, too, want to help people when I get older. But I was stunned to hear of her wealth. How could I ever dream to have a life like hers! My family doesn't make $300 a year. And to grow up in a mansion! We live in an old apartment house. We share the apartment with my father's cousins. I sleep in a room with my mother, father, and two brothers.

But I have to listen to my mother. I can dream. Many immigrant families have done well. After all, this is America. And no matter what I become when I am older, I want to help people, just like the young woman who bought our flowers.

Contrast the young immigrant girl and the young American-born woman by writing the differences in the following lists.

DIFFERENCES

Young Immigrant Girl	*Young American-born Woman*
1. ____________________	1. ____________________
____________________	____________________
2. ____________________	2. ____________________
____________________	____________________
3. ____________________	3. ____________________
____________________	____________________
4. ____________________	4. ____________________
____________________	____________________

D. Read the following selection, which contrasts going to the movies today and in an earlier generation.

What Do We Expect to Find in a Movie Theater?

Going to the movies today is a different experience from what it was in the 1930s, 40s, and 50s. Back then, movie theaters in many cities across America were like palaces. They had giant screens and could seat thousands of people at the same time. Many were filled with copies of great works of art. In some, goldfish swam in lobby pools and marble staircases led to the balconies. In others, ceilings were made to look like the sky with stars and moving clouds. Today, movie theaters are like the inside of a shoe box, with a small screen at one end and only a few hundred seats.

Movie entertainment also has changed. In the early 1950s, for example, a young person could go to the movies on a Saturday afternoon and see two full-length movies, a cartoon, the news of the week, a weekly installment of Captain Video or Batman, coming attractions, and maybe a travelog on a foreign country. For all that, the cost was 25 cents. Today, a person pays $6.00 or more and sees one movie, coming attractions, and commercials.

There is one good thing about movie theaters today. The seats are much more comfortable than in the old days. In the old theaters, the seats were close together and often had little cushioning. Today, seats recline, are better cushioned, and sometimes even have holders for soda cups.

So which do you prefer, a palace with hard seats or a shoe box with a holder for your soda? Or maybe you wait to rent a videocassette of a movie and watch it from a comfortable chair in your own palace.

Contrast movie theaters in the 1950s and today by writing the differences in the following lists.

DIFFERENCES

Movie Theaters in the 1950s	*Movie Theaters Today*
1. ______________________	1. ______________________
______________________	______________________
2. ______________________	2. ______________________
______________________	______________________
3. ______________________	3. ______________________
______________________	______________________
4. ______________________	4. ______________________
______________________	______________________
5. ______________________	5. ______________________
______________________	______________________

E. Millions of immigrants continue to come to the United States every year. Since the 1960s, a greater percentage of immigrants have come from Mexico, Central and South America, the Caribbean islands, Asia, and Africa. Do these present-day immigrants come to the United States for the same reasons that brought earlier generations of immigrants? Do they face the same problems that immigrants of an earlier period faced, or different ones?

In this exercise, you are asked to compare present-day immigrants with immigrants who came between 1880 and 1920. To complete this exercise, you may have to use an American history textbook or a current magazine or newspaper article to find out more about present-day immigrants.

Refer to Exercise B on page 62 for information about immigrants who came between 1880 and 1920.

SIMILARITIES
(Find as many as you can)

(How are present-day immigrants similar to immigrants who came to America between 1880 and 1920—their reasons for coming, the problems they faced, the successes they achieved?)

____

____

____

____

____

____

DIFFERENCES
(Find as many as you can)

(How are present-day immigrants different from immigrants who came to America between 1880 and 1920—their reasons for coming, the problems they faced, the successes they achieved?)

Present-Day Immigrants	*Immigrants Between 1880 and 1920*
____________________	____________________
____________________	____________________
____________________	____________________
____________________	____________________
____________________	____________________
____________________	____________________
____________________	____________________
____________________	____________________

CHAPTER 7

Recognizing Cause and Effect

What were the causes of the American Revolution? What effect did the invention of the railroad have on the United States? What were the causes and effects of the Great Depression of the 1930s? Such questions are asked in every U.S. history course. They introduce two important words: *cause* and *effect.* They are important because so much history is seen in terms of causes and effects. In this chapter, you will learn to recognize cause-and-effect relationships.

A *cause* is an event or action that brings about another event or action.

An *effect* is an event or action brought about by an earlier event or action.

Read the following statement to see how one event (a cause) brought about another event (an effect).

Statement 1

In 1620, as a result of religious persecution, the Pilgrims left England and sailed to America.

In this example, a cause—religious persecution—had an effect: Pilgrims left England and sailed to America. There are usually key words in a reading selection that let you know that you are reading a cause-and-effect relationship. In Statement 1, the key words are *as a result of.* Other key cause-and-effect words include *because, since, therefore, if . . . then,* and *for this reason.*

Here is another statement containing a cause-and-effect relationship.

Statement 2

In colonial America, girls were not given the same opportunity for schooling as boys because, it was claimed, they needed only to learn how to keep house and become good wives and mothers.

On the following lines, write the cause in Statement 2.

____

____

____

____

On the following lines, write the effect in Statement 2.

____

____

____

____

Statement 2 contains the key word *because.* One event happened *because* another event happened first. Here is the event that was the cause: colonial girls were expected to grow up to keep house and become wives and mothers. Here is the event that was the effect: (therefore,) girls were not given the same opportunity for schooling as boys.

Statements 1 and 2 show simple cause-and-effect relationships. Often a cause may have *multiple effects* (more than one effect), as in the following example.

Statement 3

In what came to be called the Boston Tea Party, American colonists in 1773 destroyed British tea by dumping it into Boston Harbor. In response, the British government took more direct control over the government of Massachusetts. It closed the port of Boston and passed a new Quartering Act, requiring colonists to provide housing for British soldiers. In addition, the British government allowed British soldiers accused of crimes in America to stand trial in Britain.

In Statement 3, the cause is the Boston Tea Party. On the following lines, write the effects.

____

____

____

____

____

____

What did you write? In Statement 3, there were four effects. The government of Massachusetts was put more directly under Great Britain's control, the port of Boston was closed, a new Quartering Act was passed, and British soldiers accused of crimes in America were allowed to stand trial in Britain. All four actions were in response to the Boston Tea Party.

Sometimes an effect can have *multiple causation* (more than one cause). Read the following example.

Statement 4

The American colonists organized the First Continental Congress in 1774 to protest the British action of taking more direct control of the government of Massachusetts. The Congress was directed to protest the closing of the port of Boston and the new Quartering Act. It was also to object to the new policy allowing British soldiers accused of crimes in America to stand trial in Britain.

In Statement 4, the effect is the organization of the First Continental Congress in 1774. There are four causes in Statement 4 that brought about that effect. Though worded a little differently, those four causes are the same as the four effects in Statement 3. The effects in Statement 3 become the causes in Statement 4. Very often in history, a cause brings about an effect, and in turn, that effect becomes the cause of another effect, and so on. This is what is meant by a *chain reaction* of causes and effects.

Here is how a chain reaction works.

This *cause*—The Boston Tea Party—brought about these *effects* (↓)

The government of Massachusetts was put more directly under the control of Britain.
The port of Boston was closed.
A new Quartering Act was passed.
British soldiers accused of crimes in America were allowed to stand trial in Britain.

These *effects* (↑) became *causes* (↓) that brought about

The meeting of the First Continental Congress.

This *effect* (↑) became the *cause* (↓) that brought about

The colonists' decision to *boycott* (refuse to purchase) goods made in Great Britain.

Of course, there were events that caused the Boston Tea Party and events that followed the boycott of British goods. In fact, this continuing chain reaction led to the American Revolution.

Studying a chain reaction of causes and effects shows us that important events in history rarely happen overnight or for only one reason. Like most major events in history, the American Revolution occurred for many reasons and because of developments that took place over a long period.

You have seen how important recognizing cause-and-effect relationships is to understanding American history. The following exercises will give you more practice in developing this skill.

USING YOUR SKILLS

A. Simple Cause-and-Effect Relationships. On the lines provided, write the cause and effect in each statement.

1. As a result of Alexander Graham Bell's invention of the telephone, people who live a great distance apart can speak to each other simply by talking into a telephone.

CAUSE: ______________________________

____

EFFECT: ______________________________

____

2. In 1941, Japan believed that the United States would enter World War II soon. For this reason, it made a surprise attack on the American naval fleet at Pearl Harbor.

CAUSE: ______________________________

____

EFFECT: ______________________________

____

3. If Lyndon Johnson had been able to end the war in Vietnam before the 1968 presidential election, he would have run for re-election.

CAUSE: ______________________________

____

EFFECT: ______________________________

____

4. More and more American wives are forced to find work outside the home because their husbands do not earn enough to pay all the bills.

CAUSE: ____

____

EFFECT: ____

____

5. Unfortunately, issues of race still divide the nation.

CAUSE: ____

____

EFFECT: ____

____

B. Multiple Causes and Effects. Read each paragraph. Then, on the lines provided, write the cause(s) and effect(s) stated in each paragraph. *Note:* The number of causes and effects differs from paragraph to paragraph. For example, one paragraph may have one cause and three effects. Another paragraph may have three causes and one effect.

1. The American victory at the Battle of Saratoga in 1777 is called the turning point of the American Revolution. As a result of this victory, the British lost many soldiers they could not replace, and the Americans began to think they could win the war. The victory at Saratoga also persuaded the French to sign an agreement with the Americans to give them naval and military aid.

CAUSE(S): ____

____

____

____

EFFECT(S): ____

____

____

____

2. Andrew Carnegie knew how to succeed in the steel business. He hired talented people to assist him. He produced a better grade of steel for less money than other companies charged. He forced his competitors (rivals) out of business by selling his steel for less money. For these reasons, Carnegie transformed a small steel company into a giant business worth almost $500 million.

CAUSE(S): ____________________

____

____

EFFECT(S): ____________________

____

____

3. By 1880, the railroad was the largest industry in the United States. Railroad lines stretched across the nation from the Atlantic to the Pacific. The trip from New York to California, which had taken months by wagon, could be made by railroad in less than two weeks. Land all along the railroad lines became more valuable as people sought to set up businesses near the lines. Perhaps the most amazing effect of the railroad was how it influenced time. Until the late 1800s, there were no time zones in the United States. In some states, as many as 30 cities each had different times. In the early 1880s, the railroads developed a plan that divided the country into time zones. Every place in the same time zone would have the same time. The need for the railroad companies to assign the same time to the same places on their schedules forced the United States government to accept this plan.

CAUSE(S): ____________________

____

____

____

EFFECT(S): ____________________

____

____

____

4. Americans today know more than any generation in history has known. At one time, newspapers and books were the only sources of information, provided you could read or have someone else read to you. Then came radio. You could listen to major events as they happened. Then came television, and you could see major events taking place. Now we have the computer, perhaps the greatest source of information ever invented. Home computers can instantly provide almost any kind of information imaginable, especially if they are linked to the World Wide Web. Of course, this brings up an important question. With all this information, are we any wiser than previous generations were?

CAUSE(S): ____

____

____

EFFECT(S): ____

____

____

C. A Chain Reaction of Causes and Effects. Read the following selection, which contains a chain reaction of causes and effects.

As the 13 American colonies struggled to gain their independence from Britain, they realized that they had to join together to form a working government. After a long delay, a new national government was established in 1781 under the Articles of Confederation. The new government, however, did not have the power to raise taxes, regulate trade between states, or settle quarrels between states. As Americans became more aware of these weaknesses, they began demanding changes in the Articles.

In 1787, a convention met in Philadelphia to improve the Articles. But the delegates to the convention found too many weaknesses in the Articles, and decided to draw up a new constitution instead.

After much debate, a new national Constitution was adopted and, in 1788, accepted by the states. The national government now had greater power than it had held under the Articles. Included in the new Constitution was the power to raise taxes, regulate trade between states, and settle quarrels between states. This is the same Constitution that is the supreme law of the United States today.

Complete the chain reaction of causes and effects that has been started. Use the information in the reading selection to help you.

(Cause) ....The colonists had to form a working government in order to make their struggle for independence succeed.

brought about ↓

(This effect becomes a cause) ....The establishment of a new national government under the Articles of Confederation.

brought about ↓

(This effect becomes a cause) .... 1. ______________________________

brought about ↓

(This effect becomes a cause) .... 2. ______________________________

brought about ↓

(This effect becomes a cause) .... 3. ______________________________

brought about ↓

(Effect) .... 4. ______________________________

D. A Chain Reaction of Causes and Effects. Read the following selection, which contains a chain reaction of causes and effects. Then complete the exercise.

For much of the 19th century, Americans used petroleum, commonly called "oil," to make illuminating gases, wax, and lubricating oils. Because there was money to be made from petroleum, a few Americans tried to find a way to get oil out of the ground easily. In 1859, Edwin Drake drilled the first successful oil well in the United States. His discovery of oil deposits in western Pennsylvania encouraged others to drill in nearby areas. Soon wells dotted the Pennsylvania landscape.

The discovery of an abundant supply of oil led people to seek new uses for it. In the 1890s, a giant breakthrough in the United States came with the development of a practical internal combustion engine that operated on gasoline (made from petroleum). The engine was put to use to power automobiles. With so much petroleum available, it was inevitable that gasoline-operated cars would be produced in great numbers.

At first, such cars were expensive, but soon a large number of Americans could afford them. By the 1920s, the United States had become a nation on wheels. Cities spread out, highways were built, suburbs were created, and roadside restaurants and stores were opened. The car changed the way Americans lived, worked, and traveled. Surely, Edwin Drake could not have imagined that his oil well would have such an effect on the lives of Americans.

illuminating: giving off or causing light
lubricating: making slippery or smooth
abundant: plentiful; in large supply
inevitable: sure to happen; certain

Complete the chain of causes and effects that has been started.

(Cause).................................There was money to be made from petroleum.

brought about

(This effect becomes a cause)................... People searched for a way to get petroleum out of the ground easily. In 1859, Edwin Drake drilled the first successful oil well in the United States.

brought about

(This effect becomes a cause)................... 1. ______________________________
____

brought about

(This effect becomes a cause)................... 2. ______________________________
____

brought about

3. ______________________________

(This effect
becomes a cause) .... ______________________

brought about
↓

4. ______________________

(This effect
becomes a cause) .... ______________________

brought about
↓

5. ______________________

(Effect) .... ______________________

E. Discovering the Causes and Effects. Based on what you have learned in school or from reading or watching television, complete the following:

E-1. Give three effects brought about by the following cause.

CAUSE: Thomas Edison invented the electric light bulb.

EFFECTS: 1. ______________________

____

2. ______________________

____

3. ______________________

____

E-2. Give three causes that brought about the effect stated below.

CAUSES: 1. ______________________

____

2. ______________________

____

3. ______________________

____

EFFECT: Today, the United States has a great influence on the cultures of other countries.

CHAPTER 8

Understanding Time Lines and Dates

Imagine studying the history of the United States without dates. It would be impossible. Dates tell you when events took place and help you keep track of the correct *sequence,* or order, of events. Knowing the correct sequence makes it easier to understand how one event may have influenced another.

A *time line* is a line, divided into time periods, on which events are placed in correct order. Time lines help you remember the correct sequence and show you the length of time between events. Almost all time lines are divided into equal time periods. The most commonly used time periods are:

- *decade* (10 years)
- *century* (100 years)
- *millennium* (1,000 years). *Millennia* means more than one millennium.
- *age* (period of time marked by features and events that set it apart from other periods). For example, we now live in the Space Age, when a number of nations are exploring outer space. An age may have no fixed starting and ending dates.

The time line below shows the major wars fought by the United States. It is divided into equal periods of 100 years—from 1700 to the present.

Use this time line to answer the following questions.

____ 1. The time line is divided into
(*a*) decades. (*b*) centuries. (*c*) millennia. (*d*) ages.

Which answer did you choose? You can see that the time line is divided into periods of 100 years, which are called cen-

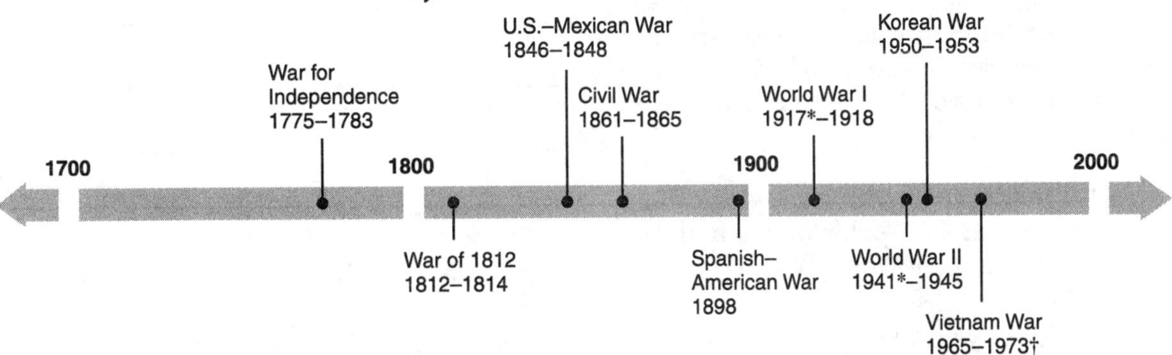

*World War I began in 1914, and World War II began in 1939. The United States did not enter either war until the years given on the time line.

†The civil war between North and South Vietnam lasted from 1955 until 1975. The dates on the time line mark the years of U.S. involvement.

turies. Therefore, the answer to question 1 is *(b)*.

____ 2. The period 1801 to 1900 is called the
(a) 17th century.
(b) 18th century.
(c) 19th century.
(d) 20th century.

Which answer did you choose? To answer this question, you have to know the years that belong to each century. The years 1 to 100 are called the first century. The years 101 to 200 are called the second century. This sequence of centuries continues from the years 201 to 300 (the third century) all the way to the years 1901 to 2000 (the 20th century). In which century are the years 1801 to 1900? You should be able to figure out that they are in the 19th century. Therefore, the answer to question 2 is *(c)*.

____ 3. Which of the following wars was fought first?
(a) Civil War
(b) Korean War
(c) Vietnam War
(d) U.S.–Mexican War

There are two ways to find this answer. First, each of these four wars is shown on the time line with the year or years during which it took place. You can see that the U.S.–Mexican War was fought between 1846 and 1848. These years are earlier than the years for the other three wars. Second, you can refer to the centuries that divide the time line. The Mexican War was fought in the 19th century. The Civil War was fought later in the 19th century, and the other two wars were fought in the 20th century. Therefore, the answer to question 3 is *(d)*.

____ 4. How many years passed between the end of World War I and the beginning of World War II?
(a) 10 years
(b) 21 years
(c) 35 years
(d) 50 years

Which answer did you choose? This question points out the need to pay attention to every detail on a time line. The time line shows the years of U.S. involvement in World War I (1917–1918) and World War II (1941–1945). But to answer this question, you have to know when World War II began rather than when the United States entered it. The asterisk (*) after 1941 refers you to a footnote below the time line. That footnote tells you that World War II began in 1939. The time line also shows that World War I ended in 1918. By subtracting the year World War I ended from the year World War II started, you will know how many years passed between the wars.

1939 (start of World War II)
–1918 (end of World War I)
21 years.

The answer to question 4, therefore, is *(b)*.

____ 5. Read the following statements:
A. The invention of the airplane in 1903 helped bring a quick end to the Spanish-American War.
B. The airplane, invented in 1903, saw its first major use in warfare in World War I.

One statement is TRUE. The other is FALSE. Explain how the time line can help you choose which statement is TRUE even if you know nothing about the events mentioned.

____

____

____

____

____

____

____

____

What did you write? You were told that the airplane was invented in 1903. According to the time line, the Spanish-American War was fought in 1898 and U.S. involvement in World War I took place between 1917 and 1918. Therefore, the airplane was invented after the Spanish–American War but before World War I. Only Statement B contains the correct sequence of events, so it must be the TRUE statement. If you wrote that finding the correct sequence of events helped you decide which statement is true, you wrote a good answer for question 6.

In this chapter, you learned that dates are important in the study of U.S. history because they tell you when events took place. You also learned that time lines help you see the correct sequence of these events. The following exercises will give you more practice in using dates and in interpreting time lines.

USING YOUR SKILLS

A. Place the letter of the correct choice next to the number of each question.

_____ 1. Which set of dates is a decade?
(a) 1781–1880
(b) 1861–1870
(c) 1896–1900
(d) 1956–1970

_____ 2. A period of history covering 1, 000 years is called
(a) an age.
(b) a century.
(c) a half-century.
(d) a millennium.

_____ 3. If the 15th century began in 1401 and ended in 1500, then the 17th century
(a) began in 701 and ended in 800.
(b) began in 1001 and ended in 1100.
(c) began in 1601 and ended in 1700.
(d) began in 1701 and ended in 1800.

_____ 4. When we say we live in the Computer Age, we mean that
(a) today many people all over the world use computers.
(b) computers have been used for many years.
(c) you have to be a certain age to operate a computer.
(d) computers will be used for thousands of years to come.

_____ 5. An event that took place from 996 to 1005 lasted
(a) one decade.
(b) two decades.
(c) one millennium.
(d) two millennia.

Use the time line on page 77 to answer questions 6 to 10.

_____ 6. The Spanish-American War took place in the
(a) 17th century.
(b) 18th century.
(c) 19th century.
(d) 20th century.

____ 7. Which war was fought first?
(a) Korean War
(b) U.S.–Mexican War
(c) World War I
(d) Vietnam War

____ 8. Which two wars took place in the same century?
(a) War for Independence and Civil War
(b) War of 1812 and World War I
(c) Spanish-American War and Vietnam War
(d) World War II and Korean War

____ 9. How many years passed between the end of the War for Independence and the start of the War of 1812?
(a) almost 20 years
(b) almost 30 years
(c) almost 40 years
(d) almost 50 years

____ 10. Some soldiers who fought in the Civil War probably gained earlier military experience in
(a) the War for Independence.
(b) the War of 1812.
(c) the U.S.–Mexican War.
(d) the Spanish-American War.

B. Using a Time Line.

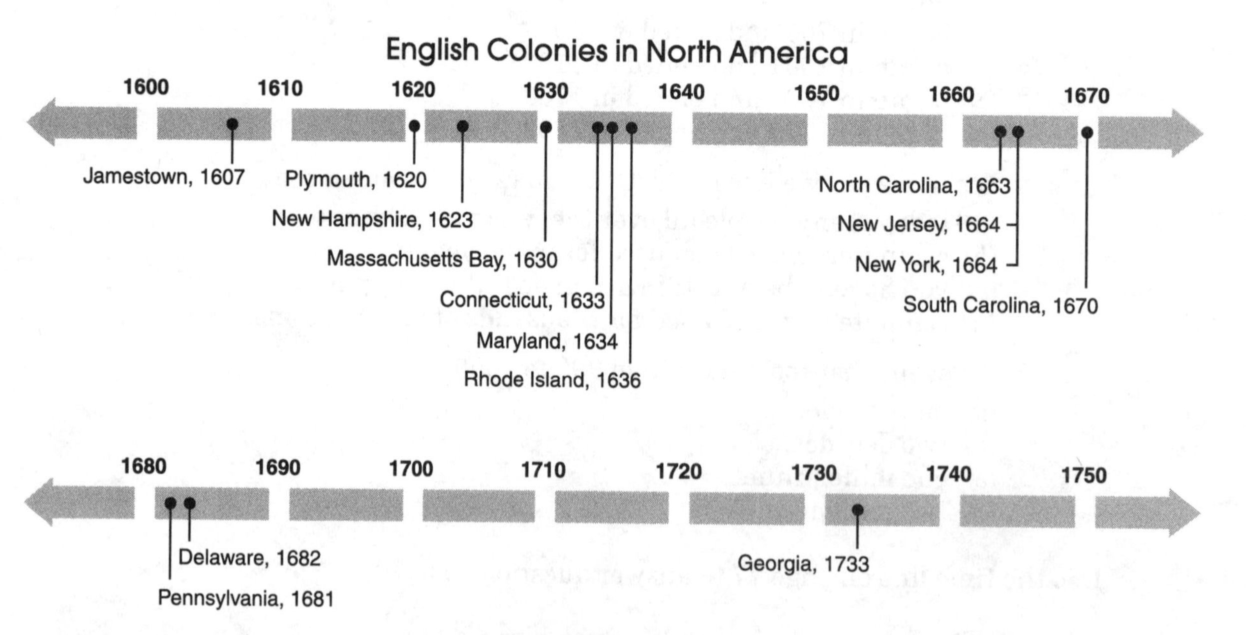

Note: The year after each colony refers to the year it was founded (first settled) by the English. New York had been settled by the Dutch in 1624, but became an English colony in 1664. In 1664, a part of New York became New Jersey. Delaware had been settled by the Swedes in 1638, but became an English colony in 1682. By 1624, Jamestown had developed into the colony of Virginia. In 1691, Plymouth joined Massachusetts Bay.

Write the letter of the correct choice on the line next to the number of each question.

_____ 1. The time line is divided into
- *(a)* decades.
- *(b)* centuries.
- *(c)* millennia.
- *(d)* ages.

_____ 2. The time line covers the entire
- *(a)* 15th century.
- *(b)* 16th century.
- *(c)* 17th century.
- *(d)* 18th century.

_____ 3. Which colony was founded before the other three?
- *(a)* South Carolina
- *(b)* Maryland
- *(c)* Pennsylvania
- *(d)* Rhode Island

_____ 4. Which colony was founded last?
- *(a)* Plymouth
- *(b)* Massachusetts Bay
- *(c)* Georgia
- *(d)* South Carolina

_____ 5. In which decade were the most colonies founded or taken over?
- *(a)* 1630–1639
- *(b)* 1660–1669
- *(c)* 1680–1689
- *(d)* 1730–1739

_____ 6. Pennsylvania was founded in
- *(a)* 1630.
- *(b)* 1681.
- *(c)* 1682.
- *(d)* 1733.

_____ 7. Which statement is TRUE?
- *(a)* The English founded colonies in each decade between 1600 and 1740.
- *(b)* The English founded or took over more colonies in the 18th century than in the 17th century.
- *(c)* More than ten colonies were founded or taken over by the English in the 17th century.
- *(d)* More than five decades passed between the founding of Jamestown and the founding of Rhode Island.

_____ 8. Which two colonies were part of the same colony before 1664?
- *(a)* Connecticut and South Carolina
- *(b)* New York and New Jersey
- *(c)* Pennsylvania and Georgia
- *(d)* Jamestown and Rhode Island

_____ 9. How many decades passed between the founding of Maryland and the founding of North Carolina?
- *(a)* nearly one decade
- *(b)* nearly two decades
- *(c)* nearly three decades
- *(d)* nearly four decades

____ 10. Which colony no longer existed by the beginning of the 18th century?
(a) Maryland
(b) New Hampshire
(c) Rhode Island
(d) Plymouth

C. Using a Vertical Time Line. This time line is called a vertical time line because the years are listed vertically (from top to bottom).

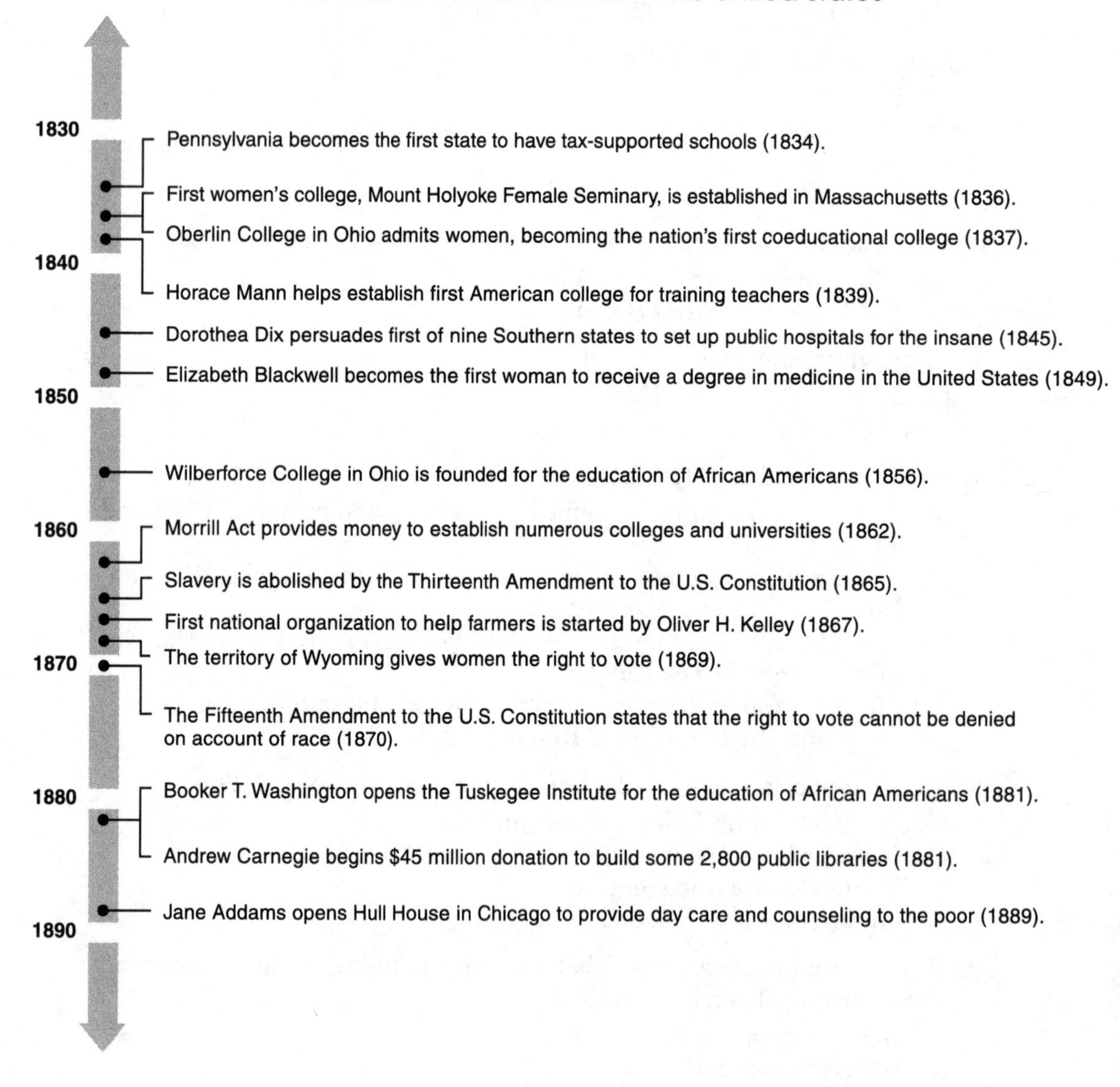

C-1. Write the letter of the correct choice on the line next to the number of each question.

____ 1. The time line covers
  (a) all of the 18th century.
  (b) most of the 18th century.
  (c) all of the 19th century.
  (d) most of the 19th century.

____ 2. Which event happened between 1840 and 1850?
  (a) Oliver Kelley began a national organization to help farmers.
  (b) The Fifteenth Amendment was added to the U.S. Constitution.
  (c) Oberlin College became the first coeducational college in the United States.
  (d) Dorothea Dix persuaded Southern states to set up public hospitals for the insane.

____ 3. Which two events happened in the same year?
  (a) Andrew Carnegie began donating to build public libraries, and Booker T. Washington opened the Tuskegee Institute.
  (b) Pennsylvania became the first state to have tax-supported schools, and Horace Mann helped establish the first American college for training teachers.
  (c) Mount Holyoke Female Seminary and Wilberforce College were founded.
  (d) The Thirteenth Amendment to the U.S. Constitution abolished slavery, and Jane Addams opened Hull House to help the poor.

____ 4. How many years passed between the founding of Mount Holyoke Female Seminary and Elizabeth Blackwell's degree in medicine?
  (a) 9 years *(c)* 13 years
  (b) 11 years *(d)* 15 years

____ 5. How many decades passed between the first tax-supported schools in Pennsylvania and the funding of colleges and universities by the Morrill Act?
  (a) almost two decades
  (b) almost three decades
  (c) almost four decades
  (d) almost five decades

C-2. Following the Sequence of Events on a Time Line.

1. Read Statements A and B.
   A. When the Civil War began in 1861, only qualified white men had the right to vote in the United States and its territories.
   B. By the time the Civil War began, qualified white women had the right to vote in any state or territory.

One statement is TRUE. One statement is FALSE. Explain how the time line on page 82 can help you choose which statement is TRUE even if you do not know about the events in the statements. Include in your answer which statement is TRUE.

____

____

____

____

2. Read Statements A and B.
   A. Elizabeth Blackwell could not have attended college without money provided by the Morrill Act.
   B. Elizabeth Blackwell could not have earned a degree in medicine in the United States before 1836.

One statement is TRUE. One statement is FALSE. Explain how the time line on page 82 can help you choose which statement is TRUE even if you do not know about the events in the statements. Include in your answer which statement is TRUE.

____

____

____

____

D. Time Line. Study the following time line.

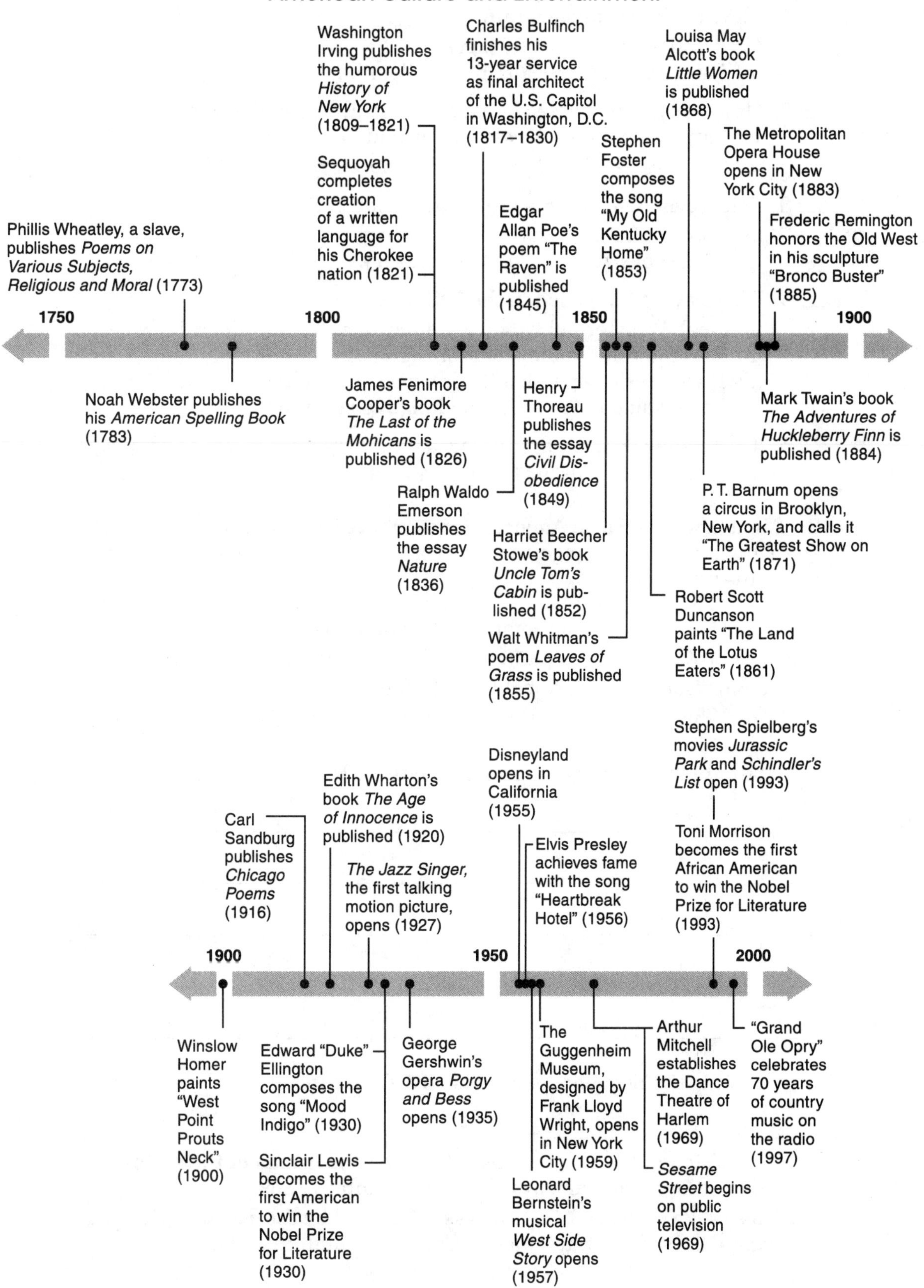

D-1. Write the letter of the correct choice on the line next to the number of each question.

_____ 1. The time line is divided into
(a) decades. *(c)* ages.
(b) half-centuries. *(d)* half-millennia.

_____ 2. How many years passed between the awarding of the Nobel Prize for Literature to Sinclair Lewis and to Toni Morrison?
(a) 25 years *(b)* 42 years *(c)* 50 years *(d)* 63 years

_____ 3. Talking motion pictures are an invention of the
(a) 18th century. *(c)* 20th century.
(b) 19th century. *(d)* 21st century.

_____ 4. Which event happened in the 19th century?
(a) Noah Webster published his *American Spelling Book.*
(b) Carl Sandburg published *Chicago Poems.*
(c) Elvis Presley recorded the hit song "Heartbreak Hotel."
(d) Sequoyah created a written language for the Cherokee nation.

_____ 5. The Grand Ole Opry first broadcast country music on the radio in
(a) 1927. *(b)* 1947. *(c)* 1977. *(d)* 1997.

D-2. The following African Americans contributed much to the cultural life of the United States. Arrange them in correct sequence according to their place on the time line.

Edward "Duke" Ellington composes "Mood Indigo."
Robert Scott Duncanson paints "The Land of the Lotus Eaters."
Toni Morrison wins the Nobel Prize for Literature.
Phillis Wheatley publishes *Poems on Various Subjects, Religious and Moral.*
Arthur Mitchell begins the Dance Theater of Harlem.

1. ____________________

2. ____________________

3. ____________________

4. ____________________

5. ____________________

D-3. Following the Sequence of Events on a Time Line.

1. Read Statements A and B.
   A. The design of the U.S. Capitol influenced the design of the state capital building in Sacramento, California, built in 1869.
   B. The design of the U.S. Capitol was influenced by the design of the state capital building in Sacramento, California, built in 1869.

One statement is TRUE. One statement is FALSE. Explain how the 1750–1900 time line on page 85 can help you choose which statement is TRUE even if you do not know about the events in the statements. Include in your answer which statement is TRUE.

___

___

___

2. Read Statements A and B.
   A. President Abraham Lincoln referred to Harriet Beecher Stowe, author of *Uncle Tom's Cabin,* as the "little woman" who started the Civil War (1861–1865).
   B. President Abraham Lincoln believed that Louisa May Alcott's novel, *Little Women,* contributed to the start of the Civil War.

One statement is TRUE. One statement is FALSE. Explain how the 1750–1900 time line on page 85 can help you choose which statement is TRUE even if you do not know about the events in the statements. Include in your answer which statement is TRUE.

___

___

___

E. Making and Using a Vertical Time Line.

E-1. The time line on page 88 needs to be completed. Write the following events in their correct place on the time line. (You may have to abbreviate as some events are too long for the line provided.)

Arnold Palmer wins his first Masters Tournament in golf (1958).
Dan Jansen wins his first Olympic gold medal in speed skating after losing in three previous Olympics (1994).
The U.S. men's gymnastic team wins the first team gold medal for the United States at the Summer Olympics (1984).
Eddie Arcaro becomes the first jockey to win five Kentucky Derby races (1952).
Hank Aaron, of the Atlanta Braves, hits his 715th career home run, breaking Babe Ruth's record (1974).
Cassius Clay (Muhammed Ali) wins the World Heavyweight Championship (1964).
Kristi Yamaguchi wins a gold medal in figure skating at the Winter Olympics (1992).
Wilma Rudolph runs the 220-yard dash in 25 seconds, a women's indoor record (1961).

Michael Jordan leads the Chicago Bulls to a sixth NBA Championship (1998).

Pete Rose, of the Cincinnati Reds, passes Ty Cobb's record by getting his 4,192nd career hit (1985).

The Green Bay Packers defeat the Kansas City Chiefs in the first football Superbowl (1967).

Maureen Connolly is the first woman to win the "Grand Slam" in tennis (1953).

Mark Spitz wins seven gold medals in swimming at the Summer Olympics (1972).

Nancy Lopez wins five consecutive golf tournaments in her first year as a professional (1978).

The New York Islanders win their fourth consecutive Stanley Cup in ice hockey (1983).

Sports in the United States

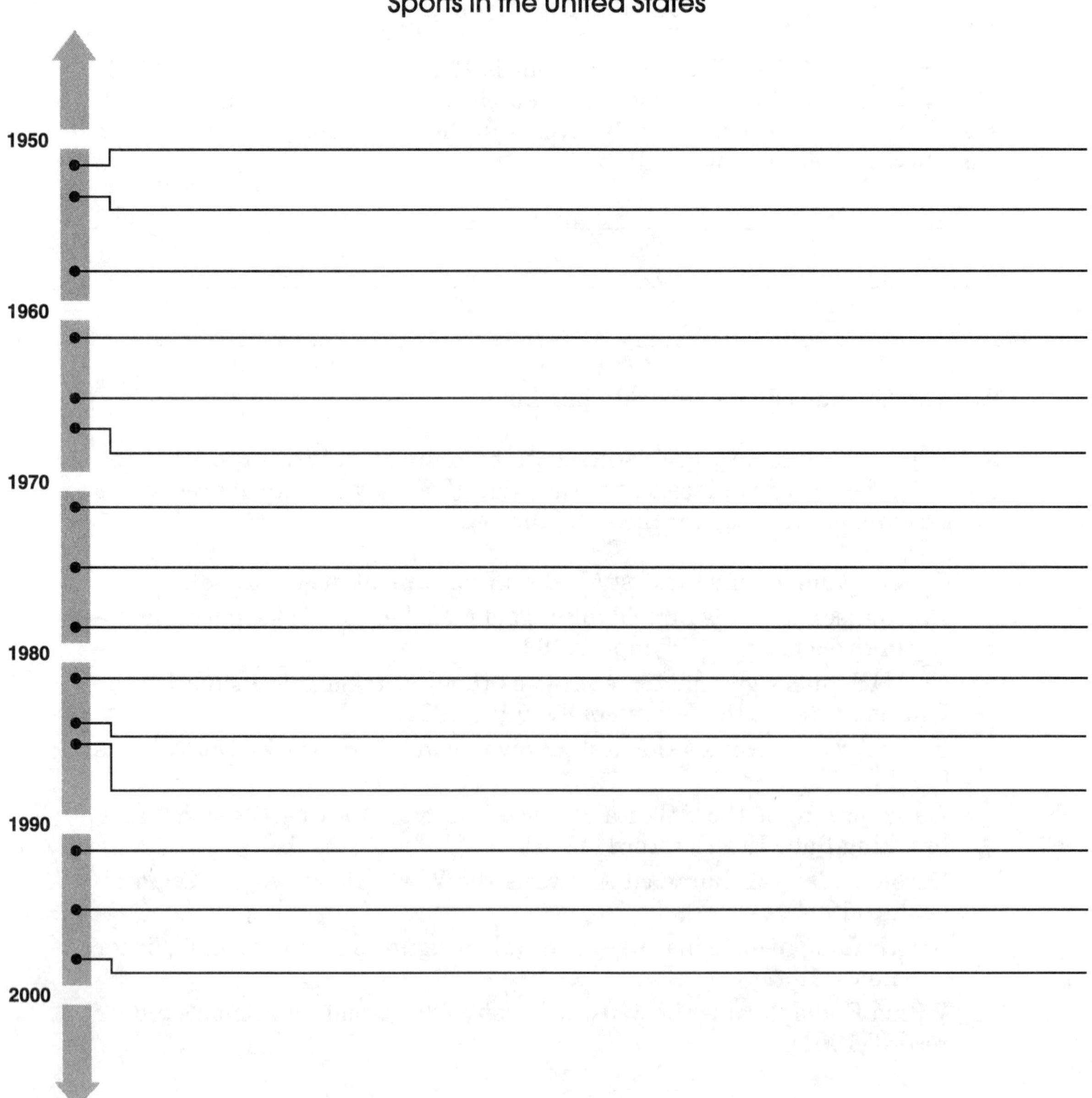

E-2. Write the letter of the correct choice on the line next to the number of each question.

_____ 1. The time line shows sports in the United States

(a) in the second half of the 19th century.
(b) in the first half of the 20th century.
(c) in the second half of the 20th century.
(d) in the first half of the 21st century.

_____ 2. The women's world indoor 220-yard dash record, with a time of 25 seconds, was run in 1961 by

(a) Maureen Connolly.
(b) Kristi Yamaguchi.
(c) Nancy Lopez.
(d) Wilma Rudolph.

_____ 3. How many years passed between Arnold Palmer's first Masters Tournament win and Nancy Lopez's first year as a professional golfer?

(a) 20 years *(c)* 35 years
(b) 25 years *(d)* 40 years

_____ 4. Which two events happened in the same decade?

(a) Cassius Clay won the World Heavyweight Championship in boxing, and Michael Jordan won his sixth NBA championship.
(b) Figure skater Kristi Yamaguchi and speed skater Dan Jansen each won an Olympic gold medal.
(c) Hank Aaron broke Babe Ruth's career home-run record, and Pete Rose broke Ty Cobb's career hit record.
(d) Mark Spitz won seven Olympic gold medals for swimming, and the United States won its first team Olympic gold medal in gymnastics.

_____ 5. Which sporting event was begun most recently?

(a) football Superbowl
(b) Kentucky Derby
(c) boxing Heavyweight Championship
(d) Masters Tournament in golf

CHAPTER 9
Taking a Test

Sometimes, you will be asked to show what you have learned in your U.S. history class. The most common way is by giving you a test. Test taking is a skill as important as any that you will learn in this book. In this chapter, you will learn how to study for a test, take it, and do well on it.

Studying for a Test

How much you need to study for a test depends on how well you have understood the work in class. The best and easiest way to study is to listen and take an active part in class each day and do your homework assignments. If you do not understand the work, ask the teacher for further explanations. If you do not pay attention in class, you will have to study more outside the class.

At home, start studying several days before a test, not just the night before. It is a good idea to read the material you are to be tested on a few times each day. By rereading and reviewing something, you have a better chance of remembering it.

You will study better without a television or radio on. Try to study alone in a quiet place. You will probably find that you study better sitting in a chair. A bed or sofa may be more comfortable, but how much studying can you do if you fall asleep?

The most important material to study is your class notes. You also need to read over parts of your textbook.

If your teacher gives a review lesson before a test, pay close attention to what is said because that information will help you remember what you learned in class. Be sure to take notes during this review lesson. After all, your teacher will probably go over topics that will be on the test.

The last, and best, thing to do the night before a test is to get a good night's sleep. A rested mind thinks much better than a tired one.

Taking a Test

On the day of a test, arrive on time and bring a pencil and a pen. Any delay in starting a test will harm your chance of success.

Here is a list of things to keep in mind when taking a test:

1. Read the directions and the questions carefully. Many students rush to answer test questions without first reading the directions and each of the questions carefully. If you do not read the directions, you may answer more questions than you have to or leave out important parts you are required to complete. Before answering any question, you should know exactly what that question is asking.
2. Plan your time so that you will be able to complete all of the questions you are required to answer.
3. Be sure to write your answers in the proper spaces.
4. Answer the easy questions before tackling the difficult ones.

5. Do not leave any question unanswered. An answer left blank is always wrong, but a good guess may be correct.

Types of Test Questions

Several kinds of questions usually appear on tests. Some questions ask you to use one or two words to complete the answers. Other questions ask you to match a word with a *definition* or a person with a description. But the most common kinds of questions are multiple choice, true or false, and essay.

Multiple Choice Questions

As shown in the following sample, a multiple choice question consists of two basic parts: the stem and the choices.

Stem { 1. The governor of New York responsible for the Erie Canal construction project was

Choices {
(*a*) DeWitt Clinton.
(*b*) Andrew Jackson.
(*c*) Robert Fulton.
(*d*) Elias Howe.

The first rule in answering a multiple choice question is to understand the stem. Try to figure out what the stem is asking before you read the choices. The stem in question 1 is simple. You have to identify the governor of New York who was responsible for building the Erie Canal. (The answer is DeWitt Clinton.) But sometimes stems require a great deal of thought before you can understand what is being asked. Would you know, for example, what the following stem is asking?

2. All of the following machines were invented in the early 1800s *except*

What do you think? All the choices are machines. You have to pick the machine that was *not* invented in the early 1800s.

Let us look at another stem.

3. A major economic difference between the North and the South in the early 1800s was

Do you know what this question is asking before you read the choices? *Major* means important. *Economic* means having to do with money or business. You need to look for an important difference between the North and the South that involves money or business.

Here is another stem. On the lines following it, explain what you think the stem is asking.

4. Which one of the following statements about tariffs would most likely have been made by a textile factory owner in New England in the 1830s?

____

____

____

____

What did you write? You should first try to understand all the key words in the stem. The key words are *tariffs* (taxes on imported goods), *most likely,* and *textile factory owner in New England in the 1830s.* In studying about the Industrial Revolution, you would have learned that factory owners in New England in the 1830s supported tariffs. Therefore, you should be looking for a statement that shows support for tariffs. The question says *most likely* because you do not know whether any factory owner made such a statement. You think that such a statement is probable, based on what you have studied about textile factories and tariffs.

Of course, stems can be written in many other ways. No matter how the stem is written, the important thing is to understand what it is asking before you read the choices. Once you understand the stem, you are ready to read the choices.

Multiple choice questions give two or more possible answers. You have to choose the best answer. In most multiple choice questions, you can easily eliminate (get rid of) one or more choices that do not fit at all. If two of the choices seem correct, you must pick the better choice. It is important to read all the choices. Choice *(a)* may seem correct, but by reading all the choices, you may find that choice *(b)*, *(c)*, or *(d)* is the *best* answer.

Study the following question to see how certain choices can be eliminated.

____ 5. The 19th-century American inventor Robert Fulton is associated with
(a) the cotton gin.
(b) television.
(c) the steamboat.
(d) the airplane.

You can start by eliminating choices *(b)* and *(d)*. Since television and the airplane were both invented in the 20th century, a 19th-century inventor could not be associated with them. This leaves choices *(a)* and *(c)*. If you remember that Eli Whitney invented the cotton gin, you can also eliminate choice *(a)*. This leaves choice *(c)* as the answer to question 5.

Study the following question to see why you should read all the choices before selecting an answer.

____ 6. Which invention had the greatest influence on the growth of business in the United States in the 1800s?
(a) telegraph
(b) reaper
(c) sewing machine
(d) railroad

Which answer did you choose? The telegraph certainly had an influence on the growth of business. So is choice *(a)* the answer? No! The question asked for the invention that had the *greatest* influence. The telegraph, the reaper, and the sewing machine all had an influence on the growth of business, but the railroad had the greatest influence. You can see by this example that you must read all four choices before you choose the *best* answer.

Here is another example to show you why you should read all the choices.

____ 7. The increase in population of many cities in the 1800s is best explained by
(a) the arrival of new immigrants.
(b) the opening of new factories in cities.
(c) the development of cities as centers of trade.
(d) all of the above.

Which choice did you pick? Choice *(a)* is one explanation for the population growth of cities. But is it the only one or the best one? Choices *(b)* and *(c)* are also explanations for the population growth. Each of these three choices gives part of the explanation. Only choice *(d)* puts all the parts together. Choice *(d)* is the *best* explanation. You had to read all the choices to see that the best answer to question 7 is *(d)*.

There are many kinds of multiple choice questions. You will have little problem answering them if you read the stems and all of the choices carefully. Remember always to choose the *best* answer.

True or False Questions

Another common kind of question is the true or false question. There is a very simple rule for answering such questions. A statement must be *completely* true to be true. If any part of the statement is false, the whole statement is false.

Read the following true or false question.

____________ Davy Crockett was killed at the Battle of the Alamo in Oklahoma in 1836.

It is true that Davy Crockett was killed at the Battle of the Alamo in 1836. It is *not* true that the battle took place in Oklahoma. It took place in Texas. Since one part of the statement is false, the whole statement should be marked false.

Sometimes you will be asked to correct the false part of a true or false statement. In the previous example, the word "Oklahoma" would be underlined and you would write the correct location of the battle (Texas) on the line to the left of the statement.

In a true or false question, you have to watch out for tricky or misleading words. Such words include "some," "many," "everyone," "no one," "never," "always." What is true of something may not be true of everything. Here is an example:

____________ All slaves, hoping to gain their freedom, welcomed the start of the Civil War.

For this statement to be true, every slave had to welcome the start of the Civil War. If one slave did not, the statement is false. Surely, at least one slave did not welcome the start of the war, for whatever reason. Therefore, the statement is false. In this example, the significant word is underlined. What other word or words could replace All to make the statement true? "Some" probably expresses too small a number of slaves. Better choices would be "Most" or "Nearly all."

Essay Questions

The third most common kind of test question is the essay question. An essay answer is written in complete sentences arranged into paragraphs. It should contain ideas and facts as well as your thoughts and opinions. You will learn how to write essays in Chapter 12. Let us now think about how to follow the directions for answering essay questions. Many students rush to answer such questions without first understanding what is wanted.

Read the following essay part of a test.

Directions: Answer two of the following questions.

1. *(a)* Give and explain three reasons why immigrants came to the United States in the early 1800s.

   (b) Are the reasons given in *(a)* different from the reasons why immigrants come to the United States today? Explain.

2. *(a)* Give and explain three ways in which Americans who lived in the early 1800s benefited from the Industrial Revolution.

   (b) Give and explain three problems caused by the Industrial Revolution in the United States in the early 1800s.

3. *(a)* How did each of the following contribute to the growth of factories in the United States in the early 1800s?
   1. the use of interchangeable parts in making goods
   2. the availability of workers in Northern cities
   3. the availability of water power in Northern states

   (b) How did each of the following affect the way businesses produced and marketed their goods in the early 1800s?
   1. steamboats
   2. railroads
   3. clipper ships

How many questions should you answer in this essay part of the test? Some students might answer all the questions just because they are on the page. But the directions clearly tell you to answer *two* questions. Some students might answer 1.*(a)* and 1.*(b)* and think they had answered two questions. In fact, they would have answered only two parts of the same question. They would still have to answer either 2.*(a)* and 2.*(b)* *or* 3.*(a)* and 3.*(b)*.

If you chose to answer 3.*(a)* and 3.*(b)*, you would have to answer all three parts of *(a)* and all three parts of *(b)*. In each essay question, answer all parts unless the directions tell you differently.

Questions 1.*(a)* and 1.*(b)* and 2.*(a)* and 2.*(b)* contain the word "explain." Some essay questions use words such as "explain," "discuss," or "describe." This means that you have to give full, complete answers including both ideas and facts as well as your own thoughts and opinions.

You have seen in this chapter that learning how to take a test is a useful skill.

Think of all the times in your life when you will be required to take a test. The following exercises will give you more practiced in test-taking skills.

USING YOUR SKILLS

A. Write the letter of the correct choice on the line next to the number of each question.

____ 1. Generally speaking, the more you listen and actively participate in your lessons each day, the
(a) more you will have to study for the test on those lessons.
(b) less you will have to study for the test on those lessons.
(c) more you will become confused about your lessons.
(d) less you will be interested in your lessons.

____ 2. A review lesson is useful because it
(a) teaches new material.
(b) takes the place of doing any studying.
(c) points out important things you should have learned in other lessons.
(d) allows you to be absent from other lessons.

____ 3. All of the following are good study habits *except*
(a) sitting in a comfortable chair rather than on a sofa or bed.
(b) studying without a television or radio on.
(c) finding a quiet place where you can be alone.
(d) leaving your studying until the last minute.

____ 4. The most important rule in taking a test is to
(a) read the directions and the questions carefully.
(b) work as fast as you can.
(c) answer all questions.
(d) spend more time on the difficult questions.

____ 5. When two choices in a multiple choice question seem to be correct, you
(a) can pick either choice.
(b) must look for another choice.
(c) must pick the choice that is *better.*
(d) should give two choices for your answer.

B. List five things you should keep in mind when you are taking a test.

____

____

____

____

____

C. Looking for the Tricky Words in True or False Questions.

All of the following statements are FALSE. Underline the tricky word or words in each statement that make it FALSE. On the lines provided, explain why you underlined the word or words.

1. No one in England believed that the 13 colonies would gain their independence.

 ____

 ____

2. President Abraham Lincoln never doubted that the Union would win the Civil War.

 ____

 ____

3. All cowboys know how to use a lasso.

 ____

 ____

4. Periods of economic slowdown always bring calls for war.

 ____

 ____

5. Today, computers are used to run every business in the United States.

 ____

 ____

D. You have learned that it is important to understand the stem of a multiple choice question before you read the choices. The following are five stems belonging to multiple choice questions. Beneath each stem, write in your own words what you think the stem is asking.

1. One source of energy used to fuel homes today is

 ____

 ____

2. All of the following contributed to the Allied victory in World War II *except*

 ____

 ____

3. A major difference between television 25 years ago and today is

____

____

4. Which statement about factories most likely would be made by a person who opposes the pollution caused by factories?

____

____

5. The improvement in medical technology today is best explained by

____

____

E. Read carefully the following essay part of a test. Then answer the questions based on the essay part.

Directions: Answer two of the following questions.

1. *(a)* Give and explain three reasons why the North believed that it would win the Civil War.
   (b) Give and explain three reasons why the South believed that it would win the Civil War.
2. *(a)* Give and explain three reasons why the United States sought to build an empire in the late 1800s.
   (b) How did the United States acquire each of the following possessions?
   1. Alaska
   2. Hawaii
   3. Puerto Rico
3. *(a)* How did each of the following contribute to the Great Economic Depression of the 1930s?
   1. overproduction of goods
   2. weather conditions
   3. personal debts

   (b) Give the purpose of each of the following New Deal programs and tell how successful it was.
   1. Federal Deposit Insurance Corporation
   2. Social Security
   3. Civilian Conservation Corps

For questions 1, 2, and 3, write the letter of the correct choice on the line next to the number of each question.

____ 1. How many questions do you have to answer in this essay part of a test?

(a) one *(b)* two *(c)* three *(d)* four

____ 2. How many questions are given in the essay part of this test?

(a) three questions, each with two parts
(b) four separate questions
(c) five questions, each with two parts
(d) six separate questions

____ 3. In answering question 2.*(b)* you

(a) may write about any one of the possessions listed.
(b) may write about any two of the possessions listed.
(c) must write about all three of the possessions listed.
(d) must write about a possession not listed.

4. In a number of questions, the word "explain" appears. What does this mean?

____

____

____

____

5. Is the following statement true or false? Explain your answer. "If I answer only 2.*(a)* and 2.*(b),* I have followed the directions correctly."

____

____

____

____

____

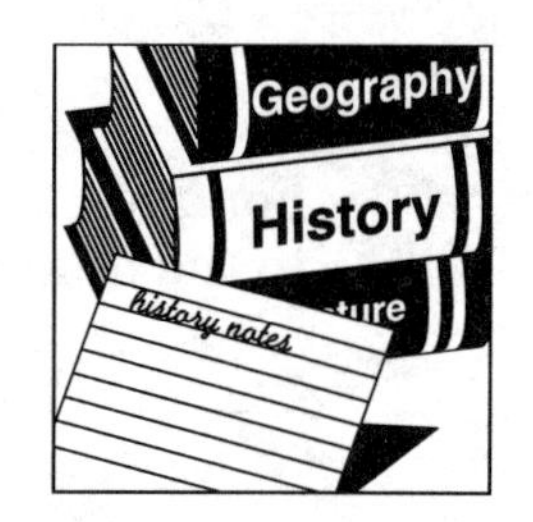

CHAPTER 10
Writing a Summary

Have you ever read something in a history textbook and a short time later forgotten what it was all about? It is not possible to remember everything you read, especially when the selection is long. Look at the selection on page 99 about the Progressive Movement at the beginning of the 20th century.

Could you read this selection and remember what it was about tomorrow or next week? Most students would find it difficult to remember all the important details. But what if you took notes while you were reading? If you wrote down the highlights—the important details—you could remember what you had read by going over your notes.

Writing a Summary

By taking notes on what you read, you can reduce many sentences to a few sentences and phrases. This skill is called *summarizing.* When a selection is long, such as the one on page 99, you should write a summary for each paragraph. Begin by stating the main idea of the paragraph—what the paragraph is all about. The main idea is often found in the first sentence, but any sentence in the paragraph may contain it. Sometimes the main idea is not found in any one sentence. When this is the case, you have to think about the meaning of all the sentences in the paragraph in order to find the main idea.

Now read Paragraph 1 of the selection on the Progressive Movement. Then see how the main idea of the paragraph has been summarized in the following sentence.

Summary of Paragraph 1

Progressives who fought for reforms only did what Americans have always done, fight for reforms.

The main idea of Paragraph 1 comes from combining the third and fourth sentences: "But I am proud to be a Progressive and proud to be fighting for the political, economic, and social reforms that this country needs. Reforms have always been a part of America's history." Instead of a paragraph of seven sentences, you now have a one-sentence summary stating the main idea. But the original paragraph contains details that would help you understand the main idea of the paragraph. To include these details in your summary, you need another sentence or a few supporting phrases. A more complete summary would look like this:

Summary of Paragraph 1

Progressives who fought for reforms only did what Americans have always done, fight for reforms.

- Jacksonian Democrats urged educational reforms, opportunities for women
- 1840s–1850s, reformers urged an end to slavery
- Progressives wanted to help farmers, city dwellers, factory and mine workers

A Progressive Plans to Fight for Reforms

Paragraph 1

Some people are filled with horror when they hear the word "progressive." They think we only know how to complain about America. But I am proud to be a Progressive and proud to be fighting for the political, economic, and social reforms that this country needs. Reforms have always been a part of America's history. In the 1830s and 1840s, Jacksonian Democrats worked to improve schools and mental institutions and to provide women with greater educational opportunities. In the 1840s and 1850s, reformers called for an end to slavery. Today, we call for reforms that will help farmers, city dwellers, factory workers and mine workers.

Paragraph 2

What reforms do we want? We want to end corruption in government by taking government away from the greedy and giving it back to the people. We want our United States senators elected directly by the people, not by state legislatures. We want women to have the right to vote. We want the giant trusts that control an entire industry broken up. We want improved working conditions in factories, mines, and shops. Child labor must end, and the government should recognize the right of workers to join unions.

Paragraph 3

How do we plan to bring about these reforms? We will shout from the rooftops. We will march, demonstrate, write books and newspaper articles, and give speeches. We will bring our cause before the American people. We will elect only Progressives to office, and we will force the government to bring about needed reforms. I have no doubt that our cause is just and that in the end we will win. Let everyone know that the word "progressive" stands for people who care about America.

You now have a better idea of what Paragraph 1 is all about. A few supporting phrases added to the summary sentence make it easier to remember more of the information.

Note that this summary was not copied word for word from Paragraph 1. Write a summary in your own words. By doing so, you will prove that you understand what you read.

Now read Paragraph 2 of the reading selection. A one-sentence summary of Paragraph 2 follows. This time, add to the summary a few supporting phrases that will help you remember the important details in the paragraph.

Summary of Paragraph 2

Progressives wanted the following reforms:

____

____

____

____

____

____

____

If the supporting phrases you wrote help you remember more details from Paragraph 2, you have written a good summary. Here is an example of what you might have written.

Summary of Paragraph 2

Progressives wanted the following reforms:

- end corruption in government
- elect senators by direct vote
- give women the right to vote
- break up giant trusts
- improve working conditions
- end child labor
- make government recognize unions

Now let us see if you can write a complete summary for Paragraph 3. Read Paragraph 3 and then write a summary that includes one sentence stating the main idea and a few phrases giving some supporting details.

Summary of Paragraph 3

____

____

____

____

____

____

____

What did you write in your summary? The main idea was contained in the first sentence of the paragraph: "How do we plan to bring about these reforms?" Most of the remaining sentences in the paragraph give examples of how Progressives planned to bring about their reforms. Here is one possible summary with details following the main idea.

Summary of Paragraph 3

The Progressives had plans for bringing about their reform.

- by marching demonstrating, writing, giving speeches, electing Progressives to office, forcing the government to act

After writing a summary for each paragraph of a long reading selection, ask yourself if there is one idea contained in all the paragraphs in the selection? In other words, what is the main idea of the entire reading selection? You should write that main idea at the end of the summary.

Write on the following lines a summary sentence that states what the entire reading selection on page 99 is about.

____

____

____

____

____

What did you write? Sometimes the title of a reading selection can help you find the main idea. Sometimes the first or last sentence in the selection may help you. At other times, you may have to think about what meaning all the sentences make together in order to find the main idea. In this reading selection, the main idea of the entire selection is stated in the second sentence of Paragraph 1: "But I am proud to be a Progressive and proud to be fighting for the political, economic, and social reforms that this country needs." The wording of your summary sentence is up to you. All that matters is that it tells you the main idea of the entire selection.

The next time you are reading something for school, write a summary of it. When you read the summary at a later time, you should be able to recall more easily the important ideas and facts contained in the reading. This skill will help you remember more of what you read.

Taking Good Classroom Notes

Taking good notes means more than writing a summary of what you have *read.* Taking good notes also means writing a summary of what you have *heard.* In your U.S. history class, your teacher may write notes on the board for you to copy, but copying notes is not the only thing you should do in class. Listening to what the teacher and other students say during a lesson may be just as important as copying from the board. You will probably be tested on what is said in your classroom as well as on notes written on the board. As you listen to everything said in your classroom, write down the important ideas and facts in your notebook. You will save some time if you use abbreviations. At the end of each lesson, ask yourself two questions: (1) What was the main idea of this lesson? (2) What important facts support that idea? Write the answers to these two questions in your notebook directly after the class notes for that day's lesson.

Taking good notes is an important skill. The following exercises will give you more practice in writing good summaries and in taking good notes.

USING YOUR SKILLS

A. Write the letter of the correct choice on the line next to the number of each question.

____ 1. The main idea of a reading selection
- *(a)* is the most important fact in the selection.
- *(b)* should contain every fact in the selection.
- *(c)* is what the selection is all about.
- *(d)* should not contain any facts.

____ 2. The main idea of a reading selection
- *(a)* is always stated in the first sentence.
- *(b)* may be stated anywhere in the selection or not at all.
- *(c)* is always stated in the last sentence.
- *(d)* is never stated in the selection.

____ 3. A good summary
- *(a)* should include the main idea and supporting facts.
- *(b)* should be as long as the original reading selection.
- *(c)* must use the exact words contained in the original reading selection.
- *(d)* must be written in one sentence.

_____ 4. It is important to take good notes in class because
(*a*) it pleases the teacher.
(*b*) you can show them to someone at home.
(*c*) notes will help you remember what you learned in class.
(*d*) you can give your notes to friends to read.

_____ 5. Which statement is TRUE?
(*a*) Teachers always write the important points of a lesson on the board.
(*b*) Taking notes of what a teacher says in class is a waste of time.
(*c*) Good students do not have to listen to what a teacher is saying.
(*d*) Listening to what a teacher says is just as important as copying notes from the board.

B. Writing a Summary. Read the following selection.

Women in Colonial America

Paragraph 1

Many of the early American colonies were first settled by men. Only after a colony was successfully established did the men allow women to come. Women were needed as workers, wives, and mothers who would help populate the colony. Often, women were brought as *indentured servants.* That is, their passage to America was paid, and, in exchange, they agreed to work on a man's farm or in his business for a certain number of years. Some women married immediately upon arriving in a colony. Their new husbands paid for their release from indentured servitude.

Paragraph 2

European women found that America was as much a man's world as Europe. They could not own property or vote. Their husbands had a legal right to any money they earned. Colonial women had few rights but many responsibilities. They had to take care of the house and help on the farm or in business. They had to raise the children and be their teachers. A few women in colonial America achieved important positions on their own, but most led lives serving and obeying their husbands.

B-1. Answer the following questions based on the reading selection. Write the letter of the correct choice on the line next to the number of each question.

____ 1. The main idea of Paragraph 1 is:
  (a) Men and women came in the first ships to America.
  (b) Some women married immediately upon arriving in a colony.
  (c) Most women were brought to colonial America as indentured servants.
  (d) Women were needed in the colonies as workers, wives, and mothers.

____ 2. Which fact supports the main idea of Paragraph 1?
  (a) Women could not own property.
  (b) Many of the early American colonies were first settled by men.
  (c) Women were often brought to colonial America as indentured servants.
  (d) Women had to educate their own children.

____ 3. The main idea of Paragraph 2 is:
  (a) Colonial women had few rights but many responsibilities.
  (b) Colonial women had no legal rights to money they earned.
  (c) Colonial women often worked as indentured servants.
  (d) Some colonial women achieved important positions on their own.

____ 4. Which fact supports the main idea of Paragraph 2?
  (a) Colonial women were expected to raise their children but not teach them.
  (b) Women were needed in the colonies as wives and workers.
  (c) Colonial women had to help on the farm but could not own property.
  (d) Men brought women to the colonies once the colonies were established.

____ 5. Which sentence states the main idea of the entire reading selection (paragraphs 1 and 2 together)?
  (a) Only after a colony was established did the men let women in.
  (b) Women were needed as workers, wives, and mothers who would help populate the colony, but they were given few legal rights.
  (c) Often women were brought as indentured servants.
  (d) Women could not own property or vote, and their husbands had a legal right to any money they earned.

B-2. Write your own summary of the reading selection. For each paragraph, write a summary that states the main idea and some supporting facts. Then write a summary sentence that gives the main idea of the entire selection. (Use the answers to questions 1 to 5 in B-1 to help you write the summary.)

Summary of Paragraph 1

____

____

____

____

____

____

____

Summary of Paragraph 2

____

____

____

____

____

____

____

Summary Sentence of the Reading Selection

____

____

____

____

C. Read the following selection. Then write your own summary.

Why Colonial America Turned to Slavery

Large numbers of laborers were required to turn the great open lands in colonial America into productive farms. Forests had to be cleared. Crops had to be planted, cared for, and harvested. There was always a lack of laborers to do the work. At first, wealthy owners of *plantations* (large farms) tried to hire Native Americans as laborers. But there were not enough Native Americans to do all the work. And many of them fled west because they did not like their working conditions. Farmers then tried to use indentured servants. Although most indentured servants were white, some were black. The first black indentured servants arrived in Jamestown, Virginia, in 1619. Like the whites, they were freed after a certain period of servitude.

When the farmers were unable to meet their labor needs with Native Americans and indentured servants, they turned to black slavery. There seemed to be an endless number of black people in

Africa who could be captured and taken to the colonies by force. Black Africans could supply all the labor needed. In the 1660s, colonial laws were passed that made all newly imported black servants into slaves for life. The slaves had no rights and were regarded as property. Their owners could even separate husbands from wives, or children from parents. To justify slavery, some colonists claimed that black Africans were inferior. They also claimed that whites had a right and a duty to capture and civilize blacks. To "civilize" them meant to teach blacks European ways and religions.

By the end of the 1600s, slaves lived in every English colony. Large numbers of slaves were brought into the Middle and Southern colonies to work on farms and plantations. The rocky soil and smaller farms of New England limited the need for slaves there. Some New Englanders, however, profited from the slave trade. They used their ships to carry slaves from Africa to the West Indies and the Southern colonies.

By the time the slave trade was outlawed in 1808, at least 350,000 Africans had been brought to the United States to live and die as slaves. It was not until 1865, after the Union victory in the Civil War, that slavery ended in the United States.

Summary

____

____

____

____

____

____

____

____

____

____

____

____

____

____

D. Read the following selection. Then write your own summary.

Muckrakers Move a Nation to Act

As America entered the 20th century, calls for political, economic, and social reforms grew loud. In large part, these calls came from journalists and novelists known as *muckrakers.* In their writings, the muckrakers exposed corruption in government, unfair business practices, and poor working conditions in mines and factories. Some people felt that the muckrakers could write only about what was wrong in America. President Theodore Roosevelt, at first, had no use for them. He was the first to call them muckrakers, after a character in John Bunyan's story *Pilgrim's Progress.* This character saw only filth on the ground and never bothered to look up to the clear sky.

One of the first muckrakers was Lincoln Steffens. In 1902, he wrote a magazine article describing government corruption in St. Louis, Missouri. This was only the first of many of his articles about corruption in city government. In 1904, he collected all the articles into one book, *The Shame of the Cities.*

Ida Tarbell investigated large corporations. In her *The History of the Standard Oil Company,* she attacked John D. Rockefeller and the way he ran the Standard Oil Company. She charged that Rockefeller used ruthless business practices to destroy any competition.

In 1906, Upton Sinclair wrote his novel *The Jungle* to expose the horrible working conditions in meatpacking plants. Although the characters were fictitious (made up), the story was based on fact, and the public knew it. Scenes of workers laboring in filthy plants shocked readers. So did descriptions of rats mixed in with the meat and diseased animals sold for food. If Sinclair's charges were true, people said, then something had to be done. As a result, Congress was forced to pass the Meat Inspection Act and the Pure Food and Drug Act of 1906.

The writings of the muckrakers brought the need for reform to the attention of the American people. Most Americans responded with a willingness to look at the ground below as well as the sky above.

Summary

E. Read the following selection. Then write your own summary.

The United States as Leader of the Free World

World War II proved to the United States that it could not isolate itself from the rest of the world. Before the war, many Americans had believed that the Atlantic and Pacific oceans were large enough to keep the world's problems at a safe distance. But four years of fighting Nazi Germany and Imperial Japan ended such isolationist dreams. If the United States wanted peace, it would have to take an active role in world affairs. For this reason, it helped to create the United Nations (UN) in 1945. With the Soviet Union, Great Britain, France, China, and 46 other countries, the United States worked to maintain world peace.

But from the beginning of the UN, the United States was at odds with the Soviet Union. The Soviet leaders sought to spread communism throughout the world. They made the Eastern European countries that they had occupied during World War II into Communist satellites. With Soviet support, North Korea and China became Communist states in the late 1940s.

The United States responded with a policy called *containment.* According to this policy, everything necessary would be done to prevent the further spread of communism. One course of action was to give economic and military aid to countries threatened by a Communist takeover. A second course of action was to form defense treaties. The United States, for example, joined other countries of the "free world" to form the North Atlantic Treaty Organization (NATO). NATO's basic principle was that an attack on one member would be considered an attack on all members.

At times, the United States and other countries of the free world took military action against aggression. The most significant example was in 1950 when UN forces repelled a Communist invasion of South Korea.

Throughout the tense years after World War II, the United States and the Soviet Union never faced each other in battle. Thus, the period is called the *cold war.* The cold war ended in December 1991, with the collapse of the Soviet Union. What has not ended is the active role of the United States in world affairs.

Summary

____

____

____

____

____

____

____

____

____

____

____

____

____

____

CHAPTER 11
Writing an Outline

The study of U.S. history requires a great deal of reading. How will you remember what you read? You could write a summary, as you learned to do in the last chapter. But you could also write an *outline*. An outline is a general plan or sketch showing only the main ideas and facts in a reading selection. In this chapter, you will learn how to write an outline.

Like a summary, an outline reduces a reading selection to a few sentences or phrases. A summary presents its information in one or more paragraphs, while an outline sets off each bit of information separately, like a series of headlines. In this way, an outline gives you a quick overview of the main ideas and arranges them to show the importance of each one.

An outline is usually divided into *topics* and *subtopics*. A topic is one of the main subjects stated in the reading selection. A subtopic is one of the subjects that are part of a topic. For example, the topic might be American constitutions, with the subtopics Articles of Confederation and United States Constitution. The partially completed outline on page 111 shows how an outline can be divided into topics and subtopics.

When writing an outline, observe the following rules:

1. Place the title above the outline.
2. Use Roman numerals (I, II, III, IV, and so on) for the main topics.
3. Use letters and numbers for subtopics in the following sequence: capital letters [A, B], arabic numbers [1, 2], lowercase letters [a, b], arabic numbers in parentheses [(1), (2)], lowercase letters in parentheses [(a), (b)].
4. Indent the first set of subtopics farther into the page than the topic. Indent each new set of subtopics farther into the page than the previous set of subtopics. (Periods are placed after all numbers and letters except those in parentheses.)

I.
    A.
        1.
        2.
            a.
            b.
                (1)
                (2)
                    (a)
                    (b)
    B.

5. Line up vertically all topics and subtopics that have the same kinds of numbers or letters.

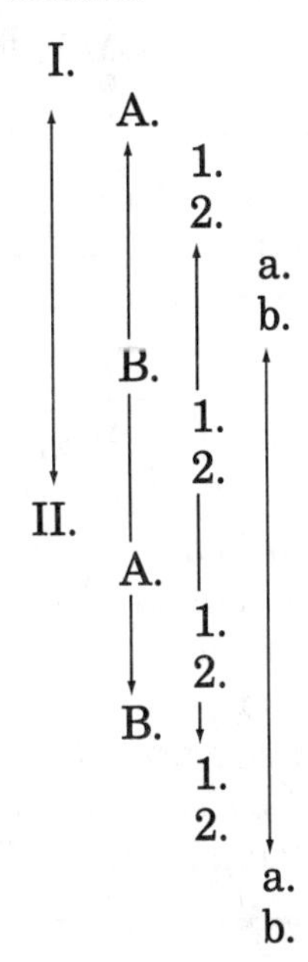

6. Use at least two subtopics for a topic or subtopic. Subtopics show how a topic or subtopic has been divided. You can never divide something into one part.

Correct: A.
    1.
    2.
B.
    1.
    2.

Wrong: A.
    1.
B.
    1.

7. Use the same kind of letter or number to show subtopics of equal importance.

Subtopics of equal importance → A. / B.

1. / 2. ← Subtopics of equal importance

8. Use a capital letter for the first word of each topic or subtopic.

Now read the following selection on the division of powers in the United States Constitution. You will then be asked to complete an outline based on the selection.

The United States Constitution: The Division of Powers

The U.S. Constitution divides power between the national (or federal) government and the state governments.

The powers given to the national government are called *delegated powers* or *enumerated powers* (so named because they are listed in the Constitution). They include the power to collect taxes, to borrow money, to regulate *commerce* (trade) with foreign nations and among states, and to coin money and punish counterfeiters, who make fake money. They also include the power to establish post offices, to punish piracies (robberies committed at sea), and to establish courts. In addition, the Constitution delegates to the national government the power to declare war and to raise and support an army and navy.

At times, the national government has tried to stretch its delegated powers by using *implied powers* found in the *elastic clause* of the Constitution. This clause states that the national government has the power "to make all laws which shall be necessary and proper for carrying into Execution the foregoing powers." ("Foregoing powers" refers to the delegated powers.) During George Washington's presidency, Congress used the clause to create the National Bank. In the 20th century, the national government has used it to regulate radio and television communications.

The state governments receive their power from the Tenth Amendment to the Constitution. That amendment states: "The powers not delegated to the United States by the Constitution, nor prohibited by it to the States, are reserved to the States respectively, or to the people." These powers are called *reserved powers* or *residual powers.* They have been used to make laws that give the states control of education, marriage and drivers' licenses, park and recreation facilities, traffic laws, and voting requirements.

Powers shared by the national government and the state governments are called *concurrent powers.* They include collecting taxes, borrowing money, building roads, maintaining courts, and operating prisons.

Complete the following outline based on the reading selection.

The United States Constitution:
The Division of Powers

I. Delegated Powers
  A. Definition: powers given to the national government that are specifically listed in the Constitution
  B. Examples:
    1. Collect taxes, borrow money, regulate commerce, coin money, punish counterfeiters
    2. Establish post offices, punish piracy, establish courts
    3. Declare war, raise and support an army and navy
II. Implied Powers
  A. Definition: power to make all laws that are necessary to carry out the delegated powers
  B. Examples:
    1. Create a national bank
    2. Regulate radio and television communications
III. Reserved Powers
  A. Definition:

____

____

____

____

  B. Examples:

____

____

____

____

IV. ______________________________

____

____

____

____

____

____

____

____

What did you write? If you followed the rules stated earlier in this chapter and the sample outline on page 109, you should have been able to complete an outline that looks like this:

III. Reserved Powers
  A. Definition: powers given to states that are neither delegated nor prohibited by the Constitution
  B. Examples: Control of
    1. Education
    2. Marriage and drivers' licenses
    3. Park and recreation facilities
    4. Traffic laws
    5. Voting requirements
IV. Concurrent Powers
  A. Definition: powers shared by the national and state governments
  B. Examples:
    1. Collect taxes
    2. Borrow money
    3. Build roads
    4. Maintain courts
    5. Operate prisons

Outlines can be much more complicated than the one given here. If you remember the rules for writing outlines, you should not have any problem.

When you have to remember a great deal of information in a reading selection, writing an outline will help you recall the information. Instead of rereading the selection, you can study the outline. Later in this book, you will see how an outline will help you write a research paper.

The following exercises will give you more practice in writing an outline.

USING YOUR SKILLS

A. Read the following selection. Then complete the outline based on the selection.

Powers Denied to the Federal and State Governments

The writers of the U.S. Constitution were just as concerned with denying power as with giving it.

Article I, Section 9, of the Constitution prevents the federal government from taking certain actions: collecting a tax on *exports* (goods sent out of the country), collecting a direct tax not based on population, passing a law favoring one state, spending money in ways not allowed by law, granting titles of nobility, and limiting certain *civil liberties* (rights). The first ten *amendments* (additions) to the Constitution, called the Bill of Rights, also deny the federal government the right to interfere with certain civil liberties. In addition, Amendments 15, 19, 24, and 26 prevent the federal government from interfering with voting rights.

Article I, Section 10, of the Constitution prevents states from taking certain actions: entering into a treaty, coining money, passing laws limiting various civil liberties, ignoring contracts, and granting titles of nobility. Without the approval of Congress, no state may collect a *duty* (tax) on imports or exports, keep troops, enter into an agreement with another state or foreign power, or engage in war. Certain amendments to the Constitution are as binding on states as they are on the federal government. Amendments 14, 15, 19, 24, and 26 prevent states from interfering with certain rights of the people.

OUTLINE

Powers Denied to the Federal and State Governments

I. Powers denied to the federal government
  A. Article I, Section 9, prohibitions:
    1. Collecting a tax on exports
    2. ______________________________
    3. ______________________________
    4. Spending money in ways not provided by law
    5. ______________________________
    6. ______________________________
  B. Amendments
    1. First ten amendments (the Bill of Rights) deny the federal government the right to interfere with certain civil liberties.

2. ______________________________

____

II. Powers denied to state governments

A. ______________________________
1. Entering into a treaty

2. ______________________________

3. ______________________________
4. Ignoring contracts

5. ______________________________

6. ______________________________

7. ______________________________

8. ______________________________
9. Engaging in war

B. ______________________________

____

B. Read the following selection. Then, on the lines provided, write an outline based on the selection.

France and Britain in North America

By the 18th century, France and Great Britain had become the two greatest powers in eastern North America. The British had established 13 colonies along the east coast of what is today the United States. The colonies were contained between the Appalachian Mountains and the Atlantic Ocean. French influence extended over a large expanse that included most of eastern Canada and land on both sides of the Mississippi River.

The British who settled in the American colonies in the 1600s and 1700s had come to stay. They brought their families or began new ones. They developed businesses and farms and thought of the colonies as their new home. Most of the French, on the other hand, came to make quick riches, usually by fur trapping. They then hoped to return to a life of ease in France. The British colonies had a much larger population than the French settlements. In 1750, the British population in America was nearly 1.5 million. The French numbered only about 70,000.

As the British population grew, more and more land was needed for farming. The British often fought Native Americans for control of the land. The French and the Native Americans were more interested in forests than in farmland. The French wanted the forest for fur trapping, and the Native Americans wanted it for hunting.

In 1754, the French and British went to war against each other. The war was called the French and Indian War by the British because many of the Indian, or Native American, tribes fought on the French side. The war ended in a British victory. By the time a peace treaty was signed in 1763, French power in North America had almost completely disappeared.

OUTLINE

____

____

____

____

____

C. Read the following selection. Then, on the lines provided, write an outline based on the selection.

The Roaring Twenties

The decade of the 1920s was a time of swift change, fast living, and a booming economy. It thus came to be called the "Roaring Twenties."

In 1920, *ratification* (approval) of the Nineteenth Amendment gained women the right to vote. They were eager to take part in society as full citizens. But for many women, full citizenship meant more than being able to vote. It also meant being able to compete with men for jobs. Many women wanted to escape the role of housewife. They looked forward to entering the world of work. Some even hoped for careers in medicine, law, banking, and big business.

Women became more independent. They changed how they dressed and conducted themselves. Traditional floor-length dresses gave way to skirts that stopped at the knees. Many women began to smoke and drink in public and go to nightclubs.

The 1920s also saw great changes in business. It was an age of machines and gadgets. Business produced the latest appliances, and department stores sold them. It was the American dream to own an electric toaster, an iron, a refrigerator, and, of course, a radio. But no machine had a greater effect on life in the 1920s than the automobile. Henry Ford's Model T turned America into a society on wheels. What better way could people forget their problems than by taking a drive in the country in their own automobile!

As working conditions gradually improved, Americans had more time off. Increasingly, they turned to sports to fill their leisure hours. Boxers such as Jack Dempsey and Gene Tunney became as famous as government leaders. Babe Ruth and Ty Cobb broke one baseball record after another. Their accomplishments helped to make baseball the "great American pastime." The sports craze spread to college campuses, where football became enormously popular.

The arrival of regular radio broadcasts in the 1920s helped build a wider audience for sporting events. In addition, American families gathered around the radio to listen to concerts, comedy shows, and late-breaking news stories.

In the 1920s, Americans wanted to be entertained—in nightclubs, at music shows, or in movie theaters. Stars such as Charlie Chaplin and Mary Pickford made movies the most popular entertainment form of the day. There were more than 20,000 movie houses in the country. In 1927, *The Jazz Singer,* starring Al Jolson, became the first major film to be made with sound.

It is no wonder that the 1920s were called the "Roaring Twenties." But beyond the roar, the new lifestyles, and the popular inventions lay some serious problems. The good times were not being shared by all Americans. And before the end of the decade, the United States would be plunged into a great economic *depression* (long period of economic hardship).

OUTLINE

D. Read the following selection. Then, on the lines provided, write an outline based on the selection.

The Black Renaissance

When most students of history hear the word "renaissance" (rebirth), they think of Italy and France, and artists such as Leonardo da Vinci and Michelangelo. But renaissance also describes certain periods in U.S. history. One such period was the Black Renaissance, a political, economic, and cultural movement among African Americans between 1910 and 1930.

During those years, more than 1.5 million African Americans migrated from the rural South to such northern cities as New York, Chicago, Detroit, and Philadelphia. For most African Americans, the South had been a world of poverty and racial *prejudice* (unreasonable dislike against a person, group, or race). In the North, there was also prejudice, but there was a better chance of employment, as well. Jobs were available in automobile plants, steel mills, and stockyards. At times, African Americans had to compete with white Americans for housing and jobs. This competition only increased the prejudice against African Americans.

In 1909, the National Association for the Advancement of Colored People (NAACP) was established to fight such prejudice. One of its founders was W. E. B. Du Bois. In an earlier generation, Booker T. Washington had advised African Americans to learn a trade or manual skill. Du Bois believed that African Americans should get a higher education and refuse to settle for status as second-class citizens. Through court cases, the NAACP attempted to bring full justice and equality to African Americans. At first, the organization had little success. But its existence showed that African Americans would not let their rights be denied.

In the mid-1920s, another major organization developed to promote African-American interests. Marcus Garvey, an immigrant from Jamaica, began the Universal Negro Improvement Association (UNIA). At its peak, this association boasted more than 500,000 members. Garvey preached that African Americans should not try to imitate whites but rather show pride in their own race, culture, and ancestry. One of his more ambitious plans was for African Americans to return to Africa. He even went so far as to set up a steamship company for that purpose. Garvey's plan came to an end in 1925 when he was sent to jail for mail fraud.

Nowhere did the cultural achievements of African Americans reach greater heights than in the Harlem section of New York City. The Harlem Renaissance grew out of the Black Renaissance. It gave birth to literature and music that enriched the lives not only of African Americans but of all Americans. In their poetry, Langston Hughes and Countee Cullen depicted the sorrowful conditions of African Americans and their hopes and dreams. Paul Robeson achieved international fame as a singer and actor. Other important entertainers and songwriters of this period included Louis Armstrong, Cabell ("Cab") Calloway, Ethel Waters, Eubie Blake, Thomas W. ("Fats") Waller, and Bessie Smith.

The Black Renaissance did not achieve full justice and equality for African Americans. They continued to experience poverty, prejudice, and discrimination. But the excitement of the Black Renaissance strengthened African-American consciousness.

OUTLINE

____

____

____

____

____

____

____

____

____

E. Read the following selection. Then, on the lines provided, write an outline based on the selection.

The United States Constitution: The Separation of Powers

According to the U.S. Constitution, the federal government is separated into *legislative, executive,* and *judicial branches.*

The legislative branch, which is called Congress, makes the laws. Congress is made up of two houses: the *House of Representatives* and the *Senate.* In order for a bill to become law, both houses have to vote for the bill.

Each of the 435 members of the House of Representatives represents more than 600,000 people in a district in the home state. Representatives are elected directly by the people, and their term of office is two years. The House of Representatives has the sole power to introduce money bills, *impeach* (charge with misconduct in office) federal officials, and elect a president when the *electoral college* has not been able to do so.

There are 100 senators, two from each state. Their term of office is six years. Originally, senators were elected by state *legislatures* (lawmaking bodies), but now they are elected directly by the people. The Senate has the sole power to *ratify* (approve) treaties, approve presidential appointments, try impeached federal officials, and elect a vice president when the electoral college has not been able to do so.

The executive branch of the government, headed by the president, carries out the laws. The president, who can be elected for only two four-year terms, is not chosen directly by the people. On election day, people vote for electors rather than for a particular candidate. The electors, who make up the electoral college, are pledged to particular candidates. They cast the official vote for a president. The number of electors in a state is equal to that state's members of Congress (two senators plus the number of representatives in the House of Representatives).

The chief responsibility of the president is to enforce the laws passed by Congress. A president can stop any bill from becoming a law by exercising a *veto* (refusal to approve), but Congress can override a veto with a two-thirds majority vote in each house. Then the bill becomes law, and the president must enforce it. It is in foreign affairs that a president has the greatest power. The president is the commander in chief of the armed forces and can establish relations with foreign governments.

In the 200 years since the U.S. Constitution was written, many executive departments and agencies have been established to assist and advise the president. Today, more than 50 departments and agencies are part of the executive branch.

In creating a judicial branch of government, the U.S. Constitution established an independent federal court system. The United States *Supreme Court* is specifically provided for in the Constitution, while all other federal courts have been established by Congress. The major federal courts established by Congress are the District Courts and the Courts of Appeals. There are nine judges on the Supreme Court, 638 judges on 91 District Courts, and 174 judges on 13 Courts of Appeals. All federal judges are appointed by the president for life, but the appointments must be approved by the Senate.

The function of the judicial branch is to serve as a check on the legislative and executive branches. The Supreme Court has the final say on whether federal laws conform to the U.S. Constitution. The function of the lower federal courts is to hear cases in which federal laws have been broken, cases involving disputes between states, and cases concerning foreign officials.

OUTLINE

CHAPTER 12
Writing an Essay

A U.S. history test will usually require more than answering multiple choice questions or true-false questions. It will require more than answers of one or two words or even a few sentences. To demonstrate your full understanding of a topic, you will be asked to write *essays.* An essay is a composition stating a personal point of view. It should contain the writer's thoughts and opinions, along with additional ideas and facts from other sources that support the point of view of the essay.

In this chapter, you will learn how to write a good essay for a test. You can use the same rules whenever you are asked to write an essay.

A good essay question on a test should ask for your thoughts and opinions as well as for information from your class notes or textbook. An essay is often divided into several parts. The first part may require more information than opinion. The remaining parts may give you a chance to express your own opinions and ideas.

Here is an essay question on the collapse of the Soviet Union in 1991. It contains two parts, 1.(*a*) and 1.(*b*). Read the questions and the two sample answers.

Question

1.*(a)* State and explain three reasons why the Soviet Union collapsed in 1991.

Answer

There are many reasons why the Soviet Union collapsed in 1991. I think that three reasons are most important.

The first has to do with events outside the Soviet Union. In the 1980s, the people of Communist Eastern Europe began demanding an end to Soviet control of their countries. This inspired the people of the Soviet Union to make their own demands for freedom. They reasoned that if Moscow's Communist leaders were unable to stop protests in Eastern Europe, they would be unable to stop them at home.

The second reason has to do with the misuse of Soviet resources. The government spent too much money on military programs and not nearly enough on producing the basic necessities of life. For example, by the late 1980s, milk and potatoes were too expensive for the average person to buy.

The third reason has to do with the failures of the Soviet leader, Mikhail Gorbachev. His reforms were too few and too late. Once the Soviet people tasted a little freedom, they wanted more of it than Gorbachev could deliver. Finally, in December 1991, he was forced to resign.

The Soviet people willingly endured many hardships as long as they had hope for a better future. By 1991, that hope was gone, and the Soviet Union collapsed.

Question

1.*(b)* What role do you think the United States played in the collapse of the Soviet Union in 1991?

Answer

The United States played a role in the collapse of the Soviet Union in two important and very different ways.

The first way involved U.S. defense policies. During the 1980s, the United States spent great amounts of money to upgrade its military defense systems. Thus, the Soviet Union was also forced to spend great amounts of money to match the U.S. military buildup. If the Soviet Union had spent that money to improve the lives of its people, its government might not have collapsed.

The second way had nothing to do with U.S. policy. Rather it concerned American culture. The Soviet government's control of television and radio could not stop the people from learning about the United States. They knew that Americans had freedom. They knew that Americans had a high standard of living and plenty of food. Young Soviets loved the music and dress styles of young Americans. The Soviet people wanted the kind of life that Americans enjoyed. In the end, the people decided that the only way to improve their lives was to get rid of their government.

The United States did not have to fire a shot to bring about the collapse of the Soviet Union. U.S. defense policies and American culture seemed able to bring about the same result.

Do you think the answers that you just read are examples of good essays? Here are the basic rules for writing a good essay. Read them to see if they were observed in the sample essays.

1. *An essay should begin with a thesis statement (a general statement that expresses the purpose of the essay).* Before you write anything specific, you should begin with a *thesis statement* to let the reader know what your essay is all about. The thesis statement in the answer to essay 1.*(a)* is: "There are many reasons why the Soviet Union collapsed in 1991. I think that three reasons are most important." On the following lines, write the thesis state-

ment that begins the answer to essay 1.(*b*).

____

____

____

____

____

____

What did you write? The thesis statement is: "The United States played a role in the collapse of the Soviet Union in two important and very different ways." This statement tells the reader that the essay writer is going to discuss the role that the United States played in the collapse of the Soviet Union.

2. *Each idea (or reason or way) given to prove the thesis statement should have its own paragraph.* A paragraph is usually made up of a group of sentences that together express one main idea. The first sentence of a paragraph is indented to let the reader know that a new idea is being introduced. In essay 1.(*a*), three paragraphs are used to discuss three different reasons why the Soviet Union collapsed. The first reason is listed below. On the lines given, list the other two.

   1. The struggle for freedom in the Communist countries of Eastern Europe inspired the Soviet people to do the same thing.

   2. ______________________________

      ____

      ____

      ____

      ____

      ____

   3. ______________________________

      ____

      ____

      ____

      ____

      ____

What did you write? The remaining two reasons are: The misuse of the country's resources left the Soviet people without the basic necessities of life. Gorbachev's reforms were too few and too late. Each reason is a new idea and deserves a paragraph of its own.

3. *Each idea (or reason or way) should be stated in a topic sentence and then explained in some detail.* The answer to essay 1.(*a*) states "The second reason [for the collapse of the Soviet Union] has to do with the misuse of the country's resources." This sentence is called a *topic sentence* because it identifies the idea to be developed. In this example, the idea is a reason. On the following lines, write the detail given in essay 1.(*a*) to explain this reason.

____

____

____

____

____

____

The essay states that the government spent too much on its military buildup and not enough on providing for the necessities of life. This detail gives the reader a better understanding of how the government misused the country's resources.

4. *A writer's ideas should make sense.* An essay must be based on clear thinking and correct information. On the following lines, write the opinion stated in essay 1.*(b)* about how the Soviet Union might have been able to avoid collapse.

____

____

____

____

____

____

What did you write? Essay 1.*(b)* states that the Soviet Union was forced to spend great amounts of money to match the U.S. military buildup. "If the Soviet Union had spent that money to improve the lives of its people, its government might not have collapsed." This statement cannot be proven because we cannot be sure that the Soviet Union might have been saved. But the statement is still a reasonable opinion. If the government had not tried to match U.S. military spending and used its resources to produce the basic necessities of life instead, perhaps the people would have given it more time. No one knows for sure.

Suppose essay 1.*(a)* had included this sentence: "The Soviet people were afraid that the United States would drop an atomic bomb on them if they did not get rid of communism." This might be the writer's opinion, but it is doubtful that such a statement could be supported by facts. We all have opinions. But in an essay, we should make reasonable statements based on facts.

5. *An essay should end with a statement that skillfully summarizes all the ideas in the essay.* A good concluding statement gives the reader an overall grasp of the important ideas in the essay. The conclusion to essay 1.*(a)* is: "The Soviet people willingly endured many hardships as long as they had hope for a better future. By 1991, that hope was gone, and the Soviet Union collapsed." On the lines below, write the conclusion to essay 1.*(b)*.

____

____

____

____

____

____

What did you write this time? The conclusion to essay 1.*(b)* is: "The United States did not have to fire a shot to bring about the collapse of the Soviet Union. U.S. defense policies and American culture seemed able to bring about the same result." This statement is a skillful summary of the essay because it leaves the reader with the final thought that winning a war is not the only way to triumph over an enemy.

As you have seen in this chapter, an essay is not just a list of facts. It is a carefully written composition combining fact and opinion. Whether you write an essay for a test or for publication, remember these five rules:

1. *An essay should begin with a thesis statement (a general statement that expresses the purpose of the entire essay).*
2. *Each idea (or reason or way) given to prove the thesis statement should have its own paragraph.*
3. *Each idea (or reason or way) should be stated in a topic sentence and then be explained in some detail.*
4. *Your own thoughts and opinions should make sense.*
5. *An essay should end with a statement that skillfully summarizes all the ideas in the essay.*

The following exercises will give you more practice in the skill of writing good essays.

USING YOUR SKILLS

A. Write an essay answering the following question.

1.*(c)* In the late 1980s, the 15 republics (states) of the Soviet Union declared their independence. Russia has emerged as the largest and most important of these republics. What kind of aid, if any, should the United States give to Russia? Explain in detail.

B. The following essay question is divided into two parts. The first part has been done for you. Write an essay answering the second part of the question.

2. *(a)* Why did the Mormons endure *persecution* (suffering imposed because of belief) in the 1830s and 1840s?

The Mormon Church was founded in New York State in 1830 by Joseph Smith. From the very beginning, it was persecuted for its religious beliefs.

Smith claimed that an angel had helped him find buried golden plates that he later translated into the *Book of Mormon.* According to Smith, the *Book of Mormon* proved that the Bible was only one of several sacred Christian texts. It also proved that certain religious truths had been revealed to Mormons but not to other Christian churches. The Mormons thus set themselves apart from other Christians, some of whom became angry and began to persecute the Mormons.

In 1839, Smith was forced to leave New York. He and his followers moved to Illinois. There they worked hard and became a strong political and economic force. Some people did not want the Mormons to have so much power and turned against them.

Strong feelings against the Mormons reached a peak when Joseph Smith taught that certain Mormons could have more than one wife. This practice, called *polygamy,* outraged many people and led to Smith's murder.

After Smith's death, Brigham Young became the leader of the Mormons. Young led them to religious freedom in what is now Utah, but they never forgot their times of persecution.

2.*(b)* If the Mormon church were founded today, would it face the same persecution that it did in the 1830s and 1840s? Explain your answer.

C. The following essay question is divided into two parts. The first part has been done for you. Write an essay answering the second part of the question.

3.*(a)* Give and explain three causes of the war between the United States and Mexico, 1846–1848.

The war between the United States and Mexico began in 1846. The war had several causes.

One cause was the dispute over the Texas boundary. The United States claimed that the southern boundary of Texas should be the Rio Grande. Mexico claimed that the Nueces River, farther north, was the true boundary.

Another cause was the failure of Mexico to pay for American property destroyed in Mexico. Americans living in Mexico had lost property in several revolutions, and they were angered by Mexico's refusal to pay for their losses.

A third cause was manifest destiny. This was the belief that Americans should extend the boundary of the United States to the Pacific Ocean and beyond. It would be accomplished by going to war against Mexico and gaining control of New Mexico and California.

These reasons help explain why the United States went to war against Mexico.

3.*(b)* If you had been living in 1846, would you have supported the war with Mexico? Explain your answer.

D. The following essay question is divided into two parts. Read the first part for background and answer the second part.

1.*(a)* Give and explain two reasons why many Americans supported colonial expansion during the late 1800s.

In the late 1800s, many Americans began to support colonial expansion.

Economic reasons led this change in public opinion. Farms and factories in the United States were producing more goods than could be consumed (used) by the American people. There was a need for new markets—new places in which to sell American goods and products. American factories also needed rubber, tin, and other raw materials that could be found only outside the United States. Many people thought that the nation's economic interests would be served by having colonies that could supply raw materials and serve as new markets.

At the same time, some Americans claimed that the United States needed colonies for military reasons. Colonies would serve as refueling and repair stations for the growing navy. The navy would protect U.S. trade routes and defend the nation in wartime.

For these economic and military reasons, many Americans were willing to seek colonies. The United States was beginning to change from a North American power to a world power.

1.*(b)* Do you think there were any other ways the United States could have protected its economic and military interests at the end of the 19th century without establishing colonies? Explain your answer.

E. The following essay question is divided into two parts. Read the first part for background and answer the second part.

5.*(a)* The civil rights movement of the 1950s and 1960s brought great changes in American society. Give and explain three examples of such changes.

The civil rights movement of the 1950s and 1960s began by seeking equal justice for African Americans.

The first great victory of the civil rights movement came in 1954. In that year, the U.S. Supreme Court decided the case of *Brown* v. *Board of Education of Topeka, Kansas.* The Court ruled that separate schools for blacks and whites were unequal schools. Therefore, they were illegal. At first, there was much opposition to the Court's ruling. In time, white schools began opening their doors to black students.

In the late 1950s and early 1960s, there was growing support for the civil rights movement. This resulted in the passage of several federal civil rights laws. These laws made racial segregation illegal in housing, employment, and transportation.

The civil rights movement became more than a struggle for the rights of African Americans. Other Americans had also been treated as second-class citizens. They began to speak up. Women, Native Americans, Asian Americans,

Hispanic Americans, and other groups demanded their right to the equal protection of the laws.

The civil rights movement began by seeking to improve the lives of African Americans. It ended up improving the lives of all Americans.

5.*(b)* Do you believe a civil rights movement is needed today? Explain your answer.

CHAPTER 13

Using Primary and Secondary Sources

What is the best way to learn history? There are different answers to this question. One very good way is to read important *documents* from the period of history that you are studying. In studying the American Revolution, you might read the Declaration of Independence. In studying the early years of the United States, you might read the Articles of Confederation and the U.S. Constitution. In studying the Civil War, you might read letters written by soldiers to their families. In studying World War I, you might read President Woodrow Wilson's speech asking Congress to declare war on Germany.

Primary Sources

Primary source is the term used to describe a document such as the Declaration of Independence or President Wilson's speech. A primary source is a firsthand account or piece of evidence. It may be an official document, a letter, a speech, a newspaper article, a diary, a cartoon, or a drawing. It is "firsthand" in that the source was produced by someone who actually experienced what is written or drawn. A soldier's written account of a battle experience is a primary source. A drawing of the battle by an artist who was there is a primary source. In this chapter, you will read several primary source documents. In other parts of this book, you will study drawings and photographs that are primary sources.

Secondary Sources

A vast number of books, stories, and drawings dealing with U.S. history have been produced over the years. Some are primary sources, and some are not. Many accounts of the American Revolution, for example, were produced by people who did not personally experience it. Either they were somewhere else at the time or they lived years after the Revolution. Such accounts are *secondary sources,* or secondhand information.

Perhaps the two most common types of secondary sources are textbooks and accounts written by *historians.* (Historians are people who study and write about history.) You may wonder how people can write about a period of history in which they did not live. Such writers use both primary sources and secondary sources to get their information.

Let us see if you can tell the difference between primary and secondary sources. Study the following list of sources that deal with the Revolutionary Period. If the example is a primary source, write **P** on the line in front of it. If the example is a secondary source, write **S** on the line in front of it.

_____ 1. *Common Sense,* the essay written by Thomas Paine in 1776

_____ 2. A drawing of a scene from the Battle of White Plains, done by a soldier who fought in that battle

____ 3. Irving Brant's book *James Madison and American Nationalism,* published in 1968

____ 4. Any American history textbook used in your school

____ 5. Benjamin Franklin's letter to John Paul Jones dated October 15, 1779

____ 6. An article entitled *200 Years Ago: New York Joins a Revolution,* published in the *New York Sunday News* on June 29, 1975

What answers did you give? Primary sources are firsthand accounts produced by people who experienced an event (in this case, the American Revolution). Examples 1, 2, and 5 were written or drawn by people who actually lived during the Revolutionary Period. These items are primary sources. Examples 3, 4, and 6 were written years later and, therefore, are secondary sources.

The following two sources deal with the Declaration of Independence. Read the sources and then answer the questions.

Selection 1

(Part of a letter from John Adams to his wife Abigail)

Philadelphia July 3d. 1776

. . . The Second Day of July 1776, will be the most memorable Epocha, in the History of America.—I am apt to believe that it will be celebrated, by succeeding Generations, as the great anniversary Festival. It ought to be commemorated, as the Day of Deliverance by solemn Acts of Devotion to God Almighty. It ought to be solemnized with Pomp and Parade, with Shews, Games, Sports, Guns, Bells, Bonfires and Illuminations from one End of this Continent to the other from this Time forward forever more.

You will think me transported with Enthusiasm but I am not.—I am well aware of the Toil and Blood and Treasure, that it will cost Us to maintain this Declaration . . .

From *The Book of Abigail and John, Selected Letters of the Adams Family, 1762–1784.* Edited by L.H. Butterfield, Marc Friedlaender, and Mary-Jo Kline.

Epocha: a long period of time marked by important events
Generations: the average periods of time between the birth of parents and the birth of their children
commemorated: remembered, honored
solemnized: made important, observed with ceremonies
Illuminations: decorations of lights

Selection 2

(A historian's account in the style of the 1930s)

The cry for independence was in the air. On June 11, 1776, the Second Continental Congress appointed a committee to draft a formal declaration of independence. One of the committee members, Thomas Jefferson, was chosen to write the declaration. On July 2, the Congress adopted a resolution presented by Richard Henry Lee, which stated that "these united colonies are, and of right ought to be, free and independent states." Two days later, on July 4, Jefferson's Declaration of Independence was adopted by representatives of the thirteen colonies. The decision of the Congress to declare the United States free and independent was met with great approval throughout the colonies. People saw the creation of the United States as a major event in the history of the human race. Perhaps no one put it better than John Adams when he wrote to his wife, "The Second Day of July 1776, will be the most memorable Epocha, in the History of America.—I am apt to believe that it will be celebrated, by succeeding Generations, as the great anniversary Festival." Adam's letter referred to the July 2 resolution passed by the Continental Congress. Nevertheless, Americans have come to celebrate their independence on July 4, the day Jefferson's Declaration of Independence was adopted.

adopted a resolution: agreed to take action on something

1. Which selection is a primary source?

____

____

____

____

____

____

What did you write? You should have said that the letter from John Adams to his wife (Selection 1) was the primary source. The letter was dated July 3, 1776, and was written by someone personally involved in events dealing with the Declaration of Independence.

Did you notice the three dots (. . .) at the end of the second paragraph of Selection 1? They show you that the reading is not complete. Only a part of the reading, called an excerpt, is being printed. The dots, called an *ellipsis,* represent the part of the reading that was left out. Sometimes you may see four dots (. . . .). The fourth dot is the period ending the sentence.

2. Why is Selection 2 a secondary source?

____

____

____

____

____

____

What did you write? Selection 2 is written in the style of books of the 1930s, more than 150 years after the writing of the Declaration of Independence. The author of this selection would not have lived during the Revolutionary Period. This writer read primary and secondary sources and used them to write this account. It is, therefore, a secondary source.

You probably found Selection 2 easier to read than Selection 1. Sometimes a primary source from an early period in U.S. history contains words that are difficult to understand today or are no longer used. The secondary source is often written in simpler, more modern language.

3. How did the author of Selection 2 use a primary source to show that Americans were pleased to declare their independence?

____

____

____

____

____

____

What did you write? The author of Selection 2 used a primary source to support the account. The primary source was an excerpt from a letter John Adams wrote to his wife, Abigail. This is the same letter printed in Selection 1. In Selection 2, the author used the letter to let us know how Americans in 1776 felt about declaring their independence.

When you read about an event in history, you should read more than one primary source and more than one secondary source. You cannot always rely on the information contained in only one primary source. The author may have been present at an event, but he or she may not have described correctly what happened. By reading a number of primary sources, you have a better chance of finding out what really happened.

It is also a good idea to read more than one secondary source because writers may disagree about the meaning of certain events. Selection 2 gives the impression that everyone was pleased with the Declaration of Independence. But other sources would show that many people in colonial America opposed the Declaration. By reading a number of secondary sources, you will have a better idea of how colonists felt about independence and the Revolution.

Primary and secondary sources can be found for any period in U.S. history. The following exercises will give you more practice in using historic documents and telling the difference between primary and secondary sources.

USING YOUR SKILLS

A. Choosing Primary and Secondary Sources. Study the following list of sources that deal with the early years of U.S. independence, between 1776 and 1791. If the source is primary, write **P** on the line in front of it. If the source is secondary, write **S** on the line in front of it.

____ 1. The Virginia Statute for Religious Freedom, passed by the House of Burgesses in 1786

____ 2. The Bill of Rights, added to the U.S. Constitution in 1791

____ 3. Carl Becker's book *The Declaration of Independence: A Study in the History of Political Ideas,* published in 1922

____ 4. A 1787 newspaper editorial in the *Pennsylvania Gazette* commenting on the Philadelphia Constitutional Convention

_____ 5. A textbook on the U.S. Constitution

_____ 6. A 1983 newspaper article in the *Los Angeles Times* discussing some recently found letters written by Thomas Jefferson

_____ 7. A drawing of the delegates to the 1787 Philadelphia Constitutional Convention done by one of the delegates

_____ 8. The motion picture *1776*

_____ 9. *The Federalist,* first published in book form in 1788 and reprinted in 1961

_____ 10. The letters of James Madison commenting on his role in writing the U.S. Constitution

B. Read the following sources dealing with the Articles of Confederation. Then answer the questions.

Selection 1

(The Articles of Confederation)

ARTICLE 1. The style of this confederacy shall be "The United States of America."

ARTICLE 2. Each state retains its sovereignty, freedom, and independence, and every power, jurisdiction, and right, which is not by this confederation expressly delegated to the United States, in Congress assembled. . . .

ARTICLE 5. . . . In determining questions in the United States in Congress assembled, each state shall have one vote. . . .

ARTICLE 8. All charges of war, and all other expenses that shall be incurred for the common defense or general welfare, an allowed by the United States in Congress assembled, shall be defrayed out of a common treasury, which shall be supplied by the several states in proportion to the value of all land within each state, . . .

ARTICLE 9. . . . The United States in Congress assembled shall never engage in a war, . . . nor coin money, nor regulate the value thereof, nor ascertain the sums and expenses necessary for the defense and welfare of the United States, . . . nor borrow money . . . nor agree upon . . . the number of land or sea forces to be raised, . . . unless nine states assent to the same . . .

ARTICLE 13. Every state shall abide by the determinations of the United States in Congress assembled . . . And the articles of this confederation shall be inviolably observed by every state, . . . nor shall any alteration at any time hereafter be made in any of them, unless such alteration be agreed to in a Congress of the United States, and be afterward confirmed by the legislatures of every state. . . .

confederacy: group of states united for a common purpose
sovereignty: total power of self-government

jurisdiction: authority to interpret and apply laws
expressly delegated: specifically given
incurred: taken on
defrayed: paid
ascertain: determine
assent: agree
abide: accept without opposition
determinations: decisions
inviolably: without change or attack
alteration: change
confirmed: approved; made valid

Selection 2

(A historian's account written in the style of the 1980s)

Let there be no mistake about it. The supporters of the Articles of Confederation liked the loose confederation under which very little power was given to the national government. They did not want to replace a strong British government with a strong U.S. government. As far as they were concerned, very little government was enough government. These supporters reminded people that the Articles of Confederation brought the American Revolution to a successful conclusion and were responsible for the Treaty of Paris, which formally ended the Revolutionary War.

Yet as the spring of 1787 approached, there were more and more calls for changing the Articles or for replacing them with a completely new constitution. Those who opposed the Articles pointed to a number of weaknesses in them. Congress found it very difficult to enact laws because a vote of 9 out of the 13 states was required to pass a law. Any attempt to change the Articles required the approval of all 13 states. The national government had no *chief executive,* such as a president, so laws had to be enforced by the states. The lack of a strong executive made the government look weak in the eyes of many foreign countries. Under the Articles, there were no national courts to handle disputes between citizens of different states. Congress could not tax the people directly; instead, it had to ask the states for money. Since Congress could not raise an army, it had to ask the states to supply troops. In the area of trade, Congress could not control trade between states or the trade of any state with a foreign country.

The weaknesses of the Articles of Confederation were too great to overcome. The convention that met in Philadelphia to address the problems of the Articles had no choice but to produce a new constitution.

1. Why is Selection 1 a primary source?

2. Why is Selection 2 a secondary source?

3. State two ways in which you can tell that Selection 1 is only an excerpt from the Articles of Confederation.

4. Why would a person read a secondary source (Selection 2) instead of an available primary source (Selection 1)?

5. In Selection 2, does the author give any opinion about the Articles of Confederation or just the facts? Explain your answer.

C. Read the following primary sources dealing with the U.S. Constitution. Then answer the questions.

Selection 1

(Part of a letter from Elbridge Gerry to the Massachusetts legislature)

October 18, 1787

Gentlemen:

I have the honor to inclose, pursuant to my commission, the constitution proposed by the federal convention.

To this system I gave my dissent, and shall submit my objections to the honourable legislature.

It was painful for me, on a subject of such national importance, to differ from the respectable members who signed the constitution: But conceiving as I did, that the liberties of America were not secured by the system, it was my duty to oppose it.

My principal objections to the plan, are, that there is no adequate provision for a representation of the people—that they have no security for the right of election—that some of the powers of the legislature are ambiguous, and others indefinite and dangerous—that the executive is blended with, and will have an undue influence over, the legislature—that the judicial department will be oppressive—that treaties of the highest importance may be formed by the president with the advice of two-thirds of a quorum of the senate—and that the system is without the security of a bill of rights. . . .

From *The Records of the Federal Convention,* edited by Max Farrand. Revised edition, Vol. III. Copyright © 1937 by Yale University Press.

pursuant to: according to
commission: the authority given to a person to carry out a particular order
federal: relating to a form of government in which power is distributed between the central government and state governments
dissent: disapproval
ambiguous: unclear; open to different interpretations
quorum: the number of people needed to make a meeting official or legal

Selection 2

(Part of a letter from Thomas Jefferson to James Madison)

December 20, 1787

. . . I like much the general idea of framing a government . . . into Legislative, Judiciary and Executive. I like the power given the Legislature to levy taxes; and for that reason solely approve of the greater house being chosen by the people directly. For tho' I think a house chosen by them will be very illy qualified to legislate for the Union, for foreign nations &c. yet this evil does not weigh against the good of preserving inviolate the fundamental principle that the people are not to be taxed but by representatives chosen immediately by themselves. I am captivated by the compromise of the opposite claims of the great and little states, of the latter to equal, and the former to proportional influence. I am much pleased too with the substitution of the method of voting by persons, instead of that of voting by states: and I like the negative given to the Executive with a third of either house, . . . I will now add what I do not like. First the omission of a bill of rights . . . a bill of rights is what the people are entitled to against every government . . . The second feature I dislike, and greatly dislike, is the abandonment in every instance of the necessity of rotation in office and most particularly in the case of the President. . . . After all, it is my principle that the will of the Majority should always prevail. If they approve the proposed Convention in all its parts, I shall concur in it chearfully, in hopes that they will amend it whenever they shall find it work wrong. . . .

levy: to impose or collect
inviolate: without change
proportional: determined by size
majority: a number larger than half of the total
prevail: win

1. Why are both selections primary sources?

____

____

____

____

2. Does Selection 2 give Thomas Jefferson's complete letter? How can you tell?

____

____

____

____

3. What did both Elbridge Gerry and Thomas Jefferson feel should have been included in the Constitution?

____

____

____

____

4. Give two reasons why Gerry opposed the Constitution.

____

____

____

____

5. Give two reasons why Jefferson supported the Constitution.

____

____

____

____

6. How do these selections prove that it is better to read more than one source when you are studying a topic in history?

____

____

____

____

D. Read the following letter written by a soldier during the Civil War (1861–1865).

July 14, 1861
Camp Clark, Washington

My very dear Sarah:

The indications are very strong that we shall move in a few days—perhaps tomorrow. Lest I should not be able to write again, I feel impelled to write a few lines that may fall under your eye when I shall be no more.

I have no misgivings about, or lack of confidence in the cause in which I am engaged, and my courage does not halt or falter. I know how strongly American Civilization now leans on the triumph of the Government, and how great a debt we owe to those who went before us through the blood and sufferings of the Revolution. And I am willing—perfectly willing—to lay down all my joys in this life, to help maintain this Government, and to pay that debt.

Sarah my love for you is deathless. . . . The memories of the blissful moments I have spent with you come creeping over me, and I feel most gratified to God and to you that I have enjoyed them so long. And hard it is for me to give them up and burn to ashes the hopes of future years, when, God willing, we might still have lived and loved together, and seen our sons grown up to honorable manhood. . . . If I do not [return] my dear Sarah, never forget how much I love you, and when my last breath escapes me on the battle field, it will whisper your name. Forgive my faults, and the many pains I have caused you.

But, O Sarah! if the dead can come back to this earth and flit unseen around those they loved, I shall always be near you; in the gladdest days and in the darkest nights . . . always, always, and if there be a soft breeze upon your cheek, it shall be my breath, as the cool air fans your throbbing temple, it shall be my spirit passing by. Sarah do not mourn me dead; think I am gone and wait for thee, for we shall meet again. . . .

(Major Sullivan Ballou wrote this letter to his wife in Rhode Island one week before he died at the First Battle of Bull Run [Manassas].)

lest: in case
blissful: happy, joyful
flit: fly, dance, flutter

D-1. Write the letter of the correct choice on the line next to the number of each question.

_____ 1. Which statement is TRUE?
(a) This is the complete letter written by Major Sullivan Ballou.
(b) This is an excerpt of a letter written by Major Sullivan Ballou.
(c) Almost all of the letter written by Major Sullivan Ballou is printed here.
(d) Parts of the letter written by Major Sullivan Ballou have been lost.

_____ 2. Major Ballou died
(a) in the first year of the war.
(b) in the second year of the war.
(c) in the third year of the war.
(d) in the fourth year of the war.

_____ 3. The letter shows that
(a) all Northern soldiers believed they were fighting a just war.
(b) most soldiers enjoy warfare.
(c) some soldiers volunteer to go into battle.
(d) Major Ballou was willing to die in battle.

_____ 4. This letter is a good primary source for proving that
(a) war can never be justified.
(b) Civil War soldiers wanted to believe they were fighting for a good cause.
(c) the wives of soldiers away in battle suffered many hardships.
(d) the Civil War was supported equally by Northern soldiers and Southern soldiers.

_____ 5. Words are sometimes added to a primary source to make it easier to understand. The inserted words are put in brackets [ ]. What word or words were inserted in this letter?
(a) blissful
(b) perfectly willing
(c) return
(d) flit

D-2. 1. What one word would you pick to describe Major Ballou's mood (feelings) as he wrote this letter? Explain your answer.

____

____

____

____

____

2. How has this letter increased your understanding and knowledge of the Civil War? Explain your answer.

____

____

E. Read the following sources dealing with the U.S. entry into World War I. Then answer the questions.

Selection 1

(President Woodrow Wilson's speech asking Congress to declare war on Germany, April 2, 1917)

. . . The present German submarine warfare against commerce is a warfare against mankind.

It is a war against all nations. American ships have been sunk, American lives taken, in ways which it has stirred us very deeply to learn of, but the ships and people of other neutral and friendly nations have been sunk and overwhelmed in the waters in the same way. . . . I advise that the Congress declare the recent course of the Imperial German Government to be in fact nothing less than war against the government and people of the United States; . . .

It is a distressing and oppressive duty, Gentlemen of the Congress, which I have performed in thus addressing you. There are, it may be, many months of fiery trial and sacrifice ahead of us. It is a fearful thing to lead this great peaceful people into war, into the most terrible and disastrous of all wars, civilization itself seeming to be in the balance. But the right is more precious than peace, and we shall fight for the things which we have always carried nearest our hearts,—for democracy, for the right of those who submit to authority to have a voice in their own Governments, for the rights and liberties of small nations, for a universal dominion of right by such a concert of free peoples as shall bring peace and safety to all nations and make the world itself at last free. . . .

universal dominion: worldwide controlling influence
concert: a plan to act together

Selection 2

(Speech by Senator George W. Norris of Nebraska against the declaration of war, April 4, 1917)

There are a great many American citizens who feel that we owe it as a duty to humanity to take part in this war. Many instances of cruelty and inhumanity can be found on both sides Men are often biased in their judgment on account of their sympathy and their interests. To my mind, what we ought to have maintained from the beginning was the strictest neutrality. . . . there are many honest, patriotic citizens who think we ought to engage in this war and who are behind the President in his demand that we should declare war against Germany. I think such people err in judgment and to a great extent have been misled as to the real history and the true facts by the almost unanimous demand of the great combination of wealth that has a direct financial interest in our participation in the war. . . . War brings prosperity to the stock gambler on Wall Street—to those who are already in possession of more wealth than can be realized or enjoyed. . . .

Their object in having war and in preparing for war is to make money. . . .

We are taking a step today that is fraught with untold danger. . . . By our act we will make millions of our countrymen suffer, and the consequences of it may well be that millions of our brethren must shed their lifeblood, millions of broken-hearted women must weep, millions of children must suffer with cold, and millions of babes must die from hunger, and all because we want to preserve the commercial right of American citizens to deliver munitions of war to belligerent nations.

From *Great Issues in American History, a Documentary Record,* Vol. II, 1864–1957. Richard Hofstadter, editor.

humanity: all human beings
inhumanity: heartless actions
patriotic: having love for and devotion to one's country
unanimous: completely in agreement
consequences: results
munitions: military weapons and supplies
belligerent: warring

Selection 3

(An article about World War I)

The scene was a familiar one in 1917—thousands of soldiers boarding trains to be taken to ships that would carry them to war in Europe, hundreds of young ladies waving American flags, cheering the soldiers as they departed.

For those Americans who supported the United States's entry into World War I, the war was a simple matter of right and wrong. Germany was sinking American ships, and it was the right of the United States to defend itself. But the war was also to be viewed as a crusade, a holy war against the forces of evil. As President Wilson stated in his declaration of war speech before Congress, the war would be a fight "for democracy, for the right of those who submit to authority to have a voice in their own Governments, for the rights and liberties of small nations, for a universal dominion of right by such a concert of free people as shall bring peace and safety to all nations and make the world itself at last free."

While most Americans supported the war effort, some saw the war as a waste of lives. If U.S. ships stayed out of troubled waters, they argued, there would be no sinkings. There were those who saw the United States's entry into World War I as nothing more than a chance for rich men to become richer. According to Senator George W. Norris of Nebraska, American involvement would bring "prosperity to the stock gambler on Wall Street—to those who are already in possession of more wealth than can be realized or enjoyed." Other critics of the war claimed that those who manufactured guns and bullets would make money while poor people's children died on bloody battlefields on the other side of the world.

Despite such criticisms, American soldiers went off to battle, and when the fighting ended on November 11, 1918, the United States could be counted on the winning side. There was jubilation as President Wilson sailed to Europe to participate in the peace conference that would formally end the war. But the excitement of the victory soon turned to feelings of frustration and betrayal. The world had not been made safer for democracy as promised. Disputes between countries had not been ended. Instead, the war to end all wars had laid the groundwork for another even more disastrous world war.

1. Which of these sources are primary? Explain your choice(s).

____

____

____

2. Does Selection 1 give President Wilson's complete speech? How can you tell?

____

____

____

3. According to Senator Norris, who would benefit from the entry of the United States into World War I?

____

____

____

4. Give two reasons why Wilson supported a declaration of war.

____

____

____

5. Give two reasons why Norris opposed a declaration of war.

____

____

____

6. Why do you think the author of Selection 3 quoted Wilson and Norris?

____

____

____

7. How does the author of Selection 3 show that there was popular support for the entry of the United States into World War I?

____

____

____

8. Can you tell from Selection 3 whether the author supported the entry of the United States into World War I? Explain your answer.

____

____

____

9. How can you tell that Selection 3 was written a number of years after World War I?

____

____

____

10. Why is it a good idea for a student of World War I to read all three selections in this exercise?

____

____

____

CHAPTER 14
Using the Library

Your textbook provides most of the information that you need to do well in your U.S. history class. But it may not give you as many details on a subject as you would like. To find out more, you may have to use your school or public library. In this chapter, you will learn how to locate information in a library.

Let us imagine that you have been given an assignment to write a report on the War of 1812. From your class notes, you already know some details:

- Congress declared war on Britain on June 18, 1812.
- The war did not end until January 1815, but it became known as the War of 1812.
- One cause of the war was that many British sailors left their ships to serve in the U.S. merchant marine. Britain, in turn, stopped U.S. ships and seized British-looking sailors, even though some of them were Americans.
- Some Americans welcomed the war as an opportunity to *annex* Canada and Florida.

For your assignment, however, you need more details about the War of 1812. It is time to go to the library.

In recent years, many libraries have used computers as a way to catalog (list) their books and other resources. Later in this chapter, you will learn how to use a computer to locate information in a library, but, first, let us study traditional ways of using a library.

Card Catalog

If your library has not computerized its catalog, it most likely uses a *card catalog.* The card catalog is a listing on cards of every book in the library. Every book is listed on at least three cards—a *subject card,* a *title card,* and an *author card.* The cards are arranged in alphabetical order in small cabinet drawers.

To find books on a topic, first look for a subject card. A subject card headed "War of 1812" would probably tell you to look under UNITED STATES—HISTORY—WAR OF 1812. When you did that, you would find the subject UNITED STATES—HISTORY—WAR OF 1812 written at the top of the card. (See Example A.) The card would be found in the drawer marked **U** (for "United").

You may find a number of subject cards on UNITED STATES—HISTORY—WAR OF 1812. Sometimes there are too many books on one subject or too many subjects beginning with the same letter to fit into one drawer. A label on each drawer gives the first three or four letters of the subjects it contains—for example, **UBA–UNG** and **UNH–UZB**. In which drawer would you find a card or cards on UNITED STATES—HISTORY—WAR OF 1812?

If you know the title of a book about the War of 1812, you can use the title card. (See Example B.) The title of the book, "The dawn's early light," is written at the top of the card. You would find this card in the drawer marked **D** (for "dawn's"). (There are so many titles that begin with the words "the," "a," or "an" that the next word in the

Example A

UNITED STATES - HISTORY - WAR OF 1812
973.52
L Lord, Walter, 1917-
The dawn's early light. New York,
W.W. Norton [1972]
384 p. illus. 22 cm.

Bibliography: p. 351

Example B

The dawn's early light
973.52
L Lord, Walter, 1917-
The dawn's early light. New York,
W.W. Norton [1972]
384 p. illus. 22 cm.

Bibliography: p. 351

Example C

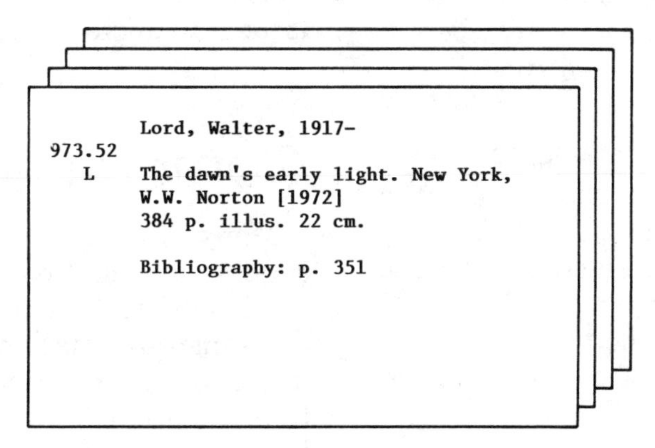

Lord, Walter, 1917-
973.52
L The dawn's early light. New York,
W.W. Norton [1972]
384 p. illus. 22 cm.

Bibliography: p. 351

title is used to determine the alphabetical order.)

If you know the name of the author whose book you want, you can look up the author's card. (See Example C.) At the top of this card is the author's last name (Lord) followed by a comma (,) and then the first name (Walter). The date 1917 is the year in which Walter Lord was born. The author's card can be found in the drawer marked **L** (for "Lord").

You can see that each card in Examples A, B, and C gives you the title and the author. Each card also gives:

1. The place of publication, the publisher, and the date of publication: New York, W.W. Norton [1972].
2. The number of pages in the book: 384 p. means 384 pages.
3. Information about illustrations in the book: The abbreviation *illus.* means that the book contains illustrations (photographs, drawings, maps, cartoons).
4. The height of the book in centimeters: 22 cm. means 22 centimeters.
5. Information about the *bibliography* and the page it is on. (A bibliography is a list of other books on the same subject.) The bibliography in this book is on page 351.
6. A number and letter to help you find the book on the library shelf: 973.52 L

A number is given to all nonfiction (true or factual) books. The letter under the number is the first letter of the author's last name. The number, which is also placed on the spine (back end) of the book, is determined by the Dewey Decimal Classification system. Under this system, history subjects have been given the numbers 900–909 and 930–999. Most of the shelves in the library are numbered according to the Dewey system. By looking up the card and finding the exact number (973.52) and letter (L) of *The Dawn's Early Light,* you can go to the shelf numbered 930–999 and locate the book.

Fiction books (made-up stories) do not have numbers on their cards. These books can be found in the part of the library marked FICTION. Fiction books are placed on the shelves in alphabetical order by the author's last name. For example, the book *Tall Ships* by John Jennings would be found on the shelves under **J** (for "Jennings").

To find out if you understand how to use the card catalog, answer the following question:

_____ 1. A book numbered 973.52 / C on a title card in the card catalog would
- *(a)* have different numbers on the author and subject cards.
- *(b)* have a title starting with the letter "C."
- *(c)* be a work of fiction.
- *(d)* be found on a shelf labeled 960–981.21.

Which answer did you choose? You should eliminate the incorrect choices first. Choice *(a)* is incorrect because the title, author, and subject cards of the same book have the same number. Choice *(b)* is incorrect because the "C" in the classification number stands for the first letter of the author's last name. Choice *(c)* is incorrect because works of fiction are not given numbers on the cards. This makes choice *(d)* correct by elimination. But why is it correct? According to the Dewey system, books numbered 960 to 981.21 deal with history. Therefore, a book numbered 973.52 would deal with history and be placed on the shelf marked 960–981.21.

Microfilm and Microfiche

Your library may list its books in the form of *microfilm.* These rolls of miniature photographs show catalog cards or book and magazine pages. Sheets of microfilm are called *microfiche.* One of them can contain the images of as many as 400 book pages.

Both forms take up much less space than bulky cabinets of cards. Most of what you have already learned about a card catalog also applies to microfilm and microfiche. You can look up books on microfilm and microfiche by subject, title, and author.

To use a microfilm or microfiche catalog, you put the film into a machine. It has a screen that lights up and enlarges the tiny print on the film. You can move the film rapidly to the item you want and then focus it to make it clear.

Computer Catalog

Many libraries now use computers to catalog information on their books and other materials. A *computer catalog* has the same information as the card catalog, microfilm, or microfiche, but it also contains additional information. For example, it shows how many copies of a book the library owns and whether those copies are "in" or "checked out." Some computer catalogs even show what is available in neighboring libraries.

Not all computer catalogs work the same way, but most are similar to the following examples.

Let us look again for *The Dawn's Early Light* by Walter Lord. In this first example, you are seated at a computer catalog that requires you to enter commands on the keyboard. The screen appears as follows:

Example 1 Screen A

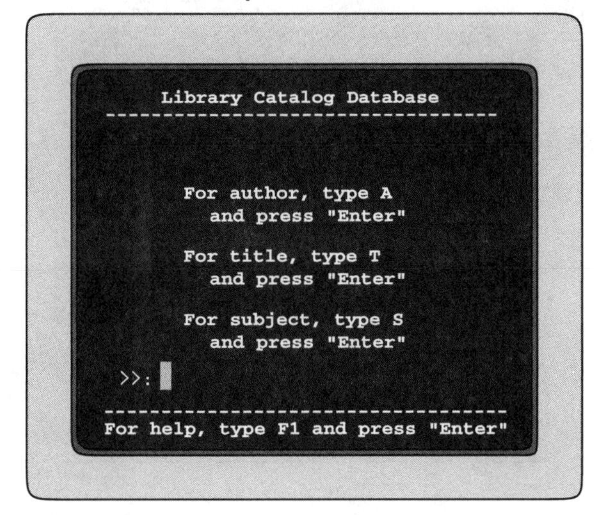

By pressing the "function" keys, such as A, T, S or F1 to F10, you can make the computer do certain things. For example, type A. On the screen, the A will appear in place of the flashing *cursor* ▌ after >>:. (The cursor will move one space to the right.) Then press "Enter" on the keyboard, and a new screen will appear. On the new screen, you will type in the author's last name, a comma, and first name, and press "Enter." Another screen will appear, listing all the works written by or about that author.

In the next example, a device called a *mouse* replaces the function keys on the keyboard. A mouse is a small two-button device connected to the computer by a wire. Using it enables you to save time and effort in typing. When a mouse is used, the computer screen appears as follows:

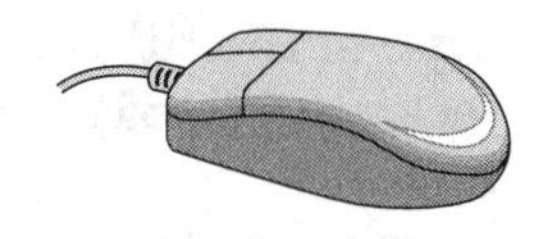

Example 2 Screen A

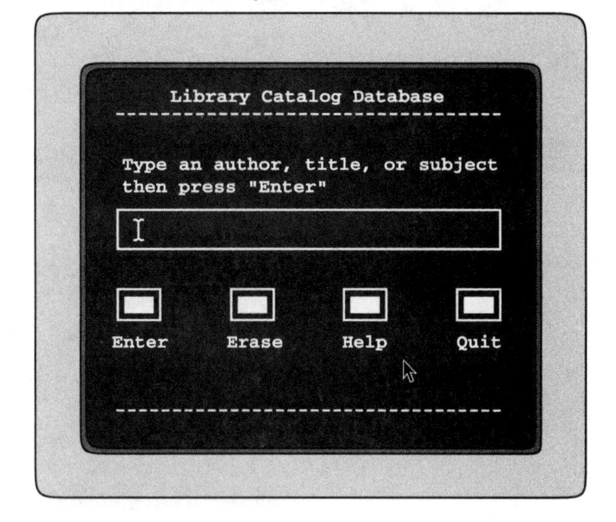

The flashing cursor in this example looks like a capital I. It is located at the far left of the rectangular box. As you type on the keyboard, the letter you type appears in place of the flashing cursor, which moves one space to the right. Let us search again for *The Dawn's Early Light* by typing in the author's name. (Always type the last name first.) You could type just Lord, but that word is so common that you would get many responses. Instead, type Lord, Walter. The instructions tell you that you should then PRESS "ENTER." You could either press the Enter key on the keyboard or use the mouse. For the rest of this lesson, let's use the mouse.

When using a mouse, you will see an arrow somewhere on the screen. By slowly moving the mouse around on the flat surface of the computer table, the arrow on your screen will also move. If you move the mouse to the right on the table, the arrow will move to the right on the screen, and so on. Move the mouse on the table until the arrow on the screen touches the *icon,* or picture, above the word Enter. (On some computer screens, the arrow turns into a hand when it touches the icon.) Then click the left button on the mouse. A screen like the following will appear:

Example 2 Screen B

The first reference states that "Lord, Walter" is mentioned in one work in the library other than the 12 titles given in the second reference. The second reference states that the library has 12 books either written by "Lord, Walter" or written about him. You want the second reference, so move the mouse on your table until the arrow on the screen touches the icon to the left of the second reference. Click the mouse and a list of titles similar to the following will appear:

Example 2 Screen C

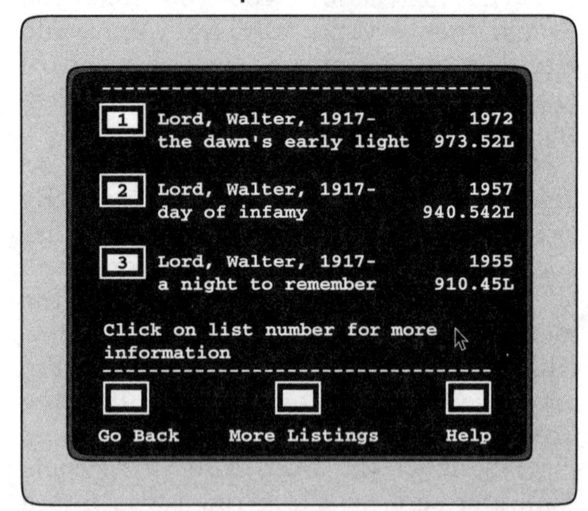

The titles are listed in the order of publication, with the most recent listed first. There may be more titles than can be shown on one screen. Instructions will show you where to click for the next group of titles. At this point, however, you could look for *The Dawn's Early Light* on shelf 973.52 L. But the screen also instructs you to click on number 1 for more information about the book. Click on number 1 and a screen like the following will appear:

Example 2 Screen D

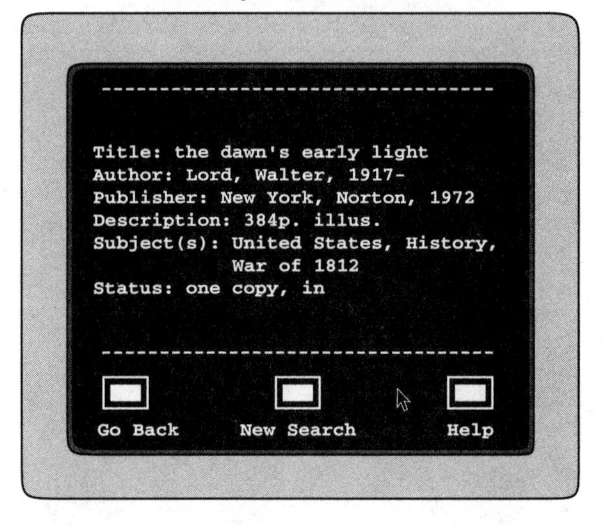

This screen gives the same information as the card catalog, microfilm, and microfiche do, plus an important additional piece of information. The library has one copy of the book, and it is on the shelves (Status: one copy, in). If the copy were checked out, you could use your time searching the computer file for another book simply by clicking the icon above Go Back.

The Go Back function will return you to the previous screen—in this case, the screen listing titles by or about Walter Lord. If you want to look for another author instead, you would click the icon above New Search. This would return you to Screen A (Example 2) on page 153, and you could type in the name of another author. Or you could type in the title of another book or the subject War of 1812. Then, by clicking the icon above Enter, you would find out if the library has the book you need.

Also on Screen A (Example 2) are the choices Erase, Help, and Quit. By clicking the icon above each word, a different operation happens. If you had made a typing mistake, Erase would clear the box so that you could retype correctly. If you were unsure how to use this computer catalog, Help would give you instructions. If you wanted to see what books were in neighboring libraries, Quit would bring up a screen for searching their catalogs.

Let's see if you understand how to use a computer catalog. Answer the following question.

____ 2. Which statement is TRUE?

(a) A computer catalog will list all the works by an author that are owned by the library.

(b) A card catalog contains exactly the same information as a computer catalog.

(c) All computer catalogs use a mouse.

(d) A computer catalog does not list works of fiction.

Which answer did you choose? A computer catalog will list all of an author's works owned by the library. So choice *(a)* could be correct. But look at the other choices in case they offer a better answer. Choice *(b)* states that the card catalog contains exactly the same information as the computer catalog. This is incorrect. Only the computer catalog, for example, can tell you if the book you want is available at the moment. Choice *(c)* is incorrect. Some computer catalogs do not use a mouse. Instead, you have to hit certain function keys on the keyboard. Choice *(d)* is also incorrect. Works of fiction can be found in the computer catalog just as they can be found in the card catalog, microfilm, and microfiche. All you have to do is type in the author's last name and first name, the title of the book, or a few words describing the subject. Choice *(a)* is indeed the correct answer.

You shouldn't hesitate to use the computer catalog if your library has one. It might look complicated to operate, but it really isn't. In fact, most students think that it's fun.

The Readers' Guide to Periodical Literature

Much information about the War of 1812 has been published in magazines rather than in books. Although computer catalogs can be used for magazine research, there is a more traditional way to locate magazines. It is by using the *Readers' Guide to Periodical Literature.* (Periodical literature is another name for magazines published weekly, monthly, and so on.)

The *Readers' Guide* is found in the REFERENCE section of a library. It is published monthly. Every third month, a quarterly is published that combines the entries for the third month and the previous two months. At the end of the year, a large volume is published that contains the entries for the entire year. In each issue of the *Readers' Guide,* authors and subjects are arranged together in one alphabetical listing. Under each author's name, you can find the title of every magazine article published by that author during the time period covered by the issue. Similarly, under each subject, you can find the title of every magazine article published on that subject during the time period covered by the issue.

The *Readers' Guide* is used mainly to find articles on current (present-day) topics. But it can also help with historical topics. For example, you can find an article on the War of 1812 in the *Readers' Guide* for 1995. The article, entitled "The Battle of Lake Erie," was published in the magazine *Smithsonian.* Its listing by subject looks like this:

LAKE ERIE, BATTLE OF, 1813
The battle of Lake Erie. B. Gilbert.
bibl (p126) il por map *Smithsonian*
v25 p24–8+ Ja '95

As you can see, many abbreviations were used. Because so many articles are listed in the *Readers' Guide,* abbreviations save space. If you forget what the abbreviations mean, they are explained in the front of each issue. Here are the explanations for the abbreviations used in the preceding example.

B. Gilbert—the author
bibl (p126)—bibliography (the page it is on)
il—illustrated
por—portrait
v25—volume number of the magazine
p24–8+—page numbers of the article. The + sign means that the article is continued on later pages of the same issue.
Ja '95—January 1995

Here is another article on the War of 1812, published in *American History Illustrated.* Its listing by author looks like this:

HUNT, GILBERT J.
The Battle of New Orleans (King James Version) [excerpt from The historical reader; biblical-style history; with introd. by Margaret Fortier] il *American History Illustrated* v28 p50–3 N/D '93

Answer the following questions based on this example.

3.*(a)* When was this article published?

____

____

(b) On which pages of the magazine can you find the article?

____

What did you write? The article was published in the November/December 1993 issue (N/D '93). The months November and December show that the magazine is published bimonthly (every two months). The article can be found on pages 50 to 53.

The *Readers' Guide* can save you a great deal of time. Instead of looking through many magazines, you can use the *Guide* to find recent articles on current and historical topics. Remember that all abbreviations used are explained in the front of each issue.

Learning how to use a library effectively is an important part of your education. In this chapter, you have learned the major ways to locate information in a library. Many other sources of information are available in a library. Your librarian will be happy to explain how to use them.

The following exercises will give you more practice in locating information in a library.

USING YOUR SKILLS

Note: To give you a sense of a real library search for a particular topic, exercises B, C, and D all deal with the War of 1812. Exercises E, F, and G all deal with the Great Depression.

A. True or False. If the underlined word or words make the statement true, write TRUE on the line to the left of the statement. If the underlined word or words make the statement false, write on the line to the left the word or words that will make the statement true.

______________________ 1. The card catalog in a library lists every book found in that library.

______________________ 2. Fiction books are placed on the shelves in the library alphabetically by the author's first name.

______________________ 3. The *Readers' Guide* is a listing of books published over a period of time.

_______________ 4. In the *Readers' Guide,* authors and subjects are arranged in two separate listings.

_______________ 5. A computer catalog can show if a book is presently available in a library.

B. Using the Card Catalog. Study the following entry in the card catalog.

```
          Caffrey, Kate
973.52
   C      The twilight's last gleaming: Britain
          vs. America 1812-1815. New York,
          Stein & Day [1977]
          340 p. illus. 25 cm.

          Bibliography: p. 327-329
```

B-1. Write the letter of the correct choice on the line next to the number of each question.

____ 1. The card shown on this page is
(a) a subject card. *(b)* a title card. *(c)* an author card.

____ 2. Kate Caffrey is the author of *The Twilight's Last Gleaming.* You can find an author card for this book in a drawer marked
(a) AAA–ADA. *(c)* KAL–KAV.
(b) CAB–CLA. *(d)* TAG–THA.

____ 3. A title card for *The Twilight's Last Gleaming* would be found in the card catalog drawer marked
(a) TAB–TX. *(c)* TOY–TUX.
(b) THA–TOX. *(d)* TWA–TZA.

____ 4. A book numbered 973.52 in the card catalog can be found on the shelf numbered
(a) 900–909.99. *(c)* 956.77–978.81.
(b) 930–956.76. *(d)* 978.82–999.97.

____ 5. Which abbreviation on the card tells you that there are drawings in the book?
(a) cm. *(b)* p. *(c)* & *(d)* illus.

B-2. Write your answers to the following questions on the lines provided.

1. How many pages are in *The Twilight's Last Gleaming?*

____

2. In which year was the book published?

____

3. In which city was the book published?

____

4. Which company published the book?

____

5. What is the height of the book?

____

C. Using the Computer Catalog. Study the following screens from a computer catalog using a mouse. Then answer the questions.

Screen A

Screen B

Screen C

Screen D

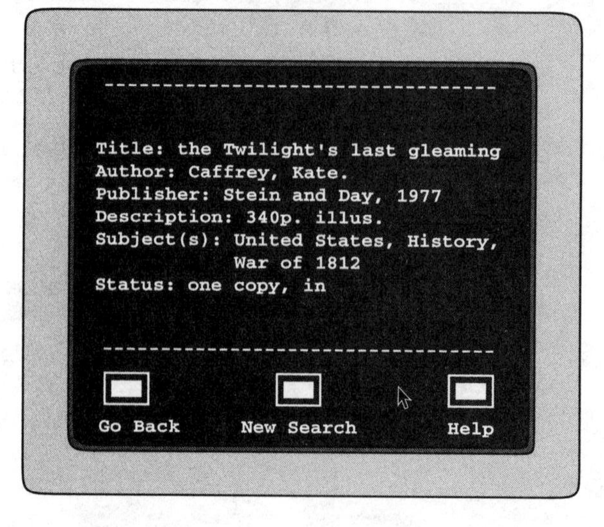

C-1. Write the letter of the correct choice on the line next to the number of each question.

_____ 1. In using a computer catalog, you can search for a book by
(a) author only.
(b) title only.
(c) subject only.
(d) author, title, or subject.

_____ 2. To find a book by author, you begin by
(a) moving the arrow to the icon above Enter and clicking the mouse.
(b) typing in the author's first name, then last name, and then clicking the icon above Enter.
(c) typing in the author's last name, comma, first name, and then clicking the icon above Enter.
(d) typing in the author's last name and then clicking the icon above Help.

_____ 3. The library has two books by Kate Caffrey. Their titles are listed on Screen C
(a) in alphabetical order.
(b) with the more recently published book listed first.
(c) according to their card catalog number.
(d) in no particular order.

_____ 4. How many copies of *The Twilight's Last Gleaming* does this library own?
(a) none
(b) one
(c) two
(d) three

_____ 5. If you were on Screen C and wanted to see Screen B, you would
(a) click on the Go Back icon.
(b) type the letter B on the keyboard.
(c) click on the Quit icon.
(d) type Go Back on the keyboard.

C-2. On Screen C, the complete title of book number 1 cannot fit in the space provided. What could you do to see the complete title on the screen?

____

____

____

C-3. Give and explain one advantage of using a computer catalog over a card catalog.

____

____

____

D. Using the *Readers' Guide to Periodical Literature.* Study the following samples of entries on the War of 1812 in the *Readers' Guide.* Then answer the questions.

Sample A

New Orleans, Battle of, 1815

Carry me back to 1815. C.G. Roberts. il *Southern Living* v31 p12 Ja '96

Sample B

United States—History—War of 1812—Naval operations

Commerce raider [Prince de Neufchâtel privateering vessel] J.S. Gordon. il *American Heritage* v46 p20+ S '95

Sample C

Lake Erie, Battle of, 1813

The battle of Lake Erie. B. Gilbert. bibl (p126) il por map *Smithsonian* v25 p24–8+ Ja '95

Sample D

Hunt, Gilbert J.

The Battle of New Orleans (King James Version) [excerpt from The historical reader, biblical-style history; with introd. by Margaret Fortier] il *American History Illustrated* v28 p50–3 N/D '93

Write the letter of the correct choice on the line next to the number of each question.

_____ 1. Which article was published in 1996?
(*a*) Sample A (*c*) Sample C
(*b*) Sample B (*d*) Sample D

_____ 2. Which two articles were published in the same year?
(*a*) Samples A and B (*c*) Samples B and C
(*b*) Samples A and D (*d*) Samples C and D

_____ 3. Which sample is an entry by author rather than by subject?
(*a*) A (*b*) B (*c*) C (*d*) D

_____ 4. In which volume of *American Heritage* was the article "Commerce Raider" published?
(*a*) 12 (*b*) 18 (*c*) 33 (*d*) 46

_____ 5. Which magazine is published bimonthly?
(*a*) *American Heritage*
(*b*) *American History Illustrated*
(*c*) *Smithsonian*
(*d*) *Southern Living*

_____ 6. Which symbol means that an article is continued on later pages of the same issue?
(*a*) + (*c*) /
(*b*) : (*d*) '

____ 7. Which article contains a map and a portrait?
(a) Sample A *(c)* Sample C
(b) Sample B *(d)* Sample D

____ 8. On which page of *Southern Living* does the article by C.G. Roberts appear?
(a) 12 *(c)* 54
(b) 31 *(d)* 96

____ 9. Which topic is the subject of two articles?
(a) Privateering
(b) Battle of New Orleans
(c) Southern living
(d) Battle of Lake Erie

____ 10. The article in Sample C is found on
(a) four pages.
(b) five pages.
(c) fewer than four pages.
(d) more than five pages.

E. Using the Card Catalog. Study the following card catalog entries, all of which deal with the same book. Then answer the questions.

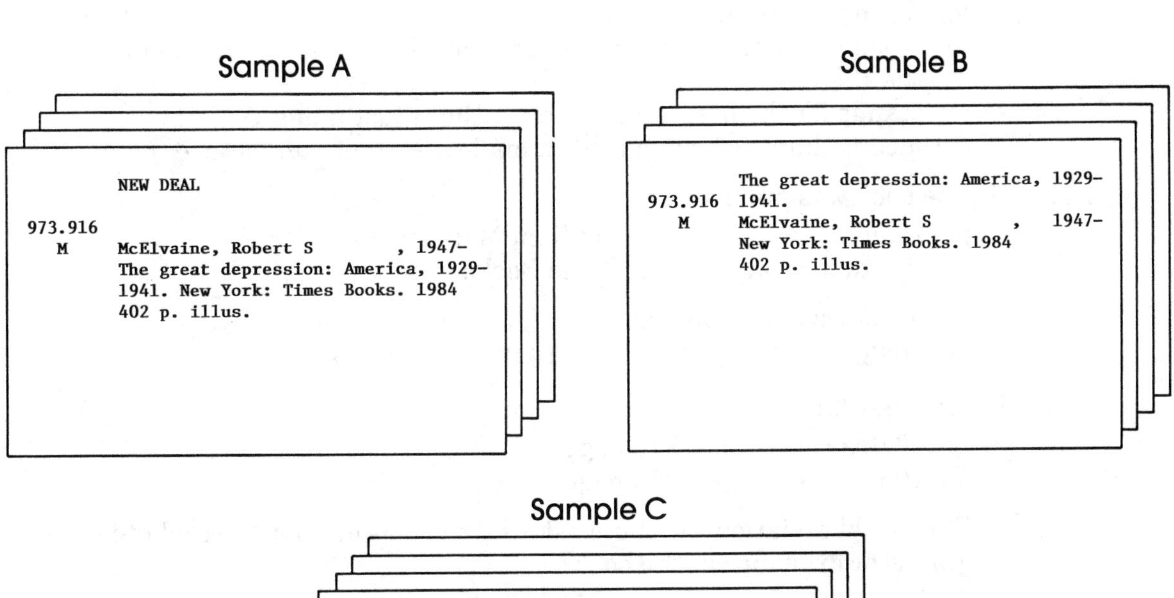

Sample A

NEW DEAL
973.916
M McElvaine, Robert S , 1947-
The great depression: America, 1929-
1941. New York: Times Books. 1984
402 p. illus.

Sample B

The great depression: America, 1929-
973.916 1941.
M McElvaine, Robert S , 1947-
New York: Times Books. 1984
402 p. illus.

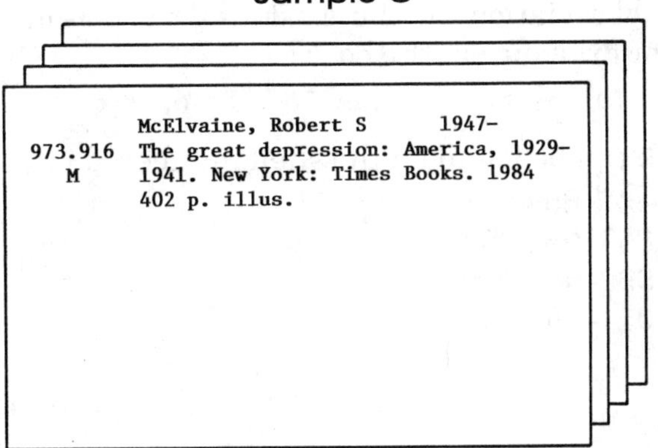

Sample C

McElvaine, Robert S 1947-
973.916 The great depression: America, 1929-
M 1941. New York: Times Books. 1984
402 p. illus.

Write the letter of the correct choice on the line next to the number of each question.

_____ 1. Sample A is

(a) a title card.
(b) a subject card.
(c) an author card.
(d) none of the above.

_____ 2. The complete title of the book is

(a) *The New Deal.*
(b) *The Great Depression.*
(c) *America, 1929–1941.*
(d) *The Great Depression: America, 1929–1941.*

_____ 3. Robert S. McElvaine is the author of the book. You can find an author card for this book in a card catalog drawer marked

(a) McCa–McGR.
(b) McGU–McMA.
(c) MAB–MOC.
(d) MOD–MRS.

_____ 4. According to the card catalog, the author

(a) was born during the Great Depression.
(b) is still alive.
(c) is dead.
(d) died during the Great Depression.

_____ 5. The M under the number 973.916

(a) has no meaning at all.
(b) means that there are more books on the Great Depression on the shelves.
(c) stands for the first letter of the author's last name.
(d) means that the book has been made into a motion picture.

_____ 6. The book was published by

(a) Doubleday.
(b) Bantam Books.
(c) William Morrow.
(d) Time Books.

_____ 7. The book was published in

(a) 1929. *(b)* 1941. *(c)* 1947. *(d)* 1984.

_____ 8. The book has

(a) 402 pages.
(b) 408 pages.
(c) 916 pages.
(d) 973 pages.

_____ 9. Which abbreviation on the cards tells you that there are photographs or drawings in the book?

(a) S *(b)* M *(c)* illus. *(d)* p.

_____ 10. The book can be found on the shelf numbered

(a) 900–921.854
(b) 921.855–951.998
(c) 951.999–980.010
(d) 980.011–999.999

F. Using the Computer Catalog. Study the following screens from a computer catalog using a mouse. Then answer the questions.

Screen A

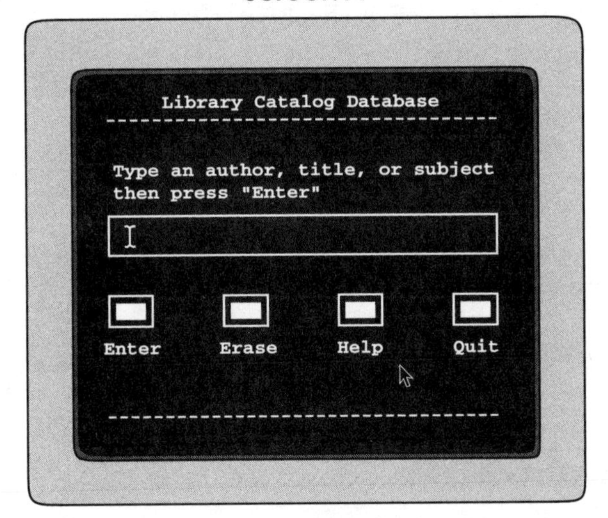

Screen B

Library Catalog Database

14 items containing "Great Depression"

Go Back
Help

Screen C

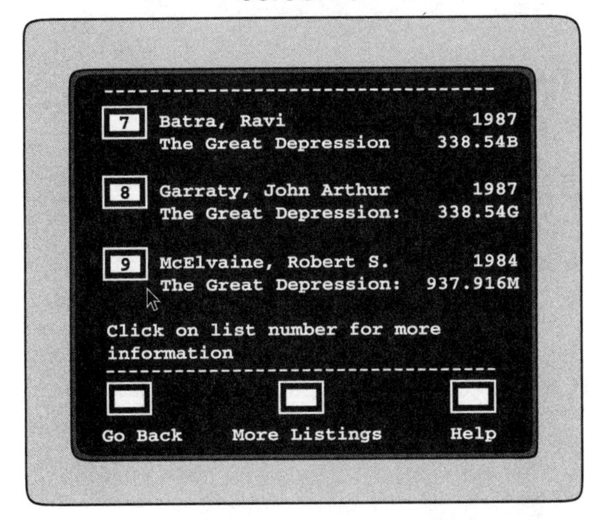

Screen D

Title: The Great Depression: America, 1929-1941.
Author: McElvaine, Robert S., 1947-
Publisher: New York, N.Y.: Times Book, 1984.
Description: 402p. illus.
Subject(s): Depression, U.S., 1929
New Deal, 1933-1812
Status: two copies, one checked out

Go Back
New Search
Help

F-1. Write the letter of the correct choice on the line next to the number of each question.

____ 1. The person using this computer was searching for a book by
  (a) year of publication.
  (b) card catalog number.
  (c) subject.
  (d) publisher.

_____ 2. To find a book by author, you would begin by typing in
(a) the author's first name, last name, and then clicking the icon above Enter.
(b) the author's last name, comma, first name, and then clicking the icon above Enter.
(c) the author's last name and then the title of the book.
(d) the author's last name and then clicking the icon above Help.

_____ 3. How many books does the library have containing information on the Great Depression?
(a) 3 *(c)* 14
(b) 9 *(d)* 38

_____ 4. Screen C does not give you the complete titles of the three books listed. You can learn the complete title of any of the books by
(a) clicking the icon next to More Listings.
(b) going to Screen B.
(c) going to Screen A.
(d) clicking on number 7, 8, or 9.

_____ 5. If you were on Screen B and wanted to see Screen A, you would
(a) click on the Go Back icon.
(b) type the letter A on the keyboard.
(c) click on the Quit icon.
(d) type Go Back on the keyboard.

_____ 6. How many copies of *The Great Depression: America, 1929–1941* does this library own?
(a) none *(c)* two
(b) one *(d)* three

_____ 7. How many copies of *The Great Depression: America, 1929–1941* are available to be taken out of the library?
(a) one *(c)* three
(b) two *(d)* four

_____ 8. If Screen D showed that no copy of *The Great Depression: America, 1929–1941* was available, you could look for another book on the same subject by
(a) starting a new search on Screen A.
(b) looking for new references on Screen B.
(c) going back to Screen C.
(d) clicking the Help icon on Screen D.

_____ 9. The complete title of book number 7 is *The Great Depression of 1990.* From this fact, you should realize that
(a) book 7 was published in 1990.
(b) the term Great Depression has been used to describe more than one period in U.S. history.
(c) all the items containing 'Great Depression' refer to the same period in U.S. history.
(d) we are living in the Great Depression today.

____ 10. Using a mouse
(*a*) means never having to type.
(*b*) requires two hands.
(*c*) slows down your search for a book.
(*d*) replaces using function keys.

F-2. List four words or phrases from Screen D that could be typed in Screen A to begin your search for *The Great Depression: America, 1929–1941.*

1. ______________________________

2. ______________________________

3. ______________________________

4. ______________________________

G. Using the *Readers' Guide.* Study the following examples of entries on the New Deal taken from several volumes of the *Readers' Guide to Periodical Literature.* Then answer the questions.

Sample A

New Deal, 1933–1939

Prosperous paupers and affluent savages. N. Eberstadt. bibl *Society* v33 p17–25 Ja/F '96

Sample B

New Deal, 1933–1939

The New Deal on Thanksgiving [FDR's attempt to change date] il *Yankee* v59 p15 N '95

Sample C

United States—History—1933–1939

FDR's lessons for Clinton. M. Barone. il pors *U.S. News & World Report* v118 p35–6 Ap 17 '95

Sample D

Goodwin, Doris Kearns

Echoes of FDR. por *Newsweek* v125 p31 Ap 10 '95

Sample E

United States—History—1933–1945

The Man of the Century [F.D. Roosevelt] A.M. Schlesinger. il pors *American Heritage* v45 p82–8+ My/Je '94

Write the letter of the correct choice on the line next to the number of each question.

____ 1. Three of the articles were published in
(*a*) 1933. (*c*) 1995.
(*b*) 1994. (*d*) 1996.

_____ 2. In which magazine did the article "The Man of the Century" appear?
(*a*) *American Heritage*
(*b*) *Newsweek*
(*c*) *Society*
(*d*) *U.S. News & World Report*

_____ 3. Which two magazines are published bimonthly?
(*a*) *American Heritage* and *Newsweek*
(*b*) *Newsweek* and *Yankee*
(*c*) *Yankee* and *Society*
(*d*) *Society* and *American Heritage*

_____ 4. In which volume of *Newsweek* was the article "Echoes of FDR" published?
(*a*) 46 (*c*) 152
(*b*) 125 (*d*) 195

_____ 5. Which article contains a picture or portrait?
(*a*) Sample A (*c*) Sample C
(*b*) Sample B (*d*) Sample D

_____ 6. Which two articles were published in the same month?
(*a*) Samples A and B
(*b*) Samples B and C
(*c*) Samples C and D
(*d*) Samples D and E

_____ 7. On which pages of *Society* does the article by N. Eberstadt appear?
(*a*) 17 to 25 (*c*) 82 to 88
(*b*) 35 and 36 (*d*) 94 to 96

_____ 8. Which article was published in November 1995?
(*a*) Sample A (*c*) Sample D
(*b*) Sample B (*d*) Sample E

_____ 9. Which sample does not give the author of the article?
(*a*) B (*c*) D
(*b*) C (*d*) E

_____ 10. Doris Kearns Goodwin is
(*a*) the subject of one of the articles.
(*b*) the author of one of the articles.
(*c*) the editor of *American Heritage.*
(*d*) the editor of *Newsweek.*

CHAPTER 15

Using Reference Books

One of the easiest ways to find detailed information on almost any subject is to use *reference books.* The ones most commonly used are encyclopedias, almanacs, atlases, fact books, and dictionaries. Reference books contain so much information on so many topics that you would not want to read them in their entirety. You just look up the information you need.

In a library, reference books are found in an area marked REFERENCE. They cannot be taken out of the library because so many people need them. Your library will probably have several different sets of encyclopedias and different kinds of almanacs, atlases, fact books, and dictionaries. If you don't find the information you want in one encyclopedia or almanac, you may find it in another.

Let us learn how to make the best use of reference books. Imagine that your teacher has asked each student to prepare a *portfolio* on one state in the United States. (A portfolio is a collection of related papers and pictures.) You have been assigned Alaska. There are many ways in which you could gather detailed information about Alaska. Begin by looking in the library at the most commonly used reference books.

Encyclopedias

An *encyclopedia* is probably the best reference book with which to start your search because it gives detailed information on almost every subject. Subjects in an encyclopedia are arranged in alphabetical order. An encyclopedia is usually divided into several books, or volumes. Volume 1 contains subjects starting with the letter "A." Subjects starting with other letters are in later volumes. The letter is printed in the back end, or spine, of the volume so that you know where to look for a certain subject. For example, in volume A you would find in alphabetical order the article on Alaska.

Sometimes there are too many subjects beginning with one letter to be contained in one volume. In that case, the information is spread over two volumes. For example, one volume may include subjects starting with the letters "Oa" and going to the letters "Om." The next volume would cover the subjects from "On" to "Oz." If there are too few subjects beginning with one letter to make up one volume, it might start with subjects beginning with one letter and end with those beginning with another letter. For example, a volume might be marked "Pr–Q." This means that the volume covers subjects starting with the letters "Pr," continues through the "P's," and then covers all subjects starting with "Q."

Some encyclopedias include a special index volume. It is usually the first or last volume. It lists in alphabetical order all the subjects covered in the encyclopedia. The index gives the volume and pages where each subject can be found. It also may tell you if an article contains illustrations.

Let us look at one encyclopedia in particular, *The World Book Encyclopedia.* The entire article on Alaska in *The World Book Encyclopedia* is 12 pages long. The last part, entitled *Study aids,* is given below. Most long articles in the encyclopedia have a *Study aids* section.

First, look at the **Outline** section of *Study aids.* It is an outline of the entire 12-page article. It shows that there are six major sections in the article: People, Visitor's guide, Land and climate, Economy, Government, and History. If you had the entire article in front of you, you would see that each section consists of paragraphs, perhaps pages, of information. You also would find maps, photographs, drawings, lists, and time lines to provide additional information and make the article more interesting. Notice also in the same excerpt

Study aids

Related articles in *World Book* include:

Biographies

Bartlett, Edward L.
Bering, Vitus
Gruening, Ernest
Muir, John
Seward, William H.

Cities and towns

Anchorage
Fairbanks
Juneau
Ketchikan
Nome
Sitka

History

Gold rush
Haida Indians
Klondike
Tlingit Indians

Physical features

Aleutian Islands
Arctic Ocean
Bering Sea
Coast Ranges
Inside Passage
Mount McKinley
Pacific Ocean
Pribilof Islands
Saint Elias Mountains
Yukon River

Other related articles

Alaska Highway
Aleuts
Arctic
Denali National Park
Elmendorf Air Force Base
Gates of the Arctic National Park
Glacier (picture)
Inuit
Kenai Fjords National Park
Kobuk Valley National Park
Lake Clark National Park
Wrangell-St. Elias National Park

Outline

I. People
- A. Population
- B. Schools
- C. Libraries and museums

II. Visitor's guide
- A. Places to visit
- B. Annual events

III. Land and climate
- A. Land regions
- B. Coastline
- C. Rivers and lakes
- D. Glaciers
- E. Plant and animal life
- F. Climate

IV. Economy
- A. Natural resources
- B. Service industries
- C. Mining
- D. Manufacturing
- E. Fishing industry
- F. Agriculture
- G. Fur industry
- H. Electric power
- I. Transportation
- J. Communication

V. Government
- A. Constitution
- B. Executive
- C. Legislature
- D. Courts
- E. Local government
- F. Revenue
- G. Politics

VI. History

Questions

What is Alaska's "Marine Highway"?
What are the basic units of local government?
Why do summer crops ripen quickly in central Alaska?
What is Alaska's most valuable mineral? What had been the state's most valuable mineral for many years?
What three groups of people lived in Alaska before Europeans arrived?
What part in Alaskan history was played by Vitus Bering? By William H. Seward?
What is the highest peak in North America? How high above sea level does it reach?
What part of Alaska was the only part of North America invaded during World War II?
Why did Alaska abolish its state income tax in 1980?

Additional resources

Level I

Fradin, Dennis B. *Alaska.* Childrens Pr., 1993.
Heinrichs, Ann. *Alaska.* 1990. Reprint. Childrens Pr., 1992.
Johnston, Joyce. *Alaska.* Lerner, 1994.
Murphy, Claire R. *A Child's Alaska.* Alaska Northwest, 1994.
Oberle, Joseph. *Anchorage.* Dillon Pr., 1990.
Wood, Ted. *Iditarod Dream.* Walker, 1996. Story of an Alaskan boy who raced in the Junior Iditarod.

Level II

Alaska Almanac. Alaska Northwest. An annual publication.
Bradley, Charles C. *Aleutian Echoes.* Univ. of Alaska Pr., 1994. Bradley's experiences in Alaska during World War II.
Fitzhugh, William W., and Chaussonnet, Valerie, eds. *Anthropology of the North Pacific Rim.* Smithsonian Institution, 1994. Discusses the Arctic cultures of Canada, Russia, and the United States.
Hedin, Robert, and Holthaus, G. H., eds. *Alaska: Reflections on Land and Spirit.* 1989. Reprint. Univ. of Ariz. Pr., 1994.
Hinckley, Ted C. *The Americanization of Alaska, 1867-1897.* Pacific Bks. 1972. Reprint. Pacific Bks., 1994.
Milepost editors. *Alaska A to Z.* Vernon Pubns., 1993.
Naske, Claus-Michael, and Slotnick, H. E. *Alaska.* 2nd ed. 1987. Reprint. Univ. of Okla. Pr., 1994.
Walker, Tom. *Alaska's Wildlife.* Graphic Arts Ctr., 1995.
Wayburn, Peggy. *Adventuring in Alaska.* Rev. ed. Sierra Club, 1994. A travel guide.

that there is a Questions section after the outline that will test you on important ideas and details included in the article.

Just in case the article on Alaska has not given you all the information you need, two other parts of the *Study aids* section may be of help. The first lists **Related articles**. These are articles found in other parts of the encyclopedia. Look for the name Seward, William H., under Biographies. Seward was the U.S. secretary of state responsible for the purchase of Alaska from Russia in 1867. If you want to know more about Seward, you can look up the related article on him. In which volume would you find it? His last name begins with "Se." One volume of *The World Book Encyclopedia* is marked "S–Sn." You would look in that volume.

At the very end of the *Study aids* section, there is a helpful list entitled **Additional resources**. These are books about Alaska. The list is divided into two categories: Level I gives less challenging books than Level II. Check the card catalog or computer catalog to see if your library owns these books.

Let us see how well you can use an encyclopedia. Answer the following questions based on the *Study aids* section of the article on Alaska.

1. What is the fastest way to find out what the article says about the natural resources of Alaska?

____

____

____

____

____

What did you write? The important point here is not to start at the beginning of the article and read every word until you come to natural resources. Check the outline. You will see that natural resources is the first topic in the section on the economy. Then flip to the page where the section on the economy begins, marked by the word ***Economy*** (in bold italic letters), and read about Alaska's natural resources. If your answer included this idea, you wrote a good response.

Let us continue by looking up the related article on William Seward. In volume "S–Sn," you will find the following article:

Seward, *SOO uhrd,* **William Henry** (1801-1872), served as United States secretary of state during the Civil War (1861-1865). He was the leading Republican in the nation in 1860, but Abraham Lincoln defeated him for the party's nomination. Seward worked for Lincoln's election and entered his Cabinet as secretary of state. Because of Seward's able administration of foreign affairs, European countries did not aid the Confederacy. He was wounded by an accomplice of John Wilkes Booth on the night that Lincoln was assassinated. He slowly recovered and continued as secretary of state under President Andrew Johnson.

Among the important tasks that Seward accomplished was the purchase of Alaska from Russia. Alaska later proved valuable to the United States and finally became a state in 1959. But at the time it was mockingly called "Seward's Folly" and "Seward's Icebox." See **Alaska** (American purchase).

Seward was born in Florida, New York, and attended Union College in Schenectady, New York. He became a lawyer in 1822. Seward won election to the state legislature in 1830 and joined the Whig Party about 1834 (see **Whig Party**). He served as governor of New York from 1839 to 1842 and became a United States senator in 1849. Seward opposed slavery and fought its spread.

Mark E. Neely, Jr.

See also **Johnson, Andrew** (Foreign relations); **Lincoln, Abraham** (Election of 1860; Foreign relations); **Trent Affair; Emancipation Proclamation** (picture).

Here are some important points about this article:

- **Seward, William Henry**—An article about a person is almost always listed with the person's last name printed first, followed by the first and middle names. You are given a pronunciation guide for the last name: *SOO uhrd. SOO* is capitalized so that you know to stress that sound.
- (1801–1872)—These dates show the years of Seward's birth (1801) and death (1872).

- Mark E. Neely, Jr.—This is the name of the person who wrote the article. It appears after the biographical section of the article.
- See also **Johnson, Andrew** (Foreign relations); **Lincoln, Abraham** (Election of 1860; Foreign relations); **Trent Affair; Emancipation Proclamation** (picture)—This section at the end of the article means that Seward is mentioned elsewhere in the encyclopedia. For example, you will find additional information about him in the articles on Andrew Johnson and Abraham Lincoln. In which volume of the encyclopedia would you find the article on Andrew Johnson?

Answer the following question:

_____ 2. In addition to the biographical article on William Seward, he is mentioned in *The World Book Encyclopedia* in at least
(a) three other articles.
(b) four other articles.
(c) five other articles
(d) six other articles.

Which answer did you choose? *The World Book Encyclopedia* tells you that there are related articles on a subject by writing "See," followed by the title of the related article. Within the Seward article, you will find "See **Alaska**" and "See **Whig Party**." There are also the four related articles listed at the end of the article: See **Johnson, Andrew**; **Lincoln, Abraham**; **Trent Affair**; and **Emancipation Proclamation**. Therefore, the answer to question 2 is *(d)*.

Dictionaries

The encyclopedia article about Seward mentions "Seward's Folly" and "Seward's Icebox." You probably know that iceboxes were used before refrigerators to keep food cold. But you may not know the meaning of "folly." To find out, you could use another important reference book, a *dictionary*. The most usual type of dictionary is an alphabetical list of words in a language with their meanings defined. Here is how the paperback edition of *The American Heritage Dictionary* defines "folly":

fol · ly (fŏl′ē) *n., pl.* **-lies. 1.** A lack of good sense, understanding, or foresight. **2.a.** An act or instance of foolishness. **b.** A costly undertaking having an absurd or ruinous outcome. [< OFr. *folie* < LLat. *follis,* FOOL.]

The entry shows that the word "fol • ly" is divided into two parts, or syllables. The respelling in parentheses shows how to pronounce the word. (On the same page in the dictionary is a key that indicates how to say each letter in the parentheses.) Next comes the part of speech, "n.," which means noun. Next, you learn that to write folly in the plural, you would drop the "y" and add "ies." Three meanings are then given. The entry ends with information on the word's origin (where it comes from); the "OFr." stands for Old French, so you know that folly comes from an Old French word, *folie,* meaning foolish.

The third meaning of folly is probably what most people meant when they called Alaska "Seward's Folly." Such an insulting term may make you want to learn more about Seward's purchase. You could check the computer catalog to see if the library has any biographies on William Seward, or you could use another kind of dictionary, the *Dictionary of American Biography.*

As you can tell from its title, the *Dictionary of American Biography* gives the life stories of famous Americans. It consists of 10 volumes (Volumes I through X). There are also additional volumes for biographies added to the collection. In Volume VIII, "Platt to Seward," you would find in alphabetical order a detailed article on the life of William Seward. The article covers eight pages and is too long to show in this book. You cannot take this reference book out of the library. Instead, you would make photocopies of the paragraphs or pages you want and put them in your portfolio.

Atlases

Earlier in this chapter, you learned that *The World Book* article on Alaska contains maps. A book that consists only of maps and information related to them is called an *atlas.* The maps may show the entire earth or only a small area of a country or a state. They may show boundaries, cities, and bodies of water. They may also show rainfall, products, altitude, and natural resources.

The maps in the *World Book* article are good, but they are all of modern Alaska. You, however, want to see what the size and shape of Alaska was when Seward bought it in 1867. To find out, you could use a special kind of atlas called a *historical atlas.* The map on page 172 is typical of maps in a historical atlas. It is taken from *The American Heritage Pictorial Atlas of United States History* and shows Alaska between 1867 and 1905. The key explains the symbols on the map.

Fact Books

You want the facts in your portfolio to be as accurate and interesting as the maps. Although the encyclopedia article on Alaska gives many interesting facts, you can also use specialized *fact books.* They contain many lists and charts (words and numbers arranged to show information on a given subject clearly and simply). One such fact book is *Facts About the Cities.* It contains detailed information about major U.S. cities on such topics as climate, population, the economy, housing, education, taxes, crime, transportation, health, tourism, and cultural resources. See the excerpt opposite from the section on Juneau, the capital of Alaska.

POPULATION

	1990	% change 1980–90	1992
Central City	26,751	36.99%	28,364

White: 80.91%
Black: 1.03%
Amer. Indian: 12.90%
Asian: 4.35%
Other: 0.80%
Hispanic: 2.51%
Male: 50.64%
Median age: 31.9
17 and under: 29.47%
65 and over: 5.18%

Native-born population: 95.15%
Language other than English spoken at home: 6.71%
Spanish spoken at home: 1.44%

ECONOMY

Total businesses (1992): 3,099
% of total state businesses: 10.3%
Labor force (16+ years): 15,405
% of total pop: 78.7%
Males: 8,124
Females: 7,281
Armed forces: 191
Civilian: 15,214
Employed: 14,482
% of total labor force: 94.01%
Unemployed: 732
% of total labor force unemployed: 4.75%
Employment by industry: 6,669; % by type:
Agriculture, forestry, & fisheries: 4.14%
Mining: 3.00%
Construction: 5.19%
Manufacturing: 2.35%
Transportation: 6.62%
Communications/public utilities: 1.87%
Wholesale and retail trade: 15.93%
Financial, insurance & real estate: 3.08%
Services, all: 29.46%
Public administration: 28.37%
Government employment: 6,737; % by type:
Local: 22.1%
State: 60.2%
Federal: 17.7%
Self-employed: 1,056
Unpaid family workers: 20

Excerpted from *Facts About the Cities,* Second Edition.

Almanacs

As good as encyclopedias, atlases, and fact books are, they are mostly hardcover books and, therefore, expensive. Not all libraries can afford new ones every year. An easy way to find the latest facts is to look in an *almanac.* Almanacs are published yearly so that their facts and figures are up to date. Because they are usually paperbound, they are less expensive than hardcover books.

An almanac contains in one volume useful and interesting facts and figures about many subjects. You will find information on art, business, countries of the world, education, entertainment, farming, geography, history, industry, religion, science, and sports, among other subjects.

Alaska Territory, 1867–1905 (without the westernmost Aleutian Islands)

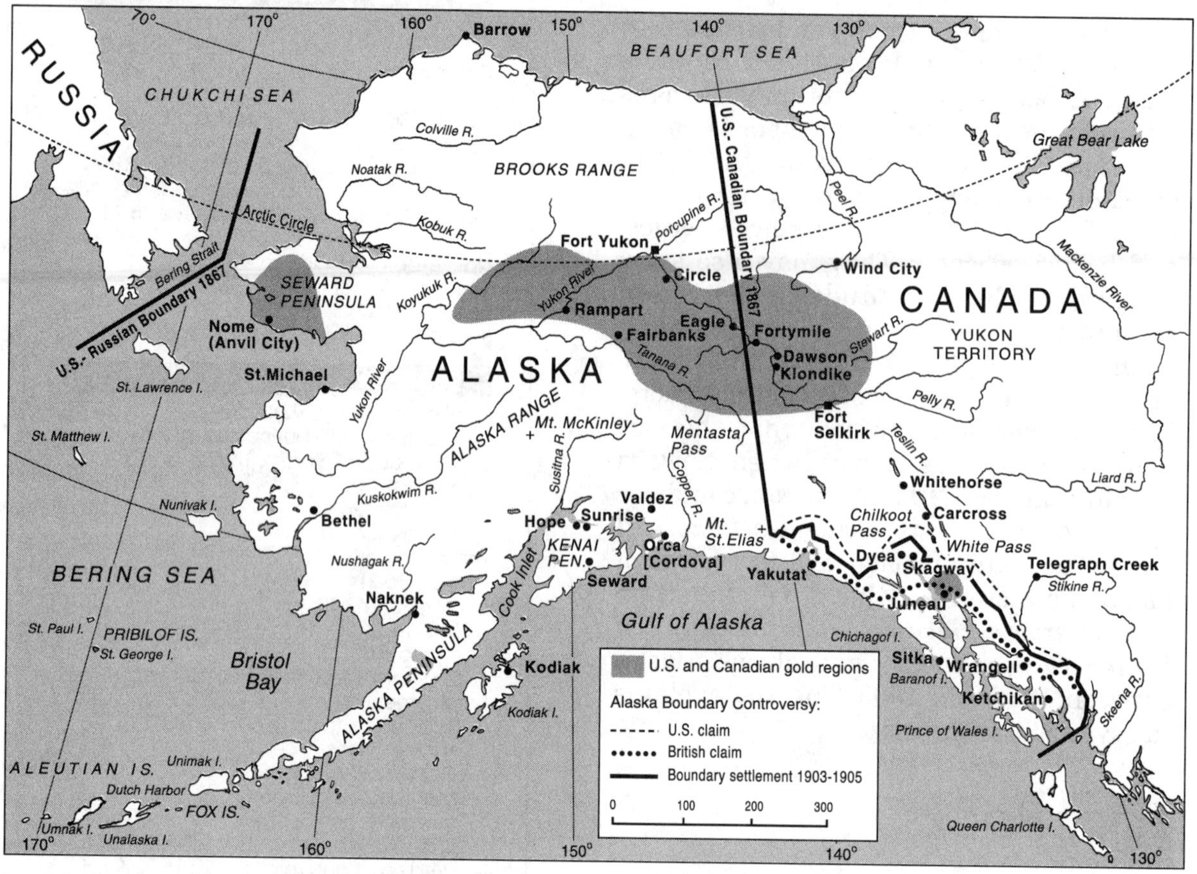

Courtesy The American Heritage Picture Collection (adapted).

Another area covered in almanacs is the states of the United States. An article on Alaska in an encyclopedia covers many pages. An article on Alaska in an almanac gives only the essential facts on one or two pages. For example, the article on Alaska on page 173 is from *The 1998 World Almanac and Book of Facts.*

Let us see what you have learned about reference books.

_____ 3. You want a brief history of Alaska, the latest population figures, and the latest figures on the number of people unemployed. The best reference book from which to learn all this is

(*a*) an encyclopedia.
(*b*) a dictionary.
(*c*) an almanac.
(*d*) an atlas.

Which answer did you choose? All of these reference books might supply the information. But you want the very latest information available in the briefest form. The best choice would be an almanac. Its articles are brief, and it is published every year. Therefore, the answer to question 3 is (*c*).

Many other reference books exist in the library. There are shelves of them that can supply you with information on any subject you can imagine. They could surely supply you with a great deal of information for your Alaska portfolio or any other school project.

The following exercises will give you more practice in using the major reference books found in libraries.

Alaska

The Last Frontier (unofficial)

People. Population (1996): 607,007; rank: 48; **Net change** (1990-96): 10.4%. **Pop. density:** (1990) 1.0 per sq mi. **Racial/ethnic distrib.** (1990): 75.5% white; 4.1% black; 15.6% Amer. Indian, Eskimo or Aleut; 3.6% Asian or Pacific Is.; 3.2% Hispanic.

Geography. Total area: 656,424 sq mi; rank: 1. **Land area:** 570,374 sq mi; rank: 1. **Acres forested land:** 129,131,000. **Location:** NW corner of North America, bordered on east by Canada. **Climate:** SE, SW, and central regions, moist and mild; far north extremely dry. Extended summer days, winter nights, throughout. **Topography:** includes Pacific and Arctic mountain systems, central plateau, and Arctic slope. Mt. McKinley, 20,320 ft, is the highest point in North America. **Capital:** Juneau.

Economy. Principal industries: petroleum, tourism, fishing, mining, forestry, transportation, aerospace. **Principal manufactured goods:** fish products, lumber and pulp, furs. **Agriculture: Chief crops:** barley, oats, hay, silage, potatoes, lettuce. **Livestock** (1996): 10,200 cattle; (1995) 30,000 reindeer; 2,000 hogs. **Timber/lumber:** spruce, yellow cedar, hemlock. **Nonfuel minerals** (est. 1996): $523 mil; zinc, gold, silver, tin, lead, sand & gravel, crushed stone. **Commercial fishing** (1996): $1.2 bil. **Chief ports:** Anchorage, Dutch Harbor, Kodiak, Seward, Skagway, Juneau, Sitka, Valdez, Wrangell. **International airports at:** Anchorage, Fairbanks, Juneau. **Value of construction** (1996): $1.0 bil. **Employment distribution** (1996): 27.7% govt.; 23.7% serv.; 20.7% trade. **Per capita personal income** (1996): $24,558. **Unemployment** (1996): 7.8%. **Tourism** (1994): $863 mil.

Finance. FDIC-insured commercial banks & trust companies (1996): 8. **Deposits:** $4.2 bil. **FDIC-insured savings institutions** (1996): 2. **Assets:** $243 mil.

Federal government. No. federal civilian employees (Mar. 1996): 11,611. **Avg. salary:** $41,547.

Energy. Electricity production (1996, kWh, by source): Coal: 229 mil; Petroleum: 1.5 bil; Gas: 2.9 bil; Hydroelectric: 1.2 bil.

Education. Pupil-teacher ratio(1995): 17.3. **Avg. teachers' salary** (1996-97): $50,647.

State data. Motto: North to the future. **Flower:** Forget-Me-Not. **Bird:** Willow ptarmigan. **Tree:** Sitka spruce. **Song:** Alaska's Flag. **Entered union** Jan. 3, 1959; rank, 49th. **State fair** at Palmer; late Aug.-early Sept.

History. Early inhabitants were the Tlingit-Haida people and tribes of the Athabascan family. The Aleut and Inuit (Eskimo), who arrived about 4,000 years ago from Siberia, lived in the coastal areas. Vitus Bering, a Danish explorer working for Russia, was the first European to land in Alaska, 1741. The first permanent Russian settlement was established on Kodiak Island, 1784. In 1799, the Russian-American Co. controlled the region, and the first chief manager, Aleksandr Baranov, set up headquarters at Archangel, near present-day Sitka. Sec. of State William H. Seward bought Alaska from Russia for $7.2 mil in 1867, a bargain some called "Seward's Folly." In 1896, gold was discovered in the Klondike region, and the famed gold rush began. Alaska became a territory in 1912.

Tourist attractions. Inside Passage; Portage Glacier; Mendenhall Glacier; Ketchikan Totems; Glacier Bay Natl. Park and Preserve; Denali Natl. Park, one of N. America's great wildlife sanctuaries, surrounding Mt. McKinley, N. America's highest peak; Mt. Roberts Tramway, Juneau; Pribilof Islands fur seal rookeries; restored St. Michael's Russian Orthodox Cathedral, Sitka; Katmai Natl. Park & Preserve.

Famous Alaskans. Tom Bodett, Susan Butcher, Ernest Gruening, Gov. Tony Knowles, Sydney Laurence, Libby Riddles, Jefferson "Soapy" Smith.

Tourist information. Alaska Division of Tourism, PO Box 110801, Juneau, AK 99811-0801; 1-907-465-2010.

Web site: http://www.state.ak.us

USING YOUR SKILLS

A. Choosing the best reference book. Which reference book would you look at first to find the following information?

Mark E for encyclopedia, D for dictionary, AT for atlas, or AL for almanac.

____ 1. The names of the two U.S. senators representing your state.

____ 2. A description of Inuit life in Alaska.

____ 3. The meaning of the word "Inuit."

____ 4. Styles of churches, synagogues, and mosques built in the United States.

____ 5. The boundary lines of the United States in 1848 and today.

____ 6. The name of the most recent winner of the Nobel Peace Prize.

____ 7. A history of baseball in the United States.

____ 8. The source of the Mississippi River.

____ 9. The origin of the word "peninsula."

____ 10. The population of Chicago for the last 50 years.

B. Using the Encyclopedia. Read the following *Study aids* section from an encyclopedia article on Hawaii. Then answer the questions.

Study aids

Related articles in ***World Book*** include:

Biographies

Cook, James
Damien de Veuster, Joseph
Dole, Sanford Ballard
Kamehameha I
Liliuokalani, Lydia K.

History

Asian Americans (History of Asian immigration)
Cleveland, Grover (Foreign affairs)
Pacific Islands
World War II (Japan attacks)

Military installations

Camp H. M. Smith
Fort Shafter
Hickam Air Force Base
Pearl Harbor Naval Base

Physical features

Kilauea
Mauna Kea
Mauna Loa
Pacific Ocean
Volcano

Other related articles

Flower (picture: Colorful leis)
Haleakala National Park
Hawaii, University of
Hawaii Volcanoes National Park
Hawaiian honeycreeper
Hilo
Honolulu
Nene
Surfing
United States (picture: Waimea Canyon)

Outline

I. People
A. Population
B. Language
C. Clothing
D. Food
E. Dancing and music
F. Schools
G. Libraries
H. Museums

II. Visitor's guide
A. Places to visit
B. Annual events

III. Land and climate
A. Hawaii
B. Maui
C. Kahoolawe
D. Molokai
E. Lanai
F. Oahu
G. Kauai
H. Niihau
I. Climate

IV. Economy
A. Natural resources
B. Service industries
C. Manufacturing
D. Agriculture
E. Mining
F. Fishing industry
G. Electric power
H. Transportation
I. Communication

V. Government
A. Constitution
B. Executive
C. Legislature
D. Courts
E. Local government
F. Revenue
G. Politics

VI. History

Questions

What are the eight main islands of Hawaii?
How and when were the islands first united?
Why are airplanes so important in Hawaii?
When did Hawaii become a state?
What is the chief crop of Hawaii?
What are the main features of the Hawaiian language?
What are Hawaii's largest service industries?
Why is Pearl Harbor important in U.S. history?
Who were the first people in Hawaii?
Why is Hawaii called the *Aloha State*?

Additional resources

Level I

Feeney, Stephanie, and Fielding, Ann. *Sand to Sea: Marine Life of Hawaii.* Univ. of Hawaii Pr., 1989.
McNair, Sylvia. *Hawai'i.* Childrens Pr., 1990.
Rayson, Ann. *Modern Hawaiian History.* Bess Pr., 1984.
Siy, Alexandra. *Hawaiian Islands.* Dillon Pr., 1991.

Level II

Budnick, Rich. *Stolen Kingdom.* Aloha Pr., 1992.
Culliney, John L. *Islands in a Far Sea: Nature and Man in Hawaii.* Sierra Club, 1988.
Daws, Gavan. *Shoal of Time: A History of the Hawaiian Islands.* 1968. Reprint. Univ. of Hawaii Pr., 1974.
Forbes, David W. *Encounters with Paradise.* Univ. of Hawaii Pr., 1992. Art portraying the Hawaiian islands from 1778 to 1941.
Nordyke, Eleanor C. *The Peopling of Hawaii.* 2nd ed. Univ. of Hawaii Pr., 1989.
Tregaskis, Mona. *Hawaii.* Compass Am. Guides, 1992.
Walker, Steven L., and Majorin, M. P. *Hawaiian Islands.* Camelback Design Grp., 1992.
Wright, Thomas L., and others. *Hawaii Volcano Watch: A Pictorial History.* Univ. of Hawaii Pr., 1992.

B-1. Write the letter of the correct choice on the line next to the number of each question.

____ 1. You would find this excerpt in the volume of the encyclopedia marked

(*a*) A
(*b*) H
(*c*) Q–R
(*d*) S–Sn

_____ 2. The subject of this excerpt is
(a) the early history of Hawaii.
(b) the economy of Hawaii.
(c) the many uses of an encyclopedia.
(d) study aids relating to the article on Hawaii.

_____ 3. You can see all the topics discussed in the article on Hawaii in the section labeled
(a) Related articles. *(c)* Questions.
(b) Outline. *(d)* Additional resources.

_____ 4. If you quickly wanted to find the number of schools in Hawaii, you would look in the section of the article with the heading
(a) People. *(c)* Government.
(b) Economy. *(d)* History.

_____ 5. In which section of the article could you find the answer to the first question in the list of questions?
(a) People *(c)* Land and climate
(b) Visitor's guide *(d)* Economy

B-2. This excerpt tells you how to find more information on Hawaii in two ways. Name them and explain how they are different.

1. ____

____

____

____

2. ____

____

____

____

C. Using the Encyclopedia. Read the following encyclopedia article on Queen Liliuokalani of Hawaii. Then answer the questions.

Liliuokalani, *lee LEE oo oh kah LAH nee,* **Lydia Kamekeha,** *LIHD ee uh KAH meh KEH hah* (1838-1917), reigned as queen of Hawaii from 1891 to 1893. She became queen after the death of her brother, King David Kalakaua. In 1893 Liliuokalani tried to restore some of the monarchy's power through the political movement called Oni Pa'a (Stand Firm). But American settlers who controlled most of Hawaii's wealth disapproved of the queen's efforts and revolted against her. A republic was established in 1894. United States President Grover Cleveland tried in vain to restore Liliuokalani to her throne. Hawaii became a U.S. territory in 1898.

Liliuokalani made two trips to the United States after she lost her throne. She is perhaps best known today for her song, "Aloha Oe," which became Hawaii's traditional farewell song. She was born in Honolulu, Hawaii.

Edward A. Lukes-Lukaszewski

See also **Dole, Sanford Ballard; Hawaii** (History).

Write the letter of the correct choice on the line next to the number of each question.

____ 1. You would find this article in the volume of the encyclopedia marked
(a) D *(c)* L
(b) H *(d)* U • V

____ 2. The author of this article is
(a) Edward A. Lukes-Lukaszewski.
(b) Sanford Ballard Dole.
(c) David Kalakaua.
(d) Lydia Kamekeha Liliuokalani.

____ 3. In using the pronunciation guide after the article's title, capitalized letters should be stressed. Large capitalized letters should be stressed more than small capitalized letters. Therefore, the correct pronunciation of Liliuokalani's name is
(a) LEE lee oo oh KAH lah nee. *(c)* LEE lee oo oh kah lah NEE.
(b) lee LEE oo oh kah lah nee. *(d)* lee LEE oo oh kah LAH nee.

____ 4. Liliuokalani was queen of Hawaii from
(a) 1838 to 1917. *(c)* 1894 to 1898.
(b) 1891 to 1893. *(d)* 1898 to 1917.

____ 5. Liliuokalani is mentioned in at least
(a) two other articles in the encyclopedia.
(b) three other articles in the encyclopedia.
(c) four other articles in the encyclopedia.
(d) five other articles in the encyclopedia.

D. Read the following statement and dictionary entry. Then answer the questions.

Statement

All 50 states have mottoes. The motto of Alaska is: North to the future. The motto of Hawaii is: The life of the land is perpetuated in righteousness. Do you know the motto of your state? If you do not understand such words as "motto," "perpetuated," and "righteousness," you can find their meanings in a dictionary. Here is *The American Heritage Dictionary* entry for "motto."

Dictionary entry

mot · to (mŏt′ō) *n., pl.* **-toes** or **-tos. 1.** A brief statement used to express a principle, a goal, or an ideal. See Synonyms at **saying. 2.** A sentence, phrase, or word of appropriate character inscribed on or attached to an object. **3.** A maxim adopted as a guide to one's conduct. [Italian, word, motto, probably from Vulgar Latin* *mōttum,* word. See MOT.]

Write the letter of the correct choice on the line next to the number of each question.

____ 1. The word "motto" has
(*a*) two syllables. (*c*) four syllables.
(*b*) three syllables. (*d*) five syllables.

____ 2. Its part of speech is
(*a*) a noun. (*b*) a verb. (*c*) an adjective. (*d*) an adverb.

____ 3. From which language does the word "motto" come?
(*a*) French (*b*) Spanish (*c*) Italian (*d*) Japanese

____ 4. How many meanings are given for "motto"?
(*a*) one (*b*) three (*c*) five (*d*) seven

____ 5. The respelling (mŏt´ō) of the word "motto" shows its
(*a*) original language. (*c*) most important meaning.
(*b*) part of speech. (*d*) pronunciation.

E. Study the following article on Hawaii from *The 1998 World Almanac and Book of Facts.* Then answer the questions.

Hawai'i

Aloha State

People. Population (1996): 1,183,723; rank: 41; **Net change** (1990-96): 6.8%. **Pop. density:** (1990) 172.5 per sq mi. **Racial/ethnic distrib.** (1990): 33.4% white; 2.5% black; 61.8% Asian or Pacific Is.; 7.3% Hispanic.

Geography. Total area: 10,932 sq mi; rank: 43. **Land area:** 6,423 sq mi; rank: 47. **Acres forested land:** 1,748,000. **Location:** Hawaiian Islands lie in the North Pacific, 2,397 mi SW from San Francisco. **Climate:** subtropical, with wide variations in rainfall; Waialeale, on Kaua'i, wettest spot in U.S. (annual rainfall 460 in.) **Topography:** islands are tops of a chain of submerged volcanic mountains; active volcanoes: Mauna Loa, Kilauea. **Capital:** Honolulu.

Economy. Principal industries: tourism, defense, sugar, pineapples. **Principal manufactured goods:** processed sugar, canned pineapple, clothing, foods, printing and publishing. **Chief crops:** sugar, pineapples, macadamia nuts, fruits, coffee, vegetables, floriculture. **Livestock** (1996): 171,000 cattle and calves; 28,000 hogs/pigs; 870,000 chickens. **Nonfuel minerals** (est. 1996): $112 mil; mostly crushed stone, cement. **Commercial fishing** (1996): $64 mil. **Chief ports:** Honolulu, Nawiliwili, Barbers Point, Kahului, Hilo. **International airport at:** Honolulu. **Value of construction** (1996): $1.8 bil. **Employment distribution** (1995): 25.4% trade; 3.2% mfg.; 36.9% serv.; 20.1% govt. **Per capita personal income** (1996): $25,159. **Unemployment** (1996): 6.4%. **Tourism** (1995): $11.6 bil.

Finance. FDIC-insured commercial banks & trust companies (1996): 14. **Deposits:** $15.2 bil. **FDIC-insured savings institutions** (1996): 5. **Assets:** $6.6 bil.

Federal government. No. federal civilian employees (Mar. 1996): 20,539. **Avg. salary:** $38,814. **Notable federal facilities:** Pearl Harbor Naval Shipyard; Hickam AFB; Schofield Barracks; Ft. Shafter; Marine Corps Base-Kaneohe Bay; Barbers Point NAS; Wheeler AFB; Prince Kuhio Federal Building.

Energy. Electricity production (1996, kWh, by source): Petroleum: 6.4 bil; Hydroelectric: 18 mil.

Public education. Student-teacher ratio (1995): 17.8. **Avg. teachers' salary** (1996-97): $35,842.

State data. Motto: The life of the land is perpetuated in righteousness. **Flower:** Yellow hibiscus. **Bird:** Hawaiian goose. **Tree:** Kukui (Candlenut). **Song:** Hawai'i Pono'i. **Entered union** Aug. 21, 1959; rank, 50th. **State fair:** State Fair in June and State Farm Fair in July.

History. Polynesians from islands 2,000 mi to the south settled the Hawaiian Islands, probably between AD 300 and AD 600. The first European visitor was British captain James Cook, 1778. Between 1790 and 1810, the islands were united politically under the leadership of a native king, Kamehameha I, whose five successors—all bearing the name Kamehameha—ruled the kingdom from his death, 1819, until the end of the dynasty, 1872. Missionaries arrived, 1820, bringing Western culture. King Kamehameha III and his chiefs created the first constitution and a legislature that set up a public school system. Sugar production began, 1835, and it became the dominant industry. In 1893, Queen Liliuokalani was deposed, and a republic was instituted, 1894, headed by Sanford B. Dole. Annexation by the U.S. came in 1898. The Japanese attack on Pearl Harbor, Dec. 7, 1941, brought the U.S. into World War II.

Tourist attractions. Hawaii Volcanoes, Haleakala natl. parks; Natl. Memorial Cemetery of the Pacific, Waikiki Beach, Diamond Head, Honolulu; U.S.S. *Arizona* Memorial, Pearl Harbor; Hanauma Bay; Polynesian Cultural Center, Laie; Nu'uanu Pali; Waimea Canyon; Wailoa and Wailuku River state parks.

Famous Islanders. Bernice Pauahi Bishop, Tia Carrera, Father Damien de Veuster, Don Ho, Duke Kahanamoku, King Kamehameha, Brook Mahealani Lee, Daniel K. Inouye, Jason Scott Lee, Queen Liliuokalani, Bette Midler, Ellison Onizuka.

Chamber of Commerce of Hawaii. 1132 Bishop St., Suite 200, Honolulu, HI 96813.

Toll free travel information. 1-800-464-2924.

Web site: http://www.hawaii.gov

Write the letter of the correct choice on the line next to the number of each question.

_____ 1. The population figure of 1,183,723 is from the year
(a) 1994. *(c)* 1996.
(b) 1995. *(d)* 1997.

_____ 2. In 1990, 61.8 percent of the racial/ethnic distribution was
(a) white.
(b) black.
(c) Asian or Pacific Is. (Islanders).
(d) Hispanic.

_____ 3. Hawaii entered the Union (became a state) in
(a) 1828. *(c)* 1929.
(b) 1898. *(d)* 1959.

_____ 4. Which fact is unlikely to change in the next ten years?
(a) chief ports
(b) electricity production
(c) the number of chickens raised
(d) bank deposits

_____ 5. Mention of the U.S.S. *Arizona* Memorial occurs in the section entitled
(a) Geography.
(b) State data.
(c) History.
(d) Tourist attractions.

F. Specialized Reference Books. From the list provided, choose the best reference book for each of the following needs, and write the title on the line provided. One reference book will not be used.

Reference Books

American Jewish Year Book
The College Board Guide to High Schools
Dictionary of Asian-American History
The Encyclopedia of Fashion
Facts about the Cities
Family Law Dictionary
Historical Documents of Presidential Elections
Peterson's Paying Less for College
The Penguin Dictionary of Saints
The Timetables of African-American History
Transportation Through the Ages

1. You want to know how people dressed in colonial America.

____

2. You want to know the number of hospital beds in Detroit, Michigan.

____

3. You want to read a speech made by Ronald Reagan when he ran for president of the United States in 1980.

---

4. You want to know about the cost of going to college.

---

5. You want to know if men and women in your state have the same legal rights in a marriage.

---

6. You want to know when the first college for blacks opened in the United States.

---

7. You want to know the name of the first American-born saint of the Roman Catholic Church.

---

8. You want to know how the coming of the railroad changed the lives of Americans.

---

9. You want to know if the Jewish population in the United States is increasing or declining.

---

10. You want to read about the camps in the United States in which Japanese-Americans were held during World War II.

CHAPTER 16
Using the Internet

In the mid-1400s, Johannes Gutenberg made the first practical use of movable type. Soon afterwards, printing greatly changed the world of learning. Books on almost every subject became widely available.

In your lifetime, another innovation has greatly changed the world of learning. It is called the *Internet.* The Internet is a network of computers that uses a system known as the World Wide Web to provide information and resources on almost every subject. Anyone in the world with a computer connected to a *modem* and a telephone line can use the Internet. (A modem is a device that allows a computer to communicate with another computer over a telephone line.) The following picture shows a computer setup, with modem and telephone connections. In the picture, the modem is a separate device, but nowadays most computers are equipped with a modem, and the telephone line is plugged directly into the modem outlet at the back of the computer.

In the last chapter, you learned how to use reference books to do research for a school project. In this chapter, you will learn how to use the Internet to do research. As in the last chapter, let us say that you have to prepare a portfolio on a particular topic. Your assignment is to use the Internet to discover details about the White House, the home of the president of the United States. You are seated before a computer, either at school, the library, or home. If the school or the library computer has access to the Internet, the computer screen will display an icon that represents the Internet. Using the mouse, move the arrow on the screen to the icon. When you click the icon once or twice, the computer will connect to the Internet.

If you have a computer at home, you may not be able to gain access to the Internet automatically. Your home computer must be connected to a modem and telephone line. In addition, you must belong to a service that provides access to the Internet. Most people use, for a fee, an Internet Ser-

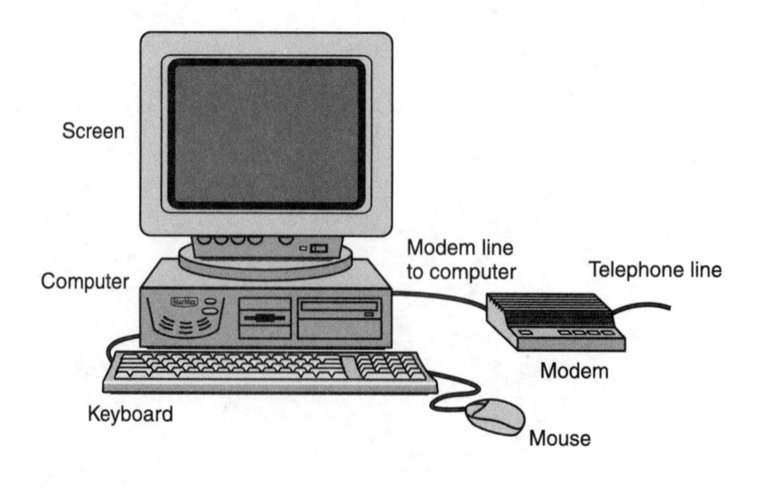

vice Provider (ISP) or an on-line service. An on-line service, such as America Online or Microsoft Network, usually provides more services than an Internet Service Provider. Therefore, on-line services usually cost more. Once you belong to an Internet Service Provider or an on-line service, an Internet icon will appear on your home computer screen. You would click it once or twice to gain access to the Internet.

The top of the first Internet screen that you access—and the top of every screen thereafter—will be similar to this one:

You will see the term Search (or Search the Internet or Search the World Wide Web). Click once or twice on the S in Search. (If the screen shows a search icon instead of the term Search, click on the icon.) A new screen will appear, presenting a list of search programs that will help you gather information on the White House. The list will probably include Yahoo!, AltaVista, and WebCrawler—three of the most popular search programs. Choose a program by clicking the small box next to the program's name until a black dot shows in the box. A wide box will appear in which you will type a word or phrase relating to your research topic.

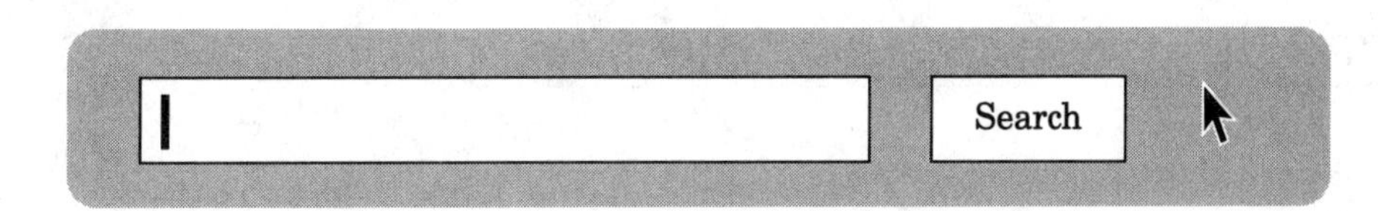

You type in White House. You move the arrow to the small Search box and click the mouse once. The search program will then list all the resources it has that match your request.

Let us say your search produced the screen at the top of the next page.

Your search has found 175 matches

Site Matches (1-9 of 175)

- Today's **White House** Press Releases
- Welcome to the **White House** - Official **White House** site.
- Harrington **House** Bed and Breakfast - This 1923 restored home on Anna Maria Island, Florida, has rooms facing the gulf, **white** sand beaches and great sunsets.
- **White House** Easter Egg - beautiful wooden eggs in honor of the traditional Easter Egg Roll at the **White House.**
- **White House** Historical Association - Christmas Ornaments.
- Write to the **White House** - Send mail to the President or Vice President by using your computer.
- **White House** Fellowships - Established by President Lyndon Johnson in the East Room of the **White House** in 1964, gives talented and highly motivated young Americans first-hand experience in the process of governing the nation.
- **White House** News Photographers' Association - TV and Still Photojournalists who cover the **White House**; based in Wash, D.C.
- **White** Moving & Storage, Inc - national and international **house**hold moving needs.

[next 20 site matches]

New Search   Options

At the top of the screen, you see the number of matches found (175). Under the number of matches, you are told how many matches appear on this first screen (1-9 of 175). Each listing on this screen (and on later screens) is a separate *Web site.* The address of each Web site is underlined, and the words matching your request are shown in bold type. By clicking any of the underlined words in the address, you will be connected to the information and resources found on that Web site.

None of the examples on the first Search screen shows a real Web site address. The real address of each site is made up of unusual words and abbreviations. The Search program gives you a simpler address. When you click this simpler address, the Search program connects you with the real address. (Later in this chapter, you will be introduced to real Web site addresses.)

Before you choose the first Web site to visit, consider limiting (narrowing) your search. Perhaps you do not want to visit all 175 Web sites. You can use the bottom of the screen to limit your search. Ignore the New Search box, which is for completely new searches. Instead, click Options. A new Search screen will offer you several options that allow you to limit your search. (These options differ from one Search program to another.) Before selecting an option, you will again have to type in White House in the wide box.

One commonly used option provides an exact match. This option will list only Web sites that match all the words in your request in the exact order in which you typed them in the wide box. So, when you request an exact match for White House, you will be offered only those Web sites that contain the word White followed immediately by the word House. You can see why this is a good option by looking at two Web sites on the first Search screen. The web site Harrington **House** Bed and Breakfast shows **House**, and its description shows **white**; but this site has nothing to do with the White House. The Web site **White** Moving and Storage, Inc. shows **White**, and its description shows **house** as part of the word "**house**hold"; but this site has nothing to do with the White House either. After you have selected your option, a new Search screen will appear. You will see that the original 175 addresses have been reduced to a much smaller number. So remember to click Options to limit your search.

There is one more important piece of information you should know before choosing your first Web site. Any Web site that you visit may contain information that is out of date or inaccurate. When doing research on the Internet, it is a good idea to see if the facts that you find on a Web site can also be found in other sources.

Now let us choose a Web site from the Search screen. You choose Welcome to the **White House**. You move the arrow to the site and click the mouse. A screen similar to the following one will appear.

Good Afternoon

Welcome to the White House

The President & Vice President:
Their accomplishments, their families, and how to send them electronic mail

Commonly Requested Federal Services:
Direct access to Federal Services

Interactive Citizens' Handbook:
Your guide to information about the Federal government

What's New: What's happening at the White House

White House History and Tours:
Past Presidents and First Families, Art in the President's House and Tours
--**Tour Information**

Site News:
Recent additions to our site

The Virtual Library:
Search White House documents, listen to speeches, and view photos

The Briefing Room:
Today's releases, hot topics, and the latest Federal statistics

White House Help Desk:
Frequently asked questions and answers about our service

White House for Kids:
Helping young people become more active and informed citizens

This opening screen is called the *home page.* Think of it as the first (and main) page of a book that contains many pages on the White House. This home page lists ten pages that will provide information and resources relating to the White House. Click any page and you will be connected to it. For example, if you click **White House History and Tours:**, the following screen will appear.

White House History and Tours

A White House History: A virtual historical tour of the White House where you can view the rooms and furnishings, past and present. See Art in the White House--A Nation's Pride, for an historical perspective of selected pieces from the White House collection.

The Presidents of the United States: A portrait and biographical sketch of each President.

The First Ladies of the United States: A portrait and biographical sketch of each First Lady.

The First Families at Home: A glimpse into the lives of families who have lived in the White House.

Tour Information: Schedules and regulations governing tours of the White House. (Subject to change)

On this screen, one click will bring forth a tour of many rooms in the White House. Another click will present a portrait and biographical sketch of each president or first lady. Another click will let you glimpse into the lives of families who have lived in the White House. Click **Tour Information**: and you will learn about visiting the White House in person.

After you visit a page, you can return to the previous page by clicking the Go-Back arrow (←) on the top of the screen. After you go back to a previous page, you can click the Go-Ahead arrow (→) to return to a page in the other direction.

If you click the Go-Back arrow (←) enough times, you will go back to the home page of the official White House Web

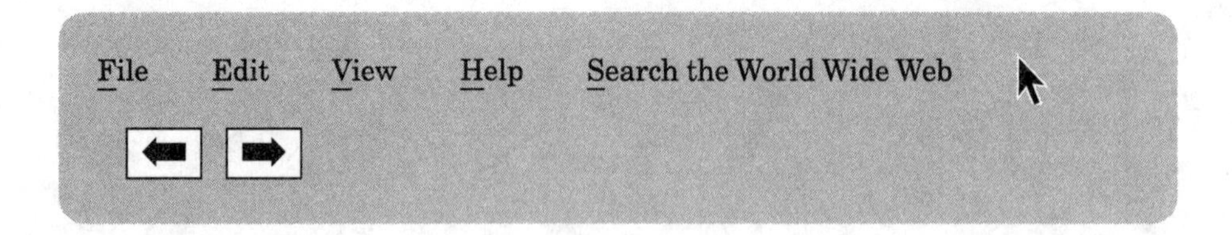

site. Click the arrow once more and you will return to the Search program list of White House Web sites. By connecting to other White House Web sites, you can learn about Christmas ornaments at the White House, Easter egg rolls on the White House lawn, presidential campaigns, presidential comments on the important issues of the day, and many other topics. In other words, a search of the Internet will gain you considerable information about the White House.

How do you get this information from the computer screen into your portfolio? If your computer is connected to a printer, you can print out what the screen shows. If you have a word-processing program on your computer, you can probably copy the material from the Web site onto your program. Then, you can edit the information before printing it so that it looks the way you want it to. With so many Web sites devoted to the White House, your portfolio will be filled with interesting details about the White House in no time. You may even feel that you have been there, talking with the president in the Oval Office.

Let us see how much you have learned about using the Internet. Answer the following questions.

1. The following list gives, in the wrong order, the steps for obtaining information from the Internet for your White House portfolio. Put them in the correct order by placing 1 next to the first step, 2 next to the second step, and so on.

    ____ *(a)* On the Search program list of White House Web sites, click the official White House Web site Welcome to the **White House**.

    ____ *(b)* Print out the material on **The Presidents of the United States:** page, and place it in your portfolio.

    ____ *(c)* Use a Search program to obtain a list of Web sites relating to the White House.

    ____ *(d)* Click the **White House History and Tours:** page.

    ____ *(e)* Click **The Presidents of the United States:** page.

What order did you pick? By looking at the screens given in this chapter and rereading the accompanying explanations, you should have come up with the following correct order: 2 *(a)*, 5 *(b)*, 1 *(c)*, 3 *(d)*, 4 *(e)*.

____ 2. Which statement about Search programs is NOT true?

   (a) Search programs list all Web sites that they can find to match your request.

   (b) The line Site Matches (1-9 of 175) on the screen on page 182 means that this screen shows only 9 of the 175 matches available.

   (c) Some Web sites found on a Search program may contain out-of-date or inaccurate information.

   (d) There is no way to narrow your search.

Which answer did you choose? All of these statements are true except *(d)*. By clicking Options in a Search program, you will find ways to narrow your search.

Let us now learn to use real Web site addresses. Earlier in this chapter, you learned that addresses such as Welcome to the **White House** are only simpler addresses that can connect you to real Web site addresses. You have probably seen many real Web site addresses in magazines and on television at the end of a program or commercial. Here is the real Web site address for Welcome to the **White House**.

http://www.whitehouse.gov/WH/ Welcome.html

This strange-looking group of words and punctuation marks is often typed in italics, as shown. It is made up of the following parts:

http:// These four letters stand for hyper text-transfer protocol. This is the method that the computer uses to go to a Web site. (There are other methods, but most Web sites have an http address.) The punctuation marks *://* must follow *http*.

www. These three letters stand for the World Wide Web. A period must follow *www*.

whitehouse. This is the name of this particular Web site. The name is typed as one word even though it is made up of two words. A period must follow *whitehouse.*

gov This part of the address gives the address a category. The abbreviation *gov* stands for government. Other Web sites use *org* for nonprofit organizations, *com* for commercial, or profit-making, organizations, or *edu* for educational institutions. No period follows this part of the address.

/WH and */Welcome.html* This part of the address gives the two paths that lead to the Welcome page of the White House Web site. A slash / must be placed before each path. To go to other pages on the White House Web site, you must use other paths. You may have to add several paths before you get to the exact page you want. For example, the page on the first families that lived in the White House has the address *http://www.whitehouse.gov/WH/glimpse/families/html/top.html. WH, glimpse, families,* and *html* are all paths that lead to the page *top.html,* where the information on the first families is found. (The four letters *html* refer to hyper text markup language, a way of writing text files so that the computer program running your Internet service can read them.)

Here are some real Web site addresses, some with paths, that would be helpful in the study of U.S. History. (*Note:* Web site addresses are often discontinued or changed. The addresses in this chapter are given as examples only.)

http://www.si.edu/nmai National Museum of the American Indian

http://www.discovery.com Discovery Channel Online

http://www.census.gov/main/www/subjects.html U.S. Census Bureau

http://www.historychannel.com History Channel Online

http://www.mapquest.com Maps of nearly every street and road in the United States

http://www.nara.gov National Archives and Records Administration

http://www.nationalgeographic.com National Geographic Society

http://www.i-channel.com/ellis/index.html Ellis Island Web Site

http://www.osv.org Recreated 1830s Sturbridge Village in Massachusetts

If you want to go to one of these Web sites, you will have to type in the real Web site address. On most Internet services, you click the F in File at the top left corner of the screen.

A box similar to this one will appear. You click the O in Open.

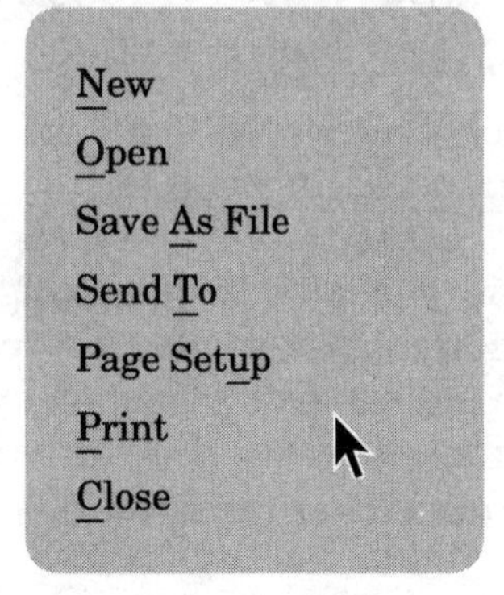

A box similar to this one will appear.

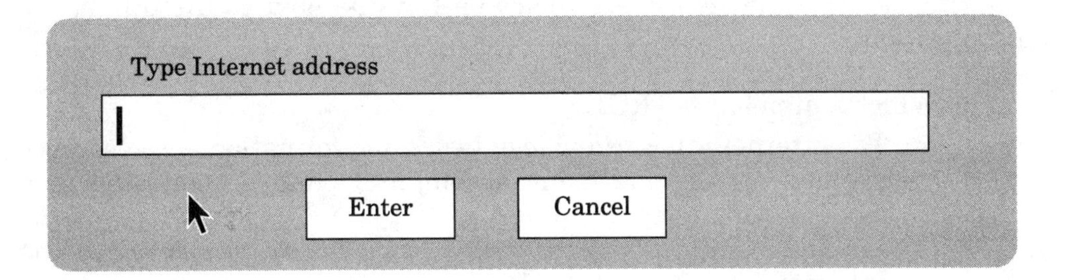

You type in the address, for example, *http://www.i-channel.com/ellis/index.html.* You click the Enter box and that Web site will open. The Web site address now appears in the address box at the top of the screen.

If the Web site does not open, you may have typed in the address incorrectly. It is very important to type the address exactly as it is given.

The following Web site address for the National Geographic Society has been typed incorrectly. Rewrite it correctly.

http:www.national geographic.org

____

____

There were three mistakes in the Web site address. First, after *http:,* you need to add //. Second, there should be no space between any letters or punctuation marks. The correct form is *nationalgeographic,* not *national geographic.* Third, the National Geographic Society, which owns this Web site, is a commercial organization. Its Web site address must end with *com* (commercial organization), not *org* (non-profit organization).

Finally, as you collect materials for your portfolio, make a list of where you found the materials. Each source on the list should include the following information, if available:

- Author's last name, author's first name.
- Titles of document and complete work (in quotation marks for an article, underlined or italicized for a book).
- Document date (day, month, year) or date of last change made to the document.
- Web site address beginning with *http://*.
- Date (day, month, year) when you copied the material from the Web site.

For example, a source might be listed as follows:

Bradsher, Keith. "Mexico: Absent from the White House Crisis List." The New York Times News Service. 9 November 1995. *http://www.latinolink.com/biz/mexx1109.html.* 3 January 1998.

In this chapter, you have learned the basic steps for searching the Internet. You now know how to use Search programs to find resources on the Internet. You know how to enter real Web site addresses. You also know how to list sources for material taken from the Internet. The following exercises will give you more practice in the skill of searching the Internet.

USING YOUR SKILLS

A. Write the letter of the correct choice on the line next to the number of each question.

____ 1. Which statement is TRUE?

(a) The Internet is a worldwide network of information and resources available to anyone using a computer that is connected to a modem and a telephone line.
(b) Anyone owning a computer is automatically connected to the Internet.
(c) To access the Internet, you must own a Search program.
(d) The Internet is a network of information and resources that is available only in the United States.

____ 2. A modem is

(a) a method that a computer uses to go to a Web site.
(b) an early model of computer.
(c) a style of writing text files so that they can be read on a computer screen.
(d) a device that allows a computer to communicate with another computer over a telephone line.

____ 3. A Search program on the Internet will list

(a) no more than 100 Web sites for each request.
(b) only Web sites that end with *html.*
(c) all Web sites that it finds to match your request.
(d) only up-to-date Web sites.

____ 4. Clicking Options in a Search program

(a) ends the search.
(b) allows you to pick a way to narrow your search.
(c) begins a totally different search.
(d) places all the matching Web sites on one screen.

____ 5. On a Search screen, the address of a Web site is

(a) underlined, with the words matching your request in bold type.
(b) underlined, with all words in bold type.
(c) in bold type, not underlined.
(d) neither underlined nor in bold type.

____ 6. If you searched for an exact phrase match of Web sites for the **U.S. Congress**, you would be given a list of sites that

(a) included a Web site for the **U.S.** Army.
(b) included a Web site on the Continental **Congress**.
(c) included a Web site on the **Congress** of Vienna.
(d) did not include any of the above.

____ 7. After you visit a page of a Web site,

(a) there is no way to return to a previous page.
(b) you can return to the previous page by pressing the Enter key on your keyboard.
(c) you can return to the previous page by clicking the Go-Back arrow (⬅) on the top of the screen.
(d) you can only return to the home page of the Web site.

____ 8. Web sites
(*a*) contain only up-to-date information.
(*b*) must, by law, be updated on a monthly basis.
(*c*) never contain unreliable information.
(*d*) may contain information that is out of date or inaccurate.

____ 9. In the Web site *http://www.mapquest.com, com* stands for
(*a*) communication.
(*b*) command.
(*c*) commercial organization.
(*d*) committee.

____ 10. In giving the source for material that you copy from the Internet, you
(*a*) should state your last name and first name.
(*b*) should state the author's last name and first name.
(*c*) should not include the date you copied the material from the Internet.
(*d*) should not include the Web site address.

B. Using Search Programs on the Internet. Study the Search listing of White House Web sites, and then answer the questions that follow.

Your search has found 124 matches

Site Matches (1-9 of 124)

- Welcome to the **White House** - Official **White House** site.
- **White House** Historical Association - Christmas Ornaments.
- Bardi's Steak **House** - close to Union Station in Toronto, Canada.
- **White House** Easter Egg - beautiful wooden eggs in honor of the traditional Easter Egg Roll at the **White House.**
- Write to the **White House** - Send mail to the President or Vice President by using your computer.
- **White House** Fellowships - Established by President Lyndon Johnson in the East Room of the **White House** in 1964, gives talented and highly motivated young Americans first-hand experience in the process of governing the nation.
- **White House** News Photographers' Association - TV and Still Photojournalists who cover the **White House**; based in Wash, D.C.
- Today's **White House** Press Releases.
- **White House** Conference on Small Business.

[next 10 site matches]

New Search   Options

1. How many matches on the White House did this search find?

____

2. How many Web sites are shown on this screen?

____

3. On which Web site will you find out about White House Christmas decorations?

____

4. Name a Web site on this Search screen that has nothing to do with the White House.

____

5. What should you do to see the next ten listings?

____

6. Explain the purpose of Options at the bottom of the screen.

____

7. How would you connect to the **White House** Fellowships Web site?

____

8. Which Web site on this Search screen provides a way to send mail to the president?

____

9. Why are **White** and **House** in bold letters every time they appear on the Search screen?

____

10. How can you start a new search?

____

C. Searching the Internet. You have to create a portfolio on the White House. The following steps will help you obtain information from the Internet for your portfolio, but they are in the wrong order. Put the steps in the correct order by placing 1 next to the first step, 2 next to the second step, and so on.

____ *(a)* After finding a list of Web sites relating to the White House, narrow your search if the list is too long.

____ *(b)* Print out the material on **The First Ladies of the United States:** page and place it in your portfolio.

____ *(c)* Gain access to the Internet.

____ *(d)* Use a Search program to obtain a list of Web sites relating to the White House.

____ *(e)* Click the **White House History and Tours:** page.

____ *(f)* Click **The First Ladies of the United States:** page.

____ *(g)* On the Search program list of White House Web sites, click the official White House Web site entitled Welcome to the **White House**.

D. Web Site Abbreviations. Match the abbreviation in Column B with what its stands for in Column A. One choice in Column B will be left over.

Column A	*Column B*
____ 1. World Wide Web	*a. http*
____ 2. Hyper test transfer protocol, the method that the computer uses to go to a Web site	*b. www*
____ 3. The end of a school's Web site address	*c. org*
____ 4. Hyper text markup language, a way of writing text files so that the computer program running your Internet service can read them	*d. edu*
____ 5. The end of a Web site address for a non-profit organization	*e. html*
	f. com

E. Making Web Site Addresses Correct. Each of the following Web sites contains two mistakes. Rewrite each Web site correctly. (All are given correctly somewhere in this chapter.)

htpp://www.discovery/com

1. ______________________________

http://www.history channel.com.

2. ______________________________

http:\\wwwosv.org

3. ______________________________

http://www.census.gov.main.www/subjects.html

4. ______________________________

http:/www.whitehouse.gov/WH/Welcome/html

5. ______________________________

CHAPTER 17

Writing a Research Paper

You have been asked to write a *research paper*—a composition that includes information from various sources. At first, such an assignment might seem overwhelming. But you already know how to use the sources in a library to research information. In this chapter, you will learn ten basic steps for turning your research into a good research paper.

Step 1: Selecting and Limiting the Subject

Avoid a subject that is too big or too general. For example, suppose you decide to write about the United States Supreme Court. So many books have been written about this subject that you might not know where to begin or end. You should limit your subject. You might decide to write about one important Supreme Court decision or about one or more of the justices who have served on the Supreme Court.

Answer the following question:

____ 1. Which title for a research paper indicates the most limited subject?
(a) The History of the United States Supreme Court
(b) How the Chief Justices Have Influenced the Supreme Court
(c) How John Marshall Increased the Power of the Supreme Court

Which answer did you choose? Since title *(c)* deals with only one person, it would be a more limited subject than either title *(a)* or *(b)*.

By limiting your subject, you can study the subject in depth. Let us imagine that you decide to write a research paper on John Marshall, who served as chief justice of the United States from 1801 to 1835. Your title will be "How John Marshall Increased the Power of the Supreme Court."

Step 2: Preparing a Working Bibliography

The next step is to prepare a list of available primary and secondary sources about John Marshall. This will be your working bibliography. You should keep track of the available sources on 3-x-5-inch index cards. As you look through the card catalog, the computer catalog, and the *Readers' Guide,* write the titles of books and articles about John Marshall on the index cards. Each book or article should have a separate index card. Next, look through some encyclopedias for articles on John Marshall. Write the title of each encyclopedia article on a separate index card.

The general rules for writing a bibliography card are listed on the following page.

Books

B
Marshall
Feinberg, Barbara Silverdick
John Marshall: The Great Chief Justice
Springfield, N.J.: Enslow, 1995

1. Card catalog number or the letter "B" (for biography) and the subject of the book
2. Author (last name first)
3. Title, underlined
4. Place of publication
5. Publisher
6. Year of publication

Magazine Articles

Kramer, Peter, Jr.
"Judicial Giant"
Newsweek August 24, 1974: 85-86

1. Author (unless no name is given)
2. Title of article, in quotation marks
3. Name of magazine, underlined
4. Date (day, month, year)
5. Page number(s)

Encyclopedia Articles

Murphy, Bruce Allen
"Constitution of the United States"
The World Encyclopedia 1966 ed.

1. Author (unless no name is given)
2. Title of article, in quotation marks
3. Name of encyclopedia, underlined
4. Year of publication and ed. (edition)

When you complete your bibliography, alphabetize the cards by author, title, or subject. Then number them on the top right corner. The first card will be 1, the second card 2, and so on. Then, you can refer to a book or article simply by the number on the top right corner of its index card.

Answer this question on preparing a bibliography:

____ 2. Quotation marks are used to enclose the

(a) title of a book.
(b) title of a magazine article.
(c) name of a magazine.
(d) name of an encyclopedia.

Which answer did you choose? By looking at the bibliography cards on this page, you can see that the titles of books and the names of magazines and encyclopedias are underlined. The titles of magazine and encyclopedia articles are enclosed in quotation marks. Therefore, the answer to question 2 is *(b)*.

Step 3: Preparing a Possible Outline

As you look at the contents of the books and articles in your bibliography, you should get a sense of the topics you want to include in your paper. The next step is to make an outline of those topics. It might look like this:

How John Marshall Increased the Power of the Supreme Court

I. Early Life
II. Education
III. As Chief Justice
IV. Important Court Decisions

As you read the books and articles in your bibliography, look for information that will help you write about the topics in your outline. If you come across a topic you had not thought of before, add it to your outline. For example, you could add: V. Early Law Career. You can change the order of the outline topics when you are ready to write your paper.

Step 4: Taking Notes

You do not have to read every page of the books and articles in your bibliography. Just read the pages that contain information needed for your paper. As you read, enter notes in your own words on index cards. Place information from only one source on each card. Write the outline topic at the top of the card. In the top right corner of the card, write the number you gave to that source (book or article) in your set of bibliography cards. Directly under the source number, write the page number on which the information is found in that source. You might want to use one color pen or pencil for the source numbers and another color for the page numbers. If you are planning to use the exact words found in a source, be sure to put quotation marks at the beginning and end of the words you are quoting.

For each topic, you should expect to have many cards like this one:

1
Important Court Decisions 399
Marbury v. Madison: Marshall claimed part of Judiciary Act violated Constitution. This decision gave the Supreme Court the right to declare laws unconstitutional. It was "a decision that..., perhaps more than any single act by a government official or branch, affected the history of the United States."

After you have assembled all the necessary information on index cards, arrange the cards in the order that you will probably use to write your paper. Once the cards are in that order, number each card (1, 2, 3, and so on) in the top left-hand corner. These numbers will help you keep to the order you have decided on.

Step 5: Writing the Final Outline

More than likely, you will come up with a new outline. For example, you may want to add subtopics to your main topics. (Be sure to follow the outline style that you learned in Chapter 11, pages 109–110).

Before writing your final outline, you must write a thesis statement and place it at the beginning of the outline. A thesis statement gives the purpose of your paper. For example, as you gather information about John Marshall, you realize that he was a very important man. One of your index cards contains the quotation "a giant ranking with George Washington and Thomas Jefferson as a founder of our nation." You decide that your paper is going to prove that John Marshall was as important as George Washington or Thomas Jefferson to the development of the United States.

Here is an example of a final outline with new topics, subtopics, and a thesis statement added.

How John Marshall Increased the Power of the Supreme Court

Thesis Statement: John Marshall was as important as George Washington and Thomas Jefferson to the development of the United States.

I. On the Road to the Supreme Court
  A. Early Life and Education
  B. Law Career
  C. Government Positions
II. On the Supreme Court
  A. Marbury v. Madison
  B. Dartmouth College v. Woodward
  C. McCulloch v. Maryland
  D. Gibbons v. Ogden
III. My Opinion of Marshall

This sample includes only major topics and subtopics. Your final outline will probably include many more subtopics.

Step 6: Writing the First Draft

Now it is time to write the *first draft* of your research paper, which will be subject to change. Use lined paper and write on every other line so it will be easy to *revise* (add or change things). If you type the draft, set your typewriter or word processor to double-space. It is not necessary to write the perfect opening paragraph now. It is important to include your thesis statement in the first paragraph.

Next, read the note cards that give information on the first topic, "Early Life and Education." Use that information to write your own story of the early life of John Marshall. Do the same for all remaining topics and subtopics.

As you write, you will need *documentation* for information from a primary or secondary source. This means that you will have to cite (state) where you found certain kinds of information—a direct quotation, someone else's ideas or opinions, and little-known facts. For instance, it is well known that John Marshall served as chief justice for 34 years. However, that his yearly salary as chief justice was $4,000 is a little-known fact and would need documentation. The rules for documenting your information will be discussed in Step 9.

Answer the following question on writing a first draft:

3. What is the purpose of writing a first draft?

____

____

____

____

____

____

____

____

____

____

What did you write? In the first draft, you use the information from your note cards to write a composition in which one idea flows smoothly into the next. This draft will let you see if your information can be formed into a complete research paper. Then, you can keep the information that is helpful and look for any new information that you need.

Step 7: Revising the Draft; Writing the Introduction and Conclusion

It is a good idea to put your first draft away for a while. When you come back to it, you will probably want to revise some of the material. You may be able to make some ideas clearer, cut out some sentences and paragraphs, or put them in a better order. As you revise, it is not necessary to rewrite the whole paper. Just make sure that each sentence, as well as each paragraph, flows smoothly into the next one. When you are satisfied with your draft, think about your introduction and conclusion. Your introduction must contain your thesis statement, stated in a way that grabs the reader's attention. The introduction must make the reader want to read the rest of the paper. Your conclusion, or closing paragraph(s), provides a good opportunity to state your own views on the subject. You may also want to summarize the main points and show how they support your thesis statement.

Step 8: Writing the Finished Paper

It is very important that your paper looks neat so that it will be easy to read. Here are some points to remember when putting your paper into final form:

1. Use good grammar and correct spelling. Consult a dictionary if you are not sure how a word is spelled.
2. Leave at least a one-inch margin on the top, bottom, and both sides of your paper.
3. In the top left corner of the first page, write or type double-spaced:

   Your name
   Your teacher's name
   The course title
   The day, month, and year when the paper is due
4. In the top right-hand corner of each page write or type your last name, followed by the page number.
5. Use the same style and format throughout your paper. For example, if you underline a heading on page 2, underline every similar heading. Make sure that the margins are the same on every page.
6. A long quotation (more than four lines) does not require quotation marks. Instead, start it on a new line, double-space it, and use a wider left margin, which will set it apart from the rest of the text. As an example, see the sample page of a research paper on page 200.

Step 9: Documentation

Documenting your information is important. First, it is a matter of honesty; you should not use another person's words or ideas without giving credit. Second, documentation shows that you did research, that you are knowledgeable about the subject, and that your opinions are worthwhile.

The usual style of documentation is called *parenthetical documentation.* That is, parentheses enclose the source of a quotation, idea, or little-known fact obtained from a primary or secondary source. Place the parenthetical documentation at the end of the quotation, idea, or fact. Here are some examples:

(Severn 36) This means that the information cited comes from a work written by a person whose last name is Severn, and that the information is found on page 36 of that work.

(114) A page number alone means that the author or title is the same as the previous source. In this example, it would mean page 114 of the work written by Severn.

(Corwin John Marshall 19) Both the author's last name and the work are given when more than one work by the same author is used in a research paper. You only have to give enough words in the title to make clear what work you are citing.

(Severn 149) Severn's work has already been cited, but another source (Corwin John Marshall 19) has just been cited. Therefore, if you want to cite Severn again, you must give his last name along with the page number.

(Johnson and Cullen 61) If there are two persons to be named for a source, you must give both last names, followed by the page number. In this example, Johnson and Cullen are editors rather than authors of a work on John Marshall.

("John Marshall" 34) This means that no author is given. "John Marshall" is the title of the magazine or encyclopedia article cited, followed by the page number.

Turn to pages 199–200 to see how these examples are placed in a research paper. The parenthetical documentation comes at the end of a sentence. With one exception, the period ending the sentence follows the parenthetical documentation. The exception is a long quotation set apart with a wide left margin. In this case, the last period comes before the parenthetical documentation.

On the last page of your research paper, write a list of Works Cited. It will give complete information for each source cited in your paper. The information can be found on your bibliography cards. The following is a sample of a Works Cited page.

Works Cited

Corwin, Edward Samuel. The Doctrine of Judicial Review. Princeton: Princeton University Press, 1914.

- - -. John Marshall and the Constitution. New Haven: Yale University Press, 1919.

Feinberg, Barbara Silberdick. John Marshall: The Great Chief Justice. New Jersey: Enslow, 1995.

"John Marshall." Encyclopedia Britannica. 1994 ed.

Johnson, Herbert A., and Charles T. Cullen, eds. The Papers of John Marshall. Chapel Hill: University of North Carolina Press, 1974.

Kramer, Peter, Jr. "Judicial Review." Newsweek 26 August 1974: 85-86.

Here are the rules for preparing a list of Works Cited:

- Write or type Works Cited centered and one inch from the top of the page.
- Arrange works in alphabetical order according to the last name of the author. Works without an author are listed by the first word of the title. If "The," "An," or "A" is the first word, then list the work by the second word of the title.
- Titles of books and names of magazines and encyclopedias are often printed in italics. In your Works Cited list, underline them rather than using italics. Also remember to put titles of magazine and encyclopedia articles in quotation marks.
- Double-space, as elsewhere.
- If you use more than one line for a work, indent the additional lines.
- If you cite two or more works by the same author, give the author's name for only the first work. For the other works, use three hyphens followed by a period in place of the name.
- If there is more than one author for the same work, list the last name of the first author, comma, first name, comma, followed by "and" and the first and last name of the second author. Repeat the first and last name format for additional authors, inserting "and" before the last author's name.
- If the person listed is the editor rather than the author, write "ed." after the person's name.

Let us see if you can write a Works Cited entry correctly.

4. List the following book as it would appear on a Works Cited page.

John Marshall: A Life in Law, written by Leonard Baker, published in New York in 1974 by Macmillan

Did you remember to underline the title rather than using italics? Refer to the Works Cited sample on page 202 to see how this source would appear in a Works Cited list.

Step 10: Proofreading

Proofreading is the checking of a finished paper for errors. It may be the easiest or the most difficult part of preparing your research paper, but it is very necessary. Your paper will require considerable effort. You may be tempted to "just get it done," but you should do the best job possible. Set your paper aside for a while, and then go back and reread it. Read slowly. You want to read the words exactly as they appear on the page, not as you remember them. Watch for spelling or typing errors. Check for confusing punctuation. Finally, make sure your paper has a logical flow that will support your thesis statement.

Turn to pages 199–202, where you can study four sample pages taken from different parts of a research paper on John Marshall. These pages are the result of following all the steps discussed in this chapter.

Being able to write a research paper is a valuable skill. You will be called upon to use this skill in school and, perhaps, later during your working career. The following exercises will give you more practice in writing a research paper.

USING YOUR SKILLS

A. Write the letter of the correct choice on the line next to the number of each question.

____ 1. In writing a research paper, you should
- *(a)* limit your subject.
- *(b)* write as much as you can on a subject.
- *(c)* write the shortest paper you can.
- *(d)* write a very general paper.

____ 2. Which is the best source to use to find available books on a subject?
- *(a)* the computer catalog
- *(b)* the *Readers' Guide to Periodical Literature*
- *(c)* an encyclopedia
- *(d)* an almanac

____ 3. Which step in writing a research paper should come before the others?
- *(a)* writing a first draft
- *(b)* taking notes
- *(c)* preparing parenthetical documentation
- *(d)* preparing a possible outline

____ 4. After you have taken notes on index cards, you should
- *(a)* arrange them by book title.
- *(b)* arrange them in the order that you will probably use to write your paper.
- *(c)* decide on the subject that you are going to write about.
- *(d)* divide the cards into book and article cards.

Turner 1

Morgan Turner

Ms. Hernandez

U.S. History

May 13, 1997

John Marshall: A Founding Father

John Marshall was born in Virginia on September 14, 1775. No one could have known on that day that he would become the greatest Supreme Court justice in the history of the United States. As chief justice, he would make the judicial branch an equal partner with the executive and legislative branches of government. Marshall was to become "a giant ranking with George Washington and Thomas Jefferson as a founder of our nation" (Kramer 85).

Yet his youth was similar to that of many boys who grew up in the frontier region of Virginia. He loved the outdoors, and he learned to hunt and fish and to climb the Blue Ridge Mountains. He did not have much opportunity for a formal education, but he loved to read. His favorite book was Blackstone's Commentaries on the Laws of England, and it has been said that that book started John on his interest in the law (Feinberg 16-17).

John Marshall was 21 years of age at the time when the Declaration of Independence was signed. He was one of the

Turner 3

John Marshall's law career began in August 1788 when he was licensed to practice law. He quickly became a successful lawyer. One Historian writes:

> Marshall's court victories were becoming legend. He might not have the manner or learning of other lawyers, but he won cases. Marshall went straight to the core of an argument and reduced it to simple terms the judges could understand. . . . (Severn 36)

John Marshall held a number of important positions in the new government of the United States, but it was not until 1801 that he received his greatest challenge. In that year, President John Adams named Marshall to be the fourth chief justice of the United States. The Supreme Court that Marshall took over was not the great body we know today. "Among the three . . . branches of government, it was a poor third, weak, neglected, and all but ignored" (114).

Through the decisions he handed down as chief justice, John Marshall turned the Supreme Court into a strong and independent branch of the federal government. Marshall was able to establish the Supreme Court as the final authority on the U.S. Constitution and to give the national government power over the states. Few other persons have had the

Turner 5

In 1801, William Marbury was appointed a judge by President Adams, who was soon to leave office. Incoming Secretary of States James Madison was ordered by President Jefferson to deny Marbury his appointment. So Marbury, using the Judiciary Act of 1789, asked the Supreme Court for an order, a writ of mandamus, to force Madison to give him the appointment.

In the Marbury v. Madison decision, Marshall declared that the part of the Judiciary Act giving the Supreme Court the power to issue writs of mandamus violated the Constitution. This decision was monumental because it made the Supreme Court the final interpreter of what the Constitution means. It also gave the Court the right to declare laws unconstitutional, thus no longer in effect. This was "a decision that more than any other act by the Supreme Court in its long history, perhaps more than any single act by a government official or branch, affected the history of the United States" (Baker 399). It was "as great an act of statesmanship as the formulation of any part of the written constitution" (Cuneo 88).

The decision was also important because it said that Marbury was entitled to his appointment as a judge. This meant that a person wronged by the government could seek his "ultimate remedy in the courtroom" (Baker 40). It had the

Turner 9

Works Cited

Baker, Leonard. John Marshall: A Life in Law. New York: Macmillan, 1974.

Corwin, Edward Samuel. The Doctrine of Judicial Review. Princeton: Princeton University Press, 1914.

---. John Marshall and the Constitution. New Haven: Yale University Press, 1919.

Cuneo, John R. John Marshall: Judicial Statesman. New York: McGraw-Hill, 1975.

Feinberg, Barbara Silberdick. John Marshall: The Great Chief Justice. New Jersey: Enslow, 1995.

Johnson, Herbert A., and Charles T. Cullen, eds. The Papers of John Marshall. Chapel Hill: University of North Carolina, 1974.

Kramer, Peter J. "Judicial Review." Newsweek 26 August 1974: 85-86.

Severn, Bill. John Marshall: The Man Who Made the Court Supreme. New York: David McKay, 1969.

Stites, Francis N. John Marshall: Defender of the Constitution. Boston: Little, Brown, 1981.

____ 5. In a research paper, type quotations of more than four lines
(a) single-spaced with a wider left margin than in the rest of the paper.
(b) double-spaced with a wider left margin than in the rest of the paper.
(c) single-spaced with the same margin as the rest of the paper.
(d) double-spaced with the same margin as the rest of the paper.

____ 6. The parenthetical documentation (Conroy 42) means that the cited material is found on page 42 of
(a) a book titled Conroy.
(b) a magazine titled Conroy.
(c) a source written or edited by Conroy.
(d) a magazine article written about Conroy.

____ 7. The parenthetical documentation (Smith Truth in Law 102) indicates that
(a) more than one book by Smith is being cited.
(b) Truth in Law is the only work by Smith being cited.
(c) Smith is the subject of the book Truth in Law.
(d) Smith is the publisher of Truth in Law.

____ 8. The sources in a Works Cited list are arranged
(a) with the most-cited sources listed first.
(b) in the order in which they are used in the research paper.
(c) in alphabetical order by the authors' last names.
(d) with the oldest sources listed first.

____ 9. In a Works Cited list, the title of a magazine article should be
(a) underlined.
(b) enclosed in quotation marks.
(c) underlined and enclosed in quotation marks.
(d) neither underlined nor enclosed in quotation marks.

____ 10. Although all of the following choices may be true, the one that gives the BEST explanation of a thesis statement is
(a) a thesis statement gives the main idea of a research paper.
(b) a thesis statement is a summary of a research paper.
(c) a thesis statement tells what the research paper is about.
(d) a thesis statement gives the purpose of a research paper.

B. To answer the following questions, refer to the sample pages of the research paper on John Marshall found on pages 199–202.

Write the letter of the correct choice on the line next to the number of each question.

____ 1. Which statement about the sample pages is TRUE?
(a) Every line is double-spaced.
(b) Long quotations are single-spaced and short quotations are double-spaced.
(c) The sources in Works Cited are single-spaced.
(d) All quotations are single-spaced.

____ 2. Which of the following sources in the Works Cited list was published most recently?
(a) "Judicial Giant," Newsweek
(b) John Marshall: A Life in Law
(c) John Marshall: The Great Chief Justice
(d) John Marshall: Defender of the Constitution

____ 3. John Marshall: Defender of the Constitution was published by
(a) David McKay.
(b) Little, Brown.
(c) Enslow.
(d) Macmillan.

____ 4. The parenthetical documentation (Kramer 85) is for
(a) a book.
(b) an encyclopedia article.
(c) a magazine article.
(d) an almanac entry.

____ 5. Which parenthetical documentation gives a source for information but NOT for a direct quotation?
(a) (Kramer 85)
(b) (Feinberg 16-17)
(c) (Severn 36)
(d) (Cuneo 38)

____ 6. The source for parenthetical documentation (114) is
(a) John Marshall: A Life in Law
(b) John Marshall and the Constitution
(c) The Papers of John Marshall
(d) John Marshall: The Man Who Made the Court Supreme

____ 7. Which of the following authors is quoted more than once on the sample pages?
(a) Francis N. Stites
(b) Leonard Baker
(c) Peter Kramer, Jr.
(d) Edward Samuel Corwin

____ 8. Which of the following authors is quoted more than once on the sample pages?
(a) Barbara Silberdick Feinberg
(b) John R. Cuneo
(c) Bill Severn
(d) John Edward Oster

____ 9. Two books on the Works Cited list were written by
(a) Leonard Baker.
(b) Bill Severn.
(c) Barbara Silberdick Feinberg.
(d) Edward Samuel Corwin.

____ 10. Which is the name of an editor of a source on the Works Cited list?
(a) Herbert A. Johnson
(b) Francis Stites
(c) Samuel Konefsky
(d) David Loth

C. Bibliography Cards. Prepare a bibliography card for each source given. Follow the rules in Step 2, pages 192–193.

1.

John Marshall: A Life in Law, a biography written by Leonard Baker, published in New York in 1974 by Macmillan

____
____
____
____
____
____
____
____

2.

"Law in History: History in Law," an article written by G. L. Fetner, printed on pages 173–183 of the March 1977 issue of *Social Education*

____
____
____
____
____
____
____
____

3.

The 1996 edition of *The World Book Encyclopedia* article titled "John Marshall," written by Charles T. Cullen

____
____
____
____
____
____
____
____

D. Taking Notes. The following is a page from *John Marshall: The Great Chief Justice,* written by Barbara Silberdick Feinberg. Read the page and then write notes on the index card as if you were gathering information for a research paper on John Marshall. Follow the rules for writing note cards in Step 4, page 194. This book should be coded as number 5 in your pile of bibliography cards.

• John Marshall

offend the senior Justice. So Adams asked former Chief Justice John Jay to return to the post. Jay turned him down because he said the Court lacked "the public confidence and respect."[1]

On January 19, 1801, President Adams turned to his forty-five-year-old Secretary of State John Marshall. Marshall was personally loyal to him, logical in his reasoning, and an excellent leader. The president said, "I believe I must nominate you," and Marshall replied that he was "pleased as well as surprized [sic]."[2] The next day, Adams asked the Senate for approval, as the Constitution required. The Senate held up the vote for a week, hoping that Adams would change his mind in favor of Paterson. As a Federalist, Marshall was too unpredictable and independent. He had even opposed the party's Alien and Sedition laws.

The president stood firm. On January 27, Marshall became the new Chief Justice by a unanimous vote. At Adams's request, he also stayed on as secretary of state for the rest of the president's term in office. He received a yearly salary of $4,000 (equal to about $33,880 today).[3] Associate Justices were paid $3,500 (equal to about $29,645 today). In 1819, his salary was increased to $5,000 (equal to about $42,350 today). For comparison, in 1993 the Chief Justice was paid $ 171,500 a year and an Associate Justice, $164,100.[4]

Over the years, the Supreme Court had been sadly neglected. On the day Adams chose Marshall, the District Commissioners wrote to Congress. "As no house has been provided for the Judiciary of the United States, we hope the Supreme Court may be accommodated with a room in the Capitol to hold its sessions until further provision shall be made."[5] The Justices met in a Senate committee room on the main floor of the Capitol for seven years. Then, they were

54

E. Parentheical Documentation. Match each parenthetical documentation in Column B with the document source it refers to in Column A.

Column A

____ 1. The only document source with two authors

____ 2. The only document source for an encyclopedia article without an author and cited for the first time.

____ 3. The only document source that is the second of two identical sources in a row

____ 4. The only document source with an author who is represented by more than one work

____ 5. The only document source for an author of one work cited for the first time

Column B

a. (Beveridge 222)

b. (Johnson and Cullen 91)

c. (313)

d. (Swindler The Constitution and Chief Justice Marshall 84)

e. ("Federalist Party" 54)

F. Works Cited. The following is a list of different sources of information on John Marshall. Arrange them as a Works Cited list.

John Marshall and Alexander Hamilton, Architects of the American Constitution, written by Samuel J. Konefsky, published in New York in 1964 by Macmillan

"Ten Builders of the Law of the Land," printed on page 7 of the October 23, 1983 issue of *Scholastic Update*

Chief Justice John Marshall and the Growth of the American Republic, written by David Loth, published in New York in 1949 by W.W. Norton

The Life of John Marshall, written by Albert J. Beveridge, published in Boston in 1916 by Houghton Mifflin

"John Marshall," an article written by Philip B. Kurland from the 1995 edition of *Encyclopedia Americana*

Works Cited

____

____

____

____

____

____

____

____

____

____

____

____

____

____

____

CHAPTER 18

Interpreting Picture Graphs, Charts, and Circle Graphs

The U.S. Constitution requires the national government to conduct a *census* every ten years. The first census, in 1790, was mainly a population count of the new nation. Today, the U.S. Census Bureau, which conducts the census, gathers the latest *statistics* (numerical information) on population, education, income, housing, and many other subjects. The government, private businesses, and individuals use these statistics to judge the past and plan for the future.

The Census Bureau also provides *estimated statistics,* or estimates, for every year between the most recent census and the present year. Though not as exact as a census, estimated statistics are based on the latest available information. The Census Bureau also provides *projected statistics,* or projections, for future years. They are based on changes that are likely to occur by a future year.

Statistics also exist for colonial America, but most of them were gathered after 1790. This was done by studying numerous sources of information about the colonial period. Where there were no exact statistics, it was necessary to make estimates. By using the best sources of information available, it was possible, for example, to estimate the population of Philadelphia in 1700.

The best way to show past, present, or future statistics is to use *graphs* and *charts.* Graphs and charts (sometimes called tables) are arrangements of symbols, words, and numbers that show information in a clear and simple way. In this chapter, you will learn how to make effective use of picture graphs, charts, and circle graphs.

Picture Graphs

Let us begin with *picture graphs.* They are so named because they give statistics in pictures or symbols instead of numbers. Picture graphs show a simple comparison of statistics that is easy to understand.

The following picture graph shows the estimated African population in colonial America from 1700 to 1770.

Africans in Colonial America, 1700–1770

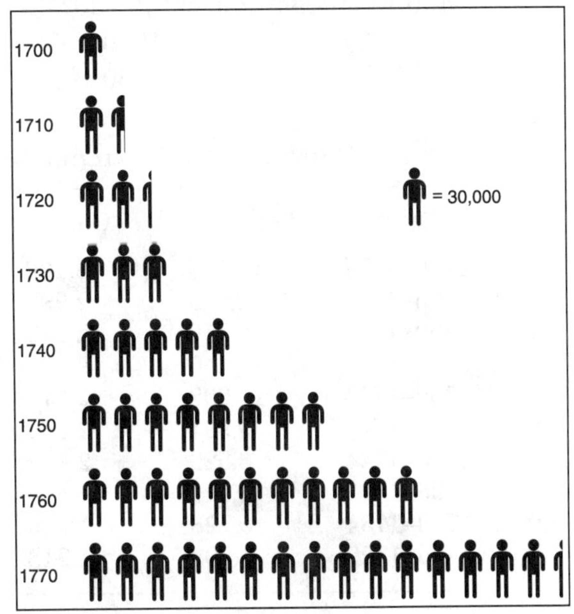

Humanlike figures represent the population numbers. A note on the graph states that each figure stands for 30,000 people. By counting the number of figures and multiplying by 30,000, you can find the African population for each of the eight years listed on the graph.

Notice that three figures are not complete. One shows two-thirds of a human figure, and two others show one-third of a human figure. Since one figure stands for 30,000 people, two-thirds of a figure stands for 20,000 people. How many people are represented by one-third of a figure? That answer will help you answer the following question.

____ 1. What was the estimated African population of colonial America in 1720?

(a) 30,000 *(c)* 100,000
(b) 70,000 *(d)* 130,000

Which answer did you choose? Two and one-third stick figures are given for 1720. Each figure stands for 30,000 people, so one-third of a figure stands for 10,000 people. In numbers, two and one-third figures would be written 30,000 + 30,000 + 10,000. The total is 70,000. Therefore, the answer to question 1 is *(b)*.

____ 2. In which year did Africans in colonial America number 150,000?

(a) 1710 *(c)* 1740
(b) 1730 *(d)* 1760

Which answer did you choose? Since each stick figure stands for 30,000 people, a population of 150,000 would be shown by five figures (150,000 ÷ 30,000 = 5). The only year with five figures is 1740. Therefore, the answer to question 2 is *(c)*.

The statistics in a picture graph are usually not exact. In fact, the African population in 1740 was not exactly 150,000. It was estimated to be 150,024. That number was rounded off to 150,000 to make it easier to draw the picture graph. Such rounding off is acceptable as long as the statistics are nearly correct.

Charts

Let us now look at charts. Study the following chart showing the number of children for each teacher in colonial Philadelphia.

The chart is divided into rows and columns. The rows go across the page (horizontally), and the columns go from top to bottom (vertically). The rows give information for 10 five-year periods, from 1725–1729 to 1770–1774. The first column lists the 10 five-year periods. The remaining four columns show specific information for each five-year period. The second column lists the population of Philadelphia for each five-year period. The third column lists the number of children, the fourth column lists the number of teachers, and the fifth column lists the number of children

Number of Children per Teacher in Colonial Philadelphia

Years	Population*	Children*	Teachers*	Children per Teacher*
1770–1774	13,115	3,106	21.2	146.5
1765–1769	12,913	2,997	23.4	128.1
1760–1764	12,710	2,979	16.8	177.3
1755–1759	12,140	2,868	20.0	143.4
1750–1754	11,298	2,675	15.2	176.0
1745–1749	9,991	2,359	8.4	280.8
1740–1744	8,529	2,029	5.4	375.7
1735–1739	6,948	1,696	5.8	292.4
1730–1734	5,728	1,425	6.2	229.8
1725–1729	4,803	1,218	5.0	243.6

*Figures are the averages of each five-year period.

per (for each) teacher. This last statistic was found by dividing the number of children (third column) by the number of teachers (fourth column). For example, for 1750–1754, if you divide 2,675 children by 15.2 teachers, you will find that there were 176 children for each teacher.

How can there be 15.2 teachers? Some charts would round off 15.2 to 15. This chart gives the exact number. What does .2 of a person mean? Notice the small asterisk (*) after each heading in columns 2, 3, 4, and 5. It refers to the footnote at the bottom of the chart. (Always pay attention to footnotes on a chart; they contain important information.) The footnote states: Figures are the averages of each five-year period. So the numbers in columns 2, 3, 4, and 5 are averages. The numbers in columns 2 and 3 were probably rounded off, but the numbers in columns 4 and 5 were not. This explains why there are 15.2 teachers for 1750–1754. The five years were added up and divided by 5.

Year	Number of teachers
1754	19
1753	17
1752	14
1751	14
1750	+12
	76 ÷ 5 years = 15.2 teachers on average

Let us see what you understand about charts. Answer the following questions based on the chart.

____ 3. How many teachers on average did Philadelphia have between 1755 and 1779?

(*a*) 20 (*c*) 21.2
(*b*) 21 (*d*) 23.4

Which answer did you choose? Find 1755–1759 in the "Years" column. Follow across the 1755–1759 row until you come to the "Teachers" column. The number given is 20.0. Is 20.0 one of the choices? Yes, because 20.0 and 20 are the same number. Therefore, the answer to question 3 is (*a*).

____ 4. Which five-year period had the largest number of children for each teacher?

(*a*) 1725–1729 (*c*) 1750–1754
(*b*) 1740–1744 (*d*) 1765–1769

Which answer did you choose? Find the "Children per Teacher" column. Look down the column until you find the largest number. That number is 375.7. In the same row as 375.7, you will find 1740–1744 in the "Years" column. This means that between 1740 and 1744, the number of children per teacher was the largest. Therefore, the answer to question 4 is (*b*).

5. Would you say that between the years 1725 and 1774 the number of children per teacher worsened, improved, or worsened some years and improved others? Explain your answer.

____

____

____

____

____

____

____

____

What did you write? Most people would say that reducing the number of children per teacher is an improvement. Your answer should state that between 1725 and 1774, the numbers improved some years and worsened others. But from 1750 on, the number of children per teacher remained below 200. So your answer should also state that there was a steady improvement after the first 25 years.

Circle Graphs

Another important graph is the *circle graph,* or pie graph. This graph is divided like the pieces of a pie. The purpose of a circle graph is to compare the different pieces, or sections. Each section stands for a certain *percentage* (%) of the whole graph. All the sections add up to 100 percent. In a circle graph divided into four equal sections, like the one that follows, each section is 25 percent of the whole graph.

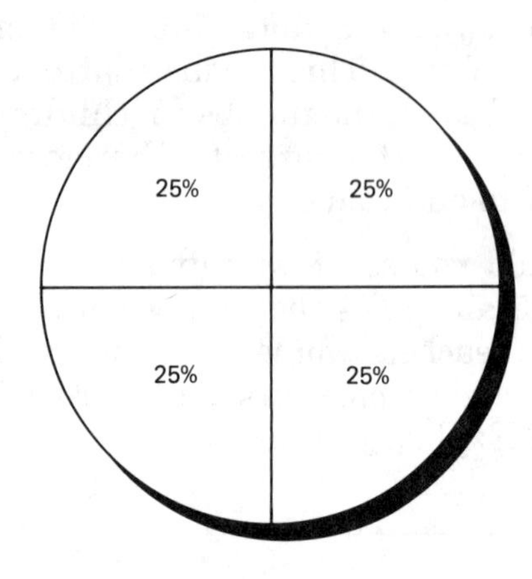

Graphs can also show different percentages. Look at the following circle graph. It shows the percentage of Harvard College graduates in 1725 who went on to various careers. Each career has a different percentage; all the careers add up to 100 percent.

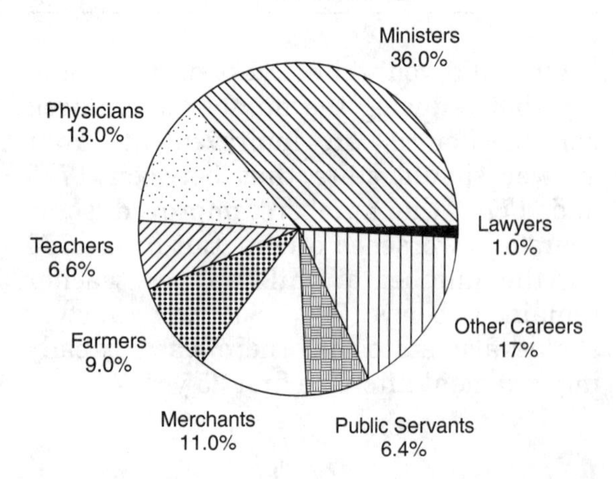

Answer the following questions based on this circle graph.

____ 6. The largest percentage of graduates became
(*a*) teachers. (*c*) farmers.
(*b*) public servants. (*d*) ministers.

Which answer did you choose this time? It is easy to see that the answer is (*d*) ministers, with 36 percent. Question 6 points out the main reason for using circle graphs. You can easily see how big a "piece of the pie" belongs to those graduates who became ministers. This image on the graph is more impressive than the percentage numbers alone.

____ 7. Teachers and public servants combined had the same percentage as
(*a*) farmers. (*c*) physicians.
(*b*) merchants. (*d*) lawyers.

Which answer did you choose? First, find the percentages for teachers and public servants—6.6 percent for teachers and 6.4 percent for public servants. By adding them, you get 13 percent, which matches the percentage for physicians. Therefore, the answer to question 7 is (*c*).

8. Does the circle graph give the number of students who graduated from Harvard in 1725? Explain.

____

____

____

____

____

What did you write? This circle graph does not give the actual number of graduates. It gives only the percentages of graduates who went on to various careers. When looking at any chart or graph, be sure that you know whether you are looking at actual numbers or percentages. The truth is that only 47 people made up the entire 1725 graduating class, but you would not know this from the circle graph.

In this chapter, you have been introduced

to graphs and charts. They are used in many books, magazines, and newspapers because they supply information quickly and easily. Knowing how to analyze graphs and charts is an important skill. The following exercises—many with census statistics—will give you more practice in developing this skill.

USING YOUR SKILLS

A. Picture Graph. Study the following picture graph. Then answer the questions.

Bales of Cotton Produced in the United States, 1810–1860

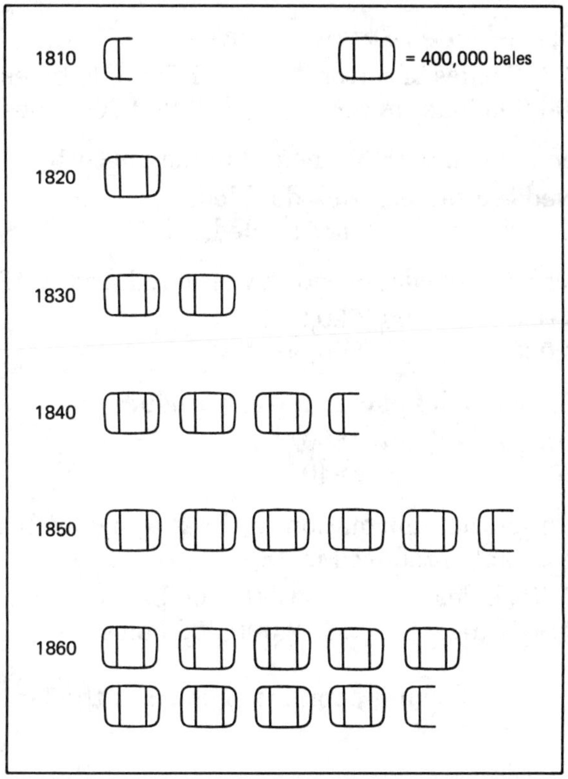

= 400,000 bales

1810

1820

1830

1840

1850

1860

Write the letter of the correct choice on the line next to the number of each question.

____ 1. The graph shows

(*a*) the number of bales of cotton produced in the United States between 1810 and 1860.

(*b*) the value of cotton produced in the United States between 1810 and 1860.

(*c*) the amount of cotton that the United States sold to other countries between 1810 and 1860.

(*d*) the quality of the cotton produced in the United States between 1810 and 1860.

____ 2. Statistics are given

(*a*) for every year between 1810 and 1860.

(*b*) for five-year intervals between 1810 and 1860.

(*c*) for ten-year intervals between 1810 and 1860.

(*d*) for twenty-year intervals between 1810 and 1860.

____ 3. The symbol ◫ stands for
(*a*) 100,000 bales of cotton. (*c*) 300,000 bales of cotton.
(*b*) 200,000 bales of cotton. (*d*) 400,000 bales of cotton.

____ 4. In 1830, the United States produced
(*a*) 400,000 bales of cotton. (*c*) 1,200,000 bales of cotton.
(*b*) 800,000 bales of cotton. (*d*) 1,600,000 bales of cotton.

____ 5. In which year were only 400,000 bales of cotton produced?
(*a*) 1810 (*c*) 1840
(*b*) 1820 (*d*) 1860

____ 6. In 1850, the United States produced
(*a*) 600,000 bales of cotton. (*c*) 1,800,000 bales of cotton.
(*b*) 1,400,000 bales of cotton. (*d*) 2,200,000 bales of cotton.

____ 7. Between 1820 and 1830, the production of cotton
(*a*) stayed the same. (*c*) doubled.
(*b*) declined. (*d*) tripled.

____ 8. How many more bales of cotton were produced in 1840 than in 1830?
(*a*) 200,000 (*c*) 600,000
(*b*) 400,000 (*d*) 800,000

____ 9. Only 200,000 bales of cotton were produced in
(*a*) 1810. (*c*) 1830.
(*b*) 1820. (*d*) 1840.

____ 10. Based on all the information in the graph, which amount of cotton was most likely produced in 1835?
(*a*) 300,000 bales (*c*) 1,500,000 bales
(*b*) 950,000 bales (*d*) 2,500,000 bales

B. Charts. Study the following population chart of the United States. Then answer the questions.

Population of the United States, 1790–1860

Year	Northeast[1]	North Central[2]	South[3]	West[4]
1790	1,968,040	—	1,961,174	—
1800	2,635,576	51,006	2,621,901	—
1810	3,486,675	292,107	3,461,099	—
1820	4,359,916	859,305	4,419,232	—
1830	5,542,381	1,610,473	5,707,848	—
1840	6,761,082	3,351,542	6,950,729	—
1850	8,626,951	5,403,595	8,982,612	178,818
1860	10,594,268	9,096,716	11,133,361	618,976

[1]Northeast includes Maine, New Hampshire, Vermont, Massachusetts, Rhode Island, Connecticut, New York, New Jersey, and Pennsylvania.
[2]North Central includes Ohio, Indiana, Illinois, Michigan, Wisconsin, Minnesota, Iowa, Missouri, and the territories of Kansas and Nebraska.
[3]South includes Delaware, Maryland, Virginia, North Carolina, South Carolina, Georgia, Florida, Kentucky, Tennessee, Alabama, Mississippi, Arkansas, Texas, Louisiana, and the Oklahoma Territory.
[4]West includes all areas west of the states and territories listed for Northeast, North Central, and South.

Write the letter of the correct choice on the line next to the number of each question.

____ 1. The chart shows
(*a*) the population of individual states between 1790 and 1860.
(*b*) the population of the four areas of the United States between 1790 and 1860.
(*c*) the white population of the United States between 1790 and 1860.
(*d*) the slave population of the United States between 1790 and 1860.

____ 2. In which year was the population of the Northeast 1,968,040?
(*a*) 1790 (*c*) 1830
(*b*) 1800 (*d*) 1840

____ 3. Which area of the United States had the largest population in 1860?
(*a*) Northeast (*c*) South
(*b*) North Central (*d*) West

____ 4. The population of the North Central area reached 859,305 in
(*a*) 1820. (*c*) 1840.
(*b*) 1830. (*d*) 1850.

____ 5. Which area on the chart includes Missouri?
(*a*) Northeast (*c*) South
(*b*) North Central (*d*) West

____ 6. In which year did the South have the largest population for the first time?
(*a*) 1790 (*c*) 1810
(*b*) 1800 (*d*) 1820

____ 7. The dashes (—) in the North Central and West columns most likely mean
(*a*) no one lived in those areas.
(*b*) the population count was too low to matter.
(*c*) no population statistics are available for those areas for certain years.
(*d*) only Native Americans lived in those areas.

____ 8. The chart shows that the total population of the United States in 1830 was about
(*a*) 7,000,000. (*c*) 11,000,000.
(*b*) 9,000,000. (*d*) 13,000,000.

____ 9. Which area and territory are correctly paired?
(*a*) Northeast—Oklahoma Territory
(*b*) North Central—Nebraska Territory
(*c*) South—Kansas Territory
(*d*) West—Oklahoma Territory

____ 10. The slave population in the South in 1850 was 3,116,629. That means that the non-slave population in the South in 1850 was nearly
(*a*) 5,900,000. (*c*) 7,300,000.
(*b*) 6,500,000. (*d*) 8,900,000.

C. Circle Graph. Study the following circle graph. Then answer the questions.

The Percentage of Southerners Who Owned Slaves in the 1800s

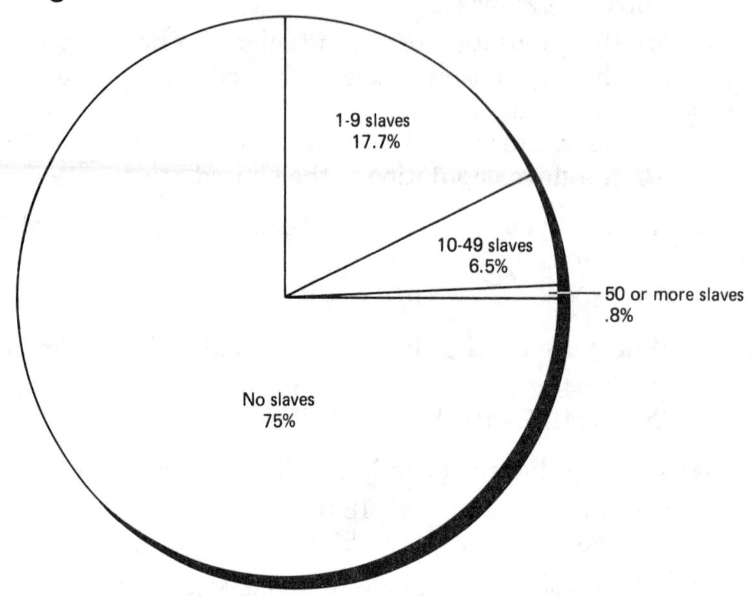

C-1. Write the letter of the correct choice on the line next to the number of each question.

_____ 1. What is the total percentage shown on this circle graph?
(a) 25%
(b) 50%
(c) 75%
(d) 100%

_____ 2. What percentage of Southerners owned between 1 and 9 slaves?
(a) .8%
(b) 6.5%
(c) 17.7%
(d) 75%

_____ 3. 6.5% of Southerners owned
(a) no slaves.
(b) between 1 and 9 slaves.
(c) between 10 and 49 slaves.
(d) 50 or more slaves.

_____ 4. A large majority of Southerners
(a) owned slaves.
(b) did not own slaves.
(c) owned at least one slave.
(d) owned more than 50 slaves.

_____ 5. What is the total percentage of Southern slave owners?
(a) 25% *(c)* 75%
(b) 50% *(d)* 100%

C-2. How might this graph support the claim that it was expensive to buy and own slaves? Explain your answer.

____

____

____

____

D. Chart. Study the following chart. Then answer the questions.

Food Prices in the United States
(Selected periods from 1891 to 1995* in dollars per pound, except for eggs per dozen and milk per half gallon)

Years	Flour	Round Steak	Bacon	Butter	Eggs	Milk	Potatoes
1991–1995	.23	3.30	1.99	1.69	.97	1.43	.33
1961–1965	.11	1.06	.72	.75	.55	.52	.07
1946–1950	.09	.79	.68	.77	.66	.40	.05
1931–1935	.04	.31	.31	.32	.33	.23	.02
1926–1930	.05	.42	.46	.54	.50	.28	.04
1901–1905	.03	.14	.18	.28	.25	.14	.02
1891–1895	.03	.12	.13	.27	.21	.14	.02

*Prices are the averages of each five-year period.

D-1. Write the letter of the correct choice on the line next to the number of each question.

_____ 1. The chart gives average food prices for
(*a*) every year from 1891 to 1995.
(*b*) every five-year period between 1891 and 1995.
(*c*) selected five-year periods between 1891 and 1995.
(*d*) selected ten-year periods between 1891 and 1995.

_____ 2. All figures are
(*a*) in dollars per pound.
(*b*) in dollars per pound, except for eggs and milk.
(*c*) in cents per dozen.
(*d*) given in percentages.

_____ 3. The average price of bacon per pound between 1991 and 1995 was
(*a*) $.68. (*c*) $1.69.
(*b*) $1.06. (*d*) $1.99.

_____ 4. The average price of round steak per pound between 1946 and 1950 was $.79. Another way of writing $.79 is
(*a*) 79 dollars. (*c*) 7 cents.
(*b*) $7.90. (*d*) 79 cents.

____ 5. Between 1950 and 1991, the average price of flour per pound increased by

(a) 9 cents. *(c)* 14 cents.
(b) 11 cents. *(d)* 23 cents.

____ 6. Which two food items decreased in price between 1950 and 1961?

(a) butter and eggs *(c)* butter and flour
(b) milk and eggs *(d)* milk and flour

____ 7. Between 1926 and 1930, a gallon of milk cost

(a) 28 cents. *(c)* 56 cents.
(b) 38 cents. *(d)* 66 cents.

____ 8. In 1893, 10 cents probably bought

(a) five pounds of potatoes.
(b) one pound of round steak.
(c) one-half gallon of milk.
(d) four pounds of flour.

____ 9. A pound of flour, a pound of butter, a dozen eggs, and one-half gallon of milk cost 92 cents between

(a) 1891 and 1895. *(c)* 1961 and 1965.
(b) 1931 and 1935. *(d)* 1991 and 1995.

____ 10. Between which two periods was there the least change in food prices?

(a) 1891–1895 and 1901–1905
(b) 1926–1930 and 1931–1935
(c) 1931–1935 and 1946–1950
(d) 1961–1965 and 1991–1995

D-2. The Great Depression began in 1929 and lasted through the 1930s. How does the chart show the worsening economic conditions during the early 1930s?

____

____

____

____

D-3. How does this chart show that butter could be called "the rich person's food"? Explain.

____

____

____

____

E. Completing a Picture Graph. The populations of seven Native American tribes are given in the following list. Place each population on the graph, using the correct number of symbols. You will not always be able to use only whole symbols. The first tribe's population has been done for you.

Cherokee	375,000	Chippewa	106,000	Pueblo	56,000
Navajo	225,000	Choctaw	87,000	Apache	50,000
Sioux	108,000			Iroquois	50,000

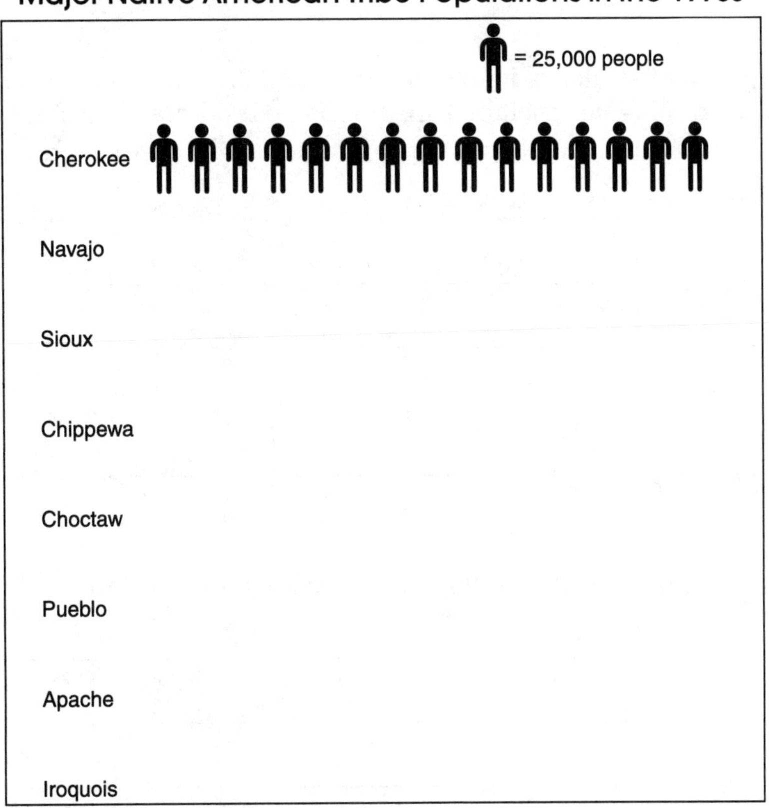

F. Chart (Averages, Projections, and Percentages). Study the chart, and then answer the questions.

U.S. Public School Enrollment
(A Century's Difference)

Year	Total[1]	Elementary[1]	Secondary[1]
2001–2005 (projected)	49,043,000	34,773,000[2]	14,270,666
1901–1905	16,071,000	15,470,800	600,200
Increase	32,972,000	19,302,200	13,670,466
Percentage increase	205%	125%	228%

[1]Figures are the averages of each five-year period.
[2]Includes kindergarten.

1. The average total public school enrollment for 1901–1906 was 16,071,000. Why is the word "average" used?

____

____

____

____

2. What group of students is included in the 2001–2005 elementary school statistics that is not included in the 1901–1905 statistics? How do you know?

____

____

____

____

____

3. In what way are the 2001–2005 statistics a guess? Explain.

____

____

____

____

4. How does the chart show that the largest percentage does not always mean the largest actual number?

____

____

____

____

G. Circle Graphs. Study the following circle graphs. Then answer the questions.

The Changing Role of Women in the Workplace

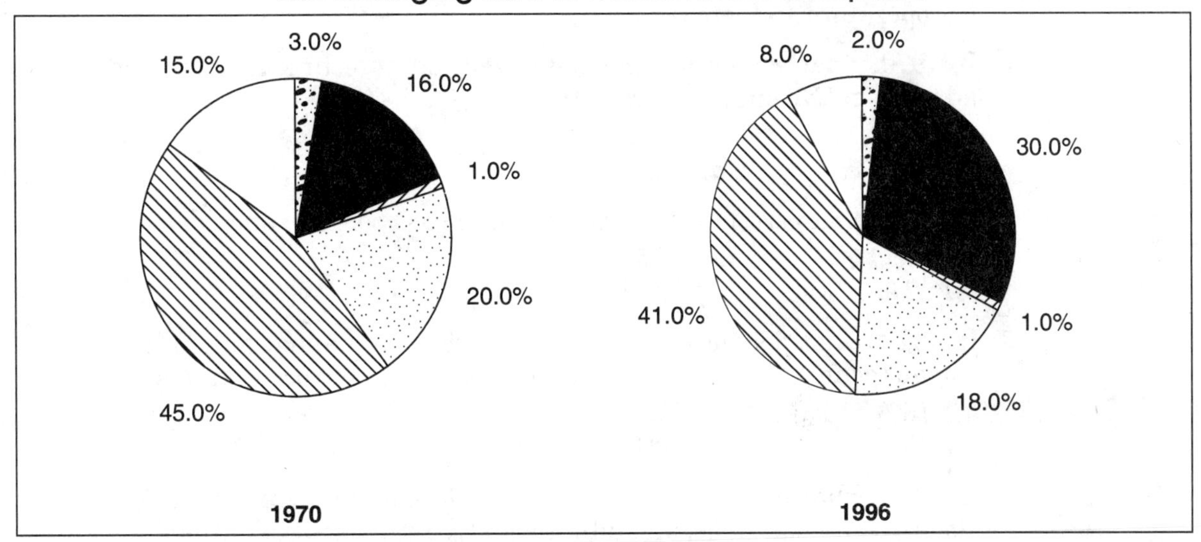

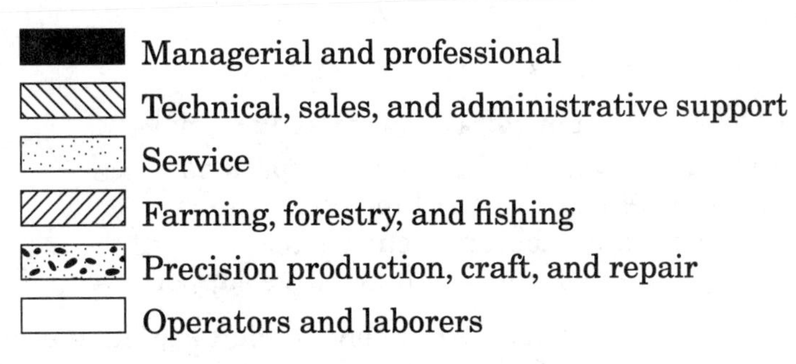

G-1. Write the letter of the correct choice on the line next to the number of each question.

_____ 1. What is the total percentage shown on each graph?

(a) 30% *(c)* 80%
(b) 50% *(d)* 100%

_____ 2. The pattern [diagonal-line pattern] stands for

(a) service occupations.
(b) managerial and professional occupations.
(c) farming, forestry, and fishing occupations.
(d) precision production, craft, and repair occupations.

_____ 3. Precision production, craft, and repair workers are represented by the pattern

(a) [pattern] *(c)* [pattern]
(b) [pattern] *(d)* [pattern]

____ 4. Which occupation would include a maid or waitress?
(a) technical, sales, and administrative support
(b) service
(c) farming, forestry, and fishing
(d) operators and laborers

____ 5. In 1970, what percentage of women worked in technical, sales, and administrative support occupations?
(a) 2% *(c)* 20%
(b) 15% *(d)* 45%

____ 6. In 1996, what percentage of women worked as operators and laborers?
(a) 8% *(c)* 16%
(b) 11% *(d)* 32%

____ 7. In 1970, what percentage of women worked in managerial, professional, technical, sales, and administrative support occupations?
(a) 16% *(c)* 61%
(b) 45% *(d)* 90%

____ 8. In 1996, what percentage of women worked in managerial, professional, technical, sales, and administrative support occupations?
(a) 30% *(c)* 71%
(b) 41% *(d)* 80%

____ 9. In 1996, 1 percent of working women were in
(a) managerial and professional occupations.
(b) farming, forestry, and fishing occupations.
(c) operators and laborers occupations.
(d) technical, sales, and administrative support occupations.

____ 10. Which occupation was the only one to increase "its piece of the pie" between 1970 and 1996?
(a) managerial and professional
(b) technical, sales, and administrative support
(c) precision production, craft, and repair
(d) service

G-2. Read the two statements, and answer the question that follows.

Statement 1

"I have had many women teachers, but three years ago, for the first time in my school's history, a woman became the principal, and last year, for the first time, a woman became the superintendent of schools."

Statement 2

"Women are rarely promoted to the top managerial positions in our company. And when they are, they don't receive the same salary as men doing the same job."

Which statement is supported by the information in the circle graphs? Explain your answer.

____

____

____

____

____

____

CHAPTER 19

Interpreting Bar Graphs and Line Graphs

In Chapter 18, you learned how to interpret statistics on picture graphs, charts, and circle graphs. In this chapter, you will learn to do the same thing with bar graphs and line graphs.

Bar Graphs

A *bar graph* uses bars of different lengths to compare statistics. In the graph below, two bars show two different sets of statistics at the same time. The graph compares the number of workers employed on farms with the number of workers employed in other occupations (non-farm workers). The first bar stands for non-farm workers, and the second bar stands for farm workers. Because this graph uses two bars, it is called a *double bar graph.*

The years covered by the graph (1820 to 1860) are listed by decade along the bottom. The numbers going up the right side (1 to 6 million) are used to determine how many workers are represented by each bar. Note that the single-digit numbers 1 to 6 on the right side represent the complete

Employed Workers in the United States, 1820–1860

numbers 1,000,000 to 6,000,000. The graph makers wanted to save space, so they replaced the six zeros in each number with the word "million." On this graph, the word "million" was put sideways next to the single-digit numbers. On other graphs, it might appear above the single-digit numbers or under the title.

You should also know that a decimal point (.) may be needed when a number is shortened. For example, the number 3.2 million appears in the first question that follows. The number 3.2 million is the same as the number 3,200,000. The number 3.22 million would be the same as 3,220,000.

Answer the following question based on the double bar graph on page 224.

____ 1. In 1850, farm workers in the United States numbered approximately (nearly)

(a) 3.2 million. *(c)* 4.9 million.
(b) 4.1 million. *(d)* 5.6 million.

What answer did you choose? First find 1850 along the bottom of the graph. Then place your finger on the top of the bar that stands for farm workers in 1850. This is the gray bar. Now move your finger across to the numbers on the right side of the graph. Your finger should stop just below the number 5 (meaning 5 million). Choice *(c)* 4.9 million is slightly less than 5 million. Therefore, the answer to question 1 is *(c)*.

____ 2. Non-farm workers increased from 1.7 million to 2.8 million between

(a) 1820 and 1830.
(b) 1830 and 1840.
(c) 1840 and 1850.
(d) 1850 and 1860.

Which answer did you choose? Look at the numbers on the right side of the graph. The number 1.7 million would be between 1 million and 2 million. Place your finger on the list of numbers between 1 million and 2 million. Because 1.7 million is closer to 2 million than to 1 million, your finger should be closer to the 2 million mark. Now move your finger across the graph until it meets the top of a white bar ▯ (The white bars stand for non-farm workers.) If your finger is on the same level as 1.7 million, it will meet the top of the bar marked with the year 1840. Follow the same steps for 2.8 million, and your finger will meet the top of the bar marked with the year 1850. So non-farm workers increased from 1.7 million to 2.8 million between 1840 and 1850. Therefore, the answer to question 2 is *(c)*.

____ 3. In 1860, the total number of workers (farm and non-farm) reached approximately

(a) 6 million. *(c)* 14 million.
(b) 10.5 million. *(d)* 18.5 million.

Which answer did you choose this time? You will find the total number of workers by adding the statistics for non-farm and farm workers. The non-farm workers' bar for 1860 is at about the 4.3 million level, and the farm workers' bar is at about the 6.2 million level. The two figures add up to approximately 10.5 million. Therefore, the answer to question 3 is *(b)*.

Percentage Bar Graphs

On page 226 is another kind of bar graph, called a *percentage bar graph.*

Each bar represents all the occupations found in a particular area of the United States. The information given is for the year 1840. Inside each bar, you can see the percentage of people who worked in certain occupations. All the percentages in each bar add up to 100 percent (%).

This kind of bar graph is used for several purposes:

1. To compare the percentage of people in one occupation with the percentage of people in another occupation.

   Example: In the South, 8.3% of the people worked in manufacturing, and 1.6% worked in trading.

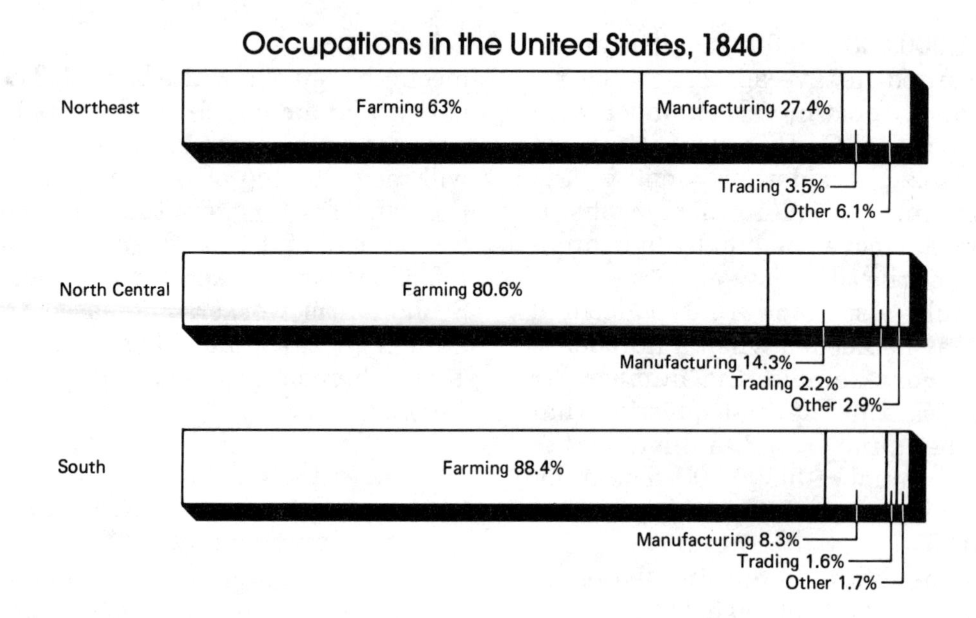

2. To compare the percentage of people in one occupation with the percentage of people in all other occupations put together.

   Example: In the North Central, 80.6% of the people worked in farming, and 19.4% worked in manufacturing, trading, and all other occupations. (The total of 14.3%, 2.2%, and 2.9% is 19.4%.)

3. To compare the percentage of people in an occupation in one area with the percentage of people in the same occupation in another area.

   Example: In the Northeast, 63% of the people worked in farming. In the South, 88.4% worked in farming.

Answer the following questions based on this percentage bar graph.

____ 4. What percentage of people in the Northeast did NOT work in farming?
   (a) 6.1%
   (b) 37%
   (c) 45%
   (d) 63%

Which answer did you choose? There are two ways to find the answer. You can add up all the percentages that do NOT deal with farming: 27.4% + 3.5% + 6.1% = 37%. Or you can subtract the percentage of farmers (63%) from the total percentage (100%): 100% – 63% = 37%. Therefore, the answer to question 4 is *(b)*.

____ 5. In 1840, most Americans worked in
   (a) farming.
   (b) manufacturing.
   (c) trading.
   (d) occupations other than farming, manufacturing, and trading.

Which answer did you choose? In each area, farming accounts for a higher percentage than all the other occupations put together. Therefore, the answer to question 5 is *(a)*.

____ 6. Which area of the United States had the highest percentage of people working in manufacturing?
   (a) Northeast
   (b) North Central
   (c) South

Which answer did you choose? Look at the percentage of people in manufacturing in each of the three areas. You can see that the Northeast had a higher percentage in manufacturing (27.4%) than the North Central (14.3%) or the South (8.3%). Therefore, the answer to question 6 is *(a)*.

Line Graphs

Line graphs use lines to show information, such as statistics. The line graph on this page is called a *double line graph* because it uses two lines, a solid line and a broken line.

The total value of U.S. exports is shown by the solid line ———. By looking at this line, you can see the value of goods sold by U.S. businesses to other countries between 1800 and 1860. But the graph also shows the value of a particular export (cotton) during the same years. The value of the exported cotton is represented by the broken line - - - - -.

The years for which statistics are given are listed in ten-year intervals along the bottom of the graph. Numbers standing for millions of dollars are listed at the right side of the graph.

Answer the following questions based on this double line graph.

____ 7. In what year did the value of all U.S. exports reach approximately 125 million dollars?

(a) 1800 *(c)* 1830
(b) 1810 *(d)* 1840

Which answer did you choose? Look at the numbers at the right side of the graph. The location of 125 (million dollars) would be just above 120. Place your finger where 125 would be. Now move your finger to the left across the graph until it meets the solid line representing the value of all exports. Where your finger meets the solid line, look at the year below it (or almost directly below it). You will see 1840. This means that in 1840, the value of all exports reached approximately 125 million dollars. Therefore, the answer to question 7 is *(d)*.

Value of Cotton Exports Compared with Value of Total U.S. Exports, 1800–1860

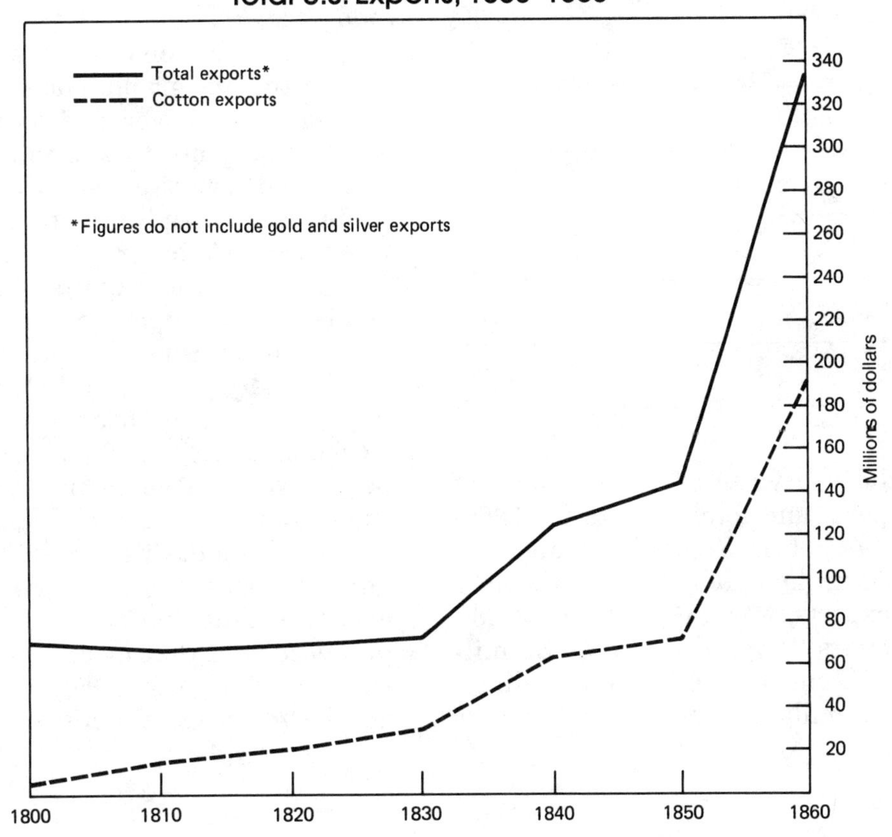

____ 8. In 1820, what was the approximate value of all exports other than cotton?

(a) 20 million dollars
(b) 32 million dollars
(c) 41 million dollars
(d) 48 million dollars

Which answer did you choose? You need to subtract the value of cotton exports in 1820 from the value of total exports in 1820. To do this, find the solid line (total exports) and the broken line (cotton exports) above the year 1820. The solid line is on the same level as 70 million dollars. The broken line is on a level slightly higher than 20 million dollars. Let us say that it is at the 22 million dollar mark. If you subtract 22 million from 70 million, the difference is 48 million dollars, the value of all exports other than cotton. Therefore, the answer to question 8 is *(d).*

____ 9. "In 1860, the value of cotton exports was more than one-half the value of the total U.S. exports." How does the graph show that this statement is correct?

____

____

____

____

____

____

What did you write? Find the value of cotton exports and total exports for 1860. The value of cotton exports was approximately 190 million dollars, and the value of total exports was approximately 330 million dollars. If you divide the 330 million in half, the answer is 165 million. Clearly, 190 million is more than 165 million, so it is correct to state that in 1860, the value of cotton exports was more than half the value of total exports.

____ 10. The line graph shows that the value of U.S. cotton exports

(a) increased steadily between 1800 and 1860.
(b) declined steadily between 1800 and 1860.
(c) stayed the same.
(d) increased some years and declined other years.

Which answer did you choose? If the line on the graph is horizontal ———, it means that the value of cotton exports stayed the same. If the line is rising ⟋, it means that the value of cotton exports increased. If the line is falling ⟍, it means that the value of cotton exports decreased. What kind of line representing cotton exports do you find on this graph? The line representing cotton exports rises in every year listed. This means that the value of cotton exports increased steadily between 1800 and 1860. Therefore, the answer to question 10 is *(a).*

Question 10 demonstrates an important use for the line graph. The line lets you see a *trend,* or an overall direction in which something is heading. One trend between 1800 and 1860, as shown on this line graph, was a steady growth in total exports after 1810. Another trend was a steady growth in cotton exports throughout the whole period. What people would have been pleased to see the total exports climb higher every year after 1810? The answer is just about everybody—business people, workers, and government officials. What people would have been displeased to see the cotton exports climb higher year after year throughout this period? The answer is anyone opposed to slavery. More cotton exports meant that more cotton was being produced, and that meant a need for more slave labor. Now you can see what a line graph can get you thinking about!

Charts and Graphs in the World of Computers

As you have learned in Chapter 18 and in this chapter, charts and graphs present information clearly and simply through the use of numbers, words, and symbols. For most people, it is easier and more time-saving to study a chart or graph than to read a lengthy selection containing the same information. Since computers produce charts and graphs easily, it is no wonder that drawing and analyzing charts and graphs are important activities in the world of computers. But computers cannot produce charts and graphs automatically. They need the help of *graphics programs,* which are available on *diskettes* and *CD-ROMs.* Once installed in the computer, such programs, often called *software,* enable you to draw lines, circles, and bars. The statistics you supply will divide those lines and shapes into any number of sections.

Let us say that you want to use a graphics program to produce the bar graph on page 224. The program would ask you to select the kind of graph you want (bar). Then it would ask you to type in the following information:

- Title (EMPLOYED WORKERS IN THE UNITED STATES, 1820–1860)
- Data that goes along the bottom of the graph (the years 1820, 1830, 1840, 1850, and 1860)
- Data that goes along the side of the graph (numbers in even million steps from 1 to 6)
- Titles for the two bars in the key (Non-farm workers, Farm workers)
- Choice of colors or patterns for each bar (white, gray)
- Statistics for each bar (These numbers would not appear on the graph but would determine the length of each bar.)

Then, with the press of a key, the computer would display the completed graph. (Actual programs may be different in some respects from this sample.)

Some computer programs produce graphs from the information on a *spreadsheet.* A spreadsheet looks like a chart, with information in columns and rows. It is so named because its information is spread out across many columns. You can select information from certain rows and columns in the spreadsheet and present it in graphic format. If you change the information on the spreadsheet, the information on the graph will change automatically to match it. Thus, the size of any bar in the graph would lengthen or shorten if the information it represents is later changed.

Let us say that the chart on page 214 is a spreadsheet. By marking (selecting) the information you wanted, you could produce the circle graph and the bar graph on page 230.

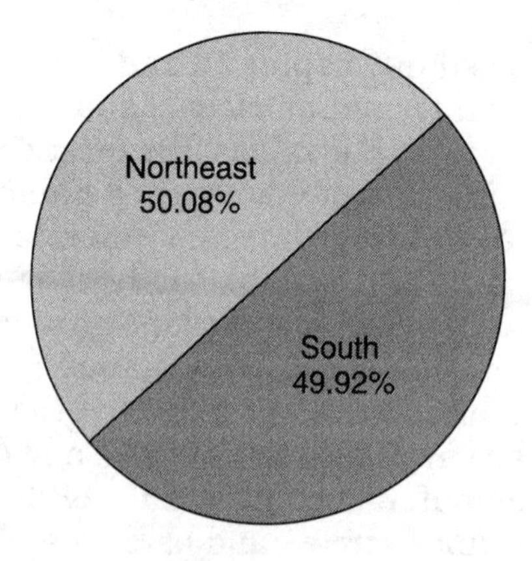

Bar Graph
Population in the South, 1840–1860

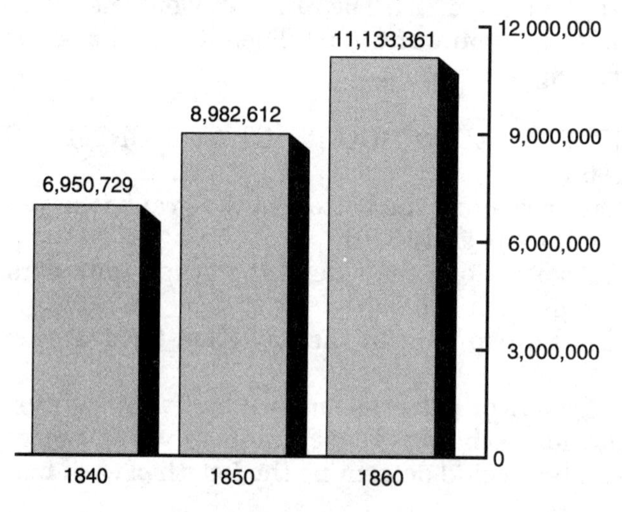

Refer to the chart on page 214, and find the information shown on the graphs. You can see that the circle graph turned the raw data of the chart into percentages. Do you think the information on the circle graph could be shown on a bar graph, and vice versa?

In addition to computer programs that produce charts and graphs, there are programs that contain ready-made charts and graphs. Many of them deal specifically with history, geography, and economics. You may have seen such charts and graphs in your school. The information in such ready-made computer programs is similar to what is found in an almanac—charts and graphs showing population, income, crops grown, available hospital beds, and so on. It is even possible to copy these charts and graphs into a word-processing program and include them in school reports and research papers. (If you do so, remember to credit the source of each chart and graph.)

Clearly, computers can do many tasks quickly and efficiently. In addition to producing graphics, as described here, computers have a wide range of other programs, from estimating and predicting outcomes to simulating (recreating) events in U.S. history.

The ability to use a computer is a very important skill that can be helpful in school and throughout your life. You live in a world of computers. Are you a part of that world yet?

You have learned in this chapter how bar graphs and line graphs show facts and other information clearly and quickly. You will come across these two kinds of graphs many times in your education and throughout your life. The following exercises will give you more practice in interpreting bar and line graphs.

USING YOUR SKILLS

A. Bar Graph. Study the double bar graph on page 232. Then answer the questions.

Write the letter of the correct choice on the line next to the number of each question.

____ 1. The chart shows the number of people who
- *(a)* immigrated to the United States between 1821 and 1870.
- *(b)* left the United States between 1821 and 1870.
- *(c)* immigrated to Europe between 1821 and 1870.
- *(d)* settled in the eastern United States between 1821 and 1870.

____ 2. The gray bar ▭ represents immigrants from
- *(a)* the United States.
- *(b)* Europe.
- *(c)* all areas of the world except Europe.
- *(d)* English-speaking countries.

____ 3. The graph shows
- *(a)* separate figures for each year between 1821 and 1870.
- *(b)* the average number of immigrants for five ten-year periods between 1821 and 1870.
- *(c)* the total number of immigrants for five ten-year periods between 1821 and 1870.
- *(d)* the total number of immigrants for 10 ten-year periods between 1821 and 1870.

____ 4. The vertical label "Thousands" means that the number 2,400 on the right side of the graph stands for 2,400,000. Therefore, the number 800 farther down on the right side stands for
- *(a)* 8,000,000.
- *(b)* 800,000.
- *(c)* 80,000.
- *(d)* 8,000.

____ 5. How many people immigrated to the United States between 1841 and 1850?
- *(a)* nearly 600,000
- *(b)* nearly 1,800,000
- *(c)* nearly 2,000,000
- *(d)* nearly 2,500,000

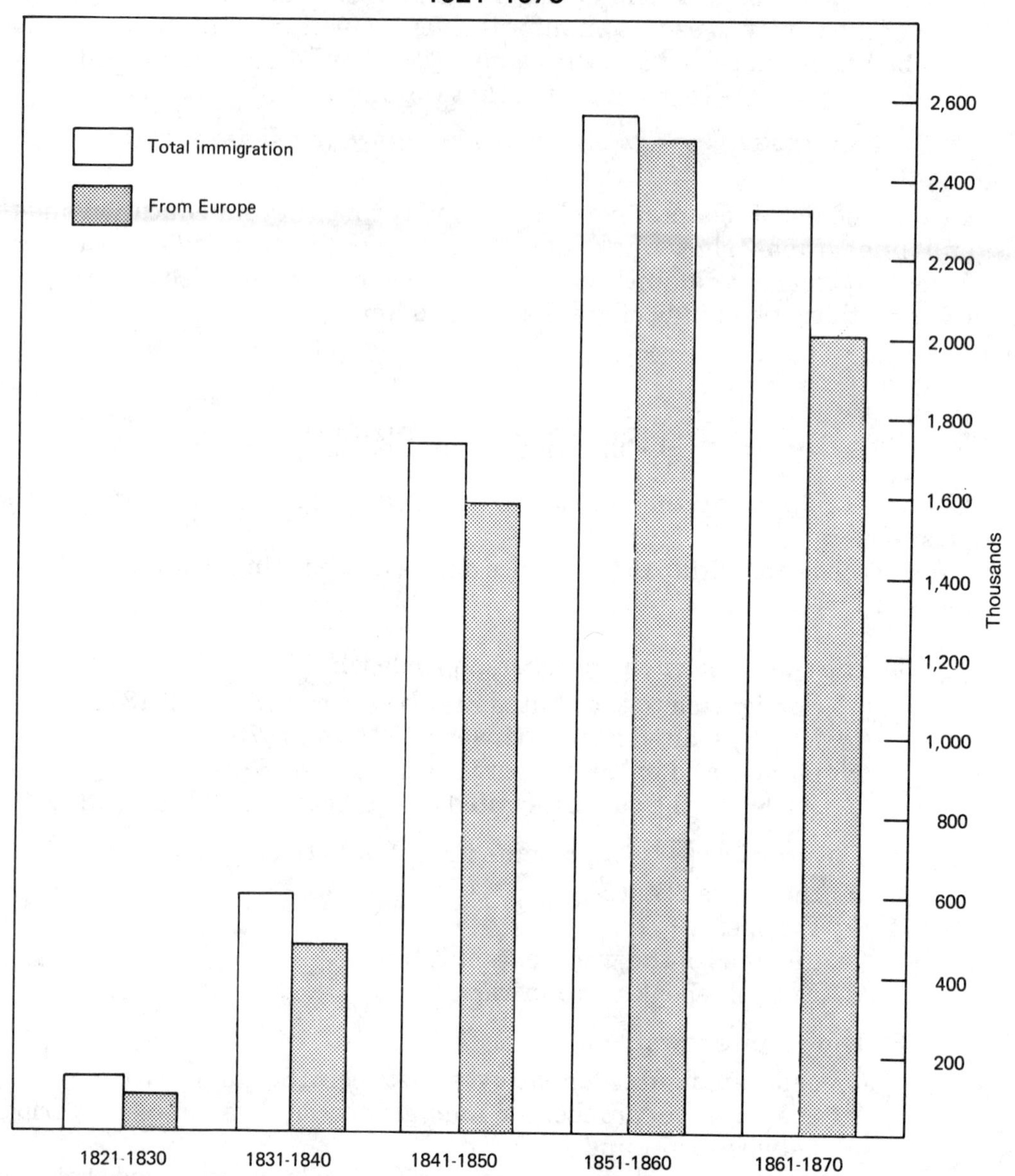

____ 6. Immigration from Europe totaled 2,000,000 in the period
   (a) 1831–1840.
   (b) 1841–1850.
   (c) 1851–1860.
   (d) 1861–1870.

____ 7. How many immigrants came to the United States from Europe between 1841 and 1860?
   (a) nearly 1,500,000
   (b) nearly 2,500,000
   (c) nearly 4,100,000
   (d) nearly 5,100,000

____ 8. Between 1861 and 1870, immigration from all areas of the world except Europe totaled approximately
(*a*) 50,000. (*c*) 200,000.
(*b*) 100,000. (*d*) 350,000.

____ 9. Which event might explain why the total immigration was less between 1861–1870 than it was between 1851–1860?
(*a*) American Revolution (*c*) U.S.–Mexican War
(*b*) War of 1812 (*d*) American Civil War

____ 10. Based on the graph, which statement is most likely to be true?
(*a*) Throughout most of the 1800s, European culture strongly influenced the United States.
(*b*) Throughout most of the 1800s, Europeans had an easy time adjusting to American life.
(*c*) Throughout most of the 1800s, most non-Europeans either lacked the means or had no reason to come to the United States.
(*d*) Throughout most of the 1800s, non-Europeans came to the United States in the same numbers as Europeans.

B. Percentage Bar Graphs. Study the following percentage bar graphs. Then answer the questions.

Sectional Assets* at the Start of the Civil War

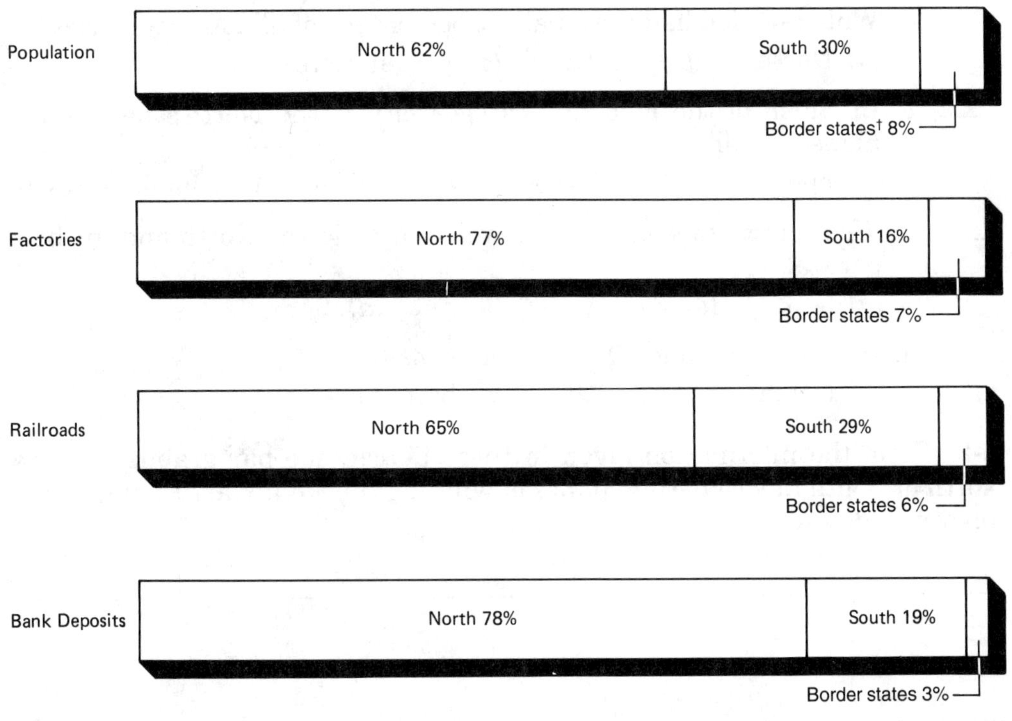

Population
North 62%
South 30%
Border states† 8%

Factories
North 77%
South 16%
Border states 7%

Railroads
North 65%
South 29%
Border states 6%

Bank Deposits
North 78%
South 19%
Border states 3%

*Advantages, property, things of value.
†"Border states" refer to Maryland, Kentucky, Missouri, Delaware, and West Virginia. They were slave states that fought on the side of the North during the Civil War. West Virginia, once part of Virginia, became a separate state in 1863.

B-1. Write the letter of the correct choice on the line next to each question.

_____ 1. These bar graphs show the
(a) percentage of population, factories, railroads, and bank deposits that belonged to the North, South, and border states.
(b) percentage of population that worked in factories in the North, South, and border states.
(c) total number of people, factories, railroads, and bank deposits in the North, South, and border states.
(d) total number of people who worked in factories and the railroad industry in the North, South, and border states.

_____ 2. What percentage of factories was located in the North?
(a) 7% *(b)* 16% *(c)* 24% *(d)* 77%

_____ 3. For which category did the South have 19% of the total?
(a) population *(b)* factories *(c)* railroads *(d)* bank deposits

_____ 4. Which section had 6% of railroads?
(a) North *(b)* South *(c)* border states

_____ 5. What percentage of population was NOT found in the North?
(a) 30% *(b)* 38% *(c)* 62% *(d)* 68%

_____ 6. Which border state was once part of another state?
(a) Maryland *(b)* West Virginia *(c)* Delaware *(d)* Missouri

_____ 7. Which section had the smallest percentage of all four categories?
(a) North *(b)* South *(c)* border states

_____ 8. In which of the following categories was the North's percentage highest of all?
(a) population *(b)* factories *(c)* railroads *(d)* bank deposits

_____ 9. What percentage of factories was located in the North and the border states?
(a) 84% *(b)* 87% *(c)* 93% *(d)* 94%

_____ 10. Which section had 19% of bank deposits?
(a) North *(b)* South *(c)* border states

B-2. From the information given in these percentage bar graphs, did the North or South have a better chance of winning the Civil War? Explain your answer in detail.

____

____

____

____

____

____

C. Double Line Graph. Study the following double line graph. Then answer the questions.

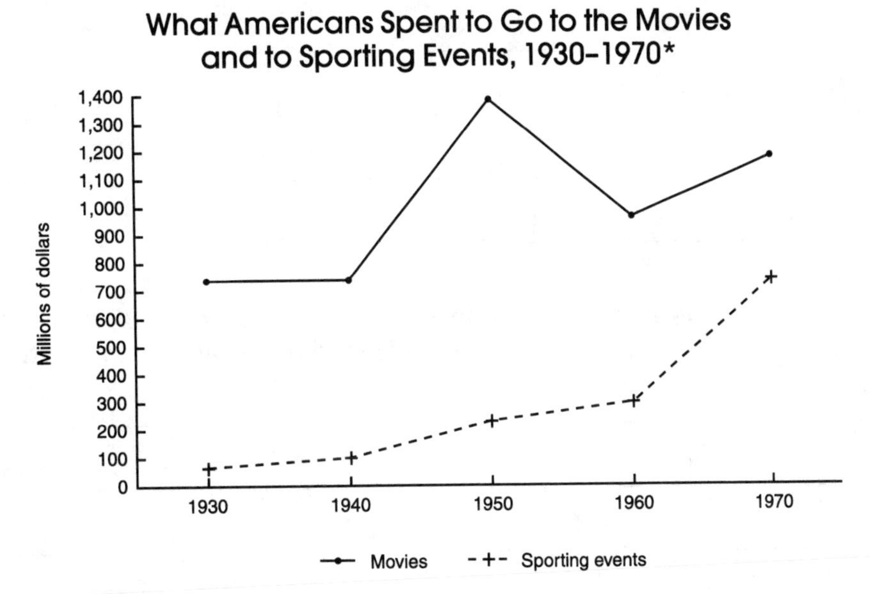

*Starting 1960, the figures include Alaska and Hawaii.

C-1. True or False. If the underlined word or words make the statement true, write TRUE on the line to the left of the statement. If the underlined word or words make the statement false, write on the line to the left the word or words that will make the statement true.

____________________ 1. $1,200 million is the same as $1.2 billion.

____________________ 2. In 1940, Americans spent about $200 million attending sporting events.

____________________ 3. In 1930 and 1960, Americans spent nearly the same amount to go to the movies.

____________________ 4. Between 1930 and 1970, sporting events *revenue* (total income from one source) increased by approximately $650 million.

____________________ 5. In 1950, Americans spent nearly $1.1 billion at the movies and at sporting events.

____________________ 6. Starting in 1970, figures included Alaska and Hawaii.

C-2. 1. What trend does this chart show concerning money spent on sporting events?

____

____

____

2. The U.S. population increased by nearly 83 million between 1930 and 1970. Do you think this increase had anything to do with the trend you stated in question 1? Explain.

____

____

____

____

C-3. Television was introduced to most Americans in the 1950s. Does the graph show how the arrival of television affected movie attendance? Explain.

____

____

____

____

____

D. Bar Graph. Study the following bar graph. Then answer the questions that follow.

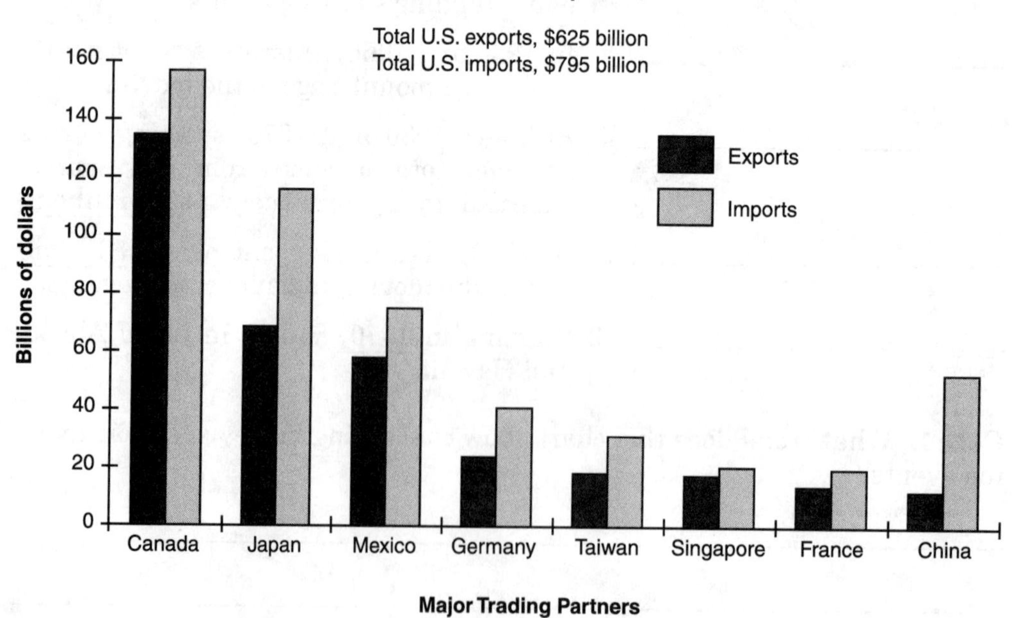

Write the letter of the correct choice on the line next to the number of each question.

_____ 1. The bar graph shows that in 1996
(a) the value of U.S. exports was less than the value of its imports.
(b) the value of U.S. imports was less than the value of its exports.
(c) the value of U.S. exports and imports was nearly the same.
(d) the value of U.S. imports was double the value of its exports.

_____ 2. Which statement is true?
(a) Imports are goods sold to another country, and exports are goods bought from another country.
(b) Exports are goods that one country buys from or sells to another country.
(c) Exports are goods sold to another country, and imports are goods bought from another country.
(d) Imports are goods that one country buys from or sells to another country.

_____ 3. Total U.S. exports for 1996 were $625 billion. That figure also can be written
(a) $625.
(b) $625,000.
(c) $625,000,000
(d) $625,000,000,000.

_____ 4. In 1996, the biggest U.S. trading partner was
(a) Canada. (c) France.
(b) Japan. (d) China.

_____ 5. In 1996, U.S. imports from Germany totaled approximately
(a) $15 billion. (c) $44 billion.
(b) $39 billion. (d) $65 billion.

_____ 6. From which country did the United States import the least amount in 1996?
(a) Taiwan (c) France
(b) Mexico (d) China

_____ 7. Which country shows the largest gap between what it buys from the United States and what it sells to it?
(a) China (c) Germany
(b) Canada (d) Japan

_____ 8. Which country buys more from the United States than it sells to it?
(a) Mexico (c) France
(b) China (d) none

_____ 9. Imports and exports were nearly equal for
(a) Germany. (c) Taiwan.
(b) Singapore. (d) Canada.

____ 10. A *trade deficit* exists when a country imports more than it exports. The size of the deficit depends on how large the difference is between the imports and the exports. In 1996, the trade deficit of the United States was

(*a*) $170 billion. (*c*) $795 billion.
(*b*) $625 billion. (*d*) $1.4 trillion.

E. Double Line Graph. Study the following double line graph. Then answer the questions.

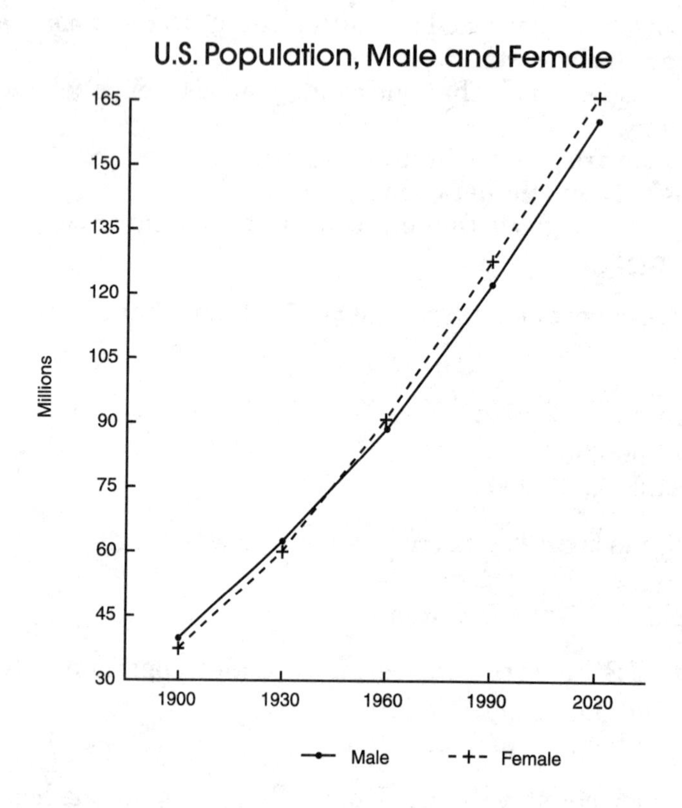

E-1. Short Answer Questions.

1. What information is represented by the broken line --------?

____

2. Using only numbers and commas, you can also write 110 million as

____

3. The female population in 1990 was approximately

____

4. In 1900, was the male or female population larger?

____

5. For which year is the population an estimate?

____

6. In 1960, the total population of the United States was approximately

____

7. In 1970, the male population was approximately

____

8. In which year were the male and female populations approximately the same?

____

9. How much did the female population increase between 1930 and 1960?

____

10. Between 1990 and 2020, the total population of the United States is projected to increase by approximately

____

E-2. What trend(s) do you see in this chart? What statistics show the trend(s)? Explain?

____

____

____

____

____

____

E-3. Why would the following people be interested in this chart?

1. Movie producer

____

____

____

2. Politician

3. Automobile manufacturer

F. Creating Percentage Bar Graphs. Read the following selection, then use the bars below to create percentage bar graphs showing age distribution for the three years given in the selection. The bars in your percentage bar graphs should look similar to those on pages 226 and 233. Give your graphs a title, and be sure to label all statistics.

A look at the 20th century shows that Americans are getting older. In 1900, as the 20th century was about to begin, 44.4 percent of Americans were under 20 years of age, 51.4 percent were between 20 and 64 years of age, and only 4.2 percent were 65 years of age or older. In 1950, 33.9 percent were under 20, 57.9 percent were between 20 and 64, and 8.2 percent were 65 or older. But in 1998, according to estimates, 28.7 percent were under 20, 58.6 percent were between 20 and 64, and 12.7 percent were 65 or older. We can only wonder how long Americans at the end of the 21st century will live.

CHAPTER 20

Interpreting Drawings and Photographs

Corbis-Bettmann

Corbis-Bettmann

George Washington and John Quincy Adams served as the first and sixth presidents of the United States. They appear above in two very different kinds of pictures. George Washington, on the left, is shown in a drawing, while John Quincy Adams, on the right, is seen in a photograph. We accept the fact that Washington looked like the person in the drawing because his appearance is similar to that in other drawings of him, and it also matches written descriptions. We know that the photograph shows Adams as he really looked because a photograph shows true-life images.

Both pictures offer more than recognizable images of past presidents. There are deeper meanings in such pictures if you know what to look for. In this chapter, you will learn how to *interpret* (explain the meaning of) drawings and photographs.

Drawings

No one knows exactly when human beings first drew pictures of themselves and their world. Over tens of thousands of years, drawings developed from simple sketches of animals on cave walls to such polished portraits as the one of George Washington shown on page 241. We rely on drawings to show us what happened during the major events in history, especially those events before the invention of photography. The drawings may have been done at the time of an event or centuries later. The most important thing to remember is that a drawing shows only what the artist wants us to see. Artists can add what they want to a drawing or leave out what they do not want us to see. Let us explore the intentions of one artist by answering the following question.

1. What do you think the artist who drew George Washington wanted us to think of Washington?

____

____

____

____

What did you write? Different answers are possible, but surely the artist was trying to show Washington as a noble man—honorable, strong, and worthy of being the first president. An artist who disliked Washington might have produced a very different drawing. Remember that we see in a drawing only what the artist wants us to see.

Photographs

The photograph of John Quincy Adams is very special. It was taken in 1848, nine years after the invention of the camera and 19 years after Adams had finished his term as president. No photograph exists of any earlier president. Adams had to sit perfectly still for several minutes as his image was slowly transferred onto a rectangular glass plate. As a result, there now exists an accurate, historical record of what the sixth president of the United States really looked like.

Fortunately, photographs have captured much of U.S. history since 1839. We can study true-life images from the Civil War, watch the settlement of the American West, and know what U.S. cities looked like through much of the 19th century. In the 20th century, the range of still photography has been expanded by motion pictures. Together, they have produced visual histories of World War I, World War II, and the landing of the first human on the moon. The magic of photographs and films will continue to show future generations what the past really looked like.

Let us look again at the photograph of John Quincy Adams to see what it can teach us. The first observation is obvious: the photograph shows what Adams looked like. Now answer the following question.

2. List two additional observations you can make about this photograph.

   a. ______________________________

   ____

   ____

   ____

   ____

   b. ______________________________

   ____

   ____

   ____

   ____

Here are some possible answers. First, you can see what Adams was wearing. His clothes are probably representative of what many men wore in the late 1840s. Second, the room where this photograph was taken seems to be decorated simply. The lamp on the table has no cord, which reminds us that oil, not electricity, lit the lamps of America in the 1840s. Something else of interest about this photograph is Adams's solemn face. Early photographs rarely show people smiling, and there are various explanations for this fact. Some people claim that such serious faces showed the effort of sitting still for several minutes while the camera took the picture. Others think that seriousness was the style of the day. Still others say that life in the 19th century was often difficult and gave few people reason to smile.

We can say with confidence that this photograph shows us exactly what Adams looked like. At the same time, we should be aware that modern computer *technology* (the materials and machines used in a given field) can change a photograph. Like artists, modern photographers can produce the pictures that they want us to see. People and objects can be removed or inserted. Frowns can be changed into smiles. Heads can be put on various bodies. Guns can be put into people's hands—or removed from them. With computer technology, the image of Adams could be cut out of his surroundings in the photograph and placed on a ride in an amusement park. He could be given a long beard or dressed in a major-league baseball uniform. It was once said that the camera does not lie. We can no longer be certain of that.

Captions

Few people would know that the man in the photograph at the beginning of this chapter is John Quincy Adams. What you see in many drawings and photographs is not enough to give you an understanding of the picture. Look at the photograph below. It shows a scene from an important period in United States history. But which event does it show? All we can see is a group of people posing for a picture. But there are questions left unanswered. Who are those people? When and where was this photograph taken? What is needed here, as is needed for Adams's photograph, is a *caption,* placed under or next to the photograph. The caption would provide details on what is shown in the photograph. Here is the caption that belongs to the photograph: "Confederate soldiers capture Fort Sumter on April 15, 1861, during what is considered the first battle of the Civil War." Now you know that this photograph has to do with the Civil War.

The Charleston Museum, Charleston, South Carolina

You know that the people in the photograph—or at least, most of them—are Confederate soldiers. (During the Civil War, the South was called the Confederate States of America, or the Confederacy. The North was called the United States of America, or the Union. So Southern soldiers were called Confederates, and Northern soldiers were called Union soldiers.) Next, you know that at the time this photograph was taken (April 15, 1861), the soldiers had captured Fort Sumter. Finally, you know that the attack on Fort Sumter is considered the first battle of the Civil War. Without the caption, you could only guess at the event shown. This is why it is important to read the caption that goes along with a picture.

Now that we know the facts, can we also look for a deeper meaning in this photograph? The soldiers look relaxed. Perhaps they think that all their battles will be as successful as their capture of Fort Sumter. In a way, these soldiers represent the feelings of many people during the early months of the war. At first, many Northerners and Southerners saw the war as a great adventure. They had no idea that it would take four long years and cause the deaths of hundreds of thousands of people. The photograph seems to show that innocence. It gives no clue to the great tragedy about to unfold.

Now look at the more modern photograph below. Does it need a caption?

This photograph includes a drawing (a billboard showing a family enjoying an automobile ride). First, answer a question about the drawing.

3. What is the message of the drawing in the photograph?

____

____

____

____

____

____

Margaret Bourke-White/LIFE Magazine © TIME Inc.

What did you write? The drawing is telling Americans that they are lucky because they have the highest standard of living in the world. It also seems to say that happiness depends on possessing all the things that American technology can produce. In particular, you need to own a car.

4. What is the message of the entire photograph?

____

____

____

____

____

____

____

____

This question is tricky. The photograph was taken during the Great Depression by a famous photographer, Margaret Bourke-White. When it first appeared in *Life* magazine in 1937, many people interpreted it as a comment on racial divisions in the United States. The white people in the car seem unaffected by the Depression. In contrast, the African Americans are on a line, with empty baskets in hand, and they seem to need something. Certainly, African Americans suffered terribly during the Depression, but so did many white Americans. It would be unfair to suggest that most white Americans were as happy during the Depression as the well-off family in the automobile. This photograph needs a caption. Here's the actual one: "Flood victims in a Negro town wait for food." Perhaps this is not the caption that you were expecting. The people are on line not because they are poor or the victims of racism but because they are victims of a flood. In fact, they look well dressed. This photograph brings up an important point: photographs may be misinterpreted. If you see a photograph of a person crying, you will not necessarily know if the tears are of joy or of sorrow. That is why a caption is often needed.

You have seen in this chapter how drawings and photographs can add to your understanding of history. Here are the points to remember when you are studying a picture:

1. Carefully study all the details of the picture.
2. Read the caption if there is one. It usually gives specific facts, such as the date and location of the scene or the names of the people shown.
3. Look for deeper meaning in the picture. Think about what it is trying to show you.

In the following exercises, you will have the opportunity to use these points in interpreting drawings and photographs.

USING YOUR SKILLS

A. Study the pictures on page 246. Then answer the questions.

For questions 1 to 4, place the letter of the correct choice next to the number of each question.

____ 1. Which statement is TRUE?

(a) Picture A is a photograph.
(b) Picture B is a photograph.
(c) Pictures A and B are both photographs.
(d) Pictures A and B are both drawings.

Picture A

The Granger Collection, New York

Black soldiers join the Union Army.

Picture B

Corbis-Bettmann

Black soldiers fight for the Union.

____ 2. Picture A shows African American soldiers
(*a*) protesting the Civil War.
(*b*) fighting for the Confederacy.
(*c*) opposing slavery.
(*d*) joining the Union Army.

____ 3. In Pictures A and B, the soldiers are
(*a*) poorly dressed and without rifles.
(*b*) dressed in full uniform and equipped with rifles.
(*c*) wearing many different kinds of uniforms.
(*d*) waiting to be given uniforms.

____ 4. In Picture A, the soldiers appear to be
(*a*) in a room. (*c*) in front of a building.
(*b*) near a field. (*d*) next to a tree.

5. In what way are Pictures A and B alike?

____

____

____

____

6. Which picture (A or B) would more likely influence people to join the army? Explain your answer.

____

____

____

____

7. How does Picture B support the following statement? "Though African Americans were asked to fight in the Civil War, they were not given positions of leadership in the army." Explain your answer.

____

____

____

____

B. Study the following drawing. Then answer the questions.

Buffalo Bill Historical Center, Cody, WY. Gift of Winchester-Western Division, Olin Corporation

Looking to make a home in the West (late 1800s)

For questions 1 and 2, write the letter of the correct choice on the line next to the number of each question.

_____ 1. You can tell that the scene in the drawing took place in the West in the late 1800s because

(a) the caption says so.
(b) no automobiles are shown.
(c) the people in the drawing look very serious.
(d) at that time it was legal to carry a rifle.

____ 2. Which statement is TRUE?

(a) You can be sure that the artist observed this scene with his own eyes.

(b) The drawing shows you only what the artist wants you to see.

(c) Drawings never show events as they really happened.

(d) You can be sure that no photograph of this scene was taken.

3. Make two lists of the belongings that the family in the drawing were taking with them. In the first list, write down belongings you can see in the drawing. In the second list, write down what you think might be found in the covered wagon.

Belongings in the drawing

____

____

____

____

____

____

Belongings that might be in the covered wagon

____

____

____

____

____

4. What do you see in the drawing that suggests that families moving west in the late 1800s expected to run into difficulty? Explain your answer.

____

____

____

____

5. In your opinion, what did the artist want people to think about when they looked at this drawing? Explain your answer.

C. Study the following drawing. Then answer the questions.

Reproduced from *A Pictographic History of the Oglala Sioux* by Amos Bad Heart Bull by permission from the University of Nebraska Press.

This scene from the Battle of the Little Big Horn was drawn by Sioux artist Amos Bad Heart Bull. The battle took place on June 25, 1876, in what is now Montana. In the course of an hour, U.S. Army General George Custer and his 264 men were killed by Sioux, led by Chief Crazy Horse.

1. Why is the caption important to understanding this drawing?

2. The significance of this drawing is that it was done by a Sioux. List at least two things in the drawing that show favorable feelings for the Sioux.

3. List two weapons used by the Sioux.

4. How does this drawing show that U.S. Army soldiers and the Sioux rode their horses differently?

5. Do you think that Sioux Chief Crazy Horse is shown in this drawing? If so, what makes you think so? Explain your answer.

D. Study the photograph on page 252.

Write an essay explaining why this photograph would disturb most Americans today.

Courtesy George Eastman House

American mine workers

E. Study the three photographs of San Francisco. Then answer the questions following.

E-1. Write the letter of the correct choice on the line next to the question.

_____ 1. The three photographs of San Francisco cover a period of
(a) 50 years. *(b)* 90 years. *(c)* 140 years. *(d)* 200 years.

_____ 2. In which photograph or photographs is San Francisco's closeness to a large body of water shown.
(a) Photograph A
(b) Photographs A and B
(c) Photograph C
(d) Photographs B and C

_____ 3. Photograph B shows San Francisco
(a) at the end of the Civil War.
(b) following the earthquake of April 1906.
(c) at the start of Word War II.
(d) during race riots in the 1960s.

_____ 4. The fact that early cameras had difficulty photographing movement might explain why Photograph A was taken
(a) when people were asleep.
(b) in daylight.
(c) on a cloudy day.
(d) when the streets were empty of people and animals.

Photograph A

Courtesy George Eastman House

San Francisco, 1856

Photograph B

Arnold Genthe, American, born Germany, 1869–1942, The burning city, San Francisco earthquake and fire, gelatin silver print, printed by Ansel Adams, 1956, April 1906, 119.1 × 31.9 cm, Peabody Fund, 1956.1098, photograph © 1998, The Art Institute of Chicago. All Rights Reserved.

San Francisco following the earthquake of April 1906

Photograph C

Matthew Frost/Corbis-Bettmann

San Francisco, 1996

____ 5. Photograph C shows that
(*a*) the people of San Francisco have no fear of future earthquakes.
(*b*) the fear of earthquakes has prevented the construction of tall buildings in San Francisco.
(*c*) San Francisco has built tall buildings despite the fear of earthquakes.
(*d*) San Francisco lies in a geographical area subject to many earthquakes.

E-2.

1. If you were alive in 1856 and saw Photograph A, would it make you want to live in San Francisco? Explain your answer.

____

____

____

____

2. Describe the destruction you see in Photograph B.

____

____

____

____

3. How does Photograph C support the following statement?

"San Francisco values its past while it builds for the future." Explain your answer.

____

____

____

____

CHAPTER 21

Interpreting Political Cartoons

Most of us are familiar with cartoons. These drawings present ideas and points of view in a simplified and exaggerated form. Most cartoons aim to be humorous. Some are meant only to amuse; others are intended to make us think or feel a certain way about an issue. They are called *political cartoons* when the ideas they express relate to history, government, or politics. Over the centuries, many cartoonists (people who draw cartoons) have expressed their feelings and opinions through political cartoons. In this chapter, you will learn how political cartoons can be used to teach important lessons in U.S. history.

To understand the meaning of a political cartoon, you have to think carefully about what is shown. For example, look at the following cartoon.

What is the message of this cartoon? It shows a snake cut into eight sections. Each section is labeled with one or two letters. Underneath is the caption: Join, or Die.

This cartoon, drawn by Benjamin Franklin in 1754, is believed to be the first political cartoon to appear in America. Its purpose was to urge the colonies to support the Albany Plan of Union. (See page 47 for a selection on the Albany Plan of Union.) Perhaps you have already figured out that the labels on the different sections are abbreviations for various colonies. M., for example, stands for Maryland, and N.E. stands for New England (Massachusetts, Connecticut, New Hampshire, and Rhode Island combined). Franklin used the illustration of a snake because, like many people in the 18th century, he mistakenly believed that a cut-up snake could grow back together. He was saying that, like a cut-up snake, the separate colonies could join together and become strong. For more than two centuries, this cartoon has inspired many other cartoons with a similar theme.

Let us look at a cartoon drawn by Thomas Nast in the 1870s. (See page 257.) It shows two of the most commonly used figures in American political cartoons. The woman is Miss Columbia, who often appeared in cartoons in the middle and late 1800s. The man is Uncle Sam, who is still a popular cartoon figure. In this cartoon, he has not yet grown the white beard seen in his later cartoon appearances.

LET THE GOOD WORK (HOUSE-CLEANING) GO ON

MISS COLUMBIA—"Uncle Sam, you keep on cleaning the ballot-box, while I give this a scrubbing—goodness knows, it needs it!"

Answer the following questions based on this cartoon.

_____ 1. The caption tells us that
- *(a)* Miss Columbia and Uncle Sam have nothing to say to each other.
- *(b)* Uncle Sam is speaking to Miss Columbia.
- *(c)* Miss Columbia is speaking to Uncle Sam.
- *(d)* Uncle Sam and Miss Columbia are speaking at the same time.

Which answer did you choose? Question 1 points out the need to read the caption, if there is one. Without a caption, this cartoon would be hard to understand. The caption states: LET THE GOOD WORK (HOUSE-CLEANING) GO ON. It also states: Miss Columbia—"Uncle Sam, you keep on cleaning the ballot-box, while I give this a scrubbing—goodness knows, it needs it!" From the caption, we know that Miss Columbia is speaking to Uncle Sam. Therefore, the answer to question 1 is *(c)*.

_____ 2. Miss Columbia is about to scrub
- *(a)* the floor.
- *(b)* the walls.
- *(c)* a door.
- *(d)* a bench.

Which answer did you choose? From the caption, you know that Miss Columbia is about to scrub something, but you have to look at the drawing to see what it is. Miss Columbia is carrying a pail and a brush. A bar of "reform soap" is on the floor next to a bench. Most importantly, Miss Columbia is looking directly at the bench as she speaks. So we know that she is about to scrub the bench. Therefore, the answer to question 2 is *(d)*.

Why does Miss Columbia want to scrub the bench? The answer is that the bench represents dishonest government officials. Miss Columbia wants to scrub them away. Who are these dishonest officials? The only words on the bench that are easy to read are "judges" and "ring." In the 1870s, when Nast drew this cartoon, the public understood that "judges" and "ring" referred to New York City judges who were illegally controlled by the Tweed Ring, led by Boss (William Marcy) Tweed. This brings up an important point. Political cartoonists usually deal with current topics and, therefore, presume that the public knows something about these topics.

3. How do you know that reforms to get rid of dishonest government officials have already begun?

____

____

____

____

____

____

What did you write? Uncle Sam is cleaning something, and the caption tells us that it is the ballot box. The caption also tells us that Uncle Sam should "keep on cleaning the ballot-box." Both the cartoon and the caption show that reforms have already begun.

In the 20th century, a commonly used figure in political cartoons has been the Statue of Liberty. During the early 1980s, major repair work was done on the statue, which inspired the following 1983 cartoon by Don Wright.

Answer the following questions.

4. According to the cartoonist, what change was made to the Statue of Liberty?

____

____

____

____

____

What did you write? First, you have to know what the real Statute of Liberty looks like. Any photograph of it will show that the statue's right arm extends up, with the right hand lifting a torch. In this drawing, however, the right hand is giving a thumb's-down (not welcome) gesture.

5. What change in U.S. immigration policy prompted Don Wright to draw this cartoon?

____

____

____

____

____

What did you write? You may think that you could not know what change was made? No specific change is mentioned in the cartoon. Clearly, this cartoonist expects you to know about the issues in the cartoon. When this cartoon was published, changes in U.S. immigration policy were being discussed on television and the radio and in newspapers and magazines. But even if you don't know the details, you can figure out the main idea. The Statue of Liberty is a symbol of the American tradition of welcoming immigrants. The thumb's-down gesture suggests that the United States no longer accepts immigrants as freely as before. Someone on the passing ship is saying that the repairs "accurately reflect immigration policy." So you can presume that the cartoonist is commenting on a recent government policy that limits immigration in some way.

6. This cartoon reflects Don Wright's personal opinion. How can we tell whether it also accurately states the facts?

____

____

____

____

____

What did you write? Wright's cartoon is clever, even humorous. But is it accurate or inaccurate? You can enjoy a cartoon and still disagree with the opinion it expresses, or realize that it does not tell the whole truth. Surely, not all Americans saw the new immigration policy of the 1980s as negatively as Wright did. To know the truth about an issue, you need to be informed about it; you should read the newspapers or follow the news on television or the radio. The more you know about an issue, the less you will be influenced by versions of it that are merely clever and humorous.

In this chapter, you have studied three political cartoons from three different centuries. Cartoons can add to your knowledge, understanding, and enjoyment of U.S. history. That is why they are included in so many U.S. history books. That is also why you should know how to interpret them. The following exercises will give you more practice in interpreting political cartoons.

USING YOUR SKILLS

A. Abraham Lincoln and the Civil War. Study the cartoon below, and then answer the questions.

1. In this cartoon, the United States is shown as a

____

2. Instead of calling Abraham Lincoln the president, this cartoon refers to him as

____

3. We know that this cartoon deals with the early days of Lincoln's presidency because

____

____

4. "Union glue" represents

____

____

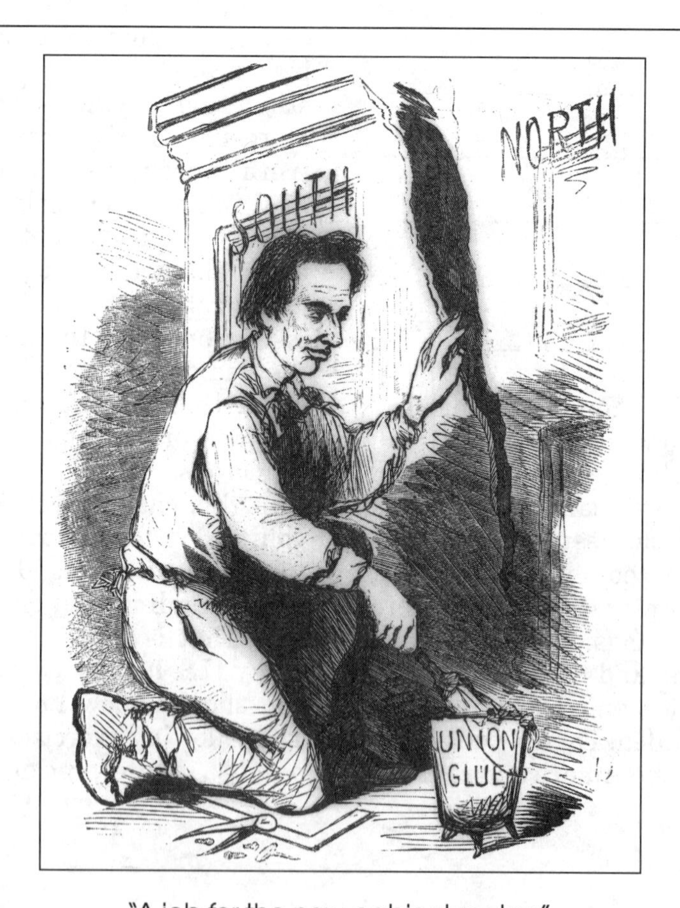

"A job for the new cabinet maker."

5. State one fact about the subject of the cartoon that the cartoonist presumes we know.

____

____

B. Thomas Nast on the treatment of minorities in the 1870s. Study the following cartoon, and then answer the questions.

THE CHINESE QUESTION.—

COLUMBIA.—HANDS OFF, GENTLEMEN: AMERICA MEANS FAIR PLAY FOR ALL MEN."

1. What is the main idea of this cartoon?

____

____

____

2. What information in the cartoon helped you to answer question 1?

____

____

____

3. Who is the woman in the cartoon, and what does she represent?

____

____

____

____

4. Give two negative comments that were made about Chinese immigrants.

a. _______________

____

b. _______________

____

5. Can you tell whether Thomas Nast was addressing a bigger issue than the treatment of one particular immigrant group? Explain your answer.

____

____

____

____

C. World War II. Study the following cartoon, and then answer the questions.

C-1. Write the letter of the correct choice on the line next to the number of each question.

_____ 1. The figure tied up is
- *(a)* Uncle Sam.
- *(b)* the president of the United States.
- *(c)* the United States Congress.
- *(d)* the king of England.

_____ 2. World War II is approaching
- *(a)* from the center of the earth.
- *(b)* on horseback.
- *(c)* across the desert.
- *(d)* in the clouds crossing the ocean.

_____ 3. The little people in the cartoon
- *(a)* want the United States to become involved in World War II.
- *(b)* do not want the United States to be involved in World War II.
- *(c)* are the cause of World War II.
- *(d)* do not believe that any war is coming.

_____ 4. From the caption, we can presume that the cartoonist believes that
- *(a)* the United States must become involved in the approaching war.
- *(b)* the main figure in the cartoon has to be kept tied down.
- *(c)* the United States can keep World War II from reaching American soil.
- *(d)* the United States can keep World War II from starting.

_____ 5. Which statement is TRUE?
- *(a)* The United States is asleep as World War II approaches.
- *(b)* The cartoonist believes that the United States is asleep as World War II approaches.
- *(c)* The cartoonist can prove that the United States is asleep as World War II approaches.
- *(d)* The groups represented by the little people in the cartoon are responsible for keeping Uncle Sam asleep.

C-2. Read the two statements and answer the question that follows:

Statement 1

"If the United States had played a more active role in world affairs, it could have prevented World War II."

Statement 2

"Some Americans thought that World War II would never reach the United States."

Which statement is supported by the cartoon? Explain your answer.

____

____

____

____

____

D. U.S. Involvement in Vietnam. Study the cartoon on page 265, and then answer the questions.

D-1. Write the letter of the correct choice on the line next to the number of each question.

_____ 1. This cartoon was first published in 1966, at the height of the debate over **escalation** (increase) of U.S. involvement in Vietnam. Therefore, the public understood that this cartoon referred to Vietnam
- *(a)* even though Vietnam is not specifically mentioned.
- *(b)* because war existed in no other part of the world at that time.
- *(c)* because Vietnam was the only war-torn area in Asia in the 1960s.
- *(d)* even though the cartoonist did not want readers to know that he was referring to Vietnam.

THE STRATEGISTS

_____ 2. The person going up the stairs wants
  (a) an end to U.S. involvement in Vietnam.
  (b) a total military victory in Vietnam.
  (c) to find a way down the stairs.
  (d) to sell arms to North Vietnam.

_____ 3. The cartoonist seems to think that the person who wants to escalate the war
  (a) is very brave.
  (b) does not see where the fighting will lead.
  (c) does not know how to fight.
  (d) is afraid to fight.

_____ 4. More than likely, the person whose head is in the sand
  (a) supports U.S. involvement in Vietnam.
  (b) is lost.
  (c) thinks that the United States should get out of Vietnam.
  (d) thinks that the war in Vietnam is morally justified.

_____ 5. According to the cartoonist, the person whose head is in the sand
  (a) is dead.
  (b) agrees with the views of the person on the stairs.
  (c) wants Americans to lead moral lives.
  (d) wants to ignore the problems of Asia.

D-2. In your own words, explain what this cartoon is saying.

____

____

____

____

____

D-3. In what way are the cartoon in this exercise and the cartoon in Exercise C saying the same thing? Explain your answer.

____

____

____

____

____

E. Equal Opportunity. Study the following cartoon, and then answer the questions.

By permission of Doug Marlette and Creators Syndicate.

1. What is the main idea of this cartoon?

____

____

____

____

2. What information in the cartoon helped you answer question 1?

____

____

____

____

3. According to the cartoonist, is the man or the woman working harder? Explain your answer.

____

____

____

____

4. This cartoon was first published in 1982. Do you believe the ideas that it expresses are true today? Explain your answer.

____

____

____

____

5. Will this cartoon still make sense if the woman is replaced by a man or woman from any minority group? Explain your answer.

____

____

____

____

CHAPTER 22

Using the Movie and Television Media

When we think of movies and television, the first word that usually comes to mind is entertainment. We expect movies and television to entertain us, to excite us, to expand our imagination. But another word could also come to mind. That word is information. Movies and television can be great sources of information. Many important events of history have become the subjects of movies and television programs. Television news shows bring the world into our homes every day. Most of us have heard the following announcement on television: "We interrupt this program to bring you a special news report." As much as we expect to be entertained by movies and television, we can also learn much from them.

In this chapter, you will develop the skill of turning two forms of *media,* movies and television, into effective tools for learning. (Media are systems of communication that also include magazines, newspapers, and radio.)

Movies

Let us first look at the kinds of movies commonly called feature films. Watching such a movie, especially one with a historical theme, requires a "critical eye." You have to ask yourself certain questions as you watch a movie that claims to be historical or factual. For example, let us say that you plan to watch *Gone With the Wind,* one of the most popular movies ever made. It deals mainly with the Southern experience in the Civil War and the rebuilding of the South after the war, a period in U.S. history known as Reconstruction. Here are some questions you might ask yourself while watching this movie.

1. What is the main idea of the movie?
2. Who are the important characters (people in a story), and do I understand what they stand for?
3. What can I learn about the story and the characters from the costumes and scenery? For example, do the costumes or the homes used in the movie show whether the characters are rich or poor?
4. How does the music make me feel about the story? Is it used to influence my opinion of a character?
5. Does the story give one point of view or many? Do all the characters get a chance to explain their feelings, or is the story seen through the eyes of only one or a few characters?
6. Is the story based on facts? Were the facts used correctly, or were they changed so much that the story is no longer historically accurate? What sources (books, magazines, encyclopedia, and so on) could I use to check the facts?

By using a "critical eye" and asking such questions, you will turn an entertaining movie into an informative one.

How well can you use your "critical eye" in the following example and questions?

Culver Pictures

Scarlett O'Hara in front of her family's plantation home, Tara, before the war.

The Kobal Collection/MGM Studios

Scarlett O'Hara and two house servants after the war, working hard to save Tara.

Example 1

Imagine that you are watching *Gone With the Wind.* The first half of the movie shows the life of privilege led by the South's wealthy plantation class before the Civil War.

The second half deals, in part, with how Scarlett O'Hara, a white Southern woman, struggles to save her family's plantation. We see her working hard in the cotton fields, wearing the same torn dress day after day. Like many other Southerners after the war, she is in danger of losing the plantation because she cannot pay the high taxes on it.

The struggle to pay the taxes and many other problems during Reconstruction are shown through the eyes of Scarlett O'Hara and other white Southerners. In time, Scarlett manages to pay the taxes and the plantation prospers.

Question 1(a)

In some stories, characters represent more than themselves. They may symbolize their country, a cause, a virtue, or an evil. In what ways does Scarlett O'Hara symbolize the South after the Civil War?

What did you write? Scarlett O'Hara and the South were on the losing side in the Civil War. Both suffered great losses. Both had to struggle to survive after the war. Scarlett O'Hara overcame her problems just as the South overcame its problems. Scarlett O'Hara prospered, and so did the South. In these ways, the character of Scarlett O'Hara symbolizes the South during Reconstruction.

Question 1(b)

Does this movie show Reconstruction from different points of view? Explain your answer.

What did you write this time? *Gone With the Wind* tells the story of Reconstruction from one point of view—that of white Southerners. A major criticism of the movie is that it does not present the views of black Southerners. Slaves are shown as childlike and devoted to their masters. The struggles they face when they are finally freed are not shown. In order to learn the complete story of Reconstruction, you need to know what newly freed slaves said about Reconstruction. You also need to know what Northerners thought. Surely, each of the three groups—white Southerners, newly freed slaves, and Northerners—would tell a different story.

Should you stay away from a movie that gives only one point of view? The answer is no, so long as you know that you are seeing only one point of view.

Documentaries

Movies such as *Gone With the Wind* are made primarily to entertain. Other kinds of movies, called *documentaries* (factual films), are made primarily to inform. Documentaries can be about one person, a group of people, or about an event or period in history. A narrator usually tells the story. Drawings and—if they exist—original photographs and films show what the narrator is talking about.

Watching a documentary also requires a "critical eye." You must ask yourself certain questions. What is the main idea of the documentary? Is music used to influence the way you think? Are different points of view given? Are facts used correctly and fairly?

A good documentary is factual. If it claims to present an issue fairly, it should show different points of view. Not all documentaries succeed in being so honest. Remember that you are seeing what the producer of the documentary wants you to see. The producer probably has a strong opinion on the subject of the documentary and may have made that opinion look like fact. This is why you have to watch with a "critical eye."

Let us see how well you can use your "critical eye" when watching a documentary.

Example 2

Imagine that you are watching a documentary on Reconstruction. The narrator states that the documentary will explore this difficult period in U.S. history. You hear President Abraham Lincoln's plan for Reconstruction as well as the Radical Republicans' plan. You hear that Lincoln and the Radical Republicans in Congress disagreed on how to deal with the South after the war. Lincoln wanted to be lenient (forgiving). The Radical Republicans wanted to punish the South severely for causing the war.

As many photographs of Lincoln and his family are shown, three historians speak favorably of Lincoln's plan for Reconstruction. Photographs of the Capitol in Washington, D.C., are shown as a single historian speaks in favor of the Radical Republicans' plan.

The narrator ends the documentary with a quote from Lincoln's Second Inaugural Address: "With malice toward none, with charity for all, with firmness in the right as God gives us to see the right, let us strive on to finish the work we are in, to bind up the nation's wounds, to care for him who shall have borne the battle and for his widow and his orphan, to do all which may achieve and cherish a just and lasting peace among ourselves and with all nations."

Question 2

Do you see anything unfair about the way this documentary was produced? Explain your answer.

____

____

Corbis-Bettmann

Corbis-Bettmann

President Abraham Lincoln and his wife, Mary Todd Lincoln

____

____

____

____

____

____

What did you write? The documentary began fairly; it gave both Lincoln's and the Radical Republicans' plans for Reconstruction. But then many photographs of Lincoln and his family were shown. Three historians favorable to Lincoln spoke. For this documentary to have been fair, an equal number of historians favoring the Radical Republicans should have given their opinions. Moreover, the Radical Republicans should have appeared on the screen as often as Lincoln and his family.

Television

Today, documentaries are more likely to be seen on television than in a movie theater. The same is true for classic movies like *Gone With the Wind.* That is why television is probably the most important of all the media. The following small but significant list of events in American life since 1960 will demonstrate the importance of television:

- September 26, 1960: Richard Nixon debates John F. Kennedy as part of the presidential campaign of 1960.
- July 20, 1969: Astronauts Neil Armstrong and Edwin Aldrin, Jr., take the first walk on the moon.
- August 9, 1974: Facing *impeachment* (charge of official wrongdoing) because of the growing Watergate scandal, Richard Nixon resigns as president.

- January 26, 1986: Space shuttle *Challenger* explodes seconds after being launched.
- June 17, 1994: Former football star O. J. Simpson, in his white Ford Bronco, is pursued by the police on the highways of southern California.

What do these events have to do with television? The answer is that all of them were seen on live television. Millions of people were able to witness them as they happened. As a result of such televised events, we now expect television cameras to be "where the action is." If anything significant happens anywhere in the world, we want to be able to turn on a television and see it "live."

Does watching television require skill? If you want to get the most out of your watching, the answer is yes. In 1960, Americans needed skill to watch and evaluate the Kennedy-Nixon debates. Skill is needed today if you want to understand a special news telecast or a television show dealing with historical or factual material.

Let us see how well you can use your "critical eye" when watching television.

Example 3

Imagine you are watching your favorite television program. Suddenly, a photograph of the White House appears on the screen. An announcer states, "We interrupt this program to bring you a special news report." The president of the United States appears, seated at his desk in the Oval Office of the White House. He greets the American people. Then he explains that he has asked for this television time to express concern over the failure of Congress to pass a budget. He expresses regret that without a budget he will be unable to pay federal workers. He announces, therefore, that he will begin tomorrow to close federal offices around the country. He urges all Americans to put pressure on Congress to pass his budget. He bids the American people goodnight. You think that your favorite program is about to resume, but a television commentator appears. She begins to interview a member of Congress, who blames the president for not reaching an agreement on the budget. The member of Congress states that the president's budget is too high, and that only Congress's version of the budget is good for the country. After the commentator asks several more questions, she thanks the member of Congress and states to the camera, "We now return to our regularly scheduled program."

Corbis-Bettmann

Bill Clinton
The White House

Question 3(a)

In using television to present his side of the budget issue, what advantage did the president have over the member of Congress?

___

___

___

___

What did you write? Television was on the side of the president in this special news report. The president was shown looking "presidential" at his desk in the Oval Office of the White House. He did not have to share the television screen with a commentator, as did the member of Congress. Seeing the president look so "presidential," some Americans might be quick to believe his side of the budget debate.

Question 3(b)

In your opinion, what could the commentator have said or done to influence viewers for or against the member of Congress?

____

____

____

____

____

____

____

____

What did you write? There are different possible answers. Perhaps the commentator asked very challenging questions. She decided how much time the member of Congress was allowed to answer each question. She was in a position to challenge those answers. On the other hand, she may have asked questions sympathetic to Congress's position. In such ways, the commentator had the power to make the member of Congress look good or bad.

As you watch a television news program, a documentary, or a historical feature film, you may decide to learn more about its subject. Your library is a good place to begin; you will find a good choice of U.S. history books there. In the case of the special news report on the budget, you might read about the issue in a daily newspaper or a news magazine. In the case of a documentary, you might read a biography of a person featured in the documentary to see if it agrees with information about the person given in the film. In the case of a movie such as *Gone With the Wind,* you might read the book it was based on to see if the movie story matches the one in the book. (It is easier to watch television or a movie than to read a book, but a book is usually much richer in details.) Finally, you might search the Internet for Web sites on topics related to your media source.

You have seen in this chapter that movies and television can be important tools for learning. The next time that you watch a movie, a documentary, or a special news telecast, be sure to use your "critical eye." The following exercises will give you more practice in the skill of watching movies and television programs critically.

USING YOUR SKILLS

A. Answer the following questions based on what you have read in this chapter.

1. List three things in a movie or television program that might influence the way you feel about one of the characters.

____

____

____

2. How do you watch a movie with a "critical eye?"

____

____

____

3. If a historical topic in a movie interests you, where can you find more information on the topic?

____

____

____

4. What is a documentary?

____

____

____

5. What should an "honest" documentary contain?

____

____

____

B. Watching a Movie. Read the following selection based on the movie *Tennessee Johnson.* Then answer the questions.

Imagine that you are watching a movie about the attempt of the Radical Republicans in Congress to remove President Andrew Johnson from office. (Andrew Johnson became president in 1865 after Abraham Lincoln was assassinated.) The basic disagreement between the Radical Republicans and Johnson is over who has responsibility for Reconstruction and how harshly to treat the Southern states.

The Radical Republicans believe that Congress should deal with the Southern states. They argue that the Southern states are conquered territories, and according to the U.S. Constitution, only Congress has the power to admit territories to the Union.

Johnson claims that the Southern states are not conquered territories—that, in fact, they never left the Union. He argues that the Civil War was the result of individual Southerners breaking federal law, and the U.S. Constitution gives the president the power to pardon people who break federal law.

Movie Star News (NYC)

Andrew Johnson being sworn in as president following the assassination of Abraham Lincoln.

The Radical Republicans see Johnson as a threat to their plans for Reconstruction. They hope to put him in a situation in which he will break a law. Then they will use that misstep to force him out of office. The opportunity comes with the passage of the Tenure of Office Act, which says that the president cannot dismiss any federal official without the consent of the Senate.

Culver Pictures

President Johnson (center) and the Radical Republicans in Congress disagree over Reconstruction plans.

Johnson feels that Congress has no right to make such a law. He understands that the U.S. Constitution gives the Senate the right to approve all presidential appointments, but it says nothing about dismissing them. Johnson decides to test the law, so he fires Secretary of War Edwin Stanton. The Radical Republicans immediately charge that Johnson should be removed from office for breaking the law. The president is impeached by the House of Representatives and placed on trial in the Senate. A vote of two-thirds of the members (36 at that time) is needed to remove the president from office.

Movie Star News (NYC)

Family and friends give support to President Johnson.

In this movie, Andrew Johnson is shown to be an honest man. He is played by Van Heflin, a handsome actor who portrayed heroes in a number of other movies. Johnson makes many

Culver Pictures

Thaddeus Stevens (seated at left) plots to convict President Johnson of impeachment charges.

speeches stating that he is only defending the U.S. Constitution from those who would destroy it. In a very touching scene, a pretty young woman tells Johnson how much she admires him for doing what he thinks is right.

Representative Thaddeus Stevens, the leader of the Radical Republicans, is shown in the movie as a grumpy, older man. He is played by Lionel Barrymore, an actor who portrayed unlikable characters in several other movies. While Johnson's speeches defend the U.S. Constitution, Stevens's speeches seek to protect the power of the Radical Republicans in Congress.

When the vote to convict Johnson is taken in the Senate, the Radical Republicans come up with only 35 votes—one short of the necessary 36 needed to remove Johnson. Stevens is shown as being totally disgusted, while the camera shows happy supporters of Johnson with tears in their eyes. As music plays in the background, the camera closes in on Johnson's face, showing a man who has fought courageously to defend the office of the president.

1. This movie shows how the Radical Republicans and Andrew Johnson disagreed over Reconstruction. Describe their disagreement.

____

____

____

____

____

____

2. How did the Radical Republicans attempt to remove Andrew Johnson from office? Answer in detail.

____

____

____

____

____

____

3. The basic theme of the movie is the struggle between Andrew Johnson and Thaddeus Stevens. Name and describe the actors who played these roles.

____

____

____

____

____

____

4. Four still photographs from *Tennessee Johnson* appear in this exercise. From these photographs and what you read in the selection, does this movie take sides in the struggle between Johnson and Stevens? Explain your answer.

____

____

____

____

____

____

5. If this description of the movie made you interested in learning more about Andrew Johnson, where could you find more information about him?

____

____

____

____

____

____

C. Watching a Political Debate on Television. Read the following selection, and then answer the questions.

The year is 1960. Vice President Richard M. Nixon and Senator John F. Kennedy are candidates for president of the United States. They have agreed to appear on television in four one-hour debates. This is the first time in U.S. history that two candidates for president are debating on television. Seventy million people are expected to watch the two men answer questions posed by reporters.

AP/World Wide Photos

TV debate between presidential candidates Senator John F. Kennedy (left) and Vice President Richard M. Nixon. The moderator is in the center, and the questioners face the candidates.

UPI/Corbis-Bettmann

Vice President Richard M. Nixon

UPI/Corbis-Bettmann

Senator John F. Kennedy

Imagine that you are watching one of the debates. You know that Nixon has more political experience than Kennedy and is more widely known. Both men were elected to the House of Representatives and the Senate, but Nixon has also been the vice president of the United States for nearly eight years.

As you watch the debate, you hear good responses from both candidates. Though Kennedy has not had Nixon's experience, he seems very knowledgeable about all the major issues of the day. You begin to pay attention to how the two men look. Nixon seems uncomfortable. He is sweating, and the television makeup on his face makes him look pale. By contrast, Kennedy looks perfectly at ease. His youth, good looks, and sense of humor create an ideal picture on the television screen.

When the debate is over, you think that Kennedy has won the debate. But later, as you talk to a friend who listened to the debate on the radio, you find out that your friend thinks Nixon won the debate.

1. In order to understand the issues discussed by the candidates in a television debate, what should a person do before watching the debate?

____

____

____

2. How might a viewer's opinion of a candidate be influenced by seeing the candidate on television rather than hearing the person on the radio?

____

____

____

____

____

3. Most historians agree on two reasons why Kennedy benefited more from the television debates than Nixon. Find the reasons in the selection and write them below.

a. ____

____

b. ____

____

4. What do you think is meant by the following statement? "The candidate who gives a better performance in a television debate may not do a better job as president."

____

____

____

____

____

5. In your opinion, how does television affect the way candidates run for political office?

____

____

____

____

____

____

____

____

D. Watching a Documentary. Read the following selection, and then answer the questions.

Imagine that you are watching a documentary about the *hippie movement* in the late 1960s. A narrator provides information about the movement. She says that many young people in the mid- and late-1960s did not feel part of *mainstream* American society (the way of life of the majority). They saw racial injustice in a society that said that all people are created equal. They criticized American involvement in Vietnam; to them it seemed like a civil war. Many young people were disturbed to see so many Americans acquiring wealth and material possessions while other Americans were poor and hungry. These young people saw all government and authority, which they called the "*establishment,*" as responsible for these problems. They began to oppose the "establishment" and sought to create a new world. They called themselves "hippies" because they thought they were "hip" (interested in new ideas).

Magnum Photos, Inc./Roger Malloch

Opposing the establishment.

Many hippies rejected the idea of steady work, saying that the world needed more love, not more money. The neat clothes and hairstyles of the early 1960s were replaced by faded blue jeans, wrinkled shirts, and long, bushy hair.

Some hippies established new types of isolated communities, called *communes.* In the communes, they tried to create a world free from greed, ambition, and competition. All who lived in the communes were expected to treat one another as loving family members and to share all possessions equally.

Magnum Photos, Inc./Henri Cartier-Bresson

Sharing food in a commune.

Drugs were a big part of the hippie movement. Many hippies saw drugs as a way to forget their problems. Marijuana was widely used, and some hippies experimented with LSD and other harder drugs.

Magnum Photos, Inc./Elliot Landy

Experiencing a sense of togetherness at the Woodstock rock concert, Bethel, N.Y., in 1969.

As the narrator explains these things, films and photographs of people and events in the hippie movement are shown. Besides listening to the narrator, you can hear historians comment on the hippie movement.

One historian claims that the hippies should have been ashamed of their actions. She says, "These were youngsters who saw problems in our society and decided to run away from them. Life comes with problems, and if these hippies did not like what was happening in America, they should have worked to improve things."

Another historian shows more sympathy for the hippies. He says, "The hippies were right to oppose racial injustice, the war in Vietnam, and America's desire for more material goods. But they felt helpless. How could they hope to get the United States government out of Vietnam? All they wanted was love and togetherness. They may not have chosen the best approach, but their hearts were in the right place."

In conclusion, the narrator tells you that the hippie movement reflected the frustration that many Americans felt during the late 1960s and early 1970s. When that frustration eased in the late 1970s, there was no longer a reason for young people to rebel. The hippie movement had run its course.

1. Why is this program called a documentary?

____

____

____

____

____

2. If a friend asked you what this documentary was about, what would you say? Answer in detail.

____

____

____

____

____

____

3. How fair do you think this documentary was in presenting different points of view about the hippie movement? Explain your answer.

____

____

____

____

____

____

4. If you were interested in learning more about something shown or stated in this documentary, what could you do?

____

____

____

____

____

E. Watching a Movie. Read the following selection, and then answer the questions.

The motion picture *All The President's Men* is based on the book of the same title, written by Carl Bernstein and Bob Woodward. The events in *All The President's Men* take place between June 1972 and August 1974. In the movie, which opened in April 1976, Bernstein and Woodward are played by two very popular actors, Dustin Hoffman and Robert Redford.

President Nixon being cheered as he leaves the House of Representatives after giving a speech.

UPI/Corbis-Bettmann

The movie begins with actual newsreel film showing President Richard Nixon at the U.S. Capitol addressing a joint session of Congress. As the president leaves the House of Representatives, he is given enthusiastic applause by the members of the Senate and the House of Representatives, justices of the U.S. Supreme Court, members of his cabinet, and distinguished visitors.

The movie then switches to the Watergate Office Building in another area of Washington, D.C. It is June 17, 1972, and five men are shown breaking into the Democratic National Headquarters in the Watergate Building. A security guard notices tape on one of the garage doors in the building. The tape is placed over the door lock to keep it from locking. The security guard calls the police, who come and arrest the five burglars.

At first, the burglary seems to be a minor incident, but Bob Woodward, a young, little-known reporter for *The Washington*

One of the Watergate burglars in the movie.

Movie Star News (NYC)

Post, wonders why these five men were trying to burglarize the Democratic headquarters. He finds out that the burglary team was made up of James W. McCord, who used to work for the Central Intelligence Agency (CIA), and four Cuban Americans. Woodward soon learns that one of the Cuban Americans has written the name of E. Howard Hunt in his address book. Hunt is another ex-CIA agent, who also worked for Charles Colson, a White House consultant.

The Kobal Collection/Warner Bros.

Reporters Bob Woodward (right), played by Robert Redford, and Carl Bernstein, played by Dustin Hoffman.

Woodward begins to wonder if anyone inside the White House knew of the burglary. Did the president or some of his advisers want information about the Democrats that could be used against them before the coming November presidential election?

We then see Woodward go to a secret meeting in a darkly lit garage. There, in the shadows, he meets a man who appears to have inside information on the Watergate break-in. We have no idea who the man is. (Later in the movie, he is referred to as "Deep Throat.") He tells Woodward to "follow the money." Woodward is not sure what the clue means, but "Deep Throat" repeats, "Follow the money."

In the meanwhile, Carl Bernstein, another reporter for *The Washington Post,* joins Woodward in investigating the Watergate break-in. Bernstein finds out that a check that was supposed to go to the Committee to Reelect the President (CREEP) was found in the bank account of one of the burglars. The two reporters decide that this is what "Deep Throat" meant by his clue, "Follow the money."

Bernstein and Woodward discuss the check with the editors of *The Washington Post,* including the managing editor, Ben Bradlee. Some of the editors say that the story is too dangerous and that few papers are bothering with it. They argue that if their newspaper accuses the White House of being involved in the burglary and cannot prove it, its reputation could be greatly damaged. But Bradlee tells Bernstein and Woodward to continue their investigation.

With Bradlee's support, Bernstein and Woodward begin to interview people who work on the CREEP. They want to know how the committee gets its money and how it is distributed.

The Kobal Collection/Warner Bros.

The reporters conferring with newspaper officials.

Many of the people interviewed are afraid to speak. Some think that they are being watched. We accompany Bernstein and Woodward as they follow dozens of leads, hoping that the next one will pay off. Finally, they meet a bookkeeper for the committee, who tells them of a secret fund being used to help win Nixon's re-election. The reporters have their first good lead.

The Kobal Collection/Warner Bros.

Woodward interviewing a lead.

UPI/Corbis-Bettmann

President Nixon taking the oath of office, January 1973.

Through further investigation, they learn that the Republicans illegally raised money to help re-elect Nixon and used some of the same money to *sabotage* (wreck) the Democrats' election campaign.

In a front-page article of *The Washington Post,* Bernstein and Woodward write of the secret fund and how it was used. President Nixon and members of his White House staff deny the charges. Despite the article, Nixon is overwhelmingly re-elected president. We see actual newsreel film of Nixon taking the oath of office before beginning his second term.

It is at this point that the action in the movie comes to an

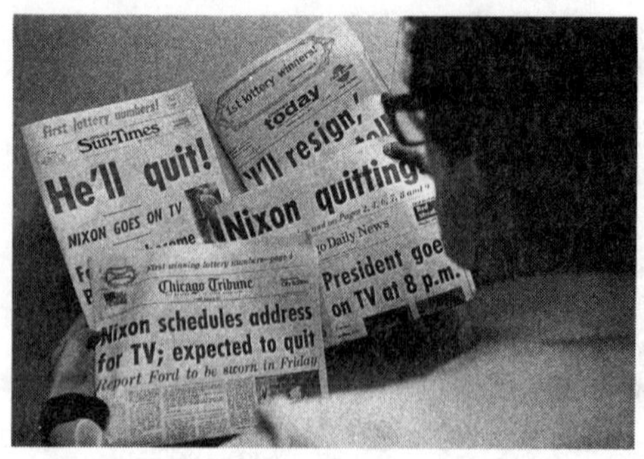

AP/Wide World Photos

Headlines predicting Nixon's resignation, August 1974.

end, and you might think that the Watergate investigation is over. But the last scene in the movie shows newspaper articles that appeared in the months following Nixon's second inauguration. The articles tell us: Bernstein and Woodward continued their investigation, the Senate and the House of Representatives began their own investigations, Nixon and his advisers were accused of covering up the Watergate break-in, pressure grew to impeach Nixon and remove him from office, Nixon's advisers were sent to prison for their involvement in the break-in and cover-up. The last newspaper article states that on August 9, 1974, Nixon resigned from the presidency. Then the movie ends.

1. The events listed below occurred in the movie *All the President's Men.* In the space provided, use these events to construct an outline.

   Nixon takes the oath of office before beginning his second term.

   Bernstein finds out that a check that was supposed to go to CREEP was found in the bank account of one of the burglars.

   President Richard Nixon addresses a joint session of Congress.

   Bob Woodward and Carl Bernstein, reporters for *The Washington Post,* investigate the burglary of the Democratic headquarters.

   Woodward and Bernstein learn that the Republicans illegally raised money to help re-elect Nixon.

   The Senate and the House of Representatives begin investigations of Richard Nixon.

   Woodward meets "Deep Throat," who tells him to "follow the money."

   Nixon is accused of covering up the Watergate break-in.

   Five men break into the Democratic National Headquarters in the Watergate Building.

   Nixon's advisers are sent to prison for their involvement in the break-in and cover-up.

   Nixon resigns from the presidency on August 9, 1974.

   Newspaper articles show how the Watergate crisis was resolved.

ALL THE PRESIDENT'S MEN (the movie)

I. ______________________________

II. ______________________________

III. ______________________________

A. ______________________________

B. ______________________________

C. ______________________________

IV. ______________________________

V. ______________________________

A. ______________________________

B. ______________________________

C. ______________________________

D. ______________________________

2. Is the following statement TRUE or FALSE? Explain your answer. *All The President's Men* tells the story of the Watergate break-in and cover-up from many different points of view."

____

____

____

____

____

3. This movie is based on a book. Why would it be a good idea to read the book even though you saw the movie?

____

____

____

____

____

4. Why do you think actual newsreel films were used in this movie?

____

____

____

____

____

____

5. How might the selection of Dustin Hoffman and Robert Redford to star in this movie influence a viewer's opinion of Bernstein and Woodward?

____

____

____

____

____

____

6. Some critics claimed that this movie gave the impression that Bernstein and Woodward were the only ones responsible for uncovering the Watergate scandal and forcing Nixon to resign. If you wanted to know the complete story of the Watergate break-in and cover-up, how could you find it out?

____

____

____

____

____

____

CHAPTER 23 Making Generalizations

We hear and make generalizations every day. We read them in newspapers, magazines, and textbooks. They can be made about our friends or the Founding Fathers, about our neighborhood or any part of the world at any time in history. A *generalization* is a general statement based on facts and true of enough people, places, or things. The first sentence in this chapter is a generalization. Although some people do not hear and make generalizations every day, enough people do so that the sentence is a valid (true) generalization. There is no exact answer as to how many people, places, or things are "enough" to make a generalization valid, except that the number should be more than half. The greater the number, the more valid the generalization is.

Unfortunately, many people make generalizations that are not supported by facts. It takes skill to make a correct generalization. Even if you have made many generalizations in your life, this chapter will improve your skill in making correct generalizations.

Let us begin with a generalization often stated in U.S. history books:

> European conquerors of the Americas in the 16th and 17th centuries had little respect for native cultures.

Documents prove that European conquerors of the Americas destroyed native cultural sights and tried to make the natives adopt European culture. Such documents are evidence that European conquerors had little respect for native cultures. But how many European conquerors acted that way? Was it some, most, nearly all, or all? For the generalization to be true, it has to be true of "enough" European conquerors. Without a doubt, some European conquerors respected native cultures, but it can be proven that most of them did not. "Most" is not an exact number, but it means more than half and is, therefore, a number large enough to make this generalization correct.

Sweeping Generalizations

A common error in making generalizations is to make a *sweeping generalization.* Using words such as "everyone," "all," and "no one," sweeping generalizations put all people into one category. They are almost always incorrect because what may be true about some or most people is rarely true about everyone. Here is an example of a sweeping generalization:

> Everyone in the Confederacy was glad to hear that Abraham Lincoln had been assassinated.

We cannot know how many people in the Confederacy welcomed the news of Lincoln's assassination, but it is reasonable to think that some people did not welcome it. Here is another example:

> You take your first flight on Safety First Airlines and have an unpleasant experience with a flight attendant. When the plane lands, you tell a friend, "Safety First Airlines hires the worst flight attendants."

You are guilty of making a sweeping generalization. You cannot judge the quality of a large airline company and the service provided by all its flight attendants by what happens on one flight.

Stereotypes

When a sweeping generalization is about a racial, religious, or ethnic group, it is called a *stereotype.* Stereotypes are almost always negative, as in the following examples:

> Jews are cheap.
>
> African Americans would rather receive *welfare* benefits (government economic assistance) than work for a living.

Neither example is supported by the facts. Documents prove that Jewish Americans give more to charity than most other ethnic and religious groups in the United States. It can also be proven that the vast majority of African Americans work for a living, and that nearly all of those who receive welfare would rather work.

Now you know what a correct generalization is and how to avoid sweeping generalizations and stereotypes. Here are four facts and two possible generalizations that can be made from them. Only one of the generalizations is supported by the facts. Can you identify it?

FACTS

1. George Washington received all of the electoral votes in the presidential election of 1789.
2. On the way to his inauguration as president in 1789, Washington was cheered by large crowds of people.
3. Washington easily won re-election in 1792.
4. Both *Federalists* and *Anti-Federalists* (the first two political parties) liked and respected Washington.

POSSIBLE GENERALIZATIONS

1. Early Americans liked and respected George Washington.
2. All early Americans liked and respected George Washington.

Which generalization is supported by the facts? All four facts support the first generalization—that a large number of people liked and respected Washington. But the four facts do not support the second generalization—that "all early Americans" liked and respected Washington. The second generalization is a sweeping generalization; it puts all people into one category. As popular as Washington was, there must have been some people who did not like and respect him.

Here is another set of facts and two possible generalizations. Only one of the generalizations is correct.

FACTS

1. U.S. coins carry the inscription "In God We Trust."
2. Daily religious programs can be seen on television and heard on the radio in most parts of the United States.
3. Mormonism, Christian Science, Jehovah's Witnesses, and the Nation of Islam are all religious *sects* begun in the United States.

4. Today, 65 percent of all Americans claim membership in a church, temple, or synagogue.

POSSIBLE GENERALIZATIONS

1. Religion is important in American life.
2. Religion matters more to Americans today than it did in the past.

Which generalization is correct? Explain why.

____

____

____

____

____

____

What did you write? The four facts support the generalization that religion is important in American life. "In God We Trust" (Fact 1) would not appear on coins unless many Americans still felt that way. Facts 2 and 3 give specific examples of the importance of religion to many Americans. Fact 4 tells us that 65 percent of Americans are members of a church, temple, or synagogue. This is nearly two-thirds, a large enough number to support the first generalization. For the second generalization to be true, however, more information is needed. Generalizations must be based on facts, not feelings, opinions, or misinformation. From the facts given, we cannot tell whether religion is more important in America today than it was in the past.

The ability to make correct generalizations is a worthwhile skill. Many writers and public speakers use generalizations because it is easier and more dramatic to state things in general rather than in specific terms. Just remember that generalizations are not supposed to be true of every person, place, or thing. They are only supposed to be true of enough of them. How many generalizations do you make in a day? The following exercises will give you more practice in making sure your generalizations are correct.

USING YOUR SKILLS

A. Choosing the Correct Generalization. In each question, study the four given facts and two possible generalizations. Then decide which generalization is supported by the four facts. On the lines provided, give the letter of the correct generalization and explain why you chose it.

1. FACTS

   (a) John Paul Jones and his ship *Bonhomme Richard* fought against great odds to defeat the British ship H.M.S. *Serapis.*
   (b) Courageous Americans left their families and farms to fight for independence.
   (c) Washington's soldiers suffered great hardships at Valley Forge during the cold winter of 1777–1778.
   (d) Despite few soldiers and poor ammunition, Washington's army scored great victories at the battles of Trenton and Princeton.

   POSSIBLE GENERALIZATIONS

   (a) All American fighting forces were very brave during the Revolution.
   (b) American fighting forces were very brave during the Revolution.

ANSWER AND EXPLANATION

____

____

____

____

2. FACTS

(a) Although the Constitution said nothing about setting up a national bank, President George Washington supported the creation of such a bank.

(b) In 1803, to double the size of the United States, President Thomas Jefferson bought the Louisiana Territory. He had once argued that the U.S. Constitution did not give a president any such authority.

(c) President Theodore Roosevelt used the power of the presidency to create national parks, although the U.S. Constitution did not specifically give the federal government the power to create parks.

(d) Trying to end the Great Depression, President Franklin Roosevelt signed laws that were later declared unconstitutional by the U.S. Supreme Court.

POSSIBLE GENERALIZATIONS

(a) Presidents have been willing to interpret the U.S. Constitution loosely to advance their policies.

(b) Presidents like to do what is popular.

ANSWER AND EXPLANATION

____

____

____

____

3. FACTS

(a) In 1832, Henry Clay stated that nearly all the successful property owners he knew were "self-made men, who have whatever wealth they possess by patient and diligent labor."

(b) Clay's colleagues in the House of Representatives continually reminded the nation that, in the United States, riches were won not by the well-born but by the hard-working.

(c) In the 1830s, William E. Dodge, a New York merchant, claimed that 75 percent of wealthy Americans came from humble beginnings.

(d) In *Democracy in America,* published in 1835, the French visitor Alexis de Tocqueville wrote that "most of the rich men" in the United States had once known the "sting of want."

POSSIBLE GENERALIZATIONS

(a) In the United States of the early 1800s, talent and hard work had more to do with becoming wealthy than did family position.

(b) In the United States of the early 1800s, wealth did not guarantee success in life.

4. FACTS

(a) In 1967, Thurgood Marshall became the first African American appointed to the U.S. Supreme Court.

(b) Ronald McNair, an African American, served his country as an astronaut until his tragic death aboard the space shuttle *Challenger* on January 28, 1986.

(c) John H. Johnson, the African-American publisher of *Ebony* and *Jet* magazines, is one of the most successful businesspeople in the United States.

(d) Oprah Winfrey, an African American, is a respected television talk-show host and actor.

POSSIBLE GENERALIZATIONS

(a) African Americans are interested only in politics and entertainment.

(b) African Americans have done well in whatever careers they have entered.

ANSWER AND EXPLANATION

5. FACTS

(a) In the 1976 presidential election, the Republican candidate received 63 percent of the vote of people who earned over $50,000 a year.

(b) In the 1980 presidential election, the Republican candidate received 64 percent of the vote of people who earned over $50,000 a year.

(c) In the 1988 presidential election, the Republican candidate received 65 percent of the vote of people who earned over $100,000 a year.

(d) In the 1996 presidential election, the Republican candidate received 54 percent of the vote of people who earned over $100,000 a year.

POSSIBLE GENERALIZATIONS

(a) Republican candidates are guaranteed the vote of wealthy Americans.
(b) Wealthy Americans tend to vote for Republican candidates.

____

____

____

____

B. Making a Generalization. Read each group of facts. Then write a correct generalization for each group.

1. FACTS

(a) In 1789, the same year in which Washington was inaugurated the first president of a free United States, slavery existed in many areas of the nation.
(b) In 1789, not one woman was allowed to vote in any election or hold any public office in the United States.
(c) In 1789, Jews and Catholics found it difficult to live and find work in some places in the United States.
(d) In 1789, land used by Indians for centuries was being taken over by white settlers.

GENERALIZATION

____

____

____

2. FACTS

(a) John Adams, a Federalist, was elected the second president of the United States in 1798.
(b) Many Americans wanted President Adams to declare war on France, but he refused.
(c) The Alien and Sedition acts, signed into law by President Adams, turned many Americans against the Federalists.
(d) John Adams lost re-election to the presidency in 1800.

GENERALIZATION

____

____

____

3. FACTS
   (a) The environmental movement, begun in the 1950s, led to the passage of the Land and Water Conservation Act in 1964.
   (b) In the 1960s and 1970s, the environmental movement succeeded in getting Congress to pass laws protecting wildlife endangered by hunting.
   (c) In the 1970s, federal, state, and local laws were passed to protect drinking water, control the spread of pesticides and other toxic chemicals, and clean up the air, rivers, lakes, and oceans.
   (d) Over the years, membership has grown steadily in such pro-environmental organizations as the Sierra Club, the Wilderness Society, the National Wildlife Federation, and the National Audubon Society.

   GENERALIZATION

   ____

   ____

   ____

4. FACTS
   (a) In 1995, Americans donated $32 billion to charity.
   (b) After every national disaster, the American Red Cross shows up to provide food, clothing, and shelter for the needy.
   (c) Every day all across America, millions of volunteers work in hospitals, schools, soup kitchens, and shelters for the homeless.
   (d) In 1993, Americans spent $4.38 trillion, of which $340 billion was spent on recreation.

   GENERALIZATION

   ____

   ____

   ____

5. FACTS
   (a) In the 1992 and 1996 presidential elections, more Asian Americans voted for the Republican candidate than for the Democratic candidate.
   (b) In the 1992 and 1996 presidential elections, more African Americans voted for the Democratic candidate than for the Republican candidate.
   (c) In the 1992 and 1996 presidential elections, more Hispanic Americans voted for the Democratic candidate than for the Republican candidate.
   (d) In the 1992 and 1996 presidential elections, more non-Hispanic white Americans voted for the Republican candidate than for the Democratic candidate.

GENERALIZATION

____

____

____

C. Presidential Generalizations. Do you agree with the following generalizations made by three presidents of the United States? Explain your answers on the lines provided.

1. Abraham Lincoln: "You can fool some of the people all of the time, and all of the people some of the time, but you can't fool all of the people all of the time."

____

____

____

____

2. Jimmy Carter: "The American people are good."

____

____

____

____

3. Bill Clinton: "There have always been things we could do together—dreams we could make real—which we could never have done on our own. . . . America has always . . . risen to every challenge."

____

____

____

____

D. Avoiding Sweeping Generalizations and Stereotypes.

D-1. Define:

1. Sweeping generalization

____

____

2. Stereotype

____

____

D-2. All of the following statements are sweeping generalizations. Some of them are also stereotypes. Explain why they would be considered sweeping generalizations (and, where it applies, stereotypes).

1. All Americans are racists.

____

____

____

____

2. Television preachers are more interested in getting your money than in saving your soul.

____

____

____

____

3. Girls think about boys more than boys think about girls.

____

____

____

____

4. The governor was arrested on bribery charges. I told you that all politicians are crooks.

____

____

____

____

5. Youngsters who come to the United States from a foreign country work harder in school than those born in the United States.

____

____

____

____

E. Making a Generalization and Proving It. Make your own generalization, and then supply three facts that prove it.

1. GENERALIZATION

____

____

SUPPORTING FACTS

1. ______________________________

2. ______________________________

3. ______________________________

2. GENERALIZATION

____

____

SUPPORTING FACTS

1. ______________________________

2. ______________________________

3. ______________________________

3. GENERALIZATION

____

____

SUPPORTING FACTS

1. ______________________________

2. ______________________________

3. ______________________________

CHAPTER 24

Drawing Conclusions and Making Inferences

In studying U.S. history, you often have to decide what other people's words mean. When you read a selection, for example, you have to decide on its meaning. If your decision is supported by the facts in the selection, you have made a correct decision. This is called *drawing a conclusion.* If your decision is only suggested by the facts in the selection, it may still be correct, but you would not say that you are drawing a conclusion. Because a decision "suggested by the facts" is less certain, you would be *making an inference.* In this chapter, you will examine the difference between drawing a conclusion and making an inference.

Drawing a conclusion means reaching a decision supported by facts. Based on these facts, no contradictory conclusion is possible. In a sense, you have already studied how to draw a conclusion in the previous chapter on generalizations. A correct generalization is a statement supported by the facts. So is a correctly drawn conclusion.

Making an inference is a more challenging skill than drawing a conclusion. Making an inference means reaching a decision suggested by facts. You "read between the lines" to interpret the facts. While a conclusion is a decision soundly supported by fact, an inference is an educated guess.

Let us begin with a simple example:

Selection 1

The president of the United States likes to go jogging. Protected by Secret Service agents, he jogs along the streets near the White House almost every day.

What conclusion can you draw? What inference can you make?

Several conclusions may be possible, but here is one: The president likes to jog on a regular basis. This conclusion is supported by two facts: (1) You know that the president likes to jog; (2) you know that he jogs almost every day.

Several inferences may be possible, but here is one: The president is accompanied by Secret Service agents almost everywhere he goes. This is a reasonable inference. If the president cannot jog without Secret Service agents, there must be few places where he can go without them. Such an inference should be provable, though not necessarily from the information given. The selection does not state that Secret

Service agents accompany the president almost everywhere he goes, but you could probably prove your inference with further research.

Here is another chance to understand the difference between drawing a conclusion and making an inference. Read Selection 2 and the two statements that follow it. Under each statement, write whether it is a conclusion or an inference, and give a reason for your choice.

Selection 2

Starting in the 1830s, certain Americans sought to improve education. Educational reformers such as Horace Mann from Massachusetts called for the establishment of free, tax-supported public education. Claiming that an educated public would make the United States a strong and prosperous country, they wanted all young people to be required to go to school. These reformers argued that free public education would give young people better job opportunities and help prevent crime. They also argued that requiring all young people to go to school would force the many immigrant groups in the United States to learn a common language as well as American customs. In time, tax-supported public schools were established in every state.

Statement 1

Educational reformers believed that free public education would solve some of society's problems.

____

____

____

____

____

Statement 2

The ideas of the educational reformers were not immediately accepted by all Americans.

____

____

____

____

____

What choices did you make? Statement 1 can be supported by facts given in the selection. The reformers thought that free public education would give young people better job opportunities, help prevent crime, and help immigrants adopt a common American way of life. From these facts, you can draw the conclusion that educational reformers believed that free public education would solve some of society's problems. So Statement 1 is a conclusion.

Statement 2 says that the ideas of the educational reformers were not immediately accepted by all Americans. This is not specifically stated in the selection, but the selection contains some key words that prompt you to assume that Statement 2 is true. The key words are "they argued" and "in time." If the reformers had to argue for free public education, at least some people opposed them. Moreover, if educational reforms were brought about only "in time," you can infer that the reformers' ideas were not immediately accepted by all Americans. Statement 2, therefore, is an inference.

So far, you have considered only valid (correct, true) conclusions and inferences. The questions following the next reading selection will test your ability to reject invalid (incorrect, untrue) conclusions and inferences.

Selection 3

Throughout history, society has cruelly treated people who suffer from mental illnesses. They were either completely ignored and left to wander the streets or locked up in jails. In jails, they were subjected to real horrors. Many doctors feared to treat them. Sometimes the mentally ill were left to run around the jails naked and unfed. Sometimes they were chained in dark cells.

In 1843, Dorothea Dix, a teacher, was invited to teach Sunday school in a jail in Cambridge, Massachusetts. She was shocked to find the mentally ill being treated like criminals. She began to visit other jails and found that the same ill treatment existed in many areas of the country.

Dix begged local governments to improve the conditions of the mentally ill. At first, few people would listen to her. But eventually, state governments began to build separate hospitals and asylums where the mentally ill could be decently housed and given help.

1. Which valid conclusion can be drawn from the selection?
   (a) Very little was done before the 1840s to help the mentally ill improve their lives.
   (b) Before the 1840s, there were very few mentally ill people in the United States.
   (c) Most of the mentally ill preferred to live in jails rather than on the streets.
   (d) Jails were overcrowded throughout the 1840s.

Which answer did you choose? There are a number of facts to support the conclusion in choice *(a)*. The selection says that throughout history the mentally ill were either completely ignored or subjected to horrible conditions in jails. So choice *(a)* is a valid conclusion. Choice *(b)* is an invalid conclusion because there is no information in the selection about how many people were mentally ill before the 1840s. Choice *(c)* is an invalid conclusion because there is no information about where the mentally ill preferred to live. Choice *(d)* is an invalid conclusion because there is no information about how crowded the jails were in the 1840s. Therefore, choice *(a)* is the only valid conclusion because it is based on facts given in the selection.

2. Circle the word VALID if the statement is a valid inference. Circle the word INVALID if the statement is an invalid inference. Explain your choice on the lines provided.

Statement

The writer of Selection 3 supported Dix's efforts to improve the lives of the mentally ill.

VALID INVALID

EXPLANATION

____

____

____

____

____

What answer did you choose? The writer did not specifically state support for Dix's reform efforts. But you should assume this support because the writer uses compassionate phrases such as "cruelly treated" and "subjected to real horrors." Moreover, the writer does not criticize Dix's efforts. You can thus infer a degree of support for them. So the statement is a valid inference.

3. Circle the word VALID if the statement is a valid reference. Circle the word INVALID if the statement is an invalid statement. Explain your choice on the lines provided.

Statement

Before Dorothea Dix visited the jail in Cambridge, Massachusetts, no one cared how the mentally ill were treated in jails.

VALID INVALID

EXPLANATION

____

____

____

____

____

____

Which answer did you choose this time? You cannot assume that before Dorothea Dix visited the jail in Cambridge, Massachusetts, no one cared how the mentally ill were treated in jails. Many people may have cared but did not have the courage to act as Dix did. There is not enough information in the selection to justify making the statement in question 3, so you must regard it as an invalid inference.

You can draw conclusions and ordinarily make inferences from everything you hear and read. In using these two skills, you will better understand what you hear and read and what a speaker or writer is trying to tell you. The following exercises will give you more practice in drawing conclusions and making inferences.

USING YOUR SKILLS

A. Drawing Conclusions and Making Inferences. Read each selection and the two statements that follow it. One statement is a conclusion based on the facts in the selection. The other one is an inference based on what is suggested by the facts in the selection. Under each statement, write whether it is a conclusion or an inference, and give a reason for your choice.

Selection 1

In the 1830s, more people than ever attended the theater. The wealthier classes, who had always attended the theater, began to complain that the new theatergoers made it difficult to enjoy the plays. According to the wealthier classes, the new theatergoers smelled, talked out loud during performances, and, worst of all, spit anywhere they wished.

Statement 1

In the 1830s, ticket prices were more affordable for a larger number of people.

____

____

____

Statement 2

In the 1830s, the wealthier classes did not welcome the growing number of new theatergoers.

____

____

____

Selection 2

In the 1840s, Ralph Waldo Emerson wrote that everyone had a right to be trusted, to be loved, and to be respected.

Statement 1

Emerson believed that each person is important and should be treated fairly.

____

____

____

Statement 2

Emerson believed that slavery is evil.

___

___

___

Selection 3

The struggle for women's rights and for reforms in the prison and education systems began in the early 19th century. At the same time, a growing number of Americans began to see slavery as a great evil.

Statement 1

When injustice is done to you, you are more likely to see the injustice done to others.

___

___

___

Statement 2

The early 19th century saw increased demands for social reform.

___

___

___

Selection 4

In what can only be described as a brilliant move, the U.S. Congress passed the Homestead Act of 1862. The government wanted to develop the vast area of land that it controlled west of the Mississippi River. According to the Homestead Act, a plot of 160 acres would be given to any person 21 years of age or older who paid a small registration fee and lived on the land for five years. By 1890, 80,000,000 acres had been settled by almost 400,000 families, who were able to have their own farms.

Statement 1

Many Americans welcomed the passage of the Homestead Act of 1862.

Statement 2

Without the Homestead Act or some similar program, the American West would not have been settled as quickly as it was.

Selection 5

In the years following the Civil War, Americans developed a taste for beef. Cattle owners in Texas seized the opportunity to produce larger herds of cattle. It became the job of cowboys to move the herds of cattle from the plains of Texas to the railroad stations of Kansas. From Kansas, railroad cars transported the cattle to meatpacking plants in Chicago, and from there, the beef was sent to markets in the East.

Statement 1

Cowboys played an important role in the growth of the cattle industry in the United States.

Statement 2

In the period following the Civil War, railroad service capable of transporting large herds of cattle did not exist between Texas and Chicago.

B. Drawing Conclusions. Read the selection and then answer the questions.

Do human beings control the events of their day, or do events control human beings? Modern historians like to ask this question when discussing President Jimmy Carter and the Iranian hostage crisis.

Jimmy Carter was unfortunate to be president at the time of the revolution in Iran. In 1979, Mohammad Reza Pahlavi, the shah of Iran, was overthrown and left the country. The Ayatollah Ruhollah Khomeini, a religious leader, gained control of the government. The shah had introduced many modern practices to his country, but many Iranians saw them as destructive to their traditional Muslim way of life. The shah had also been very repressive and refused to allow any political opposition. The Ayatollah Khomeini promised to restore to Iran strict rule by Muslim law. He wanted to bring the shah back to Iran for trial, and he severely criticized the United States because it had been a strong supporter of the shah.

When the deposed shah fell ill with cancer, President Carter allowed him to come to the United States for medical treatment. The supporters of the revolution in Iran became furious when they heard that the shah had entered the United States. Some of these *revolutionaries* then seized the U.S. embassy in Teheran, the capital of Iran, and held by force the Americans working there. Thirteen of these *hostages* were soon released, but the revolutionaries said they would not free the remaining 53 hostages until the shah and his wealth were returned to Iran. President Carter refused their demands, and for 444 days, the Americans remained in Teheran as hostages. During that time, Carter used a variety of official and unofficial channels to bring about their release. These efforts did not succeed. In desperation, he even supported a commando-type rescue raid, but the raid failed.

After the shah died in 1980, the United States and Iran began more serious discussions about how to release the hostages. By that time, Iran wanted an end to the hostage problem. Its trade had been hurt by boycotts imposed by the United States and other countries. It also had become involved in a war with Iraq.

The Iranians finally agreed to release the 53 hostages if the United States promised to return nearly $8 billion in Iranian assets to Iran. The United States accepted, and the hostages were freed on Inauguration Day, January 20, 1981. The exact moment of release came 33 minutes after Carter had ceased to be president and Ronald Reagan had been sworn in as the new president.

For his handling of this crisis, many historians give Jimmy Carter very low marks. They claim that he was not strong enough. But the real question is: What president would have been strong enough? Who could have achieved more? The hostage crisis is a perfect example of how events can control human beings. There was little else that Carter could have done. A military invasion of Iran would have resulted in the death of many U.S. soldiers and the 53 hostages. Carter did as well as anyone could have under the circumstances. And in the end, all 53 hostages came home.

Write the letter of the correct choice on the line next to the number of each question.

____ 1. The shah of Iran was
- *(a)* very popular in the United States.
- *(b)* the elected ruler of Iran.
- *(c)* a dictator.
- *(d)* a religious leader.

____ 2. Which conclusion can be drawn from the selection?
- *(a)* The author of the selection knows Jimmy Carter personally.
- *(b)* The author of the selection is a member of the Democratic party.
- *(c)* The author of the selection is not critical of how President Carter handled the hostage crisis.
- *(d)* The author of the selection feels that President Carter could have done a better job in handling the hostage crisis.

____ 3. The Iranians attacked the U.S. embassy in Teheran because
- *(a)* they had not been able to seize the Soviet embassy.
- *(b)* they were furious that the shah had been allowed to enter the United States.
- *(c)* the U.S. embassy was holding Iranian hostages.
- *(d)* the U.S. embassy was hiding some members of the shah's family.

____ 4. Which conclusion can be drawn from the selection?
- *(a)* The hostages were released because the Iranians were afraid of Ronald Reagan.
- *(b)* The Ayatollah Khomeini ordered the attack on the U.S. embassy.
- *(c)* President Carter was a good friend of the shah of Iran.
- *(d)* The hostage crisis became a problem for Iran as well as for the United States.

____ 5. Which conclusion can be drawn from the selection?
- *(a)* Historians do not like to comment on presidents while they are still in office.
- *(b)* Historians like to predict how history will judge past presidents.
- *(c)* Many historians think that President Carter handled the hostage crisis as well as anyone could have.
- *(d)* Many historians do not share the author's views on President Carter's handling of the hostage crisis.

C. Drawing Conclusions and Making Inferences. Read each selection and the two statements that follow it. One statement is a conclusion based on the facts in the selection. The other one is an inference based on what is suggested by the facts in the selection. Under each statement, write whether it is a conclusion or an inference, and give a reason for your choice.

Selection 1

Early in his presidency, Ronald Reagan called the Soviet Union an "evil empire." He requested and received from Congress great amounts of money to upgrade U.S. nuclear and military readiness in case the "evil empire" attacked. At the same time, the Soviet government was spending ever-increasing sums to maintain its own nuclear and military defenses. The two countries seemed to be competing to see who could spend more on defense.

The competition became too great for the Soviet Union. Communism was not working. The most basic foods, such as potatoes and milk, were becoming too expensive for the average person to buy. By the mid-1980s, the new Soviet leader, Mikhail Gorbachev, realized that his country needed to spend less on bombs and more on improving people's lives.

But events were already moving too fast. The Soviet people were tired of the failures of communism, tired of having more bombs than food. At first, a few of the 15 Soviet republics declared their independence, but in December 1991, Gorbachev was forced to resign, and the remaining republics became independent. Since then, 12 of the former republics have joined in the new Commonwealth of Independent States.

The "evil empire" had collapsed without the United States having to fire a shot.

Statement 1

The defense policies of President Reagan contributed to the collapse of the Soviet Union.

____

____

____

____

Statement 2

Communism in the Soviet Union did a better job building nuclear bombs than producing adequate supplies of potatoes and milk.

____

____

____

Selection 2

Ever since the first Spanish explorers set foot in the New World in the late 15th century, Hispanic peoples have been a part of U.S. history. One has only to look at the many U.S. cities and states with Spanish names to see the Hispanic influence on the development of this country. Yet, for most of U.S. history, Hispanic Americans have had very little political influence on the national level. Hispanic Americans have been elected to political office in states and local communities, but not one has been elected president or appointed to the U.S. Supreme Court; very few have been elected to Congress. While recent presidents have appointed some Hispanic Americans to executive and judicial posts, Hispanic Americans have not received their fair share of such appointments.

In the last 40 years, new waves of Hispanic immigrants have arrived to enrich the United States. As their numbers grow in the coming years, Hispanic political influence is bound to increase.

Statement 1

Despite all the centuries during which Hispanic Americans have been in America, their political influence is not as strong as it should be.

____

____

____

Statement 2

Until recently, presidents have not felt any great need to please Hispanic American voters.

____

____

____

Selection 3

Look at what President Bill Clinton has to face. There are cries for reform in government, reform of the health care system, and reform in education on all levels. Some of the public want stronger measures to be taken against crime, discrimination, and unemployment. Others want the government to encourage foreign trade, technical and industrial growth, and the arts and sciences. Still others demand protection of the environment, renewal of inner cities, and repair of bridges and roads. Divided public opinion about foreign policy must be considered, too. Should we intervene, or not intervene, in the problems of other countries? And which countries?

The list goes on. The president holds meeting after meeting with his staff. He greets a continual flow of distinguished visitors to the White House. He entertains world leaders at home and travels to meet with them abroad. His every move is under public scrutiny (inspection). So are those of his wife and daughter. The concern not to offend someone or some group arises every time he speaks, whether formally or informally. The possibility of assassination looms. Why does Bill Clinton want to be president—and for two terms, no less?

Statement 1

A person who wants to be president of the United States has to be willing to face many challenges.

____

____

____

Statement 2

Bill Clinton welcomes the challenges of the presidency.

____

____

____

D. Deciding Whether an Inference Is Valid or Invalid. An inference is valid if it is a reasonable assumption based on the given facts. An inference is invalid if the given facts do not suggest or support such an assumption.

Read the selection and then answer the questions.

Religion in American Life

Not so long ago, the phrase "God Is Dead" was heard in many areas of the United States. The phrase was used to suggest that religion was no longer a force in American life. Individuals would be free to practice their religious beliefs, as guaranteed by the First Amendment, but the important issues of the day would not be influenced by religious considerations.

Today, the phrase "God Is Dead" is rarely heard. Once again, religion is being openly acknowledged as a major force in American life. Important religious issues have become major political issues. Fundamentalist Christians preach that Americans should return to what are often called traditional American values. Such Christians are disturbed by the breakdown of American family life and want spoken prayer to be part of public school education again. Black Muslim leaders and black Protestant ministers, who have long used their pulpits to speak out against racial injustice, are increasingly calling for new economic programs to help the poor. Likewise, the American bishops of the Roman Catholic Church have joined the call to show more concern for the poor.

Many observers feel that the increasing importance of religion in the United States is also based on more personal reasons. A growing number of Americans want more meaningful lives. They have come to believe that there is more to life than just striving for success. For example, Jewish leaders report that many young and successful Jews have turned to traditional Jewish values and practices to find more fulfillment in their lives.

If religion continues to influence American life, recent events in U.S. history have also influenced religious thought. As women gained more rights in the 1960s and 1970s, those rights were reflected in religious practices. Although it was once rare for women to be ordained as religious leaders, many Protestant denominations and some branches of Judaism now permit and encourage the ordination of women.

The return of religion as a force in American life can also be seen in the words and actions of political leaders. While president, Jimmy Carter often spoke publicly of the importance of religion in his life. Presidents Ronald Reagan and George Bush supported prayer in the public schools as well as other causes advanced by fundamentalist Christians. President Bill Clinton is seen frequently, Bible in hand, going off to Sunday church services.

The growing influence of religion has not pleased everyone. Some people fear that if one religious group becomes too powerful politically, it may be intolerant of people with differing religious views. Such critics ask, "How much influence should religious beliefs have on public policy?" and "Whose beliefs should have that influence—Protestants, Catholics, Jews, Muslims, Hindus, or Buddhists?"

Public opinion polls show that most Americans want religious values to be reflected in public policy. The challenge before the American people is to see that public policies are tolerant of people with different points of view.

Circle the word VALID if the statement is a valid inference. Circle the word INVALID if the statement is an invalid inference. Explain your choice on the lines provided.

1. Americans are more likely to agree on the existence of God than on how to worship God.

   VALID INVALID

EXPLANATION

____

____

____

2. Fundamentalist Christians believe that the return of prayer to the public schools will strengthen American family life.

   VALID INVALID

EXPLANATION

____

____

____

3. Most Americans prefer to keep their religious beliefs to themselves.

   VALID INVALID

EXPLANATION

____

____

____

4. Today, many more women than men are seeking to be ordained as ministers or rabbis.

   VALID INVALID

EXPLANATION

____

____

____

5. Most Americans want the president of the United States to have strong moral principles.

   VALID INVALID

EXPLANATION

____

____

____

E. Drawing Your Own Conclusion and Making Your Own Inference. Read the following conversation. Then draw your own conclusion and make your own inference based on the conversation. On the lines marked EXPLANATION, explain your reasons for drawing such a conclusion and for making such an inference.

MS. WILSON: Good morning, Mr. Oliver. Have you heard that the town board is going to discuss passing an English-only ordinance?

MR. OLIVER: Not that again!

MS. WILSON: I must admit I don't want the United States becoming like other countries where everything has to be written in several languages.

MR. OLIVER: English is taking over the world. It's the international language of business, trade, computers, and the arts. Believe me, it's not going to lose its favored place in the United States.

MS. WILSON: I hope you're right. . . . But the other day I was at the fruit and vegetable market, and I was about the only one speaking English. I felt like a foreigner . . . and I was born here.

MR. OLIVER: So I guess you'll be going to the town board meeting.

MS. WILSON: Rest assured, I won't be the only person there.

YOUR OWN CONCLUSION

____

____

EXPLANATION

____

____

____

YOUR OWN INFERENCE

____

____

EXPLANATION

____

____

____

CHAPTER 25
Solving Problems

Many people think it must be exciting to be the president of the United States. They see the president as a person of great power and importance. They rarely think of the many problems a president must solve.

All our presidents have had to face problems, make difficult decisions, and act on them. Solving problems is a skill that students of U.S. history need as much as presidents do. In this chapter, you will learn how to solve problems by the same methods used by some U.S. presidents. In the last exercise in this chapter, you will have an opportunity to solve a current problem facing the United States.

Let us begin by looking at a problem that President Thomas Jefferson faced in 1803. Napoleon Bonaparte, the ruler of France, was willing to sell the vast Louisiana Territory to the United States for $15 million. (See map below.) Jefferson had to decide whether to buy the territory from France.

Why would this purchase be a problem for Jefferson? The answer is that Jefferson believed in *strict interpretation* of the Constitution. In other words, he felt the U.S. government should exercise only those powers specifically given to it in the Constitution. According to Jefferson, nothing in the Constitution gave the U.S. government the power to buy new territory. So he had a problem. Should he interpret the

Louisiana Territory, 1803

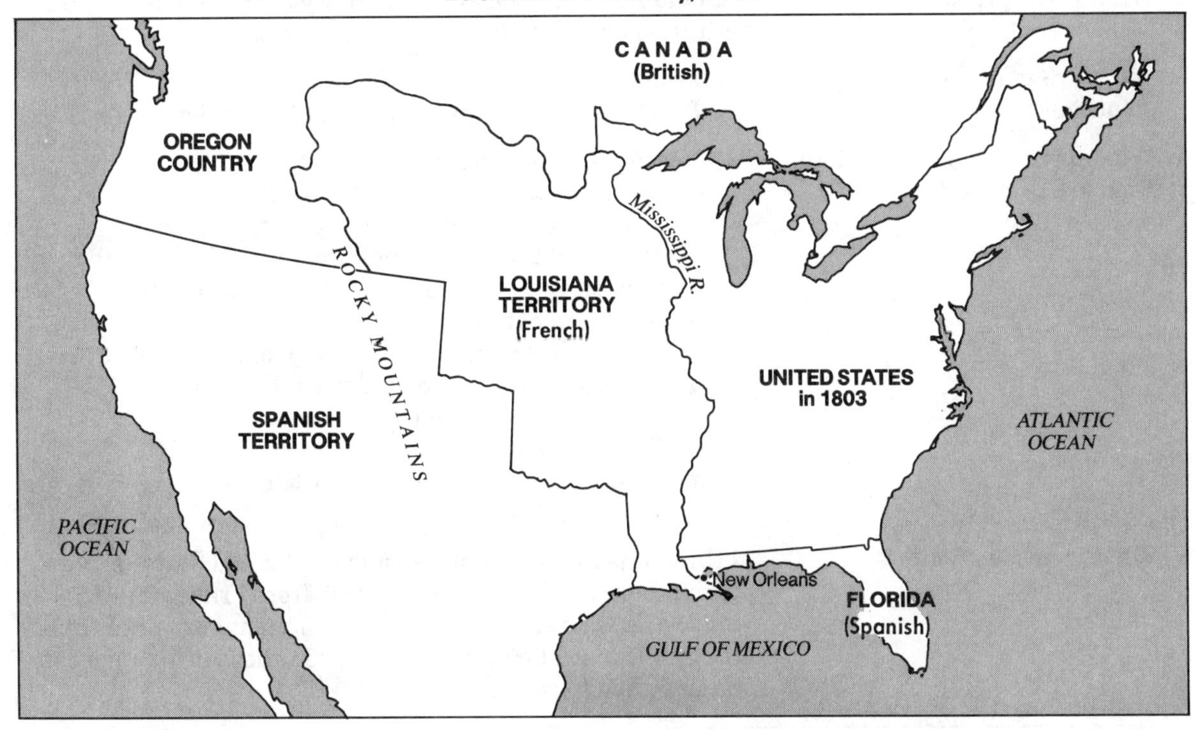

Constitution strictly and not buy the Louisiana Territory? Or should he adopt a policy of *loose interpretation,* stretch the power of the government, and buy the territory?

Jefferson studied the problem. He began by considering all the reasons why he should not buy the Louisiana Territory. First, he believed that the Constitution did not specifically give him the right to make the purchase. Second, he did not know if the United States was strong enough to control so much additional land. Third, he would have to spend $15 million, an amount of money far greater than the total government expenses for a year. Fourth, the purchase would give the United States only one thing it really wanted—the right to use New Orleans as a trading port.

Then Jefferson considered the reasons why he should purchase the territory. First, it would be an entirely peaceful way to double the land area of the United States and give the country room to expand. Second, it would give the United States almost complete control of the Mississippi River, including the port city of New Orleans. Both the river and the port were vital (necessary) to the trading interests of the western United States. Third, although $15 million was a large sum, it was a bargain price for so much land. Fourth, the country would gain power and prestige by increasing in size. Fifth, the territory would provide additional room for settlers and Native Americans from east of the Mississippi.

What decision do you think Jefferson made? After studying both sides of the problem, Jefferson decided to purchase the Louisiana Territory.

The steps that Jefferson took to solve his problem are the same steps that you should take when trying to solve a problem of your own. The following table shows those steps in question form, along with

Solving a Problem

Steps	*Jefferson's Answers*
1. What important terms should I know to study this problem?	Territory, purchase, strict interpretation, loose interpretation.
2. What is the problem?	Should I buy the Louisiana Territory even though the Constitution does not give me that specific power?
3. What are some possible solutions?	1. I could buy the Louisiana Territory. 2. I could turn down the offer to buy the Louisiana Territory.
4. What do I need to know before I make a decision?	1. Reasons for the purchase: *a.* To double the size of the United States *b.* To have room to expand without going to war *c.* To control the Mississippi River and New Orleans *d.* To spend only $15 million for a vast territory 2. Reasons for not making the purchase: *a.* To keep to a strict interpretation of the Constitution *b.* To avoid the difficulties of controlling so much additional land *c.* To save $15 million *d.* To make a huge purchase only to obtain trading rights at New Orleans
5. What is my decision?	I think it is in the best interest of the United States for me to purchase the Louisiana Territory from France for $15 million. It is a rare opportunity and a great bargain. I think that presidential power as specified in the Constitution can be stretched to cover this purchase.

answers that Thomas Jefferson might have made.

Now let us use these steps to solve a problem that President John F. Kennedy faced in 1962. Read the following selection, which will give you background information on the problem. You will then be asked how you would solve the problem and read how President Kennedy dealt with it.

In the late 1950s, revolutionary leader Fidel Castro seized power in Cuba, establishing the first Communist state in the Western Hemisphere. (A map of Cuba appears on page 320.) Thousands of Cubans fled to the United States as Castro imprisoned or executed anyone who opposed his government.

In January 1961, the United States broke off diplomatic relations with Castro's government. Nevertheless, with financial and technical assistance from the Soviet Union, Cuba turned into one of the strongest military forces in Latin America. The United States feared that Cuba would easily be able to export communism to other troubled areas in the region.

Now pretend that you are President John F. Kennedy. In the spring of 1961, you approve a plan to use 1,500 Cuban *exiles* (Cubans resettled in the United States) to invade Cuba and overthrow Castro. But the invasion, which lands at a place called the Bay of Pigs, is a disaster. The Cuban people, for the most part, remain loyal to Castro, and the invading exiles are easily defeated. Your administration is greatly embarrassed by this failure.

In the summer of 1962, Cuba again becomes a problem. You learn that Nikita Khrushchev, leader of the Soviet Union, has sent military weapons and advisers to Cuba. Perhaps the failed Bay of Pigs invasion makes him think that he can extend Soviet influence over Cuba without risking U.S. interference.

You receive intelligence reports that the weapons being installed in Cuba are offensive (first-strike) missiles capable of reaching the United States. You cannot tolerate the presence of Soviet missiles just 90 miles from U.S. soil. You have to respond.

Some of your advisers favor an air strike to destroy the missiles or an invasion of Cuba. But how large an invasion would be needed to guarantee success? You do not want another failure like the Bay of Pigs. And what if the Soviets come to Cuba's aid? Will you have caused World War III?

Other advisers recommend a naval *blockade* to cut off all access to Cuba's ports, along with a demand that the missiles be removed. Such a move would force Khrushchev to take the next step. But what if he tries to move Soviet ships past the U.S. blockade? What if he refuses to remove the missiles?

Only one thing is certain. You cannot allow the missiles to remain in Cuba. Are there other possible solutions? How will you solve this problem?

Step 1

What important terms should I know to study this problem?

___

___

___

What did you write? In order to study a problem, you must know the meaning of every word or term that relates to the problem. If you do not understand a particular word or term, look up its meaning in a reference book. For example, you may have written "Communist state," "Western Hemisphere," "diplomatic relations," "exile," "offensive missiles," and "naval blockade" for your answer to Step 1. You can find their meaning in a dictionary, an encyclopedia, or a U.S. history textbook.

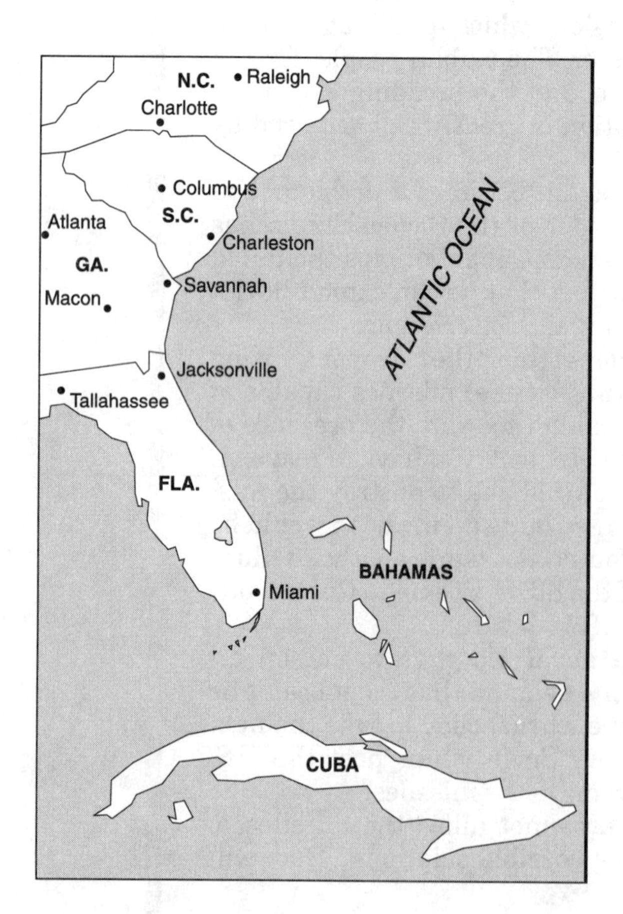

Step 2

What is the problem?

___

___

___

What did you write? You must know exactly what the problem is before you try to solve it. In this case, it is the threat to the United States of Soviet offensive missiles on Cuban soil. Here is one way in which you could have worded the problem: How should the United States deal with the presence of Soviet offensive missiles on Cuban soil?

Step 3

What are some possible solutions? (List at least two possible solutions.)

___

___

___

___

___

What possible solutions did you come up with? One possible solution is to use an air strike to destroy the missiles. Another possible solution is to invade Cuba and destroy the missiles. A third solution is to put a naval blockade around Cuba and demand that Khrushchev remove the missiles. Once you think of possible solutions, the next step is uncover information that will help you decide which solution is the best one.

Step 4

What do I need to know before I make a decision?

___

___

____

____

____

____

____

____

What did you write? When you are solving a problem, you may have to do a great deal of research and seek the advice of a number of people. In this example, the facts listed in the selection can help you make a reasonable decision: (1) The Bay of Pigs invasion failed; a successful invasion would require a major effort. (2) The Soviet Union may come to the aid of Cuba after a U.S. invasion, which will pose the risk of a major war. (3) The United States cannot allow Soviet missiles in Cuba, which is just 90 miles from Florida. (4) A naval blockade of Cuba will force the Soviets to make the next move; if Khrushchev sees that the United States is determined, he may back down.

With these facts, you are ready to move to Step 5.

Step 5

What is my decision? (Include reasons why you have made this decision.)

____

____

____

____

____

What did you decide? In Step 3, three possible solutions are mentioned. Do the facts you considered in Step 4 support one of these solutions? The first possible solution is to use air strikes to destroy the missiles, but this will cause death and destruction and may turn world opinion against the United States. The second possible solution is to invade Cuba and destroy the missiles, but after the Bay of Pigs disaster, the United States will have to launch a major invasion that guarantees success. Is the use of so much military power necessary to solve this problem? The third possible solution is to blockade Cuba and make the Soviet Union make the next move. Any fighting that follows may well be blamed on the Soviets.

President Kennedy's solution was to order a naval blockade of all military shipments to Cuba and demand that the missiles be removed. Soviet ships carrying military cargo approached Cuba but stopped at sea before reaching the U. S. naval blockade. The next move was up to Khrushchev. After consideration, Khrushchev ordered the Soviet ships to turn around and go home. He then agreed to remove the missiles from Cuba, providing that the United States promise not to invade Cuba. The United States accepted Khrushchev's proposal and the crisis was over. Most observers credited Kennedy with a great strategic victory over the Soviet Union. He had forced the Soviets to remove their missiles from Cuba.

In solving a problem, you might add one more step to the five already given. Step 6 might be worded, "Is my decision working?" As you watch your decision in action and uncover new information, be ready to make any changes that will make your solution work better.

Every one of us must solve problems throughout our lives, whether we are the president or students in a U.S. history class. If you follow the steps given in this chapter, you will have a good chance of arriving at thoughtful and reasonable solutions.

The following exercises will give you more practice in learning the skill of solving problems.

USING YOUR SKILLS

A. Solving a Problem the Right Way.

1. Why should you understand the important terms relating to your problem before you state the problem?

____

____

____

____

2. In solving a problem, how many possible solutions should you consider? What information should you get before deciding for or against a possible solution? Explain.

____

____

____

____

3. In the examples in this chapter, only five steps in solving a problem were emphasized. What sixth step should you also take, and why is it important to take it?

____

____

____

____

B. Imagine that the year is 1832 and you are President Andrew Jackson. You are asked to solve the problem presented in the following selection. Read the selection and then try to solve the problem. Use the five steps to solving a problem given at the end of the selection.

> In 1791, President George Washington signed a treaty with the Cherokee, one of the largest Native American tribes in the Southeast. The treaty recognized the Cherokee as a separate nation who were allowed to govern their own land and make their own laws.
>
> The state of Georgia, where most of the Cherokee land was located, never fully approved of the treaty. It continually sought to gain control of Cherokee land. After gold was discovered on

Cherokee land in 1828, Georgia officials became even more determined to remove the Cherokee from their land.

The Cherokee appealed to the U.S. Supreme Court to force Georgia to respect the 1791 treaty. In 1832, Chief Justice John Marshall and the Supreme Court ruled that the treaty was still valid. Only the national government had jurisdiction over Cherokee territory, the Court said, and Georgia must respect the treaty.

Now pretend that you are President Andrew Jackson. The Cherokee are pleased with Chief Justice Marshall's decision and they turn to you to enforce the Supreme Court's decision. But you disagree with the decision. Two years ago, you persuaded Congress to pass the Indian Removal Act. This act called for the Cherokee, as well as other southeastern Native American tribes, to give up their lands and resettle west of the Mississippi River.

You believe that the Native Americans' land is too valuable to be left to them. Most Georgians, and probably most Americans, agree with you. You also believe that state governments will continue to seize Native American land and that the national government will not be able to prevent the takeovers. In your opinion, the offer to move the Cherokee and the other tribes is a generous one that will allow the Native Americans to maintain their way of life and live in peace.

But the Cherokee do not want to give up their lands. They argue that their homes and farms are there and that the land is the burial place of their *ancestors* and, therefore, sacred to their people. They want you to respect the 1791 treaty signed by an earlier president and declared valid by the Supreme Court.

The entire country wants to know how you will deal with this issue. How will you solve this problem?

Step 1

What important terms should I know to study the problem? (Write the terms and their meanings on the answer lines. You may want to use a dictionary, an encyclopedia, or the glossary on page 333 of this book.)

____

____

____

____

Step 2

What is the problem?

____

____

Step 3

What are some possible solutions? (List at least two possible solutions.)

____

____

____

____

Step 4

What do I need to know before I make a decision?

____

____

____

____

Step 5

What is my decision? (Include reasons why you have made this decision.)

____

____

____

____

(If you want to compare your decision with President Jackson's solution to the problem, look up Andrew Jackson in an American history textbook or an encyclopedia.)

C. Imagine that the year is 1951 and you are President Harry S. Truman. You must solve the problem presented in the following selection. Read the selection, and then try to solve the problem. Use the five steps to solving a problem given at the end of the selection.

On June 25, 1950, troops from Communist North Korea cross the 38th parallel and invade South Korea. When the United Nations sends troops from several member countries to aid South Korea, all of the troops are placed under the command of U.S. General Douglas MacArthur.

MacArthur had served as commander of the U.S. Armed Forces in the Pacific during World War II. He was responsible for

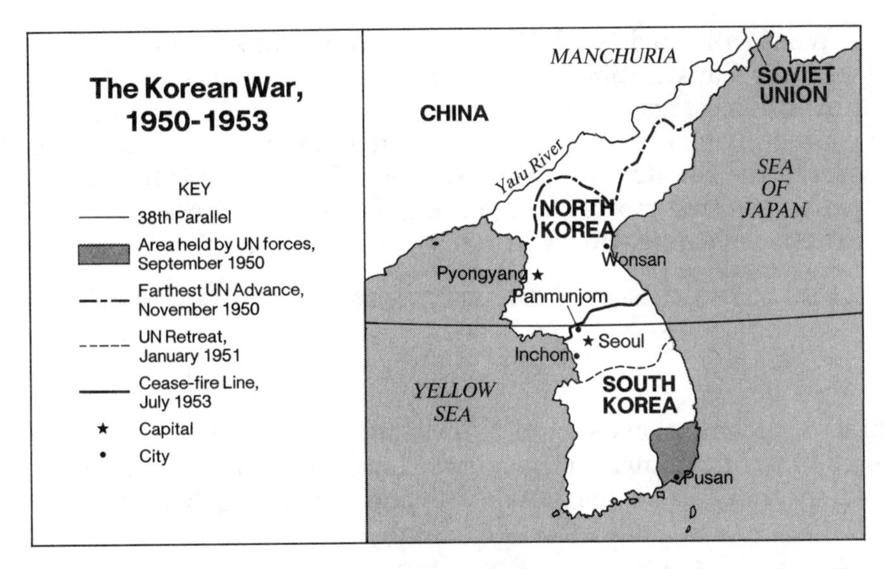

the occupation of Japan after the war and was given much of the credit for turning postwar Japan into a prosperous, democratic country. MacArthur's successful military record makes him the likely choice to lead the United Nations forces in the defense of South Korea.

Within several weeks of MacArthur's arrival in Korea, his troops are able to push the invaders back into North Korea. With permission from the United Nations and from you, the president, MacArthur crosses the 38th parallel with his troops and moves deep into North Korean territory. He intends to defeat North Korea and unite it with South Korea. But on November 26, 1950, some 300,000 Communist Chinese soldiers come to the aid of North Korea. They attack MacArthur's troops and force them to retreat. The Chinese attack is so successful that MacArthur once again finds himself south of the 38th parallel.

General MacArthur now turns to you, the president. He insists that the quickest way to end the war is to attack Communist China. He suggests using atomic bombs to destroy industrial and transportation centers there. He asks your permission to cross the Yalu River and invade Chinese territory. Other military advisers tell you such an invasion would be a mistake. Omar Bradley, chairman of the Joint Chiefs of Staff, says that getting involved in a war in China would be "the wrong war, at the wrong place, at the wrong time, and with the wrong enemy." You are also told that a war with China would most likely bring in the Soviet Union, which has a mutual assistance pact with China.

You tell MacArthur that you do not want to extend the war by invading China, but he insists that the invasion is necessary. He writes to newspaper publishers and congressional leaders, hoping that they will use their influence on you. MacArthur claims that we must crush communism in Asia before it becomes impossible to do so, and he argues that a limited war fought only in Korea is a waste of American lives. "There is no substitute for victory," he says.

> What will you do with MacArthur? You cannot let him run the war. The Constitution makes you the commander in chief of the armed forces, not one of your generals. Yet MacArthur is one of your best generals—a distinguished military leader who has served the country well. You are also aware that public opinion polls show that most Americans support MacArthur's call for an invasion of China. How will you solve this problem?

Step 1

What important terms should I know to study the problem? (Write the terms and their meanings on the answer lines. You may want to use a dictionary, an encyclopedia, or the glossary on page 333 of this book.)

____

____

____

____

Step 2

What is the problem?

____

____

Step 3

What are some possible solutions? (List at least two possible solutions.)

____

____

____

____

Step 4

What do I need to know before I make a decision?

____

____

____

____

Step 5

What is my decision? (Include reasons why you have made this decision.)

____

____

____

____

(If you want to compare your decision with President Truman's solution to the problem, look up Harry S. Truman, the Korean War, or Douglas MacArthur in an American history textbook or an encyclopedia.)

D. Imagine that the year is 1956 and you are President Dwight D. Eisenhower. You must solve the problem presented in the following selection. Read the selection, and then try to solve the problem. Use the five steps to solving a problem given at the end of the selection.

The 1950s is a time of fear that communism will spread throughout the Middle East. The United States does not want to see the Arab countries of the Middle East become Soviet satellites, as most countries of Eastern Europe did in the late 1940s. It is important to the United States and the other countries of the "free world" that the Suez Canal and the oil fields of the Middle East stay in friendly hands.

U.S. relations with the Arab countries of the Middle East are complicated by U.S. support for the state of Israel. When Israel became a nation in 1948, the Arab countries surrounding the new Jewish state refused to accept its existence. Displeased by U.S. support of Israel, a number of Arab countries are threatening to develop closer ties with the Soviet Union.

Gamal Abdel Nasser is elected president of Egypt in 1954. For a time, he makes deals with both the United States and the Soviet Union. But as Nasser's threats against Israel increase, the United States begins to limit its sale of military weapons to Egypt. Nasser immediately goes to the Soviet Union for his military needs. In turn, the United States, Britain, and France withdraw their offer to finance construction of the Aswan High Dam on the Nile River. (The dam is part of Nasser's plans to increase food production in Egypt.)

In retaliation, Nasser seizes control of the Suez Canal, which has been operated by a joint British and French company. Nasser says that the canal rightfully belongs to Egypt. He claims that the tolls collected from ships using the canal will be used to build the Aswan Dam. At the same time, Nasser announces that he will not allow Israeli ships through the canal.

Britain and France then attack and take control of the canal area, while Israel attacks and takes control of the Sinai Peninsula area of Egypt. The Soviet Union threatens to come to the

The Middle East

aid of Egypt and even to use missiles against Britain and France, if necessary.

You, as president, are greatly disturbed that Britain, France, and Israel have attacked Egypt without consulting you. You do not approve of Nasser's seizure of the canal, but you do not want to risk World War III over the issue.

A resolution calling for a cease-fire and an immediate withdrawal of British, French, and Israeli soldiers from Egyptian soil is introduced in the United Nations. It is supported by the Soviet Union. Should the United States support or oppose the resolution? Britain, France, and Israel are your allies. There are times when you need their support, and this is a time when they need your support. But you do not want to anger the Egyptians and their Arab neighbors. You do not want to push them any closer to the Soviet Union. How will you solve this problem?

Step 1

What important terms should I know to study the problem? (Write the terms and their meanings on the answer lines. You may want to use a dictionary, an encyclopedia, or the glossary on page 333 of this book.)

____

____

____

____

Step 2

What is the problem?

___

___

___

Step 3

What are some possible solutions? (List at least two possible solutions.)

___

___

___

___

Step 4

What do I need to know before I make a decision?

___

___

___

___

Step 5

What is my decision? (Include reasons why you have made this decision.)

___

___

___

___

(If you want to compare your decision with President Eisenhower's solution to the problem, look up Dwight D. Eisenhower or the Suez Crisis in a U.S. history textbook or an encyclopedia.)

E. Solving a Problem. From the following list, pick ONE of the current problems facing the United States. You may have learned about this problem from a newspaper, magazine, or television program. Solve the problem by using the five steps that are given.

Poverty
Homeless People
Unemployment
Racism/Discrimination
AIDS
Crime
The Breakdown of Family Life
Child Abuse
Pollution
Americans Without Health Insurance
Illegal Immigrants
Getting Americans to Vote
Illegal Drugs

Step 1

What important terms should I know to study the problem? (Write the terms and their meanings on the answer lines. You may want to use a dictionary, an encyclopedia, or the glossary on page 333 of this book.)

____

____

____

____

____

____

Step 2

What is the problem?

____

____

____

____

Step 3

What are some possible solutions? (List at least two possible solutions.)

____

____

____

___

___

___

Step 4

What do I need to know before I make a decision?

___

___

___

___

___

___

Step 5

What is my decision? (Include reasons why you have made this decision.)

___

___

___

___

___

___

GLOSSARY

The definitions relate directly to the way the term or phrase is first used in the text.

age (noun) period of time, such as the Space Age, marked by features and events setting it apart from other periods.

aggression attack or assault, such as the invasion of one country by another.

allies supporters; people or countries joined together for a common purpose.

almanac reference book, published yearly, containing useful and interesting facts and figures on many subjects.

altitude height above sea level.

amendment addition to or change in a law or constitution.

ancestor family member or relative who lived many years ago.

annex (verb) add, attach, or take over something, such as a territory.

archipelago group of islands near each other.

assets advantages, property, things of value.

atlas reference book containing maps.

author card card in a library card catalog listing a book's author first across the top.

bar graph graph in which bars of different lengths are used to compare facts or statistics.

basin wide, deep area of land, sometimes enclosed by mountain ranges.

bay large body of water that is part of a lake or ocean and usually surrounded partly by landforms.

belligerent (adjective) warring, engaged in war.

bibliography list of additional books on a particular subject.

blockade (noun) surrounding of a place to prevent entry and exit.

boycott (verb) refuse to purchase goods in order to punish or force a change.

canal human-made stretch of water connecting two larger bodies of water.

cape point of land extending into the sea.

caption brief explanation accompanying a picture or cartoon.

card catalog listing on cards of every book in a library, with a separate card for each book.

cardinal (direction) any of the main points of the directional compass: north, south, east, or west.

cause (noun) event or action that brings about another event or action (effect).

CD-ROM compact disc read-only memory; a round, flat disk containing a great deal of information. When placed into the CD-ROM drive of a computer, the disk allows a computer to access its information.

cease-fire military order to stop fighting.

census official count of a population.

century period of 100 years.

chain reaction situation in which a cause brings about an effect and, in turn, that effect becomes a cause for another effect, and so on.

chart (noun) arrangement of words and numbers showing information clearly and simply.

chief executive person responsible for enforcing the laws and running the government.

circle graph graph that shows percentages by dividing a circle into sections that look like pieces of a pie; a pie graph.

civil liberties rights guaranteed to the people of the United States by the Constitution and its various amendments.

coastline land all along the edge of a body of water such as an ocean or lake.

cold war period of unfriendly, warlike relations—but no battlefield combat—between the United States and the Soviet Union, from the end of World War II until the collapse of the Soviet Union in 1991.

commerce trade; buying and selling of goods.

commune (noun) group of people, not necessarily related, living together as a family and sharing their goods.

communism system of government in which one party controls the state-owned means of production; belief that private property should be abolished.

Communist (noun) one who believes in communism.

comparing examining how things are alike and how they may be different.

computer catalog computer listing of every book in a library.

conclusion decision based on the information provided.

concurrent powers powers shared by the national and state governments.

confederacy group of states united for a common purpose. Capitalized, it is the name of the South during the Civil War.

containment policy of preventing the spread of an enemy's power or influence.

continent any of the largest landforms on the earth, such as Asia or North America.

contrasting examining how things are different.

culture way of life of a group of people; the customs, beliefs, art, and language of people.

culture area geographical place where people have the same or a similar way of life.

cursor blinking line on a computer screen that shows where the next letter typed will appear.

decade period of 10 years.

definition meaning of a word.

delegated powers powers specifically given to the national government by the Constitution; enumerated powers.

delta large area of fertile soil at the mouth of a river.

depression long period of economic decline.

dictionary reference book. The most usual type is an alphabetical list of words in a language, with their meanings defined.

discrimination unfair treatment of people because they are members of a certain group.

diskette small, square-shaped disk containing computer programs or files. When placed into the disk drive of a computer, it allows the computer to access its program or files.

document (noun) original or official paper.

documentary factual film or television program dealing with a particular person, event, or period of history.

documentation proof; collection of documents gathered to prove something.

double bar graph graph that uses two bars to show two different sets of statistics at the same time.

double line graph graph that uses two lines to show two different sets of statistics at the same time.

downstream direction in which a river flows.

duty tax.

effect (noun) event or action brought about by an earlier event or action (cause).

elastic clause clause in the Constitution used to expand the delegated powers of the national government.

electoral college group of people elected by the voters of each state to cast official votes for president and vice president.

encyclopedia reference work, usually divided into several books (volumes), giving detailed information in alphabetical order on almost every subject.

enumerated powers powers specifically given to the national government by the Constitution; delegated powers.

escalation increase by stages (step by step).

essay (noun) composition stating a personal point of view.

"establishment" group or groups in a society that control the society.

estimated statistics numerical data about the past or present that is believed to be correct but not officially accepted.

executive branch one of the three parts of the federal government. It is headed by the president, and its main purpose is to enforce the laws.

exile (noun) person forced to leave his or her homeland and settle elsewhere.

exports (noun) goods sent out of a country.

fact true statement; something that happened.

fact book reference book containing detailed information on a particular subject.

federal relating to a government in which power is distributed between the central and state governments.

first draft first attempt at writing, subject to change and correction.

generalization broad, general statement based on enough people, places, or things to make it true.

graph (noun) arrangement of symbols, words, and numbers showing information clearly and simply.

graphics program computer program designed to draw the lines, circles, and bars needed to produce charts and graphs.

gulf large body of water that is part of an ocean and usually surrounded in part by landforms.

hill high, rounded landmass, usually lower than a mountain.

hippie movement period in the late 1960s in which dissenting people (hippies) used actions and dress to protest against established ideas in the United States.

historian person who studies and writes about history.

historical atlas reference book containing maps that show what the world looked like in different historical periods.

historical map map showing what a part of the world looked like at an earlier time.

historical population map map showing how many people lived in a particular part of the world at an earlier time.

historical product map map showing what goods were produced in a particular part of the world at an earlier time.

home page opening (first) screen of a Web site on the Internet, used to greet visitors and direct them to other pages on the site.

hostage person held by force, usually in exchange for money or another person.

House of Representatives one of the two houses of Congress. The number of representatives elected from each state is based on the state population.

icon (computer) small picture or symbol on a computer screen representing a program (word processing, games, etc.) or function in a program (save, cut, copy, etc.). When an icon is selected, the computer goes to the program or performs the function represented by the icon.

impeach charge a public official with misconduct in office.

impeachment formal charge made against a public official for misconduct in office.

implied powers powers not specified in the Constitution but inferred from it.

indentured servant person who earned passage to America by promising to work for a sponsor for a number of years.

independence freedom, liberty, self-government.

inference process of reaching a decision suggested, but not proved, by the information provided.

intermediate direction any of the directions—northeast, southeast, southwest, northwest—in between cardinal directions.

Internet network of computers that uses the World Wide Web to provide information and resources on almost every subject. Connection to the Internet requires a computer, modem, telephone line, and service that provides access.

interpret explain the meaning of something.

island body of land completely surrounded by water.

isthmus narrow strip of land connecting two large landforms.

judicial branch one of the three parts of the federal government. It is headed by the U.S. Supreme Court, and its purpose is to interpret the Constitution and the laws.

jurisdiction authority to interpret and apply laws.

key (of a map) list explaining the information on a map.

lake body of water completely surrounded by land.

legislative branch one of the three parts of the federal government. It is headed by the Congress, and its purpose is to enact laws.

legislature branch of elected officials having the power and authority to make laws.

line graph graph using lines to display information, such as statistics.

loose interpretation (of the Constitution) use by the national government of implied powers not specifically stated in the Constitution.

mainstream term applied to the typical and average way of life.

manifest destiny 19th-century belief that Providence (God) chose the United States to govern all land from the Atlantic Ocean to the Pacific Ocean and beyond.

media systems of mass communication, such as newspapers, magazines, radio, and television.

microfiche sheet of microfilm containing a number of separate photographs.

microfilm roll of miniature photographs, each showing a catalog card or a book, magazine, or newspaper page.

migration movement of people (or animals) from one country or place to another.

millennium (*pl.* millennia) period of 1,000 years.

modem device allowing a computer to communicate with another computer over a telephone line.

mountain landmass much higher and steeper than nearby areas.

mountain range group of mountains close together in a row.

mouse (computer) small device, usually with two buttons, connected to a computer by a wire. Clicking on the buttons replaces typing.

mouth (of a river) place where a river ends.

muckrakers name given to early 20th-century writers who exposed corruption in government, unfair business practices, and poor working conditions in mines and factories.

multiple causation two or more events causing one effect.

multiple effects two or more events or actions brought about by one event or action.

munitions military weapons and supplies.

nationalist (noun) person devoted to his or her country.

negotiate seek an agreement through discussion and compromise.

New Immigration term referring to the 23 million immigrants who came to the United States between 1880 and 1920.

ocean any of the largest bodies of water on the earth, such as the Pacific Ocean.

Old Immigration term referring to the 10 million immigrants who came to the United States between 1830 and 1860.

opinion something a person believes to be true or a point of view a person holds.

outline (noun) plan or sketch of a reading selection showing only its main ideas and facts.

parenthetical documentation style of documentation for research papers in which the source of a quotation, idea, or little-known fact is enclosed in parentheses and placed at the end of the quotation, idea, or fact.

peninsula body of land extending into the sea and almost completely surrounded by water.

percentage part of a whole based on 100; part or share.

percentage bar graph bar graph in which each bar contains several pieces of numerical information shown in percentages, with the percentages on each bar adding up to 100 percent.

persecution suffering imposed on a person or group, usually because of political or religious beliefs.

picture graph graph in which statistics are given in pictures or symbols instead of numbers; also called a pictograph.

plains areas of level or rolling land.

plantation large farm with many workers who usually live there; in the United States, found mostly in the South.

plateau high, flat landmass.

political cartoon cartoon expressing ideas relating to history, government, or politics.

polygamy practice of having more than one wife at a time.

population density map map showing the average number of people living on a certain area of land, usually a square mile.

population distribution map map showing how many people live in a particular area, such as a state or territory.

portfolio collection of related papers and pictures.

prairies plains that are good for growing crops or raising animals.

prejudice (noun) dislike of a person or group, usually on account of race, religion, or gender.

primary source firsthand account or evidence.

projected statistics numerical data predicted for future years and based on the likely course of change.

proofreading checking of a finished paper for errors.

quorum number of people needed to make a meeting official or legal.

ratification approval, endorsement.

ratify approve; vote in favor of.

reference book book such as an encyclopedia or almanac containing information on a particular topic or on many topics.

research paper formal composition using information from a number of sources.

reservation (for Native Americans) area of public land set apart by the U.S. government for use by a Native American tribe.

reserved powers powers belonging to the states (those not given to the national government nor denied to the state governments by the Constitution).

residual powers another way of saying reserved powers.

revenue income, especially a large amount.

revise change, rewrite.

revolutionary rebel; supporter of quick, often violent change.

river natural stream of water flowing through land.

sabotage (verb) wreck or damage on purpose.

sea large body of water that is usually part of an ocean and usually partly surrounded by landforms. (Some seas are completely surrounded by land.)

sea level surface of the ocean waters.

secondary source secondhand information; information not directly from an original source.

sect body of people with beliefs that differ from those of many other people.

Senate one of the two houses of Congress. It is made up of two members from each state.

sequence (noun) arrangement of events in the order in which they took place.

software programs that make a computer run or allow a user to perform various operations, such as making a chart or writing a letter.

source (of a river) place where a river begins.

sovereignty total freedom from outside control; independence.

spreadsheet chart containing information in columns and rows, so named because its information is spread out across many columns.

statistics numerical data (information) collected for study and interpretation.

strait narrow stretch of water connecting two larger bodies of water.

strict interpretation (of the Constitution) use by the national government of only those powers specifically stated in the Constitution.

subject card card in a library card catalog listing the subject of the book first across the top.

subtopic subject that is part of a topic.

summarizing reducing many ideas to a few important points.

Supreme Court highest federal court in the United States; head of the judicial branch of the national government.

sweeping generalization broad, general statement that puts all people, objects, or ideas into one category. Such a statement is usually incorrect because what may be true for some or most people (objects, ideas) is rarely true for all.

technology materials and machines in a given field and the know-how to use them.

territory part of the United States not included in any state but organized with its own lawmaking body; an area controlled by or belonging to a country.

thesis statement statement placed at the beginning of a research paper's outline giving the purpose of the paper.

time line line divided into time periods on which events are placed in correct order.

title card card in a library card catalog listing the title of the book first across the top.

topic main subject covered in a reading selection.

trade deficit amount by which a country's imports exceeds its exports.

treaty formal agreement in writing between two or more countries.

trend general direction in which something is heading.

tributaries smaller rivers that flow into a large river.

upstream direction against the flow of a river.

valley long, narrow area of land, usually formed by a river.

veto (noun) refusal to approve or sign a bill, thereby keeping it from becoming a law.

volcano mountain with an opening in the top or side through which melted rock, steam, and ashes are forced out from inside the earth.

Web site file (set of data on a particular subject) on the World Wide Web.

welfare economic assistance provided by the government to people in need.

INDEX